The Leader's Dilemma

How to Build an Empowered and Adaptive Organization Without Losing Control

By Jeremy Hope, Peter Bunce and Franz Röösli

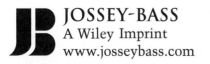

JOSSEY-BASS
A Wiley Imprint
www.josseybass.com

This edition first published 2011

© 2011 John Wiley & Sons, Ltd

Under the Jossey-Bass imprint, Jossey-Bass, 989 Market Street, San Francisco CA 94103-1741, USA

www.jossey-bass.com

Registered office

John Wiley & Sons Ltd, The Atrium, Southern Gate, Chichester, West Sussex, PO19 8SQ, United Kingdom

For details of our global editorial offices, for customer services and for information about how to apply for permission to reuse the copyright material in this book please see our website at www.wiley.com.

A catalogue record for this book is available from the British Library.

ISBN 978-1-119-97000-2 (hardback)   ISBN 978-1-119-97557-1 (ebk)

ISBN 978-1-119-97050-7 (ebk)   ISBN 978-1-119-97051-4 (ebk)

Set in 9.5/13 pt Zapf Elliptical by Sparks – www.sparkspublishing.com

Printed in Great Britain by TJ International Ltd, Padstow, Cornwall, UK

Contents

Foreword   v

Preface   vii

Some definitions   ix

Introduction
The organization as an adaptive system   1

1 **Principle #1 – Values**   33
Bind people to a common cause, not a central plan

2 **Principle #2 – Governance**   57
Govern through shared values and sound
judgment, not detailed rules and regulations

3 **Principle #3 – Transparency**   89
Make information open and transparent; don't restrict and control it

4 **Principle #4 – Teams**   105
Organize around a seamless network of
accountable teams, not centralized functions

5 **Principle #5 – Trust**   121
Trust teams to regulate and improve their
performance; don't micro-manage them

6 **Principle #6 – Accountability**   139
Base accountability on holistic criteria and peer
reviews, not on hierarchical relationships

7   **Principle #7 – Goals**   157
    Set ambitious medium-term goals, not short-term fixed targets

8   **Principle #8 – Rewards**   179
    Base rewards on relative performance, not fixed targets

9   **Principle #9 – Planning**   203
    Make planning a continuous and inclusive
    process, not a top-down annual event

10 **Principle #10 – Coordination**   225
    Coordinate interactions dynamically, not through annual budgets

11 **Principle #11 – Resources**   239
    Make resources available just-in-time, not just-in-case

12 **Principle #12 – Controls**   257
    Base controls on fast, frequent feedback, not on budget variances

13 **Implementation insights**   283

14 **Make management change your legacy**   305

Notes   309

Index   325

Foreword

This book addresses a paradox about the nature of management in large organizations. On the one hand, the pace of change in the business world today feels faster than it has ever been. There is plentiful evidence of corporate failure, there is widespread distrust of senior executives, and there are many observers calling for dramatic changes in how organizations are run. On the other hand, the standard "command and control"-based model of management, the one that has served us for more than a century, continues to dominate the business landscape.

This is not a new paradox. Every generation of management researchers and consultants argues that we need to make profound changes in how work gets done, and since at least the 1930s the primary emphasis has been on such themes as empowering workers, flattening hierarchies and creating greater levels of trust. And, yet, for all the careful research, and for all the evidence that some companies are experimenting with new ways that appear to offer a better way, the amount of real and lasting change is small. When we look at the *management* systems for getting work done in large organizations today – how we motivate people, control activities, and set objectives – they are little different from the ones used by our grandparents.

Some management books try to sidestep this paradox: they focus on the things that are changing in the business world and leave readers to figure out what to do differently; or they provide a new perspective on the paradox. Other books focus on one part of the story only, perhaps giving some new techniques for motivating employees or measuring performance. But in *The Leader's Dilemma* Jeremy Hope, Peter Bunce and Franz Röösli avoid any such tactics.

First of all, they take on the whole challenge – the organization as a complex system of interconnected parts – and they make it clear that you cannot just cherry-pick the ideas that suit you. Rather, you have to see how all the different parts of the story connect to each other, and think through the consequences of your actions. Second, they confront the paradox that large organizations seem immune to the changes that they need to make. Their argument is alluded to in the subtitle of the book: *How to build an empowered and adaptive organization without losing control.* The way forward, they argue, lies on the knife-edge between anarchic self-organization on the one side, and traditional command and control on the other.

The Leader's Dilemma lays out an agenda for change in large organizations built around 12 principles, such as "bind people to a common cause, not a central plan" and "make planning a continuous and inclusive process, not a top-down annual event." All of these principles will be familiar to a business audience, but the point is that while the words are frequently used, they are rarely enacted. So Hope, Bunce and Röösli provide lots of examples of how these principles can be applied in practice: well-known companies like Southwest Airlines and Whole Foods Market, and lesser-known companies like Sydney Water Corporation and Tomkins.

Their agenda is all about putting people first – about building an adaptive system around the needs and aspirations of employees, not treating the organization as an "obedient machine." The curious thing about this agenda is that it didn't emerge from an HR conference, or from a class in organizational behavior at a business school; it came out of an industry group called the "Beyond Budgeting Round Table," or BBRT, founded by Jeremy Hope, Robin Fraser and Peter Bunce a decade ago.

The BBRT is a group of finance and accounting professionals, all with personal experience of the limits to traditional top-down, fixed-target based budgeting. Inspired by a few enlightened companies such as Svenska Handelsbanken, they sought to find alternatives to the traditional budgeting process. But such is the interconnected nature of large organizations that a rethinking of budgeting quickly led to a rethinking of the entire management architecture of large organizations.

This book is the result of that process. The authors are professionals who wouldn't normally have started from a "people"-focused agenda but ended up there because it was the only possible place to end up if you want to make organizations more effective over the long term. The authors also understand deeply how difficult it is for those in positions of power to loosen up on the levers of control. So this is an important book: it offers a synthesis of a lot of recent thinking about how to improve management in large organizations, and it provides a clear agenda for change. If you are interested in building an adaptive and progressive company, this book gives you the ideas and inspiration to make it happen.

Julian Birkinshaw
Professor of Strategic and International Management
London Business School

Preface

One summer Albert Einstein's students complained that the questions on this year's exam paper were no different from those on the previous one. "Well, yes," said Einstein, "the questions were indeed the same. What the students needed to understand, however, was that the answers had changed!" If the question on today's management exam paper is "How does the way we manage need to change to meet today's challenges?" then the answers are indeed different from those most leaders would have given a few years ago.

The traditional "command and control" management model was never perfect. In an industrial age when suppliers could sell all their output to eager customers, business leaders could "plan and control" their way to the future. Annual plans and budgets were negotiated with the corporate center; all divisional and line managers had to do was to follow the plan and meet the numbers. This model was already in trouble in the 1990s as customer loyalty collapsed in the wake of globalization, privatization and the Internet revolution, but in the credit crunch of 2007–9 it turned into a liability as organizations failed to anticipate and respond to the economic eruptions that engulfed world markets. The trouble is that increasing levels of uncertainty and turbulence are here to stay.

Another crucial change is that the next generation of managers weaned on Facebook and YouTube are used to sharing just about everything with their families and friends. But when they enter the workplace they are faced with antiquated systems and closed mindsets that make transparency and sharing so difficult. There is little doubt that to attract and keep the best people in the future, leaders will need to make their organizations more engaging, transparent and fulfilling places to work.

This book is about rethinking how we manage organizations in a post-industrial, post-credit crunch world where, according to strategy guru Gary Hamel, innovative management models represent the only remaining source of sustainable competitive advantage.[1] It is also about releasing people from the burdens of stifling bureaucracy and suffocating control systems, trusting them with information and giving them time to think, reflect, share, learn and improve.

It is an outcome of the work we have been engaged in for over 10 years in the "beyond budgeting" movement (we use "budgeting" as another term for "command and control" management). In our 2003 book *Beyond Budgeting* Jeremy Hope and Robin Fraser set out 12 principles that represented the "best of best practices" at that time. These have stood the test of time. This book provides more depth and case examples based on these principles. We have also integrated these principles with "systems thinking" and illustrated how they enable organizations to become more empowered and adaptive.

This book is aimed at leaders who want to change their management cultures and build organizations that will adapt, improve and endure for generations to come.

No book is completed without the help and support of many people. We would like to acknowledge the support of Robin Fraser, Steve Player, Bjarte Bogsnes and Steve Morlidge, who have not only contributed to this book but also been instrumental in pushing the boundaries of Beyond Budgeting. We would also like to thank many Beyond Budgeting members who have generously given their time to facilitate case studies and interviews that we have drawn on extensively throughout this work. Also, our publisher Rosemary Nixon and her team have given us expert guidance throughout the process. Our sincere thanks go to them all.

Some definitions

It is important that we all share the same understanding of what key terms mean throughout this book. For example, many people find it difficult to distinguish between a budget, a target, a goal and a forecast, yet a clear definition of these terms *as they are applied in practice* is crucial for designing and implementing any management model. It is also fundamental to reading this book. Our definitions are set out below and are applied throughout.

A *management model* describes how an organization sets goals and strategy; how it motivates and rewards people; how it steers its course through plans, budgets and forecasts; how it makes decisions and allocates resources; and how it measures and controls performance.

A *command and control management model* assumes that an organization has many layers of management and that strategy and key decisions are highly centralized. Targets, plans, budgets, resources and controls flow down the hierarchy in the form of annual instructions, and subsequently flow back up the hierarchy in the form of results. The annual budget coordinates all plans and resources and is the "glue" that holds the management model together. We use the word "budgeting" as a generic term for command and control management, and thus "beyond budgeting" means beyond command and control toward a management model that is more empowered and adaptive.

An *adaptive management model* assumes that an organization has few layers of management and that strategy and key decisions are devolved to front-line teams who have the scope and authority to respond rapidly to emerging threats and seize new opportunities as they arise. Fixed plans and budgets are usually replaced with more flexible systems including quarterly business reviews and rolling forecasts. The glue that holds the organization together is fast, open and transparent information.

A *target* is usually short-term (often one year) and fixed. It invariably becomes a fixed performance contract between one organizational level and another. In the cultural climate of many organizations, such contracts or commitments must be met, which often leads to undesirable behavior.

A *goal* is usually aspirational and set over the medium term (two to five years). A goal should stretch managerial ambition so that an organization or work unit maximizes its performance potential, as opposed to making incremental performance improvements over the previous period.

A *budget* is a plan expressed in financial terms against which performance will be measured. It is a tool for allocating scarce resources and for committing managers to a predetermined financial outcome, usually on an annual basis. It also acts as a constraint on spending and a basis for evaluating management performance and rewards. A budget also defines authority levels and influences how managers behave in large organizations.

A *plan* is a set of actions that derive from a strategic review and aim at improving the performance of the organization or any of its subsets such as divisions or front-line teams.

A *forecast* is a financial view of the future derived from a manager's best opinion of the "most likely outcome," given the known information at the time it is prepared. Thus it should be unbiased, reflect all known events (good and bad), and, of course, be realistic. It should also be a moving window (or rolling forecast) that always looks between 12 and 24 months ahead.

The organization as an adaptive system

What ultimately constrains the performance of your organization is not its operating model, nor its business model, but its management model.[1]

Gary Hamel, *The Future of Management*

Most of you will remember Aesop's fable about the tortoise and the hare who decide to have a race on a sunny day. The brash, confident hare thinks he has won the race before it even starts and decides to have a nap under a tree half way through. But when the hare awakes, the tortoise is at the finish line.

Too many business leaders think and act like hares. They think they can grow shareholder value at unrealistic rates each year by setting aggressive targets and incentives and then (like the hare) "predict and control" their future results through detailed budgets and short-term decisions. Tortoises don't make such promises, predictions or assumptions. Instead they keep their eye on the path ahead and continuously improve their performance. Tortoises always win in the end. Their aim is to adapt to changing conditions, beat their peers and endure over long periods of time. The best organizations are adaptive systems that continuously learn, adapt and improve.

Unfortunately, in the business world, when tortoise-type organizations appoint new leaders they can turn into hares. Royal Bank of Scotland (founded 1727), Citigroup (1812), Lehman Brothers (1850), Washington Mutual (1889), Merrill Lynch (1914) and AIG (1919) had all adapted and endured for, in most cases, a century or more but collapsed when a new leadership generation changed the way they were managed. The result was the credit crunch of 2007–9, when trillions of dollars were wiped off corporate balance sheets, leaving governments around the world with no option but to step in with taxpayers' funds to avoid a catastrophic collapse of the financial system.

What followed was the worst recession since the 1930s. Everyone is asking the same questions: How did it happen? How did the banking sector, full of mature organizations with long histories of steady growth and run by highly professional people, suddenly collapse? Why did governance and regulatory systems fail so badly? Who is accountable? What lessons can we learn? And how do we prevent it from happening again?

Commentators have pointed their fingers at naïve central bankers, inept regulators, unrealistic ratings agencies, passive politicians, greedy executives, aggressive salespeople, unscrupulous mortgage brokers and short-selling hedge funds. While all these actors in this tragedy (or was it a farce?) are culpable in one way or another, the roots of the crisis lie elsewhere. They are deeply embedded in the management model itself. Hijacked by financial engineers a few decades ago, lent credence by academics and pseudo-management science, and seized upon by macho leaders and private equity partners, it was a slow-burning fuse waiting to explode.

The harbingers of this crisis were visible several years ago when Enron, World-Com and many other large corporations collapsed, triggering the Sarbanes-Oxley (SOX) legislation. Like today, fingers were pointed at greedy executives and inept regulators but, also like today's crisis, the root causes lay in a corrupt culture and a flawed management model.

If you doubt this conclusion, think about how the typical management model works.[2] Like the hare in the fable, leaders sit down once a year and plan the annual race: "What target will excite the market and boost the share price? Fifteen percent growth in earning-per-share feels good, so that's what we'll choose." The next step is to cascade this target down the organization so each division, business unit, function and department owns a piece of it. Tough negotiations take place as the less pliable managers protest that such growth is impossible. But most meekly accept the target and hope for the best. The incentive scheme helps to win them over. Once the budget is agreed the leadership team, just like the hare, thinks the race is over. They have done their job. Investors like the target and the share price responds favorably. Execution is a given.

The trouble is that this "predict and control" view of management is increasingly unhinged from reality. What happens if customer demand takes an unexpected turn for the worse (or even for the better)? What happens if there is a fire or flood, or a key supplier suffers a serious problem? What happens if a new competitor enters the market or an existing competitor changes prices or introduces a new "killer" business model? What happens if commodity prices, interest rates or inflation indexes gyrate up or down? In 2008, who predicted that the price of oil would drop from $147 per barrel to under $40 within six months, or that consumer demand for cars and property would fall by 30 to 40 percent within a similar period? There are many uncertainties that can derail the most carefully crafted targets, plans and budgets, and they are becoming more common and exaggerated over time. Many leaders have been forced to reset and recalibrate targets and budgets many times as they have tried to maintain some semblance of control.

The decline and fall of "command and control"

The traditional management model is commonly known as "command and control." As Figure I.1 illustrates, strategy is translated into targets, budgets and incentives that are cascaded down the organization, directing and dictating what

FIGURE I.1 The command and control model

people do. Each division, function and department is then accountable for meeting their numbers and must explain any variances from plan to a higher authority.

The command and control model is under pressure for many reasons. The switch in power from the supply chain to the demand chain (including marketers, consumers, designers and retailers) is forcing all suppliers to be more innovative in order to meet changing customer needs. The life cycles of products, strategies and business models are shrinking, placing greater pressure on the speed of response and continuous renewal of strategies. Entry costs into many different markets are falling as more products and services are delivered digitally. And innovation has moved from the exclusivity of the R&D department to anyone, anywhere, anytime.

Centralized, inflexible (command and control) organizations find it difficult to compete in this world of fast adaptation, continuous innovation and customer participation. They were designed for producing affordable products and services through standard processes as efficiently as possible. But merely being efficient is no longer a sustainable competitive position in the global economy. Everyone now works in a global labor force: there will always be someone cheaper than you. So the key to competitive advantage is differentiation. To avoid the "me-too" commodity trap, the focus of innovation is moving from products to services and from the exclusivity of the R&D department to employees, customers and business partners.

Differentiation can be applied in many areas, including how products are produced, delivered and consumed. Customers' needs increasingly go beyond the standard product or service, and they are prepared to pay more to satisfy them. Opportunities exist in every product and market category to provide more options from the basic product to the full menu. In fact, in some cases (e.g. cars), the standard product is nothing more than a loss leader. The profit comes from value-added options and finance packages. Being able to satisfy wide-ranging customer needs at the lowest cost is today's opportunity.

Another problem facing the centralized organization is that the Facebook generation is not prepared to be told what to do. In their personal lives they are used to fast, open collaboration between colleagues, and they are bringing these expectations into the workplace. They want to know about values, goals, plans and results. They want more engagement and fulfillment. And they are only willing to contribute their passion and creativity if the climate is one that encourages transparency and trust. It is clear that the rules of the management game have changed and there is no going back.

But the final (and perhaps fatal) blow has been delivered by the credit crunch. How has the command and control model become so toxic that a generation of macho leaders, financial engineers and private equity investors were able to use it to pursue the maximization of short-term shareholder value and personal wealth at almost any cost, destroy so many great organizations and take the whole financial system to the brink of collapse?

To answer this question, let's retrace the history of savings and loans organizations (known as "building societies") in the UK.

How the pursuit of "shareholder value" ruined many large UK Building Societies

One of the authors was born and raised in a part of northern England where many small savings and loans organizations were major features of the business land-scape, with names such as "Halifax" (now part of HBOS and recently acquired by LloydsTSB) and "Bradford and Bingley" (now part nationalized and part owned by Spanish bank Santander). Building societies were owned by and existed for the benefit of their depositors and borrowers (their members). Indeed, their original purpose was to raise money through deposits and lend that money to their members (usually within the same community) to buy a house. Apart from occasional mergers, they grew steadily (within the limits of their income) and some (like the Halifax) became giants of the industry. Their aim was to adapt and endure, and for over 150 years they achieved this purpose admirably. But in the 1980s their world changed.

In 1986 a new Act of Parliament was passed to allow building societies to "de-mutualize." This meant that they could convert their status to banks and become listed companies. In the 1990s, driven by the prospect of directors and members making capital gains from the listing of the shares, many took advantage of this Act and became public companies. All seemed to start well. But over the next decade new "professional" highly paid managers arrived and took action to "maximize shareholder value," "implement niche strategies," "align management incentives," "leverage the asset base," "create off-balance-sheet vehicles," "trade in innovative financial products" and "manage risk."

Their aim was to reach their goal (now to "maximize shareholder value") as quickly as possible, so that within a few years they would make the company so attractive that they could either acquire other companies or be acquired themselves. Whichever path was taken (and whether the company continued to exist or not), shareholders (and managers) would win. And in an age of deregulated markets, low interest rates, rising property prices, "innovative" financial products and gullible borrowers, everything was looking rosy. Shareholder values were booming, financial bonuses were exploding and mortgages were flying out of the door as borrowers who were previously excluded from the market were able to buy cheap products based on little or no evidence of secure income. But in 2007 their world changed again.

In August 2007, one of the more aggressive former UK building societies, Northern Rock, collapsed. Its high-growth oriented business model, based on raising short-term debt to fund aggressive growth in mortgage sales, ceased to function. And by September 2008 many of its UK rivals including RBS (Royal Bank of Scotland), HBOS, Alliance & Leicester and Bradford & Bingley had either been nationalized or taken over by more stable institutions.

In less than 15 years after the building societies became public companies, their smart operators, educated at the best universities and business schools, had decimated a whole industry, leaving shattered communities and thousands of angry employees and shareholders wondering what went wrong. In a bizarre twist to the banking tale, it emerged that in the same week that news broke of the collapse of RBS its former chief executive, Sir Fred Goodwin, had asked for and received a doubling of his pension fund before he would agree to leave the bank. This took his pension to £16 million, which will pay out £693,000 annually for life.[3]

The same drama was playing out elsewhere, particularly in the United States as Bear Sterns, Lehman Brothers, Washington Mutual, Countrywide Financial, AIG, Merrill Lynch, Citigroup, Fannie Mae and many other financial services organizations collapsed and were forced to seek government help. Even the great Goldman Sachs was in trouble. In less than a generation, all these tortoise-like organizations had turned into hares. They thought that making money was easy. All they had to do was set aggressive targets, underpin them by even more aggressive bonuses and wait for profits to increase and share values to rise.

The downward spiral of decline – what went so disastrously wrong?

The decline and fall of command and control management didn't happen overnight. It was a gradual deterioration. Here are some of the key steps along this fateful journey:

- **"Shareholder value" became an obsession.** One of the reasons why many organizations have gone off the rails is that their leaders lost sight of why they were in business. While they all no doubt had mission statements with all the right words in them, what came across to employees and customers was that the only purpose in evidence was to maximize short-term shareholder value. But if organizations are seen as purely money-making machines, then we are all in trouble. Of course they need to make money to reinvest and renew the business and make a decent return on the risk capital invested, but this shouldn't be *why* they are in business. Indeed, if the purpose is perceived as only making money, then it should come as no surprise that people act in their own self-interest. Nor should it surprise anyone that power, greed and corruption are the outcomes.

- **Aggressive targets and incentives encouraged the wrong behavior.** The rise in "pay-for-performance" over the past 20 years has reinforced a culture of "business is about making money" and "management is about meeting the target." CEOs in particular have been treated by the media like celebrity athletes (many have agents and lawyers as part of their "team") who appear to be more interested in maximizing their short-term rewards than in longer-term success. Many executives at failed banks used accounting trickery and financial engineering to meet aggressive targets, achieve large bonuses and satisfy demanding shareholders. Like drugs, targets and incentives are addictive. But also like drugs, they come with many side effects.[4] They provide the illusion that leaders can "predict and control" future outcomes in a fast-changing, highly unpredictable world. Target-setting is often a game of charades that rewards skilled political operators rather than the best team-builders or innovative thinkers. While many leaders would no doubt argue that targets and incentives stretch and motivate, the evidence suggests that they stifle innovation and growth as well as drain energy and demotivate people. The result is unhappy customers and underperforming companies.[5]

- **Regulation and risk management has failed.** Why didn't the regulatory system work? One reason is that rules don't change behavior. Almost without exception, all the firms that collapsed had unqualified financial statements.[6] When confronted with more regulations, large companies employ lawyers to work out how to get around them. Moreover, large companies are more likely to capture the most talented professionals, who are able to run rings around their counterparts in regulatory authorities. The reality is that too many organizations continue to operate in a gray area between what's right or wrong and too often step over the wrong side of the ethical line. When a short-term profit opportunity beckons, there is always a way to "explain away" the ethical dilemma or the risk. All the time and money spent on regulation and compliance has failed to change management mindsets, leaving a culture of self-interest, unethical behavior and outright fraud intact.[7] In July 2010 Citigroup agreed to pay a $75 million penalty for repeatedly making misleading statements in earnings calls and public filings through 2007. Apparently, Citigroup said it had reduced its investment banking unit's exposure to subprime-mortgage-backed securities to $13 billion or less, when the actual exposure was closer to $50 billion.[8] In the UK, corporate fraud losses hit a record £1bn in the first half of 2010, with about 49 percent of these frauds occurring in the finance and insurance sectors.[9]

- **Central control is more difficult and expensive.** In repeated attempts to realign strategy, structure and systems over the past 20 years or so, many leaders have expanded their control systems as increasing numbers of standard setters, compliance officers, risk managers, performance controllers, project leaders, internal consultants, quality controllers, customer relationship managers, business analysts, management advisors and many other back-office management positions have proliferated. And most of these new roles have come with expensive IT systems, training courses and management controls. The management control bureaucracy can often represent several layers of management: the people who work there do little else but handle information and make decisions that link high-level strategy with low-level execution. The levels of waste can be astonishing.[10]

- **Trust has declined.** The public perception of large corporations is at its lowest point in recent history. Just 33 percent of European and 40 percent of US consumers say that they trust large global corporations to act in society's best interest all, most, or even some of the time.[11] Too many organizations use the creativity of their people not to develop new business models and products to attract new customers but to think up as many (often devious) ways as possible to squeeze more profit from existing customers without offering much in return. For example, a substantial proportion of retail banking profits comes from penalizing customers for breaking arbitrary, complicated rules about minimum balances, credit limits and payment deadlines. Mobile phone companies make much of their money out of the minutes we don't use. Hotels and travel operators make it hard to find out about discounts or upgrades, and some airlines have computer algorithms that run so often that it is impossible to identify what the "normal" price of a flight ought to be. A "surveillance" culture is emerging as leaders use technology to check the time their people spend online, the time it takes to answer the telephone, and the time it takes to complete a call to a customer. Computer spyware and even cameras are used to check their every movement. The result is even less loyalty and more cheating.

- **Employees are neither engaged nor empowered.** In the 1970s and 80s "empowerment" was a concept that exercised the minds of many leaders. Though some leaders used the right words, their actions were undermined by intractable middle managers and suffocating control systems that demanded obedience to the plan. Little has changed. A 2007 Towers Perrin survey of nearly 90,000 employees worldwide found that only 21 percent felt fully engaged at work (meaning they're willing to go the extra mile to help their companies succeed) and 38 percent were disenchanted or disengaged. The result is an "engagement gap" between the discretionary effort companies need and what people actually want to invest, and companies' effectiveness in channeling this effort to enhance performance. That negativity has a direct impact on the bottom line. Towers Perrin found that companies with low levels of employee engagement had a 33 percent annual decline in operating income and an 11 percent annual decline in earnings growth. Those with high engagement, on the other hand, reported a 19 percent increase in operating income and 28 percent growth in earnings per share.[12] The result is that too few people are engaged in strategy and innovation, which remain exclusive, top-down processes. And frontline teams now spend increasing amounts of their time on annual budgets, irrelevant reports, burdensome administration and unnecessary meetings.

The failure of the command and control model means that the wrong story is being told about business. Joe Public hears more about excessive pay, defective products and environmental disasters than about the huge contribution that businesses all over the world make to the well-being of everyone. Where would we be without life-saving drugs, flat-screen TVs, laptops, mobile phones, low-cost airlines and so on? None of these breakthroughs could have been achieved by individuals working alone. They all needed thousands of people to collaborate effectively within and across large corporations to bring new products and services to market. There is an urgent need to eradicate the root causes of bad behavior and enable leaders to tell a more uplifting and inspiring story about business today.

Rethinking the management model

All these problems have been festering for many years. Successive leaders trying to solve them have spent billions of dollars on reorganizations, downsizing programs and management tools. But few have succeeded. The trouble is that the problems are *systemic.* They are embedded in management theories and mental models that most leaders base their management practices upon. For over 100 years these theories and models have been derived from some variant of "classical economics" and "command and control" management, both of which assume that the primary role of managers (agents) is to maximize value for shareholders (principals).

In his landmark 1962 book *Strategy and Structure* Alfred Chandler explained that the reason this command and control model proved so powerful was that it emphasized the decentralization of responsibility to operating divisions whose activities were planned, coordinated and controlled by a strong corporate center – the "general office," in Chandler's terms – which also made the decisions about resource allocation. He showed how the management process created by this organization allowed companies to apply their resources more efficiently to opportunities created by changing markets and developing technologies.[13]

The command and control model has been subject to much criticism over recent years for focusing on the hierarchy rather than the customer and requiring high costs to support its bureaucratic control systems. However, we must remember that, like mass production, it served 20th-century companies and their customers reasonably well, as productivity and living standards were steadily improved. Throughout this time, when manufacturing was a much larger part of most economies than it is today, employees served machines and simply did what was specified in their employment contract. Their knowledge was of little value. They were just cogs in a huge wheel that was driven from the center.

In today's service- and digital-based economy, however, machines serve people, and human knowledge is increasingly needed and valued. Most innovations come from employees rather than specialist research departments.[14] The reason for this dramatic role reversal is that to compete in today's fast-changing markets organizations need to attract and keep the best people, innovate continuously, respond rapidly to change, satisfy customer needs at the lowest cost and act ethically. These new competitive imperatives are not easily met by command and control organizations. Creativity cannot be centrally planned and controlled, and leaders are finding that they have little choice but to devolve power and responsibility to people closer to the customer.

But if employees are expected to take responsibility for decisions and be accountable for their actions, they need a framework that gives them the freedom and confidence to act and that guides them to the right choices. This framework should tell them something about the purpose of the business. It should tell them why they should give their time and commitment to this organization. It should tell them about what the organization values and the principles that govern relationships with colleagues both within the organization and with external parties. It should inform them about goals and performance expectations. It should inform them about the operating boundaries within which they should work. And it should tell them about the support, information and resources they will receive to enable them to perform.

Business schools: the pursuit of misguided models

None of these changes come naturally or easily to leaders that have attended the top business schools or risen through the ranks of most large corporations over the past 25 years. Despite the pioneering work of many great social scientists (such as McGregor and Maslow), it seems to be the economic and financial theorists (such as Williamson and Friedman) that leaders have most closely followed and whose ideas they have applied. The late management scholar Sumantra Ghoshal believed that many of these theories and ideas developed in leading business schools have done much to sustain command and control thinking and practice, leading to many of the problems we are experiencing today. Ghoshal summarized them in the following way: "In courses on corporate governance grounded in agency theory, we have taught our students that managers cannot be trusted to do their jobs – which, of course, are to maximize shareholder value – and that to overcome 'agency problems,' managers' interests and incentives must be aligned with those of the shareholders by, for example, making stock options a significant part of their pay. In courses on organization design, grounded in transaction cost economics, we have preached the need for tight monitoring and control of people to prevent 'opportunistic behavior.' In strategy courses, we have presented the 'five forces' framework to suggest that companies must compete not only with their competitors but also with their suppliers, customers, employees, and regulators."[15]

Ghoshal also took issue with the "scientific" model adopted by many business schools (an approach that economist Friedrich Hayek described as "the pretense of knowledge"). As Ghoshal noted, this pretense has demanded theorizing based on partialization of analysis, the exclusion of any role for human intentionality or choice, and the use of sharp assumptions and deductive reasoning."[16] The aim was to turn management into a "real" science like physics (Ghoshal was originally a physicist). He believed that this pseudo-scientific approach has far-reaching consequences. Because human behavior and relationships can't be modeled, they are conveniently ignored. So you simply end up with equations based on financial numbers (often with simple "cause-and-effect" relationships). This explains why so many managers practice "management by numbers."[17] Ghoshal's scathing attack came together in this evocative statement:

"Combine agency theory with transaction cost economics, add in standard versions of game theory and negotiation analysis, and the picture of the manager that emerges is one that is now very familiar in practice: the ruthlessly hard-driving, strictly top-down, command-and-control focused, shareholder-value-obsessed, win-at-any-cost business leader."[18]

Economics: a failure to embrace new thinking

While management thinking has been treading water for decades, economic thinking has moved on. Author of *The Origin of Wealth* Eric Beinhocker believes that business leaders can learn many lessons from these recent shifts. "Traditional economic theory sees the economy as a rubber ball rolling around the bottom of a large bowl," explains Beinhocker. "Eventually the ball will settle down into the bottom of the bowl, to its resting, or equilibrium point. The ball will stay there until some external force shakes, bends, or otherwise shocks the bowl, sending the ball to a new equilibrium point. The mainstream paradigm of economics over the past hundred years has portrayed the economy as a system that moves from equilibrium point to equilibrium point over time, propelled along by shocks from technology, politics, changes in consumer tastes, and other external factors.[19] Thus the dynamism of the economy comes from a process of equilibrium, then shock, then new equilibrium, then shock, then new equilibrium, and the economy moves from one *temporary equilibrium* to another."[20] This is known as "punctuated equilibrium."

But according to the scientific community, economic thinking is in some sort of time warp. In the early 1980s a number of scientists and economists decided to get together at the Santa Fe Institute and compare notes. One of the physicists commented that looking at economics reminded him of his recent trip to Cuba. As he described it, in Cuba you enter a place that has been almost completely shut off from the Western world for over 40 years by the US trade embargo. For the physicists, much of what they saw in economics had a similar "vintage" feeling to it. It looked to them as if economics had been locked in its own intellectual embargo, out of touch with several decades of scientific progress, but meanwhile ingeniously bending, stretching and updating its theories to keep them running.[21]

The same observation can be made about management thinking: after all, most management and accounting theory is derived from classical economics. Like traditional economists, most business leaders (and academics) have been living in their own "Cuba," blissfully ignorant of progress in scientific thinking about how systems work (we'll get to a definition of a "system" shortly).

For example, most business leaders still view the organization as an obedient machine with levers that can be pulled to change efficiency, speed and direction. Its origins go back to Sir Isaac Newton's model of the physical world as a clocklike mechanism – one gear turns, which makes another gear turn, and so on. This notion of cause-and-effect addresses one of the deepest human fears – that of losing control. Most managers still use machine metaphors for business change such as "reengineering the parts" and getting the organization to "fire on all cylinders." Author of *Leadership and the New Science* Margaret Wheatley put it this way:

> *"Amid all the evidence that our world is radically changing, we still think of organizations in mechanistic terms, as collections of replaceable parts capable of being reengineered. We act as if even people were machines, redesigning their jobs as we would prepare an engineering diagram, expecting them to perform to specifications with machinelike obedience. Over the years, our ideas of leadership have supported this metaphoric myth. We sought prediction and control, and also charged leaders with providing everything that was absent from the machine: vision, inspiration, intelligence, and courage. They alone had to provide the energy and direction to move their rusting vehicles of organization into the future."*[22]

From clockwork to complex systems

But, according to Beinhocker, the dream of a clockwork universe ended for science in the 20th century, and is ending for economics in the 21st. The economy is too complex, too nonlinear, too dynamic and too sensitive to the twists and turns of chance to be amenable to prediction over anything but the very shortest of terms.[23] While Beinhocker is talking about the economy as a whole, the same point is valid for its subsets, including organizations of every kind.

Other traditional economic assumptions have also been under attack in recent years. Whereas traditional economists still believe in functional integration, agency theory, and "rational economic man" (someone who only responds to "carrot and stick" performance drivers such as targets and incentives), a new breed of "behavioral" economists such as Herbert Simon, Daniel Kahneman and Amos Tversky have shown that while people are intelligent in their decision-making, they are intelligent in ways very different from the picture presented by traditional economics. Real people are actually quite poor at complex logical calculations, but very good at quickly recognizing patterns, interpreting ambiguous information and learning. Real people are also fallible and subject to biases in their decision-making. Finally, they engage in what Herbert Simon called *satisficing*, whereby one looks for a result that is "good enough" rather than the absolute best.[24]

While economists were pursuing their vision of the economy as an equilibrium system, physicists, chemists, and biologists during the latter half of the 20th century became increasingly interested in systems that were far from equilibrium, that were dynamic and complex, and that never settled into a state of rest. Beginning in the 1970s, scientists began to refer to these types of systems as complex systems. In brief, a complex system is a system of many dynamically interacting parts or particles. In such systems the micro-level interactions of the parts or particles lead to the emergence of macro-level patterns of behavior. Beinhocker uses the example of a whirlpool to explain this behavior: "A single water molecule sitting in isolation is rather boring," he notes. "But if one puts a few billion water molecules together and adds some energy in the right way, one gets the complex macro pattern of a whirlpool. The pattern of the whirlpool is the result of the dynamic interactions between the individual water molecules. One cannot have a whirlpool with a single water molecule; rather, the whirlpool is a collective or 'emergent' property of the system itself."[25]

Systems thinking: acting on the whole rather than the parts

Organizations are like whirlpools. Despite the fine words in mission statements and strategy documents, it is the thousands of decisions taken every day by hundreds of managers that create (or destroy) value for customers and ultimately shareholders. Innovation, adaptation and collaboration are increasingly seen as emergent properties of the collective organization culture (i.e. the values, norms, standards, and processes that connect people together to create and deliver products and services to customers).

As Fitjof Capra explains in his synthesis of "systems thinking" *The Web of Life,* "systems thinking" does not concentrate on basic building blocks but rather on the basic principles of organization. "Systems thinking" is "contextual," which is the opposite of analytic thinking. Analysis means taking something apart to understand it; systems thinking means putting it into the context of the larger whole," notes Capra.[26] He emphasizes the point that living systems are integrated wholes whose properties cannot be reduced to those of smaller parts. Their essential or "systemic" properties are properties of the whole, which none of the parts have. They arise from the "organizing relations" of the parts, i.e. from a configuration of ordered relationships that is characteristic of that particular class of organisms, or systems. Systems properties are destroyed when a system is dissected into isolated elements.[27] What is destroyed when a living organism is dissected is its pattern. The components are still there, but the configuration of relationships between them – the pattern – is destroyed, and thus the organism dies.[28]

Meg Wheatley believes that the correct scientific metaphor for management should draw on *quantum* rather than Newtonian physics. She makes the same point as Capra: that one of the key differences is a focus on holism rather than parts. Systems are understood as whole systems, and attention is given to *relationships within those systems* (the root meaning of the word "system" derives from the Greek *synhistanai*, "to place together"). To understand things systemically literally means to put them in context, to establish the nature of their relationships.[29]

"When we view systems from this perspective," notes Wheatley, "we enter an entirely new landscape of connections, of phenomena that cannot be reduced to simple cause and effect, or explained by studying parts as isolated contributors. We move to a land where it becomes critical to sense the constant workings of dynamic processes, and then to notice how these processes materialize as visible behaviors and forms."[30]

Seeing businesses as adaptive systems

There are numerous types of "systems" including biological systems (for example, the human body), mechanical systems (a thermostat) and social systems (a business organization). A complex system is usually made up of many smaller systems or subsystems. For instance, a business organization is made up of many processes and subprocesses that continuously connect and combine to achieve a goal (such as satisfying customer needs).

Seeing social systems such as business organizations as complex, adaptive systems has profound implications. As cybernetics expert Steve Morlidge explains, "Instead of viewing them as functional machines whose performance can be optimized, they are in reality creative, adaptive entities that explore, experiment and learn over time, changing their goals and strategies, and transforming themselves and their environment. This means that instead of basing our strategies and actions on *prediction*, with the development and implementation of a plan designed to take us from 'here and now' to 'there and then,' we have to adopt more frequent monitoring and reassessments, with an awareness and capacity to change course to make use of what works and discard what doesn't. This is an approach that recognizes the constant need to learn about what is happening and to try to make sense of it as quickly as possible."[31]

Systems theory tells us that the traditional mechanical model *cannot* be effective, except in a very stable environment. As Steve Morlidge explains, Ross Ashby's Law of Requisite Variety, formulated in the 1950s, sets out the necessary relationship between the complexity of the environment, the flexibility of a control system and the specificity of the goals imposed on the system. The more complex the environment, and the "tighter" the targets, the more flexibility the control system must have: "only variety can absorb variety." Failure to provide "requisite variety" will result in instability (boom and bust) and ultimately system failure. The only way out is to "game the system," such as artificially injecting flexibility by other means (in other words, by cheating). Given a complex environment, Ashby's Law tells us, the only way that complex organizations *can* be successfully controlled is through exploiting the capacity of a system for self-organization and self-regulation. In other words, we need to adopt an organic model.[32]

An alternative model based on adaptive systems

Within the context of this book it is only possible to scratch the surface of "systems thinking," but even so, it offers a viable alternative theory to the mechanistic view that has underpinned management thinking and practices for too long and should now be consigned to history. To summarize, there are four principles that we can use as the foundation stones of an alternative management model:

1. Organizations are whole systems (the whole system rather than the parts determines performance).

2. Organizations are webs of relationships that are unpredictable (rather than cause-and-effect relationships that are predictable).

3. Organizations are self-organizing and self-regulating (they don't require central coordination and control).

4. Change is best seen as integrative and adaptive rather than project-driven and reactive.

How different organization models lead to different management models

These contrasting models of how organizations work have major implications for management thinking and practice. Table I.1 shows how the "obedient machine"

TABLE I.1 Contrasting models

Organization model	Organization as an obedient machine	Organization as an adaptive system
	Organizations are made up of a collection of replaceable parts (parts determine the performance of the whole)	Organizations are whole systems (the whole system determines performance)
	Organizations comprise "cause-and-effect" relationships that are predictable	Organizations are webs of relationships that are unpredictable
	Organizations need central planning, coordination and control	Organizations are self-organizing and self-regulating
	Change is reactive and project-driven	Change is integrative and adaptive
	↓	↓
Management model	Command and control	Adaptive management
	Aim is to bind people to a plan	Aim is to bind people to a cause
	Governance is based on rules and regulations	Governance is based on values and judgment
	Information is bounded and restricted	Information is unbounded and transparent
	Natural organization form is functional hierarchy	Natural organization form is team-based network
	Teams are micro-managed	Teams are trusted to make decisions
	Teams are accountable for narrow targets	Teams are accountable for holistic success criteria
	Goal is to meet a short-term fixed target	Goal is to continuously improve relative to peers
	People are rewarded based on meeting short-term targets	Teams are rewarded based on relative improvement
	Strategy is an annual top-down event	Strategy is a continuous and inclusive process
	Plans are coordinated centrally through annual planning cycles	Plans are coordinated locally based on dynamic interactions
	Resources are available just-in-case	Resources are available just-in-time
	Control comes from centrally agreed budgets	Control comes from fast, frequent feedback

view leads to command and control management and the "adaptive systems" view leads to a different set of principles that we have called "adaptive management." We believe that the 12 principles of adaptive management sit comfortably with systems thinking.

The organization-as-an-obedient-machine model takes leaders down the pathway of shareholder value maximization, short-term targets (and "fixing" the results);

individual financial incentives; employee contracts; central planning, coordination and control; central resource allocations and budgetary control. The core assumption is that everything is controllable if an organization can be broken down into its constituent parts and the right steering mechanisms and metrics used to ensure that each part achieves its optimum performance (each part is likely to have its own target and measures independent of others). If there is a problem with any part, a range of "tools" can be used to "fix" or "re-engineer" the problem. But focusing on each separate part is likely to lead to dysfunctional behavior as one unit tries to improve its performance at the expense of another (this is known as "sub-optimization").

If the organization is struggling to satisfy shareholder expectations it appoints a new CEO who can apply the necessary "shock treatment" in terms of restructuring, re-engineering and reorganization. In other words, like the "punctured equilibrium" view of the economists, many analysts and boards believe it is the direct action of "heroic" leaders (the "shock" to the system) that creates the necessary dynamism, innovation, change and value creation. Too many leaders believe that they are responsible for changing the organization. So when the engine is misfiring they bring in the organizational "fixers" with their toolboxes full of spanners and levers that can retune the necessary parts. Few have any faith that the people actually doing the work might have a view about how it can be improved.

This machine-like model represents the current "management cockpit" view of leadership – a sort of 21st-century computer game in which a few leaders at the center control the actions of hundreds of front-line managers by monitoring variances against a fixed plan in "real time." In this model, measurement replaces management. The aim is to design judgment out of the system. Many leaders see this vision as the ultimate goal of technology – a sort of holy grail of IT and accounting.

But there is deep cynicism about these approaches based on machine-like assumptions. It is increasingly tough (and expensive) to keep strategies, structures and systems in constant alignment in a fast-changing world. Change is invariably reactive and disruptive; endless restructuring, reorganizing and re-engineering programs come and go with, in most cases, temporary relief but little longer-term effect. Employees are small cogs in this giant organizational wheel of fortune. The result is that leaders consistently fail to connect with their people and thus miss the opportunity of harnessing a potentially huge store of "free" knowledge and creativity.

The alternative view is that organizations are adaptive systems, and this model takes us down a different pathway. The organization has a noble purpose beyond shareholder value: the goal is to adapt and endure. People are motivated by self-fulfillment rather than money; they work in self-managed teams; information is unbounded and transparent; and control comes from fast, frequent feedback.

The leader's dilemma

Many leaders buy into the adaptive systems view. Most have visions of building "strategy-focused," "quality-driven," "lean and agile," "team-based" and "customer-focused" organizations. They all want to cut bureaucracy and empower their people. They all want to manage strategies instead of budgets and adapt to each new reality rather than be a slave to the plan. But few can see a way to do this within the management models they have inherited. This is the leader's dilemma: how can he or she dismantle the bureaucracy and budget and build empowered and adaptive organizations, yet maintain coordination and control? What does an alternative management model look like, and how do they get from where they are today to where they want to be in three or five years from now?

Early visionaries of the adaptive model

Today's leaders can take comfort from the fact that they are not alone, nor are they pioneers. The early life forms of a management model based on adaptive systems have been around for quite a long time. A few visionary leaders such as Herb Kelleher at Southwest Airlines (USA), Taiichi Ohno at Toyota (Japan), Jan Wallander at Handelsbanken (Sweden), William Davidson at Guardian Industries (USA), Bill Gore at W.L. Gore & Associates (USA), Götz Werner at dm drogerie-markt (Germany), Egon Zehnder at Egon Zehnder International (Switzerland), John Mackey at Whole Foods Market (USA) and Ken Iverson at Nucor Steel (USA) have always passionately believed in empowering people with information and providing them with the scope, authority and support to make key decisions.

These leaders have been successful primarily because they focused their attention (either explicitly or implicitly) on creating wealth over the longer term. They were also deep thinkers and introduced a different belief system to their organizations. They rejected command and control management and promoted leaders who naturally adopted a style that emphasized purpose, values, humility and ethics, inspiring people to raise their performance. As well as being open and accessible, they were also good listeners. It is a leadership style encapsulated in this statement by Southwest Airlines founder Herb Kelleher: "Leadership is being a faithful, devoted, hard-working servant of the people you lead and participating with them in the agonies as well as the ecstasies of life."[33]

In more recent times, a group of organizations across industries and geographies have decided to follow the same path as these visionary leaders. Though for most of them the elapsed time is insufficient to draw firm conclusions about their long-term success, the initial signs are positive. These organizations include American Express (USA), Statoil (Norway), HCL Technologies (India), Telenor (Norway), Telekom Malaysia (Malaysia), Coloplast (Denmark) and Hilti (Liechtenstein).

Figure I.2 illustrates the shape and important features of the "adaptive" management model. The major change is that the traditional organizational pyramid is turned on its side to face the customer. Accountability flows from left to right across three teams: The *executive team* is the C-level suite responsible for setting business purpose, high-level goals and strategic direction as well as challenging other teams to maximize their performance. *Support service teams* such as design, production, logistics, supply chain, finance, human resources, marketing and information technology are responsible for serving and supporting value centers. *Value center teams* are responsible for formulating and executing strategy and for

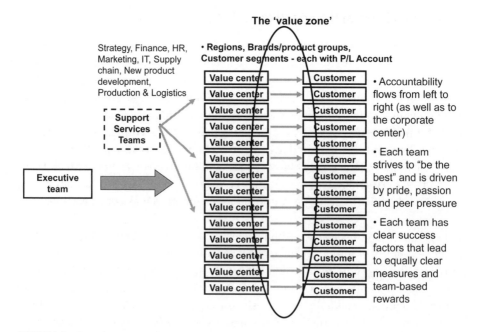

FIGURE I.2 The adaptive management model

continuously improving their performance against peers. They invariably have their own profit and loss accounts and are typically created around businesses/ markets, brands/product groups and regions/countries. In knowledge- and service-based organizations, value is no longer created in the R&D department or the head office suite. It is created in the "value zone," that is, at the interface between a company and its customers.

The 12 principles of adaptive management

The 12 principles of the adaptive management model and how you can embrace them represent the next 12 chapters of this book and are summarized here.

Principle #1 – Values: Bind people to a common cause, not a central plan

- **Command and control management:** Leaders accept that their job is to act as managers ("agents") for shareholders ("principals") in the pursuit of maximizing shareholder value. Academics call this "agency theory" and it enables them to build elegant mathematical models that can be applied to the enormously complex economic, social and moral issues related to the governance of giant public corporations that have such enormous influence on the lives of thousands – often millions – of people.[34] They also believe that clear mission and strategy statements that underpin shareholder value will cause employees to give their total commitment, and that detailed plans and budgets will enable managers to predict and control future outcomes. Meg Wheatley reminds us of the assumptions behind the machine-like metaphor. "We assume," she notes, "like good machines, we have no desire, no heart, no spirit, no compassion, no real intelligence – because machines don't have any of that. The great dream of machines is that if you give them a set of instructions, they will follow it."[35]

- **Adaptive management:** Leaders don't accept that shareholders' interests are paramount. Most shareholders can sell their stocks far more easily than most employees can find another job. In every substantive sense, employees of a company carry more risks than do shareholders. Also, their contributions of knowledge, skills and entrepreneurship are typically more important than the contributions of capital by shareholders, a pure commodity that is perhaps in excess supply.[36] Leaders recognize that all stakeholders (including shareholders, employees, customers, suppliers, partners, communities and government) need to be kept in a healthy balance. Such a delicate balancing act needs a governance framework underpinned by a noble purpose, and clear values and boundaries that support local decisions. Leaders believe that it is the pride, passion and peer pressure as well as shared rewards that drive people to achieve extraordinary results. They adopt a "coach and support" management style that places performance responsibility on the shoulders of front-line people. It is this continuous involvement in planning and execution that builds motivation and commitment and leads to ambitious strategies and continuous improvement. They are the foundation stones of the adaptive management model.

Principle #2 – Governance: Govern through shared values and sound judgment, not detailed rules and regulations

- *Command and control management:* Leaders believe they can govern the organization through detailed rules and regulations. They appoint compliance officers and risk managers to ensure that their people keep within the guidelines. They manage risk through risk registers and mathematical models and by setting "risk appetites" that enable managers to take a view on which risks to insure against (either fully or partly) and which to accept. They appoint highly paid executives to oversee risk and ethical behavior.

- *Adaptive management:* Leaders believe that risk models and processes are only one half (and not the most important half) of the governance and risk management challenge. While they also have sophisticated processes, they rely more on understanding the management model and ensuring that the risk drivers are set at the right levels (not too high, not too low). They operate within a culture of truth, transparency and trust that guides actions throughout the organization. They believe that risk management should not be a specialist back-office function but a management core competence supported by management-friendly models and processes. But they rely more on sound judgment underpinned by well-designed processes and fast feedback. When they make mistakes, they learn and move on.

Principle #3 – Transparency: Make information open and transparent; don't restrict and control it

- *Command and control management:* Leaders believe that information can be "restricted and controlled" so that people only "see what they need to see." They believe that the primary beneficiaries of information are people at the center. And they accept a culture of "treating and spinning" information to make it look better than it really is. The trouble is that each person's interpretation is different and that restricting information dissemination in this way denies the organization the richness of different views.

- *Adaptive management:* Leaders accept that information in the digital age can no longer be tightly controlled, so they promote information flows to new levels of openness and transparency. They believe that if everyone can see the same information at the same time, then the right decisions will be made more quickly and teams will be more aware of their performance compared with others. In order to achieve this they have understood that all the numbers within the organization should stick to "one truth" and be transparent: they should be seen by everyone in their raw state without people "treating" them or painting pictures that are designed to mislead. This gives everyone confidence in the numbers and supports decision-making. The outcome is more transparent and reliable information and more ethical reporting.

Principle #4 – Teams: Organize around a seamless network of accountable teams, not centralized functions

- *Command and control management:* The objective in the functional organization is to optimize the efficiency of each operating part using interrelated plans and budgets. Leaders design their organizations around hierarchies of authority, encouraging every function and department to focus on their own actions and results. They believe that if every part performs to its optimum capability then the whole organization will maximize its performance. Hierarchical command and control cultures devalue diversity, distrust self-organization and dismiss ideas of interdependence. Author of Profit for Life Jay Bragdon believes that command and control cultures kill the spontaneity living systems need to realize their full creative potential.[37]

- *Adaptive management:* Leaders see systems less like clockwork mechanisms and more like communities of self-managed teams that connect and combine to deliver customer value. They design systems and sub-systems that are tied together in a network of supplier–customer relationships. Every system has a network of supplier–customer relationships and the aim is to improve the whole system so that the organization can deliver a high-quality product and service to a customer. They don't use financial targets to link systems together. They look at the design of each system and check that it is achieving its purpose at the optimum speed, highest quality and lowest cost.

Principle #5 – Trust: Trust teams to regulate their performance; don't micro-manage them

- *Command and control management:* Leaders ensure that local managers have to "go up the line" before a decision can be made. They assume that only people at the center have the experience and wisdom to make good decisions. That's what leaders are paid to do.

- *Adaptive management:* Leaders believe that the more that strategic capability is spread around the organization and the more diversity there is, the stronger the organization will be. Leaders accept that for teams to be made accountable for performance they need the scope and authority to make decisions. That's why they transfer the accountability for planning and decision-making to front-line (value center) teams who are more likely to produce imaginative strategies and be committed to their successful execution. Front-line teams need to feel part of the problem and the solution. But this does not mean that senior executives have no influence. Their role is to set high standards, expectations and benchmarks to stretch ambition and performance, and then to challenge local teams to ensure that their goals and plans are sufficiently ambitious, yet robust and realistic. This is much more than delegation. It is a radical change in the power base as front-line teams are trusted to take the right decision to continuously improve performance.

Principle #6 – Accountability: Base accountability on holistic criteria and peer reviews, not on hierarchical relationships

- *Command and control management:* Accountability is focused on "pleasing the boss" and meeting agreed personal targets. As in a sports team, the leader is clearly accountable to the owners for the team's performance and will expect to be fired if results fail to meet expectations. But lower down the organization accountabilities become less clear, particularly at the seams in the hierarchy, where a vacuum exists. This is often filled with smart political operators who are able to pin accountability on anyone but themselves.

- *Adaptive management:* In the adaptive organization leaders are able to see more clearly where accountabilities should lie and how the information and reporting systems should flow. They switch accountability for performance from a few high-profile individuals to many small teams, and from pleasing the boss to pleasing the customer. It is not physical structures that change but the accountabilities of each team and the relationships between them. Rethinking team-based accountability is the platform for the adaptive management model.

Principle #7 – Goals: Encourage teams to set ambitious goals; don't turn goals into fixed contracts

- *Command and control management:* For decades, goal-setting has been promoted as a magic bullet for improving employee motivation and setting "stretch" goals. In 1990 Locke, Latham, Smith & Wood wrote the bible on Goal Setting Theory in which they noted that across hundreds of experiments, dozens of tasks and thousands of participants across four continents, the results are clear: compared to vague, easy goals (e.g. "do your best"), specific, challenging goals boost performance.[38] Targets are set on the basis of financial and, more often than not, "negotiated" numbers between superiors and subordinates before the start of the year. They are fixed for the year ahead and represent the key component of the annual fixed performance contract. All actions are then focused on meeting the numbers. But in their paper "Goals Gone Wild: The Systematic Side Effects of Over-Prescribing Goal Setting"[39] Lisa D. Ordóñez et al. argue that goal-setting has been over-prescribed and has powerful and predictable side effects. They conclude that rather than being offered as an "over-the-counter" salve for boosting performance, goal-setting should be prescribed selectively, presented with a warning label and closely monitored.[40] In a follow-up interview, Max Bazerman noted that "when we factor in the consistent findings that stretch and specific goals both narrow focus on a limited set of behaviors while increasing risk-taking and unethical behavior, their simple implementation can become a vice."[41] Our observations over the past 20 years confirm this view.

- *Adaptive management:* Setting targets and "fixing" the system to meet them is a particularly pernicious outcome of machine-like thinking. But in adaptive evolutionary systems, agents (such as trees and birds) have only one goal in mind: to be the fittest in their peer group and thus have the best chance of enduring and prospering over the long term. This goal is also appropriate for the corporate world (though it doesn't mean being the best every year; every company has its ups and downs). As many leaders have discovered, if you define success as some measure of relative improvement, you are likely to encourage different behavior as managers have little option but to keep improving performance until the last day in the year. "Being the best" (firm or team) is the new mantra of success. The result is a virtuous circle of high standards and continuous improvement. In other words, only with hindsight do agents in evolutionary systems know who has adapted and endured sufficiently to make it to each successive generation. This eradicates much of the "gaming" that goes on around meeting a predetermined number. Peer pressure drives performance. It doesn't require annual targets or contracts. It is simply relentless. Each team sets its own aspirational goals (typically two to five years ahead) but these are not treated as commitments or contracts. The only commitment is to keep improving.

Principle #8 – Rewards: Base rewards on relative performance, not fixed targets

- *Command and control management:* Leaders believe in the power of individual rewards. They see people as an important part of the organization machine whose performance can be "fine-tuned" by changing extrinsic motivators such as fixed targets and financial inducements. They assume that managers are motivated and fairly rewarded if the right mix of targets and incentives is put in place. Thus rewards are linked to a fixed outcome agreed in advance. The assumed benefits are that managers "know where they stand and what number they have to meet." All they have to do is achieve the target and bonus. These beliefs can be encapsulated in the expression "Do this and you'll get that." Its management origins come from piecework – the more repeatable tasks you perform, the more you will earn. However, relating pay to performance when individual output can be precisely measured is one thing, but applying this approach to complex modern organizations where success is more dependent on design, innovation, quality and customer service is another.

- *Adaptive management:* Leaders understand that employee recognition is more powerful than incentive compensation. To the extent that rewards are used, they are based upon the progress that both teams and the firm as a whole make toward achieving medium-term goals (using a range of metrics). Performance evaluation is made "with hindsight" in the light of how a team performed over the period against peers and benchmarks. Some leaders dispense with local rewards altogether and use one group-wide profit-sharing scheme based on a formula related to the competitive performance of the firm. In all cases they have seen a reduction in "gaming" behavior (with no fixed contract, there is little point in gaming).

Principle #9 – Planning: Make planning a continuous and inclusive process, not a top-down annual event

- *Command and control management:* Leaders believe that future outcomes can be predicted and controlled. They place strategy at the center of the management system as they embrace the "strategy-focused organization." But this approach tends to devalue continuous innovation and fast response. The traditional planning process is either top-down (prepared by leaders or central planning departments) or sometimes bottom-up (with local teams preparing their plans and then negotiating and agreeing them with superiors). Many plans are based on departmental improvements that are not necessarily in accord with strategic objectives. After many months of discussion, the resulting plan provides clear guidelines that tell people what they have to do in the year ahead and their performance is measured against the plan.

- *Adaptive management:* Leaders believe that the world is increasingly unpredictable and thus requires continuous planning. In practice, leaders review the medium-term outlook (usually a two-to-five-year horizon) every year and the short-term outlook (typically, five to eight quarters ahead) every quarter (or, in some cases, in response to specific events). Both cycles are aimed at continuously improving performance against peers and prior years. Responsibility for these reviews is devolved to front-line teams. The role of group executives is to set strategic objectives and medium-term goals and then challenge the plans and initiatives that managers propose to ensure their core assumptions and risks are reasonable and represent the best options available.

Principle #10 – Coordination: Coordinate interactions dynamically, not through annual budgets

- *Command and control management:* Leaders link functional and departmental plans through the central coordination of budgets. For example, they ensure that production and sales are in tune and that marketing has the resources to support the sales plan. At that point each unit plan connects with another, leading to a coherent plan for the whole firm. When key assumptions change, the whole plan often needs to be changed and coordinated all over again.

- *Adaptive management:* MIT professor of learning Mitchel Resnick likens the organization of the future to the movement of bird flocks. Most people assume, he notes, that birds play a game of follow-the-leader: the bird in front of the flock leads and the others follow. Indeed, people assume centralized control for almost all patterns they see in the world. But that's not necessarily so. In the case of bird flocks, most don't have leaders at all. Rather, each bird follows a set of simple rules, for example, matching its velocity to that of other birds around it, and keeping a safe distance from the birds on either side. A bird flock is one of many phenomena organized without an organizer, coordinated without a coordinator.[42] By substituting organization teams for birds, and seeing how they coordinate their actions within a clear framework of principles and values (rather than rules and regulations) and operate within equally clear strategic guidelines (rather than specific plans), you can begin to see how a new type of adaptive organization can emerge. Thus the organization acts as an integrated system (rather than a number of disparate parts) pursuing a common strategy.

Principle #11 – Resources: Make resources available just-in-time, not just-in-case

- *Command and control management:* Leaders allocate resources on the basis of budget contracts negotiated in advance. The benefit is that at that time all resources are allocated to one unit or another. No further management attention is then needed until the following year's budget review. But allocating resources "just-in-case" they are needed generates huge amounts of waste as teams spend their resources whether required or not.

- *Adaptive management:* In nature all byproducts of one natural system are nutrients for another. There is no waste. One way to cut waste in business is to make resources available and accessible to front-line teams as and when required through "fast-track" approvals and easier access to operational resources. The onus is on teams to use their resources productively or face the consequences. Some organizations have developed an "internal market" whereby resources can be acquired by front-line teams from central services providers when they need them at an agreed price.

Principle #12 – Controls: Base controls on fast, frequent feedback, not budget variances

- *Command and control management:* The theory of organizational control is rooted in simple machines. If the engine is not going fast enough, we allow more steam in and the situation is resolved. This thinking has led managers to believe that they can control their performance from the center. They do this by agreeing contracts with each business unit and then monitoring performance against them. Any variances must be explained. They rarely look beyond the next fiscal year-end.

- *Adaptive management:* Over the last 30 years there has been a considerable amount of work done attempting to apply the insights of systems theorists to control in the biological and social world. Most notable is the work of Stafford Beer, who created the "Viable Systems Model" based on a model of the autonomic nervous system and how it regulates activity in the most complex organization known to us: the human body.[43] According to Beer, the task of performance measurement is to monitor, in real time, those variables that are relevant to the viability of the organization. Rather than comparing actuals to arbitrary targets, processes are set up to detect signs of incipient instability – a failure to respond to perturbations in the existing environment or adapt effectively to changes in the environment. Instead of machine-like controls and "hard" numbers, what matters to real-world managers is fast, frequent and relevant feedback. The focus of measurement is on self-improvement rather than top-down control.

The future of management is based on "empower and adapt"

Like Aesop's fable, the moral of the management story is that it is better in the long run to act like a tortoise rather than a hare. You can't win a marathon through a series of 100-meter sprints. Tortoises are the world's longest-living creatures. Longevity should also be the aim of business organizations. But this means continuous adaptation. Every time, steady organic growth based on satisfying customers at the lowest cost through great products and processes trumps short bursts of dramatic boom and bust based on mega-mergers and acquisitions, share buy-backs and aggressive targets and incentives. But if a few years ago you had tried to convince the directors and shareholders of Bear Sterns, Lehman Brothers, Merrill Lynch, AIG, Northern Rock, HBOS and Bradford and Bingley, you would have been given short shrift. The problem is that the leaders of these companies (and they are not alone!) believe in a management model that encourages them to act like a hare rather than a tortoise. It is a hare-brained model!

This book is not about implementing new regulations or tools to "fix" a few broken parts. It is about unleashing huge amounts of ambition, courage, creativity and collaboration within your organization. It is about learning from a few pioneers how to make your organization feel and act more like a community with a common purpose that is free, open, accessible and interactive. It is about turning the organization on its side to face the customer and ensuring that accountability is clear and information is transparent. And it is about building a business that is free from the burdens of stifling bureaucracy, aggressive targets, misaligned incentives, stifling budgets and suffocating controls and enables and encourages people to think, reflect, collaborate, learn and improve.

Web 2.0 has changed everything

Many leaders would like to make these changes but feel trapped inside their suffocating command and control management models. Change is difficult and can take a long time. But aspiring leaders have been dealt a new deck of cards. What has changed everything is the power, speed and connectivity of Web 2.0. If Web 1.0 was about the web as an information source, then Web 2.0 is about the web as a platform for participation and connectivity that includes such social networking sites as wikis and blogs that aim to facilitate creativity, collaboration and sharing among users. Web 2.0 is a dynamic peer-to-peer network with everyone potentially connected to everyone else. It is the ultimate democracy. Everyone has a voice. The problems of disparate information systems and disconnected controls are receding. Controls can be at the front line and at the corporate center at the same time. Effective empowerment can be achieved without the negative side effects. Knowledge can be shared instantly. It is now much easier to change than before.

The emergence of Web 2.0 provides a framework for harnessing the ideas of thousands of people who can now interact and coordinate their actions in real time across large, complex organizations and even whole ecosystems using the latest communications technology. As long as people have a common understanding of what they are trying to accomplish, everyone will act with a common purpose without needing to be told what to do. Not everyone needs access to all the detail, but everyone does need access to meaningful summaries and indicators of business activity and performance in each area of the company. And this information needs to be kept current, hour by hour and day by day.

The adaptive management model looks and feels more like Web 2.0. It is radically decentralized, with many more decisions being made at the periphery rather than the center. There are no negotiated fixed targets and incentives linked to them. There is less bureaucracy. Change is more natural and adaptive. People have far more knowledge at their fingertips as well as access to tools and models that enable managers to make fast decisions as they constantly adapt to customers' needs and changes in the competitive environment. Everyone is expected to contribute to the innovation process and participate in strategy and business improvement.

The challenge: tackling entrenched mindsets

So far, management in the 21st century doesn't feel that different from management in the 20th century. This book aims to change that perception. But tackling entrenched mindsets and overturning decades of accepted management practices will not be an easy challenge. It takes time, courage, patience, perseverance and dedication. Most business leaders are not geared for that. They want things to happen quickly because they are likely to be in the job for only a short time and they want to reap the benefits on their watch. But as many business leaders are discovering, it is a winning formula in an increasingly unpredictable and competitive world. Leaders need to get their thinking straight before launching into major change programs that typically aim at "fixing" particular problems. They need to act on the whole system rather than its parts. This isn't another "improvement project." It's a new way of thinking about management in the 21st-century organization.

KEY POINTS

- Look at your organization in the mirror. Does it look like a traditional multi-divisional organization in which top management is assumed to be the fountain of knowledge, strategic planner and resource allocator; middle managers are the controllers; and front-line managers are the implementers? This so-called "command and control" model stifles sharing and innovation and requires high costs to support the bureaucracy. It assumes that leaders can predict and control performance outcomes by setting targets and budgets and turning them into hundreds of "fixed performance contracts" that every team must meet. But, as we have seen in the banking crisis, in an uncertain and fast-changing world this expensive model is more likely to lead to unethical behavior and poor performance.

- Learn about "systems thinking" and develop new management models and metaphors that will help you to rethink a number of management practices and processes. For example, understanding that organizations are adaptive systems rather than obedient machines (or tortoises rather than hares) will help you to persuade others that management thinking and practice needs to change.

- Look for a better, more inspiring way to harness the knowledge and creativity of your people. Implement governance systems that encourage the right behavior (such as ambition, team-working and sharing) as well as foster a culture of transparency and trust.

- Adopt the 12 principles of the adaptive management model. Treat them as a set of guidelines that will help you to build your own model. But don't "cherry-pick" those you like and those you don't. They come as a package which, although it can be translated and implemented in different ways and implemented at different speeds, represents a complete and coherent alternative model.

- Take advantage of the latest technology. Use social networking systems and the power of Web 2.0 to enable your people to share knowledge and ideas. With hundreds of people involved in thinking about strategy and preparing plans, the likely outcome is more likely to be more creativity and more opportunities for breakthrough thinking. We are entering what some researchers call the "innovation economy." You owe it to your organization to build a management model that encourages continuous innovation.

## CHAPTER 1

Principle #1 – Values
Bind people to a common cause, not a central plan

People are social beings. They naturally collaborate with one another to learn, experiment, innovate, and optimize their value-added capacities. When companies trust employees, value their expertise, and give them greater flexibility to self-organize, they become energized. When they can also work toward shared goals and visions that affirm their values and beliefs, they become passionate.[1]

Joseph H. Bragdon *Profit for Life*

The value of values at Southwest Airlines

In the early 1970s Rollin King and Herb Kelleher got together and decided to start a different kind of airline. They began with one simple notion: if you get your passengers to their destinations when they want to get there, on time, at the lowest possible fares, and make sure they have a good time doing it, people will fly your airline. What began as a small Texas airline has grown to become one of the largest in the United States. Today, Southwest Airlines flies over 100 million passengers a year to 72 cities all across the country, and they do it more than 3200 times a day.[2]

Southwest's business model has been copied by all the low-cost airlines that have sprung up around the world over the past 20 years. It focuses on short-haul flights (average distance 653 miles) at convenient times through the day with gate turnaround speeds that continue to amaze competitors. It does not provide meals or in-flight movies and uses inner-city rather than major airports (where feasible). It aims to be easy to deal with as well as offering great value for money, and it meets these customer expectations most of the time. In an industry that has lost billions of dollars in recent years, Southwest has remained profitable. In fact, the performance record of Southwest Airlines is stunning. Not only has it been consistently profitable (a major challenge in the airline industry) and been the most cost efficient airline, but it is usually at the top of the independent customer satisfaction ratings in America. It is also one of the most admired airlines in the world and consistently one of the most admired companies and best "corporate citizens" in America.

A unique corporate culture

The key to Southwest's success is its unique corporate culture, and its architect is former CEO Herb Kelleher. Kelleher is a heroic figure in the American tradition. He fought and won against all the odds to get Southwest off the ground. Since then he has led the Southwest crusade and created and personified the Southwest culture. When asked how he kept this entrepreneurial spirit going, Kelleher replied: "I always felt that our people came first. Some of the business schools regarded that as a conundrum. They would say: Which comes first, your people, your customers, or your shareholders? And I would say, it's not a conundrum. Your people come first, and if you treat them right, they'll treat the customers right, and the customers will come back, and that'll make the shareholders happy. There's no difficulty in visualizing that. We've always tried to be sensitive to the needs of our people and recognize the things that are important to them in their personal lives. At Southwest Airlines, you can't have a baby without being recognized ... You can't have a death in your family without hearing from us. If you're out with a serious illness, we're in touch with you once every two weeks to see how you're doing. We have people who have been retired for 10 years, and we keep in touch with them. We want them to know that we value them as individuals, not just as workers. So that's part of the esprit de corps."[3]

After around 30 years at the helm, Herb Kelleher decided to take a back seat (since 2008 he has been Chairman Emeritus). In 2004, former CFO and a Southwest employee for over 20 years Gary Kelly was appointed as CEO (he is also now President and Chairman) and Laura Wright stepped up to become CFO. Between them, they have steered Southwest through some of the stormiest waters the organization has faced in its history. Like Kelleher, Kelly believes in the integrity of people. How the Sarbanes-Oxley Act has been interpreted by some companies is typical of his thinking. "One of my pet peeves," notes Kelly, "is that it is rules-based. Rules create loopholes, and human nature is to exploit those. Ultimately it is all about integrity. You can't legislate integrity. You can't force human behavior."[4]

"Our company has a soul"

Kelly has also inherited Kelleher's passion and pride in the business. "Our company has a soul," said Kelly in a recent interview. "We have a mission that people believe in. We really believe we are giving Americans the freedom to fly. It's a cause and it allows for a sense of pride in our individual employees to be associated with Southwest Airlines. Sports are an overdone analogy, but I'm a University of Texas Longhorn alumni and I couldn't be more proud to be that and to have our team go to the national championship. And that's the way Southwest Airlines employees feel about Southwest … I was talking to my brother last night. He doesn't work for Southwest but people, when they learn that his brother does, they say, 'Hey, that is the greatest company. You know, they're such a strong brand and a wonderful company to work for.' So there is an emotional attachment by our people and it's hard to put your finger on exactly what that is. But more than anything, Herb Kelleher cares about that. I care about it and it is real. And I do think that sets us apart. We have, year in/year out, the strongest brand rankings of most airlines and that's without offering some of the perceived amenities like first class and some of the other frills – just real people working hard to deliver a high-quality product in a very friendly and caring way."[5]

Leaders at Southwest are the cheerleaders of ambition and improvement. They continuously urge their people to think the unthinkable and look for improvements where they do not seem possible at first sight. "Being the best" sums it up. As Gary Kelly said in the March 2008 edition of LUV Lines (the company's internal magazine), "I am most grateful for our unsurpassed culture, a strong culture of love, care, responsibility, accountability and respect. Our culture also is about being the best: the best place to work; the best operations; and the best customer service."

Since its inception, Southwest has religiously stuck to a clearly defined purpose: to make a profit, achieve job security for every employee, and make flying affordable for more people. In 2007 Gary Kelly restated the company's purpose in this way:

- Be the safest and most reliable airline in the world

- Be the best place to work, with the best team of people

- Offer customers the greatest air travel value by combining the lowest fares, as enabled by the lowest cost and highest productivity, with the preferred customer service experience

- Be the preferred carrier in the markets we serve in terms of schedule, seat capacity, and customers

- Provide financial and job security for our employees, and excellent financial returns to our shareholders.

Hiring and developing the right people

But most employees are cynical about words on "mission" statements. What does "provide financial and job security for our employees" mean when employees become victims of reorganizations and downsizing as soon as the hard times come around? When Hurricane Katrina devastated New Orleans – Southwest Airline's largest hub – the company's service to the city dramatically dropped from 57 flights a day to just two. But while the City of New Orleans was forced to lay off workers, Southwest was able to offer the option of relocation to all of its 250 New Orleans employees. "This proves we are living up to trust," said Gary Kelly. "You have to have great employees, and you can't do that without trust. Trust isn't about jet engines or airports; it's about people and building relationships with them."[6]

In 2007, Southwest employees received 43,386 customer commendations and 18,140 internal commendations (a 19.5 percent increase over the previous year) for their Positively Outrageous Service (and the ratio of commendations to complaints was 4.6 to 1). Customer service is indeed a way of life at Southwest. "Looking forward," notes President Emeritus Colleen Barrett in a message to employees, "we face some even more difficult challenges, and while we can't control the price of fuel, we can control the way we treat our customers. I ask you to remember that, in this world of instant communications, each of us is constantly on stage, and every customer is a potential reporter. Let's give them something positive to report!"

The key to Southwest's responsibility culture is that it hires the right people – those that have the right attitude. As Kelleher has said, "If you don't have a good attitude, we don't want you, no matter how skilled you are. We can change skill level through training. We can't change attitude."[7]

Communication is a core competence at Southwest. Whether it's in a memo, LUV Lines, other newsletters (from each division such as Ground Operations), a training program, an ad campaign or an awards ceremony, there are multiple ways that guiding principles and other key messages are spread around the organization. Over the years, these have been internalized by employees so they know instinctively what represents good judgment and what makes common sense.

A simple structure for success

Both Kelleher and Kelly recognized that Southwest's strengths lie in its simple structures and systems (for example, no matrix management, few acquisitions and lack of complex budgeting and reporting systems) and always listening to its people. The management focus has always been on improving processes and encouraging the right behavior rather than following the plan and managing budgets. Clarity, simplicity, transparency and trust are the key words that describe Southwest's management approach.

With no more than four layers between a front-line supervisor and the CEO, Southwest is indeed a flat organization largely devoid of micro-management. But it has maintained layers of supervisors that many other ("downsized") organizations have dispensed with. These supervisors often help younger employees grow up. It supports the family atmosphere. There is roughly a ten-to-one employee-to-supervisor ratio.

Local decision-making

One of the reasons why managers are so dedicated to the company is that Southwest has treated them with dignity and respect, even when they've made big mistakes. Senior executives can't of course anticipate all of the situations that will arise at the stations across the organization. But the message is clear. Kelleher put it this way: "Hey, we can't anticipate all these things, you handle them the best way possible. You make a judgment and use your discretion; we trust you'll do the right thing. If we think you've done something erroneous, we'll let you know – without criticism, without backbiting."[8]

While people are trusted to do their jobs to the best of their ability, leaders also know that trust is fragile and reciprocal. How Southwest reacted in the immediate aftermath of 9/11 is a classic Southwest story of maintaining trust with employees. After 9/11, when the federal government shut down the airlines for three days and uncertainty about the future of the industry loomed heavy, Gary Kelly noted that "we were the only airline not to announce layoffs that week and not to use our employees as pawns. We could have downsized and taken that opportunity to wring more profits out or get more costs out of our system. We also didn't go back to our employees and demand pay cuts or cut their benefits or take their retirement plans … When it is all said and done, for me that is that kind of thing I will be most proud of."[9]

While front-line people at Southwest have the scope and authority to make decisions, they are also accountable for the outcomes. It doesn't take five or seven signatures to get things done. Station managers have huge operational responsibilities. Each station (the team that runs operations at each airport) functions like an independent business unit, and managers are responsible for setting the tone of the station and ensuring that Southwest's culture is protected and promoted. Crucially, however, there is a "no blame" culture. There are many stories about managers taking an initiative that cost the company money – in some cases, hundreds of thousands of dollars – only to be told, "You made a decision; it turned out to be the wrong one; but tomorrow is another day. Let's learn from it and push on."

With such a trusting and transparent culture, a financial analyst once asked Kelleher if he was afraid of losing control. Kelleher's reply took the analyst by surprise. He told him that "I've never had control and I never wanted it. If you create an environment where the people truly participate, you don't need control. They know what needs to be done, and they do it. And the more that people will devote themselves to your cause on a voluntary basis, a willing basis, the fewer hierarchies and control mechanisms you need. We're not looking for blind obedience. We're looking for people who on their own initiative want to be doing what they're doing because they consider it to be a worthy objective. I have always believed that the best leader is the best server. And if you're a servant, by definition you're not controlling."[10]

Southwest is one of those rare and special organizations that lives up to its hype. Its management processes enable it to adapt to constantly changing markets and other unpredictable events. There are no fixed performance contracts to drive people toward meeting outdated plans and numbers, to stifle innovation, and to focus on achieving revenue and cost targets at the expense of customer service.

For such a large organization, Southwest is about as simple and straightforward as you can get. There is only one company (no subsidiaries), one market, a strategy that is simple to understand, one interdependent team whose members all get rewarded for success, one set of principles and values that never changes, and only a few measures of success, which everyone understands.

What lessons should we learn from Southwest?

What the Southwest story tells us is that even in the US, where the cult of shareholder value has been at its strongest, a large organization can consistently beat its peers by putting values and ethics before short-term profits and placing its people before customers and shareholders. In other words, values matter, and they can be a source of long-term competitive advantage.

Be open and honest, and trust your people

While most organizations have mission statements that give the impression they are as committed as Southwest to serving their people and their customers, that's where the similarity ends. Their management models, styles and actions follow a different agenda. From the employee perspective, power remains firmly at the corporate center and their actions are strictly governed by detailed rules, targets, budgets, inspections and performance appraisals. "Trust" and "transparency" are empty words as leaders are less than truthful not only with their employees but also with customers, investors and other stakeholders.

Make customer service a way of life

You only have to look at most of the other airlines around the world. Most are trapped inside "command and control" management models. So when hard times come around (as they frequently do in the airline industry) they resort to downsizing, layoffs and mergers and acquisitions. While the Internet has made it easier for customers to book flights, it has also enabled airlines to cut customer service. To change or cancel a flight or obtain a refund is usually a nightmare. Call-center agents have no discretion to make decisions. Leaders of most airlines are constantly under pressure to deliver short-term profits to long-suffering shareholders. British Airways used to have a reputation for excellent customer service. But now its leaders are constantly locking horns with their pilots, cabin crews and baggage handlers and negotiating lower-cost deals with sub-contractors for catering and cleaning.

Involve your people in key changes

No doubt their leaders would say, "What choice do we have? High legacy costs from the days before low-cost competition mean that we need to downsize and cut costs across the board." The reality is that they have the wrong management model.

What would Herb Kelleher do? He would probably say to his employees that "we are all in this together." He would lay great emphasis on the company's purpose and tell his people that they come before customers and shareholders. He would revisit the company's mission statement and tell everyone that the company will now be managed according to an inviolate set of values including trust, transparency, integrity, respect, fun, and even love and care.

But he would not duck the cost problem. He would likely say that "our costs are 40 percent too high and this is why." He would immediately open up the information system to all employees. He would probably start by cutting top management salaries and bonuses and say that from here on there will only be one group-wide profit share that will only pay out if the company performs well against its peers. He would say that "we are also slashing bureaucracy and back office costs and diverting a higher proportion of resources to front-line teams – pilots, cabin crews and ground crews." He would give each team far greater scope and authority to make decisions and tell them that no longer will they need five signatures to get resources or improvement projects approved. In other words, he would bring the whole company together, share its problems and invite ideas for improvement.

Build a culture based on transparency and trust

But this is fiction. While most leaders have responded by cutting budgets and tightening the coils of central control, the evidence suggests that attending to the organization's culture may be a better approach. As we learned from the South-west story, when leaders build a culture based on transparency and trust people are inspired, become passionate about it, want to live up to it and demand it from others. It involves a deep feeling of satisfaction and even joy. We will hear about many other organizations in this book that have operated with such a management model for decades and have built robust and enduring companies that consistently beat their peers on just about any metric you care to name. They have also built enviable reputations for being great places to work for, buy from and invest in. The public sector is also catching on. A number of US state governors are now placing contracts, minutes of meetings and detailed financial statements on their websites and placing transparency at the core of their management models. Not only does this build trust with taxpayers, who can now readily see how their taxes are being spent, but it also acts as a deterrent against unethical behavior, corruption and fraud.[11]

The success of an adaptive organization depends on front-line teams having the confidence to respond rapidly to unpredictable events without approval from senior people. That's why clarity of purpose and values are so important. Principle #1 represents the foundation stone of the adaptive organization. It takes leaders down a path of "cultural" governance based on purpose and values rather than "compliance" governance based on rules and regulations.

Implementation guidelines

- Agree a noble purpose above and beyond shareholder value.
- Establish clear and inviolate values based on truth, transparency and trust.
- Use a written constitution if this helps to clarify the issues.
- Communicate values at every opportunity.
- Include "values" in the performance evaluation system.
- Place ethics before profit.
- Promote a culture of love and care.

Agree a noble purpose beyond shareholder value

Great leaders believe passionately in the organization's purpose or "reason for being," but this is a far cry from the classic economic model in which the overarching objective of the firm is to maximize shareholder's wealth. Most of their managerial actions (both short-term and long-term) are made with this in mind. This is a model in which individuals are assumed to be self-interested, rational decision-makers driven by economic goals, and economic relationships (with employees, suppliers, customers and external partners) are governed by binding contracts. But above all, it is a mechanistic model subject to mathematical formulae where costs, volumes and profits can be optimized according to market conditions. People lower down the organization don't need to understand its purpose – they simply do what is specified in their job description.

In the second half of the 20th century it has been the "mission statement" that has been increasingly used to define purpose and values. But such statements are often too bland to convey deep meaning and end up being ignored by employees. Jeffrey Abrahams reviewed 301 corporate mission statements from America's top companies and noted that the words most frequently used were: service (230 times); customers (211); quality (194); value (183); employees (157); growth (118); environment (117); profit (114); shareholders (114); leader (104); best (102).[12] Author Stephan Haeckel invites us to consider this hypothetical mission statement: "We will strive to provide the highest return to shareholders and offer the highest quality products and services, while achieving the highest customer loyalty and the highest employee satisfaction." As Haeckel notes, this company intends to be all things to all people, and its statement offers no clues to employees about ordering priorities. When the need to compromise and make choices arises, as it inevitably will, the statement will give employees no clear basis for making decisions and no help in determining how to make the necessary trade-offs.[13]

Pursuing the wrong goal

Moving away from the organization's purpose can have serious consequences. When UK chemicals company ICI – Imperial Chemical Industries as it was known in its more illustrious days – saw its job as practicing the "responsible application of chemistry," it became phenomenally successful. Later, under pressure from fractious investors, it declared its mission to be: "the industry leader in creating value for customers and shareholders through market leadership, technological edge and a world competitive cost base." It then proceeded to go on a disastrous buying spree, which culminated in ICI falling into the hands of the Dutch firm Akzo Nobel a few years ago.[14]

When Citicorp merged with Travelers in 1999 to create the sprawling bank conglomerate Citigroup, the joint CEOs held a press conference. John Reed, Citicorp's CEO, declared: "The model I have is of a global consumer company that really helps the middle class with something they haven't been served well by historically. That's my vision. That's my dream." His joint CEO, Travelers' Sandy Weill, rapidly interjected and stated that, "My goal is increasing shareholder value." Reed, with his old-fashioned, oblique way of running a business, was sidelined.

Just a few years later, Citigroup was in trouble and Weill was forced out. Within a decade, Citigroup was forced into the arms of the US government.[15]

What these stories tell us is that by pandering to rapacious shareholders, firms are not just trying to come up with the results too quickly – they're actually pursuing the wrong goal. It's not just about numbers and targets and synergies – it's about great products, happy customers and loyal staff. As economist John Kay says, no one will be buried with the epitaph "He maximized shareholder value."[16]

Despite what they might say, few people are able to fully commit themselves to a mission statement, plan or even their job. To engage people in the process of stretching performance and taking risks has to involve something more than "doing their job." It must involve their emotional commitment. Management guru Henry Mintzberg explains why plans do not, by themselves, build commitment: "The problem is that planning represents a *calculating* style of management, not a *commitment* style. Managers with a committing style engage people in a journey. They lead in such a way that everyone on the journey helps shape its course. As a result, enthusiasm inevitably builds along the way. Those with a calculating style fix on a destination and calculate what the group must do to get there, with no concern for the members' preferences."[17]

A purpose that "grabs" people

An organization's purpose should be expressed in terms that "grab" people. It should make them proud to tell their family and friends who they work for and what the organization produces. These "soft" or emotional bonds make all the difference between people giving 40–50 percent or 80–90 percent of their effort and creativity.

Take Whole Foods Market, whose CEO John Mackey regularly speaks at college campuses across the US trying to persuade young people that business, profits and capitalism aren't forces of evil. He calls his concept "conscious capitalism." "Whole Foods has a deeper purpose," he says. "Most of the companies I most admire in the world I think have a deeper purpose." He continues, "I've met a lot of successful entrepreneurs. They all started their businesses not to maximize shareholder value or money but because they were pursuing a dream. It's not that there's anything wrong with making money," notes Mackey, "it's one of the important things that business contributes to society. But it's not the sole reason that businesses exist. Just like every other profession, business serves society. They produce goods and services that make people's lives better. Doctors heal the sick. Teachers educate people. Architects design buildings. Lawyers promote justice. Whole Foods puts food on people's tables and we improve people's health. And we provide jobs. And we provide capital through profits that spur improvements in the world. And we're good citizens in our communities, and we take our citizenship very seriously at Whole Foods."[18]

Like Mackey at Whole Foods, the founders of UK optical retailer Specsavers also believe in "conscious capitalism." Founders Doug and Mary Perkins had a goal of providing "affordable fashionable eye care for all." They never saw making money as their primary objective; they established the business to make it possible for everyone in the UK to have easy access to quality eye care. They deliberately built their business model in such a way that their business partners – the store owners – took the lion's share of the profits. Now Specsavers has 1400 stores in 10 countries and they have never closed a store.[19]

Performance: more than the bottom line

The problem that many leaders have is that investors want to talk about the bottom line. But what if we lived in a world where companies didn't measure their performance only in terms of revenue and profitability? What if pharmaceutical companies reported on their bottom lines, along with the familiar figures, the number of lives saved by their drugs every quarter, and food companies reported the number of children rescued from malnutrition? What if companies issued separate stock based on social returns, and people could buy the shares of those that saved more lives than others, or sell the shares of energy companies that polluted more than their competitors? What if, by raising "social capital" and investing it in sustainable businesses without a profit motive, companies could reach into new markets, expanding their core businesses at the same time they improved lives? That's the world that Muhammad Yunus, the winner of the 2006 Nobel Peace Prize, envisions.[20] Maybe this is a glimpse into the future of corporate accountability and measurement.

There is evidence to suggest that when the CEO makes it a priority to balance the concerns of customers, employees and the community while also taking environmental impact into account, employees perceive him or her as visionary and participatory. They report being more willing to exert extra effort, and corporate results improve. This finding is based on recent survey data gathered from 520 business organizations in 17 countries, many of them emerging markets.[21]

Establish clear and inviolate values

When global banking group HSBC decided to charge UK students a monthly fee for "free" overdrafts, there was a rebellion orchestrated by the National Union of Students who created a "protest site" on Facebook. When over 5000 students joined the protest within days, HSBC was forced to retract the action it had taken. With the meteoric rise of the blogging and Facebook generation, someone, somewhere can see a problem and tell the whole world in an instant. The punishment now meted out to offenders ranges from being "named and shamed" as an unethical company to jail sentences of up to 25 years for people who commit outright fraud. The result is always bad and sometimes catastrophic.

As this story tells us, it is increasingly costly and difficult for leaders to take decisions that are not supported by other stakeholders. That's why establishing a set of values that will govern how an organization is managed and what it regards as inviolate is a critical step in rethinking the management model. The best organizations have only a few core values. These rarely, if ever, change. They use values to send clear messages to all employees that unethical behavior and poor standards will not be tolerated. "By putting our values first, business success will follow. Without these values, there is no success at all," said Paul O'Neill, Chairman and CEO of US aluminum company Alcoa.[22]

There is little doubt that establishing a set of values that govern how an organization is managed and what it regards as inviolate is a critical step in recruiting the right people and tightening up governance standards. In 2003 researchers from the Stanford Business School and the University of California published a survey of more than 800 people with MBA degrees from 11 leading North American and European business schools. Ninety-seven percent of respondents said they would take a 14 percent pay cut to work for an "ethical" company – a contradiction of the traditional culture's supposition that money is what ultimately counts. Intellectual challenge topped the list as the most important attribute for MBAs in accepting a job. The financial package was only 80 percent as important as intellectual challenge.[23]

Core values at Handelsbanken

At Swedish bank Handelsbanken all new employees learn its seven core values:

- *Profits come from customers, not products.* There is no emphasis on marketing and/or selling products. The emphasis is finding and keeping satisfied, profitable customers. Branches "own" customers whatever their size. The selection of the right customers determines the productivity and profitability of the branch. One of the key factors in maintaining low costs is the selection of the right customers.

- *Managers have responsibility with accountability.* Managers have no excuses. The branch is responsible for its profitability and has the power to change what needs to be changed. Managers know if they are performing well or not so well.

- *People are honest and open.* There is no scope for sweet-talking away bad results. The figures speak, and speak clearly for themselves.

- *Stick to the knitting.* Many banks aim to become financial supermarkets. At Handelsbanken the aim is to develop supreme banking professionals offering good sound up-to-date advice to their customers.

- *Identify and eliminate unnecessary costs.* While the bank maintains some of the traditions associated with the sector (such as private dining rooms), it is anything but ostentatious. Modest living and value-for-money pervade the bank and promote a favorable image to customers. The sense of cost consciousness is apparent everywhere.

- *Promote from within.* The bank develops its own leaders. It takes a long time to become a good banker and understand the corporate culture in all its facets. Handelsbanken aims to recruit the right people and keep them forever.

- *Don't copy others.* In a fast-changing marketplace there is a temptation to copy what others are doing – a process of cross-pollination often promoted by the consulting community. Handelsbanken is not afraid to be different. In fact, it sees being different as a major virtue.

These values were a key element in the company's decision not to engage in the so-called "casino banking" that enabled many other banks to generate huge (but, as it turned out, illusory) profits and led up to the 2008 crash. The view of Handelsbanken's leaders was that these activities did not fit with the company's values or provide any benefit to its customers.

But no matter how many words are written in codes of practice, value statements and strategic plans, it is how people are recognized and rewarded and how an organization spends its money that tell you most about its culture. If it rewards and promotes managers who will do anything to meet their numbers (as at Enron), then getting people to work together in teams will be hard to achieve. If it spends money on limousines, lavish head offices and executive perks (as at WorldCom), then asking people to increase their effort will likely fall on deaf ears. Operating teams across the organization need standards and guidelines within which they can operate and make decisions that are consistent and coherent with the company's strategy and direction. In command and control organizations this is done through the annual plan and budget. But in adaptive organizations it is clarity of purpose, strong values and sound judgment that enable leaders to strike a fair balance between freedom and control.

Use a written constitution if this helps to clarify the issues

Following on from a clear purpose and inviolate values, there usually needs to be some form of written constitution that sets out the company's operating principles. These principles govern relationships, behavior and the interaction between managers at different organizational levels. Shared values are not only important: the success of an adaptive organization depends on them. These are the universal principles of fairness, justice, honesty, integrity and trust. Haeckel lists the following guidelines for building clear, robust principles:

- They should establish boundaries for permissible behavior, governing (not dictating) decisions, activities and accountabilities

- They must be unambiguous and can therefore be formulated in statements beginning with "we will never" or "we will always."

- They are usually qualitative rather than quantitative

- They apply to all groups and units under the authority of the issuing agent

- They lend themselves to objective tests for compliance

- They are likely to endure for at least a few years

- They are devised (rather than just approved) by policy-making executives

- Violating them results in serious system consequences.[24]

A written constitution at John Lewis Partnership

In 2010 the John Lewis Partnership, one of the UK's most respected and successful retailers, employed 72,000 people and had revenues of £7.4bn. Though John Lewis is a partnership owned by its partners/employees, it is totally open with financial information. You can even see its current weekly sales figures on its website. The partnership has a strong employee-centric culture. It also has a written constitution. The foreword to this constitution (last updated in July 2009) is revealing:

"Not many companies have a written constitution. Ours does, for two reasons. The first is historical. The Partnership exists today because of the extraordinary vision and ideals of its Founder, John Spedan Lewis. He believed an "industrial democracy" where employees shared knowledge, power and profit was a better form of business. That vision was set out in a written Constitution – a framework to define the Partnership's principles and the way it should operate. The Constitution has been revised on a number of occasions since then, in order to keep it fresh and up to date. Nonetheless, this latest edition is a direct connection to his original inspiration – it defines what we are. The second looks forward. The challenge for Partners today is to prove that a business which is not driven by the demands of outside shareholders and which sets high standards of behavior can flourish in the competitive conditions facing a modern retailing business. The Constitution provides the Principles and Rules within which we aim to demonstrate, through Partners, customers and profit, that we are a better form of business.

This Constitution identifies that the "happiness of all its members" relies on their "worthwhile and satisfying employment in a successful business." To achieve this we aim to give all Partners a relevant, consistent and rewarding experience during their career. This experience is based on the Partnership and Partners themselves delivering three commitments: taking responsibility for our business success, building relationships Powered by our Principles and creating real influence over our working lives. These commitments place on us all the obligation to improve our business in the knowledge that we share the rewards of success.

The Constitution also addresses the role of the Partnership in society, defining our responsibilities to customers, suppliers and to the environment. The Partnership must change constantly to fulfill its ultimate purpose. The Constitution ensures these changes remain true to our principles and will allow us to pass on to our successors a business they too will be proud to work in."[25]

To illustrate the scope of the constitution we have set out its contents page below:

CONTENTS

Foreword
Part 1 – Introduction
Part 2 – Principles

Purpose
Power
Profit
Members
Customers
Business relationships
The community
Part 3 – Rules
Section 1 – How power is shared
General
The Partnership Council
Purpose and authority
Constituencies and elections
Other members of the Council
Council business
Elections by the Council
Finance of the Council
Procedures
Divisional Councils

Local Forums
The Partnership Board
The Chairman
*Section 2 – Partners' rights and
  responsibilities*
Happiness of members
Relationships
Employment conditions
Pay
Security of employment
Grievances and appeals
Amenities and social activities
Pensions
Journalism
The Partners' Counsellor
The registries
Section 3 – Responsibilities to others
Customers
Suppliers
Competitors
Public service
The law
The environment
*Section 4 – Amendment and
  interpretation*

Communicate values at every opportunity

It is not sufficient just to agree and write about values. They must also be communicated in every possible way. Whole Foods CEO John Mackey explains what this means: "It doesn't matter if an organization has a higher purpose if the leadership doesn't understand it and seek to serve it. The various stakeholders of an organization, especially employees and customers, look to the leadership to 'walk the talk' – to serve the purpose and mission of the organization and to lead by example. It is especially important that the CEO and other senior leadership embody the higher purpose of the organization."

"As the co-founder and CEO of Whole Foods Market, I'm the most visible person in the company. One of the most important parts of my job is touring our stores and talking to our team members, customers and suppliers. I know that in virtually everything that I say and do, our team members are always studying me, trying to determine whether they can trust me and the mission of the company. I'm always on stage. So walking the talk is very important. I try to communicate the mission and values of Whole Foods Market at every opportunity and I try to live those core values myself with complete fidelity. Fidelity to the mission and values builds trust, while any deviation from these ideals undermines trust. High-trust organizations and hypocritical leadership are mutually exclusive."[26]

Employee health and safety constitute a vitally important indicator of caring, particularly in manufacturing where there is often exposure to injury and harmful substances. When Paul O'Neill became CEO of Alcoa in 1987 he decided to make this issue the company's highest priority – one that would be addressed in top-level meetings even ahead of profit. So embedded has this objective become that today Alcoa reports its lost workday accident rate to all employees and stakeholders in real time. The rate hovers near 0.2 – significantly better than the national average for all manufacturers of 2.2.[27] In more recent times, Alcoa has gone even further. "We have to go beyond zero injuries," noted William J. O'Rourke in the Environment, Health & Safety Audit Report 2002. "We have to send employees home healthier than they came to work. We do that through wellness and fitness programs that give them physical, emotional and work-life support."[28]

Nucor Steel serves employees by giving them a sense of empowerment over their work lives, creating a team environment in which people freely exchange ideas and coaching, and maintaining an open-door policy to division leaders. At Nucor steel mills there are no employee time clocks – there is only a work ethic that arises from within each individual team as it strives to surpass its production goals. Employees write their own job descriptions and are given wide latitude to self-organize around tasks as they see fit. The presumption behind this system is that plant workers closest to the action care about collective welfare of their teams, are intelligent and can therefore be trusted to do the right thing. What makes the system work is a culture of accountability. People understand that their teams and divisions will stand or fall on their own merits. In the words of former CEO Ken Iverson, "There's no cavalry waiting to ride to the rescue ... There's just you and the people working with you."[29]

Include values in performance evaluation

Replacing old values with new ones, no matter how well crafted and prepared, will have little effect unless leaders champion and constantly reinforce them.

The litmus test of any set of values is that senior executives promote those that live the values and discipline those that don't. Jack Welch did this in spectacular fashion at GE when he dismissed managers who made their financial targets but failed to live up to GE's values. He surprised his audience when, at one celebratory meeting of senior managers, he said, "Look around you: there are five fewer officers here than there were last year. One was fired for the numbers, four were fired for [lack of] values."[30] Former Handelsbanken CEO Arne Mårtensson was asked was what his role in the devolved organization. He replied, "To constantly talk to our people and reinforce our principles and values. There is a constant need to resist the forces of centralization."

Norwegian oil and gas company Statoil made it clear that abiding by its values would form a key element of the performance appraisal process. As Beyond Budgeting project leader Bjarte Bogsnes explains, "These are the beliefs that guide the company's operations and the foundation on which it is building its future. The key to effective devolution is crystal-clear values and principles. The new management style can only operate effectively if there is high trust (and open information), but if this trust is breached, then the sanctions are clear – people will not survive. We are ruthless on policy violations that usually lead to dismissal. We have a simple 'ethics test' so that people know whether or not their action is acceptable. They just need to ask the following question: Is it acceptable if the results of their actions appear on the front page of the newspaper? If yes, go ahead. If no, don't do it."

To support these changes, Statoil changed its performance appraisal system. Whereas previously managers were assessed on how well they met their financial targets, now 50 percent of the bonus is based on meeting a range of key performance indicators and 50 percent on meeting the company's values using a peer review process.

Place ethics before profit

For years, Dell's seemingly magical power to squeeze efficiencies out of its supply chain and drive down costs made it a darling of the financial markets. Now it appears that the magic was at least partly the result of a huge financial illusion. In July 2010 Dell agreed to pay a $100m penalty to settle allegations by America's Securities and Exchange Commission (SEC) that, in the SEC's words, the company had "manipulated its accounting over an extended period to project financial results that the company wished it had achieved."

According to the commission, Dell would have missed analysts' earnings expectations in every quarter between 2002 and 2006 were it not for accounting shenanigans. This involved a deal with Intel, a big microchip-maker, under which Dell agreed to use Intel's central processing unit chips exclusively in its computers in return for a series of undisclosed payments, locking out Advanced Micro Devices, a big rival. The SEC's complaint said Dell had maintained "cookie-jar reserves" using Intel's money that it could dip into to cover any shortfalls in its operating results.

The SEC says that the company should have disclosed to investors that it was drawing on these reserves, but did not. And it claims that, at their peak, the exclusivity payments from Intel represented 76 percent of Dell's quarterly operating income, which is a breathtaking figure. Small wonder, then, that Dell found itself in a pickle when its quarterly earnings fell sharply in 2007 after it ended the arrangement with Intel. The SEC alleges that Dell attributed the drop to an aggressive product-pricing strategy and higher than expected component prices, when the real reason was that the payments from Intel had dried up.[31]

Ethical reporting was also far from the minds of Lehman executives as they struggled to maintain credibility in the market in the years leading up to the company's demise in 2008. From 2001 onwards the company resorted to a piece of accounting trickery known as "repo 105" ("repo" is short for repurchase). This enabled leaders to book short-term loans from other banks as "sales," temporarily removing about $50 billion of assets from its balance sheet (usually at the end of each quarter), helping to make it look better than it really was. What is so strange about this affair is that it was only the UK arm of Lehman that had permission (via its lawyers and thus its auditors) to carry it out: its US lawyers and auditors ruled against it. As the following email (later discovered by examiners) showed, Lehman executives knew this was unethical:

> "It's basically window-dressing."

> "I see ... so it's legally do-able but doesn't look good when we actually do it? Does the rest of the street do it? Also, is that why we have so much BS [balance sheet] to Rates in Europe?"

> "Yes, no and yes."[32]

It is hardly surprising that few investors have much confidence in the numbers that most public companies produce. Nor are these problems confined to external reporting. "Gaming" and unethical reporting are pervasive within many

organizations today. Selling products on sale-or-return; shifting funds between accounts to avoid budget overruns; showing normal expenditure as an "exceptional"
(non-recurring) cost; and using contract labor to avoid exceeding headcount limits
are just a few of the popular "games" played by managers at every level of the
organization.

Many accountants see the "sexing up" of accounts as a perfectly legitimate practice
(provided they stay within some defensible interpretation of generally accepted
accounting principles). Indeed, it is one of their most prized skills. As most experienced accountants are aware, you can make profit statements and balance sheets
sing and dance to different tunes at different times depending on your purposes.
The effects of fudging, manipulating and spinning the numbers, like an addictive drug, can give managers a temporary fix – they can even be convinced that
they change reality – but the problems quickly return as the next reporting period
comes around.

Aggressive performance contracts reinforced by financial incentives are probably
the number-one cause of over-zealous risk-taking and unethical financial reporting in organizations today. One accounting professor described the Fannie Mae
debacle as "the kind of thing that shakes your confidence in financial statements."[33]
The lesson is that setting unrealistic earnings targets and then resorting to every
conceivable means (whether fair or foul) to meet them is likely to end badly, as
it has done for thousands of shareholders and employees in companies that have
been destroyed by these actions.

Promote a culture of love and care

Of course "love and care" are not the first qualities you associate with large
commercial organizations. In fact, many organizations would be described in
diametrically opposite terms. But as organizations make the transition from cold
and efficient "command and control" organizations to ones built on "empower
and adapt," love and care are exactly the qualities that need to come to the fore.
Both words appear on Southwest Airlines' list of values. Whole Foods CEO John
Mackey is passionate about these qualities. This is what he said in a recent essay
on *Creating the High Trust Organization:*

"Ultimately we cannot create high trust organizations without creating cultures
based on love and care. The people we usually trust the most are the people that
we also believe genuinely love and care for us. All too often, love and care are
not qualities that we associate with organizations. We tend to look for love and

friendship with our families and friends, but not from our work. Why is this? Many people believe that love and care in the organizational setting interfere with efficiency and get in the way of making the 'tough but necessary' decisions that the organization requires for success. This type of thinking reflects our own lack of integration of love and care in our own lives. We have created an artificial barrier that is holding back our own personal growth and the full potential of our organizations."

He goes on: "Fear is the opposite of love. When fear predominates in the organization, love and care cannot flourish. The opposite is also true – love and care banish fear." Mackey provides some suggestions that will hopefully stimulate further thinking on this incredibly important goal of creating more love and care in our organizations:

- The leadership must embody genuine love and care. This cannot be faked. If the leadership doesn't express love and care in their actions, then love and care will not flourish in the organization. As Gandhi said: "We must be the change that we wish to see in the world."

- We must "give permission" for love and care to be expressed in the organization. Many organizations are afraid of love and care and force them to remain hidden. Love and care will flow naturally when we give them permission and encourage them.

- We should consider the virtues of love and care in all of our leadership promotion decisions. We shouldn't just promote the most competent, but also the most loving and caring leaders. Our organizations need both and we should promote leaders who embody both.

- We must cultivate forgiveness rather than judgment and condemnation. Too many organizations believe that judgment of others and criticizing failures are essential for creating excellence. While striving for excellence is important for all organizations, this can be done at a higher level of consciousness – without condemnation. Forgiveness doesn't mean condoning mistakes and failures. It simply means that we help the other person to learn from their mistakes through non-judgmental feedback and encouragement.

- Consider ending all your organizational meetings with "appreciations." This is something that Whole Foods Market has been doing for 25 years with wonderful results for spreading love and care. Give everyone participating in the meeting the opportunity to voluntarily appreciate and thank other members in the group for services they have contributed or qualities that are admired.

This one simple cultural practice of appreciating our fellow Team Members moves us out of judgment and fear into the consciousness of love."[34]

Conclusions

Some of the strongest words to be heard at the World Economic Forum's annual meeting in Davos, Switzerland, in January 2010 came at the start of the global event when French president Nicolas Sarkozy called for a fundamental rethink of capitalism in the aftermath of the financial crisis. "We need deep, profound change," he said in his keynote speech, adding that he wished to see a "moral dimension" restored to free trade. "Were we not to change, we would be showing tremendous irresponsibility," he stated. It was a powerful opening to the meeting, in tune with its theme: "Improve the State of the World: Rethink, Redesign, Rebuild."[35]

The primary work of leaders is to release the energy and unleash the knowledge that often lies fallow within their people. This demands a governance framework that strikes the right balance between central compliance and control and local enterprise and freedom. Few organizations have achieved this balance. There is much more work to be done.

KEY POINTS

- Frame the organization's purpose in teams of social or community benefits that provide real meaning to employees and other stakeholders. Explain to people that consistent profitability (better than peers') is essential to grow and sustain the business, but this is not the purpose of the organization. Once agreed, communicate the purpose on all the company's printed materials and websites.

- The best organizations have only a few core values. These rarely, if ever, change. Use values to send clear messages to all employees that unethical behavior and poor standards will not be tolerated.

- Consider a written constitution. Frame the company's values in terms of "always" and "never." Make it clear that abusing values has serious consequences. Agree clear operating boundaries within which teams can operate autonomously (e.g. territories, markets, channels).

- It is not sufficient just to agree and write about values. They must also be communicated in every possible way. It doesn't matter if an organization has a noble purpose if leaders ignore it and fail to serve it. Leaders need to "walk the talk" of purpose and values and constantly reinforce the message at every opportunity.

- Consider including values in the performance evaluation system (for example, in peer reviews). This is particularly appropriate in the transitional phase of implementing the new model.

- Place ethics and reputation before profit. Actions that (sometimes unwittingly) damage a company's reputation can undo years of work patiently building governance and control systems and leave a trail of devastation that can last for many years. The reality is that the (temporary) rewards are never worth the risks. Educate everyone that a company's "license to operate" must be protected at all costs. Anyone breaking this rule should face dismissal.

- Promote a culture of love and care. Of course love and care are not the first qualities you associate with large organizations. In fact, many organizations would be described in diametrically opposite terms. But as organizations make the transition from "command and control" to "empower and adapt," love and care are exactly the qualities that rise in importance.

## CHAPTER 2

Principle #2 – Governance
Govern through shared values and sound judgment, not detailed rules and regulations

I've never had control and I never wanted it. If you create an environment where the people truly participate, you don't need control. They know what needs to be done, and they do it.'[1]

Herb Kelleher, Chairman Emeritus, Southwest Airlines

The limitations of risk management at BP

On April 20, 2010 in the Gulf of Mexico, BP's Deepwater Horizon oil rig exploded, killing 11 people and devastating the local environment as well as many communities that depend on fishing and tourism. Even though the rig and many of the workers were subcontractors, BP's CEO Tony Hayward took immediate responsibility and was determined to show the world that BP could handle such a disaster as well as any major organization. But after an inept performance in front of US investigators and the world's media, he became the most hated man in America, then lost his job. But this was the least of BP's problems, as the Obama administration was determined to make BP pay for every penny of damage, initially demanding that the company place $20 billion into an escrow account. BP's share price collapsed by over 40 percent and in late July 2010 the company announced that it had taken a pre-tax charge of $32.2 billion (including the $20 billion escrow compensation fund).

The 2010 disaster in the Gulf of Mexico is one of the greatest calamities ever to befall a commercial organization (although many of us remember the 1984 Bhopal disaster in India when gas from a pesticide plant owned by Union Carbide killed thousands of people – Greenpeace cites 20,000 total deaths as its conservative estimate). Why did it happen? Why didn't BP know what to do? Why was there no contingency or scenario plan? Why didn't BP do a better job of protecting its reputation? Why didn't its models anticipate such a disaster? And what are the lessons for other organizations?

Were profits placed ahead of safety?

These are questions that BP executives are probably still asking. We have no insider knowledge, so we can only examine the problems from the published information. But there seems to be much circumstantial evidence that the culture at BP placed cost and profit before safety and the environment. In its analysis of BP's records, a team of Wall Street Journal reporters made this evaluation:

"In an internal communication in early 2009, Neil Shaw, then-head of BP's Gulf of Mexico unit, lauded Atlantis' operating efficiency, saying it was '4 percent better than plan' in its first year of production. It was part of a success story that Mr. Shaw said had enabled BP to become the number-one oil producer in the Gulf. But a former BP engineer said the Gulf of Mexico operation under Mr. Shaw became focused on *meeting performance targets which determined bonuses for top managers and low-level workers alike.* The engineer says even small costs got targeted: BP no longer provided food at lunch meetings, and eliminated the fruit bowls that were offered as part of a healthy-living drive a few years earlier. BP vigorously denies putting savings ahead of safety. In a statement, BP said its cost-cutting should be seen in the context of the sharp fall in oil prices in 2008 which squeezed all oil companies' profits. BP says executives are judged on the safety record of their units, not just on financial or production criteria."[2]

The Gulf of Mexico disaster did not come out of the blue. BP grew rapidly under the leadership of John Browne, CEO from 1995 until his premature retirement in 2007. He transformed BP from a conservative, fairly dull, mid-ranking oil company into an entrepreneurial global giant. Browne preached about governance and sustainability for over a decade (and BP was consistently ranked at the top of many sustainability indexes), yet in the last five years it has been hit with a refinery explosion in Texas that killed 15, a fine for safety violations at a refinery in Ohio, a major oil pipeline leak in Alaska, a US Justice Department probe into suspected manipulation of oil prices and of course the 2010 calamity in the Gulf of Mexico.[3]

After his appointment as CEO Tony Hayward immediately set out to reduce the complexity of the organization, restructure divisions and cut administration and support functions. Investment in renewable energy was scaled back. A geologist by training, with a scientist's focused mind, Hayward said that, above all, his purpose was to focus "like a laser" on safe and reliable operations. His recent statement in BP's 2009 annual report reflects the recognition of risk: "Risk remains a key issue for every business, but at BP it is fundamental to what we do. We operate at the frontiers of the energy industry, in an environment where attitude to risk is key. The countries we work in, the technical and physical challenges we take on and the investments we make – these all demand a sharp focus on how we manage risk."[4]

Was there a failure to embrace risk at the highest levels?

But the rhetoric in the boardroom was a long way from the reality on the ground. Going back some years, Oberon Houston was a rising star in BP's engineering management group who saw at first hand BP's approach to safety. Reports say Houston was distressed that layoffs "seemed to target the best and most seasoned engineers, [and BP] had slashed the maintenance budget for the vast and aged Forties Alpha platform [which suffered a near blowout] to a dangerous, even reckless extent. Senior BP management focused so heavily on the easy part of safety – holding the hand rails, spending hours discussing the merits of reverse parking, and the dangers of not having a lid on a coffee cup – but were less enthusiastic about the hard stuff, investing in and maintaining their complex facilities." To his credit, Houston walked the walk, and left the company.[5]

Despite Hayward's "laser-like" dedication to safety, it appears that BP failed to embed a risk management culture into its management systems. Like many other large organizations, it focused on implementing better internal compliance and control systems. It had many detailed measures on the performance of the rig. No doubt it embraced terms such as "enterprise risk management" and appointed chief risk, chief compliance and chief ethics officers. The picture that emerges is that huge sums were spent on risk management and control, but the focus was on writing reports and checking boxes rather than enabling key people to form judgments and take effective action. BP is not alone. These problems are endemic to most large organizations.

Despite all the attention on risk management and health and safety issues, the messages sent to front-line people were to meet the stretch (production and financial) targets and achieve the maximum bonuses. It is instructive that one of the first actions taken by BP's new CEO Bob Dudley in October 2010 was to change the bonus formula. Bonuses for the fourth quarter of 2010 for BP staff will be based *solely* on how employees perform in terms of safety and risk management. "We are taking this step in order to be absolutely clear that safety, compliance and operational risk management is BP's number one priority, well ahead of all other priorities," he noted.[6]

Risk management: treating the symptoms rather than the disease

Internal compliance and control has traditionally been a dour back-office world inhabited by process designers, inspectors, auditors and lawyers. Its elevation to the Star Chamber of management resulted from a number of corporate disasters in the 1990s and 2000s, including Maxwell Communications, Atlantic Leasing and Polly Peck in the UK and Enron, WorldCom and Tyco in the USA. In 1992 the Cadbury code in the UK established the principle that senior management is responsible for maintaining an effective internal control system. In the US, the Committee of Sponsoring Organizations of the Treadway Commission (COSO), a group of professional associations of US accountants and financial executives, redefined "internal control" to cover not just controls relating to financial accounting (the typical focus of auditors) but also regulatory compliance matters and operations more generally. This expansion and formalization of the internal control agenda was crucial, and the COSO legacy is evident in subsequent guidance documents, particularly the Turnbull Report in the UK.

But the reality is that appointing chief "risk" and "ethics" officers, providing employees with more courses on ethics and risk management, focusing on screening for the "right" employees, implementing more "spyware" in the office and investing more on computer security is treating the symptoms rather than the disease.

Standardized process: the illusion of control

The trouble is that corporate governance, compliance and risk management become *standardized processes*. While this might sound a reasonable approach, it often gives leaders the impression that a potential "compliance," "ethics" or "risk" problem is being well managed when this may be a long way from the truth. The problem is that when rules define what's right or wrong, anything that is not specifically forbidden is allowed, leading to valuable time being spent on circumventing the rules or explaining away the risks. Few people are looking for the *unknown unknowns*. And even fewer are consistently placing ethics before profits. As long as the process passes stringent audit tests, they are in the clear.

What drives good leaders to pay lip-service to transparency and ethical issues rather than treat them seriously? One explanation is an incremental decline into a gray area of "what's acceptable," "within tolerance" or "up to industry standard." An investigation into the US space shuttle Challenger disaster of 1986 found that there was not one mistake but a series of mistakes over many years that led managers into believing they were "within tolerance," despite their existing knowledge of defects in the O-rings. The culture at NASA was all about success and the pressure to succeed crept steadily upwards, thus lowering the bar on what was acceptable.

The problem is that if people follow written rules rather than inviolate values, there is always a temptation to work around problems rather than make a fast and firm decision to say "no." In this gray area, people will interpret rules in ways that suit their purposes. For example, they will select the lowest-cost supplier despite the fact that they are sourcing products from businesses that don't have acceptable health and safety standards. They will offer a bribe to a customer to win a large order. They will cut the plant maintenance budget to meet the numbers, thus placing their people in greater danger. In a macho "meet the numbers" culture, there are no ethical dilemmas. "Hard" bottom-line benefits and vested interests will trump "soft" values and principles every time.

Without clear values and principles that are constantly reinforced by leaders, people will make their own choices based on their interpretation of ethical norms and how they will be affected personally. They will weigh up the chances of being detected (and the punishment they will receive if caught) if they consciously cross the line. This is a dangerous position to be in, as corporate and personal reputations can take years to build, only to be blown away in a few moments of madness – as Tony Hayward discovered to his dismay.

According to Professor Michael Power, author of *The Risk Management of Everything*, the private world of organizational internal control systems has been turned inside out, made public, codified and standardized and repackaged as "risk management." In this way, a blueprint for extending the reach of risk management into every aspect of organizational life has been created. Internal control systems are also highly problematic. Not only is it difficult to define their effectiveness, which is in principle unknowable, but, more crucially, a growing obsession with internal control (a mutation of the earlier audit explosion) may itself be a source of risk.[7]

Power identifies two primary problems with risk management. First, internal control systems are organizational projections of controllability which may be misplaced; such systems are only as good as the imaginations of those who designed them. Second, internal control systems are essentially inward looking and may embody mistaken assumptions of what the public really wants reassurance about. Risk management and certifications of the effectiveness of internal control systems may do little to enhance public trust in senior management of organizations. While practitioners are well aware of the limitations of these systems, "better" control systems continue to be regarded as politically acceptable solutions to a crisis, even where it is well known that such systems would not have prevented the crisis in question.[8]

To illustrate why relying on rules and procedures can give a false sense of security, Power uses the example of the auditor who discovered a major fraud when he noticed that a purchase invoice was not folded. Audit procedures include methods for vouching for the arithmetical accuracy of such documents, for agreeing the numbers to the accounts, and for agreeing the "independent" nature of the invoice. But no amount of such processes could allow one to see what this auditor saw: that if an invoice is not folded, it probably did not arrive in the mail. And why would this be significant? Enquiries later revealed that it was being fraudulently constructed by the company to create a fictitious transaction. An auditor concerned solely with official process would not see the purchase invoice in this larger way, a vignette for how risk management processes can be risky.[9]

Quality controls: failing to learn the lessons

The emphasis on following "rules and procedures" in risk management is similar to the approach taken by the quality movement over the past 25 years. Its recommended method of implementation was (and still is) as follows:

1. Look at your current organization to see how it compares with the requirements of the Standard.

2. Decide what corrective action is needed to conform to the Standard.

3. Prepare a program of work.

4. Define, document and implement new management systems and procedures.

5. Prepare a quality manual.

6. Hold a pre-assessment meeting (to help the client establish their suitability for going forward to assessment and thus registration).

7. Pass the assessment test (the inspector determines whether the organization conforms to its documentation).

8. Register.

Quality assurance, according to the standard, is a way of managing that prevents non-conformance and thus "assures quality." While quality standards were initially about *product*, over time they have mutated into *management*. As UK occupational psychologist John Seddon notes, it is standardizing not *what* is made but *how* it is made. Which management team would not declare its commitment to quality or internal control? But do they know what it means? The Standard encourages managers to think of "quality" and "business as usual" as separate and distinct. It helps managers avoid the revelation that quality means a wholly different view of management. Instead, the organization *"shall appoint a management represen- tative who, irrespective of other responsibilities, shall have defined authority and responsibility"* [for ISO 9000]. Key to the regime is auditing. The standard requires organizations to conduct internal quality audits to *"verify whether quality activities comply with planned arrangements."*

Seddon believes that ISO 9000 is not improving organizations because it is based on bad theory. Underlying it are concepts of specification and control, rather than those of understanding and improvement (the heart of real quality). Customers will recognize that ISO 9000 has led organizations to focus on procedures rather than service, encumbering the service experience. Managers point to the excessive bureaucracy and work whose only purpose is to meet the requirements of their ISO 9000 assessor.[10]

The nagging contradiction at the core of risk management

The lessons from both quality management and regulatory compliance tell us that at the core of risk management is a nagging contradiction. As Professor Michael Power explains, "On the one hand there is a functional and political need to maintain myths of control and manageability, because this is what vari-ous interested constituencies and stakeholders seem to demand. Risks must be made auditable and governable. On the other hand, there is a consistent stream of failures, scandals and disasters which challenge and threaten organizations, suggesting a world which is out of control and where failure may be endemic, and in which the organizational interdependencies are so intricate that no single locus of control has a grasp of them."[11]

While rules, regulations and internal compliance systems have proliferated in recent years, there has been less focus (and understanding) of the key drivers of (unacceptable) risk-taking. One primary cause is the elevation of targets, incen-tives and measures over process controls and management judgment. It is the contract to deliver stretch targets in a short time period (typically a year), often reinforced by high financial incentives, that drives excessive risk-taking and fraudulent practice.

Effective risk management is a critical element in the adaptive organization. If front-line teams are empowered to take important decisions and regulate their own performance, they need clear guidelines about what risks are acceptable and how to evaluate them. At the executive level, risk management is equally important. Lead-ers need to act on the management model itself to ensure that the drivers of risk are set at the right levels and that their policies are clearly stated and communicated. Principle #2 aims to strike a balance between risk management as a well-designed process and risk management as a core element of the management culture.

Implementation guidelines

- Build a diverse and empowering board.
- Engage the board in risk management.
- Understand the key drivers of risk.
- Promote a culture of truth, transparency and trust.
- Define success in terms of continuous relative improvement.
- Appoint inspirational leaders who empower rather than control.
- Promote leaders from within.
- Focus on the person, not the pay.

Build a diverse and empowering board

The pressure to meet the numbers at every level of the organization is causing people to prostitute their professional ethics – in order to keep their jobs in some cases.

This extract from a telephone conversation between WorldCom CFO Scott Sullivan and CEO Bernie Ebbers tells us a great deal about the unacceptable face of corporate governance: "This monthly financial review just keeps getting worse and worse. The copy, the latest copy that you and I have, already has the accounting fluff or junk that's already in the numbers. With the numbers being, you know, off as far as they were, I didn't think that this stuff was already in there."[12]

The real worry is that these standards are more prevalent than many of us realize. Of course, we are not suggesting that most boards are like WorldCom under Ebbers and Sullivan. In fact, most are well-intentioned and ethically sound. But they probably fail to take time out to look at their own performance. How effective are they? Do they really add value? Does everyone contribute? Jeffrey Sonnenfeld believes that good governance can't be legislated, but it can be built over time. His formula for success is based on five factors:[13]

- *Create a climate of trust and candor.* Share information in time for people to read and digest it. Rotate board members through small groups and committees so they spend time together and with a range of company personnel. And work to eliminate polarizing factions.

- *Foster a culture of open dissent.* Don't punish mavericks or dissenters. Dissent should not be confused with disloyalty. Alternative views are an opportunity for learning and testing strategies and plans.

- *Utilize a fluid portfolio of roles.* Don't allow directors to become trapped in rigid, typecast roles.

- *Ensure individual accountability.* Give directors specific tasks that require them to report back to the board with proposals and plans for a particular problem or opportunity.

- *Evaluate the board's performance.* Examine directors' confidence in the integrity of the enterprise, the quality of boardroom discussions, the credibility of reports, the level of interpersonal cohesion and the degree of knowledge. Also look at individual initiative, levels of participation and energy levels.

Three surveys conducted by McKinsey covering institutional investors in Asia/ Pacific, Europe, the US and Latin America show that three-quarters of all investors believe that board practices are as important as financial performance. Over 80 percent say they would pay more for the shares of a well-governed company than for those of a poorly governed one with a comparable financial performance.[14]

Author David Nadler neatly encapsulates the difference between well and poorly constituted boards. "Everyone knows what most boards have been," he notes, "gentlemen's-club-era relics characterized by ceremony and conformity. And everyone knows what boards should be: seats of challenge and inquiry that add value without meddling and make CEOs more effective but not all-powerful."[15] This perfectly describes how organizations such as Southwest, Whole Foods and Specsavers operate. They know the role of the board is to set the climate and context within which value creation can take place. But they do not believe that the board on its own "creates value" (though it can destroy value). And they are particularly wary of large acquisitions, grand strategies and rosy forecasts.

It is no coincidence that these organizations have all grown organically. They know that it would take years to inculcate thousands of newly acquired employees in the cultural values they cherish. They prize and protect their values and ethical standards more than anything else. They recruit the right people, then devolve strategy to them. They trust their front-line people to anticipate and deal with events as they arise. While they are tolerant about honest mistakes – even when they lead to significant losses – they have zero tolerance levels on ethical issues. This is why they are ahead of their rivals. But it is a tough sell to non-executive directors, external analysts and industry regulators who are fixated on agreeing a plan and then controlling performance against it.

Engage the board in risk management

While the board cannot know the details of every decision being taken and the risks involved, it can agree and communicate a clear policy about how it views risk. Defining "risk appetite," "risk tolerance" or simply "setting the tone at the top" are all expressions that attempt to define how the board views risk. And given the potential disasters that lurk around the corner, any self-respecting board should escalate risk monitoring to the top of its agenda rather than delegate it to a subsidiary function. The board should also support its risk officers and risk management team rather than appear to be in conflict with them.

Many banks were guilty of overriding their risk officers and sending the wrong messages to the organization.

HBOS: failing to listen to advisors

Take the failed UK bank HBOS. Paul Moore, a former partner of KMPG and head of group regulatory risk at HBOS between 2002 and 2005, accused the bank of "a total failure of all key aspects of corporate governance" and said that he was repeatedly rebuffed and thwarted when he tried to register concern. He also pointed the finger of blame firmly at Sir James Crosby, the former chief executive of HBOS (he later became deputy chairman of chief investments regulator the Financial Services Authority and a senior adviser to the UK government). In his submission to a parliamentary committee Mr Moore said that he warned HBOS it was growing too fast, warned that it was culturally indisposed to being challenged and warned that its sales culture was "significantly out of balance with their systems and controls." He also said that he told the board the bank needed to slow down, but that he was overruled by the then finance director when he tried to get his views put in writing in the board minutes. After being sacked, Moore went to an industrial tribunal, at which point HBOS settled for "substantial damages."[16]

Clearly the "risk appetite" as expressed by the board at HBOS in the heady days leading up to the crash was far greater than its chief risk officer recommended.

Citigroup: failing to understand risk exposure

HBOS was not alone. According to an article in the *New York Times*, in September 2007, with Wall Street confronting a crisis caused by too many souring mortgages, Citigroup executives gathered in a wood-paneled library to assess their own well-being. There, Citigroup's chief executive, Charles O. Prince III, learned for the first time that the bank owned about $43 billion in mortgage-related assets. He asked Thomas G. Maheras, who oversaw trading at the bank, whether everything was OK. Mr Maheras told his boss that no big losses were looming. For months, Mr Maheras's reassurances to others at Citigroup had quieted internal concerns about the bank's vulnerabilities. But this time, a risk-management team was dispatched to more rigorously examine Citigroup's huge mortgage-related holdings. They were too late, however: within several weeks, Citigroup would announce billions of dollars in losses.

According to a former Citigroup executive, Mr Prince started putting pressure on Mr Maheras and others to increase earnings in the bank's trading operations, particularly in the creation of collateralized debt obligations, or CDOs – securities that packaged mortgages and other forms of debt into bundles for resale to investors. Because CDOs included so many forms of bundled debt, gauging their risk was particularly tricky; some parts of the bundle could be sound, while others were vulnerable to default.

"Chuck Prince going down to the corporate investment bank in late 2002 was the start of that process," a former Citigroup executive said of the bank's big CDO push. "Chuck was totally new to the job. He didn't know a CDO from a grocery list, so he looked for someone for advice and support. That person was [Robert] Rubin. And Rubin had always been an advocate of being more aggressive in the capital markets arena. He would say, 'You have to take more risk if you want to earn more.' It appeared to be a good time for building up Citigroup's CDO business. As the housing market around the country took flight, the CDO market also grew apace as more and more mortgages were pooled together into newfangled securities. From 2003 to 2005, Citigroup more than tripled its issuing of CDOs, from $6.28 billion to more than $20 billion, and Mr Maheras and others on the CDO team helped transform Citigroup into one of the industry's biggest players. Firms issuing the CDOs generated fees of 0.4 percent to 2.5 percent of the amount sold – meaning Citigroup made up to $500 million in fees from the business in 2005 alone. Even as Citigroup's CDO stake was expanding, its top executives wanted more profits from that business. Yet they were not running a bank that was up to all the challenges it faced, including properly overseeing billions of dollars' worth of exotic products."[17]

UBS: failing to control risk

If further evidence was needed that boards aren't playing enough of a risk management role, it can be found in a report on Swiss bank UBS published just before the financial meltdown.

"Shareholder Report on UBS's Write-Downs" was an April 2008 report commissioned by the board of this top-tier Swiss bank to examine how it lost approximately $40 billion in 2007. The assessments were damning; they charged senior UBS management with a "failure to demand holistic risk assessment," a "failure to manage [its] agenda," and a "lack of succession planning." Additionally, the report excoriated the firm's risk management controls and testing methodologies, asserting "complex and incomplete risk reporting," "lack of substantive assessment," "inadequate systems," "lack of strategic coordination" and "inability to accurately assess valuation risk on a timely basis." As for the board, its processes also lacked accountability for evaluating the firm's risk exposures, assessments and management. In other words, according to the report, the UBS directors were as guilty as the management they ostensibly supervised of failing to confront risk.[18]

Paying lip service to risk management

Like HBOS, Citigroup, UBS, Lehman Brothers and many other failed banks, the "tone at the top" and "risk appetite" were for rapid expansion to maximize profits and bonuses. Higher risk naturally led to higher rewards. The board paid lip service to risk management but never took the advice of its officers seriously. According to Bruce Caplain, Managing Director for Internal Audit at The Blackstone Group, Lehman Brothers had a strong risk management function, yet its Risk Committee (a sub-committee of the board) only met twice per year. Further, while the make-up of the board was quite impressive, the experience of board members in managing businesses such as Lehman's was thin.[19]

According to author Michael Schrage, among bailed-out or failed companies in the US, from General Motors and Citigroup to AIG, Fannie Mae and Goldman Sachs, no boards or independent directors stand accused of illegally breaching their fiduciary charges. The same is true, at least so far, for BP, Toyota and other companies whose operational missteps have led to massive litigation and losses. In all these cases, as far as the courts and regulators were concerned, the boards did their duty. They merely followed the law and the customs of the moment.

Schrage believes that the passive board – which obeys the law but does not provide meaningful oversight – is a hindrance and handicap for any corporation. In accounting terms, its oversight is mere overhead. Even when boards are more active, their involvement tends to focus on pressuring CEOs for better financial performance; it's not clear that they provide the needed function of overseeing risk and identifying questionable behavior. Conversely, the value of a well-managed board's oversight role has never before been so apparent in facilitating a company's own health and longevity.[20]

Many organizations try to set out formal risk appetite controls whether they are for the organization as a whole or for specific risks. For example, they may say that no more than 10 percent of investments will be in a certain currency, or that arms will not be dealt, or that new offices will not be opened in countries with inflation above 4 percent, or that actual losses from operational incidents will not be more than 5 percent of revenues in any one month.

But according to risk management expert Matthew Leitch, "risk appetite" controls have been oversold, creating the seductive impression that if only a board can "articulate its risk appetite" in some simple statement, number or graph, then that can be communicated to everyone in the organization and will eliminate bad risk taking at every level and in every decision, as if by magic. "This is not realistic," notes Leitch. "These controls have to be designed carefully for particular types of decisions by particular groups or individuals. There is no magic bullet."[21]

This does not mean that boards have little influence. They need to have overall oversight. Michael Schrage believes that fiduciary oversight should be less about managing increasingly detailed "compliance checklists" than about enabling simple processes and practices: encouraging directors to collaborate on behalf of shareholder concerns.[22] This does not mean designing scorecards with hundreds of risk indicators. Instead it means continuously monitoring the bigger picture and evaluating not just isolated risks but the possibility of one risk triggering another. For example, if interest rates increase, sub-prime borrowers – many of whom have teaser, or floating, rates – will not be able to make their mortgage payments. They will default on their mortgages, causing a rash of foreclosures, thus pushing housing prices down and diminishing the value of mortgage-backed securities, which in turn causes significant losses to holders, and so on. This is a familiar story. Most banks and financial firms focused on each event as a separate risk occurrence rather than a cause and effect. Effect was limited to a specific risk, and not correlated to other risks.[23]

Three recommended practices for boards

Schrage recommends three practices that would elevate the board's risk competence while giving key stakeholders more involvement in risk oversight.

- The creation of an explicit risk manifesto articulated by the board: a set of principles that describe and govern how directors will define and oversee enterprise risk management.

- The establishment of small teams of talented executives that would prioritize and present future risk scenarios that the board could then ponder.

- The use of the "wisdom of crowds," as James Surowiecki puts it, through shareholder outreach, by having boards elicit and solicit risk concerns and insights from their shareholder communities.[24]

Schrage believes that these innovations in board practice would offer unambiguous benefits, and they could be put into place by boards today, without waiting for regulatory change. They would make exercising oversight easier, especially for independent directors (those who are not executives or employees). For shareholders, these innovations would promote transparency by offering greater visibility into how the board and management are operating. They would make companies more accessible, giving shareholders ways to reach board members and to share their concerns. And they would provide greater rigor for companies in proactively defining, assessing and confronting the threats that are embedded in enterprise behaviors.[25]

Understand the key drivers of risk

What drives big-name firms to take excessive risks including breaking the law? In an article entitled "Why 'Good' Firms Do Bad Things: The Effects of High Aspirations, High Expectations and Prominence on the Incidence of Corporate Illegality," researchers Yuri Mishina *et al.* cite several factors, including unrealistic expectations from analysts and shareholders, and unrelenting pressure on executives to exceed quarterly sales and profit targets. The authors find that prominent firms, rather than feeling secure in their status, face persistent pressure to maintain or improve their performance. As high-profile success becomes harder to sustain, managers increasingly engage in illegal behavior to fulfill external expectations and internal aspirations. (The authors focused solely on instances of corporate illegality, not examples of personal greed.)

The study examined 194 US manufacturing firms that were traded on the S&P 500 between 1990 and 1999. The researchers looked at newspapers, SEC documents and sources like the Corporate Crime Reporter, a legal newsletter that tracks company criminal and civil wrongdoing – and they discovered almost 500 incidents of corporate illegality. They found that companies were more apt to skirt the rules *after* they had already gained significant public recognition. In addition, the more a firm exceeded its stock price or performance expectations (measured as return on assets), the more likely it was to be involved in illegal activities. This was particularly true for prominent companies – defined as those that earned a spot on *Fortune* magazine's "Most Admired Companies" list. According to the authors, the results suggest that when performance soars beyond aspirations, executives are more willing to take on risk to maintain their upward trajectory. Another proposed explanation is that a successful and prominent management team may develop a sense of infallibility and feel that laws don't apply to them.[26]

Daniel Vasella, CEO of Swiss pharmaceuticals company Novartis, spoke for many frustrated CEOs when he said that "the practice by which CEOs offer guidance about their expected quarterly earnings performance … has become so enshrined in the culture of Wall Street that the men and women running public companies often think of little else. They become preoccupied with short-term 'success,' a mindset that can hamper or even destroy long-term performance for shareholders."[27]

Three types of risk

Harvard professor Robert Simons points out that firms are particularly exposed to three types of risk: *growth* (pressures for performance, rate of expansion and inexperience of employees); *culture* (rewards for risk taking, resistance to bad news and level of internal competition); and *information management* (transaction complexity and velocity, gaps in diagnostic measures and degree of decentralized decision-making).[28]

- **Pressure points due to growth**. The critical issues here are whether executives and managers are under intense pressure to deliver on stretch targets. Senior executives often feel under pressure to grow even when market forces are against them. If organic growth is limited, they typically turn to mergers and acquisitions. According to a 2003 IFAC report that analyzed a number of failed companies, the top three common problems were: (1) a lack of ethics at the top, (2) aggressive targets and incentives, and (3) mergers and acquisitions that fail.[29] The second growth pressure point is the rate of expansion. Are operations expanding faster than the organization's capacity to invest in more people and technology? The third point is the inexperience of employees. When large numbers of people are taken on too quickly, the organization can find that its checks and controls are overwhelmed and circumnavigated, leading to inexperienced people being given too much responsibility too quickly. The result is invariably dissatisfied customers and falling profits.

- **Pressure points due to culture**. The critical pressure here comes from the misalignment of incentive compensation. If people stand to receive huge financial rewards based on, for example, accounting profits, sales deals, acquisitions, mergers and alliances, they are more likely to cut corners and take excessive risks. In other words, as the rewards for entrepreneurial behavior rise, so do the risks. Derivatives traders on huge bonuses are more likely to take excessive risks. The answer is to rely less on extrinsic performance drivers (such as fixed targets and financial incentives) and more on intrinsic performance drivers (such as pride, passion and peer pressure). The second problem is the resistance to bad news. In highly centralized systems, leaders do not like surprises, so managers will do what they can to avoid unscheduled meetings to explain problems. The longer that problems are left to fester and grow, the greater will be their impact on the bottom line. The third problem is internal competition. This is at its most virulent during the budgeting process, when business units compete for resources and project approvals. Too often it is the best political operators who get the lion's share of resources, leaving more innovative projects gathering dust in the file. The result is project proposals (including forecasts and risk assessments) that lack rigor and a lack of innovation and growth.

- **Pressure points due to information management**. Most firms don't know where they are today. It is often mid-month before managers know how they performed during the previous month. If managers don't get the right information at the right time, they cannot make effective decisions. While managers have large volumes of data and reports, they have little knowledge and few insights. They know how many lightbulbs they bought over the past year, but they don't know which products or customers are profitable, or the impact of major risks and whether or not to insure against them. Another point concerns the transparency of information. If information only goes to those people that "need to know," in a form dictated by senior executives, then the checks and balances that come from full transparency will be compromised. Yet another problem is the level of decentralization. Without integrated systems and a culture of openness and transparency, problems at remote locations can be left undetected and unchecked.

Define success in terms of continuous relative improvement

The key drivers of risk are all within the control of the board. How they set goals, incentives and performance measures drives the types of behavior just described. The answer is not to "do the wrong things less aggressively" but to stop doing them completely.

Enlightened leaders have rejected fixed targets and "managing the numbers." Instead, they set goals relative to peers and market movements. Dutch electronics giant Philips has recently decided to abandon setting a fixed annual growth target, preferring to peg its sales and profits forecasts to the health of the global economy. In a recent strategy update, the company said it would aim to grow its top line at least 2 percent faster than global gross domestic product, rather than set an absolute target as it has in the past.[30]

The focus on continuous relative improvement provides a *context* for setting strategic direction and evaluating success. Dr Jan Wallander, former CEO of Handelsbanken, framed the target-setting debate in this way: "The fundamental purpose of a firm in a market economy is to deliver as high a return on capital invested in the company as possible. A company is successful and will survive if it gives a higher return than other companies in the same field. The real target is thus not an absolute sum in dollars and cents but a relative one. Beating the competition is the real target. Comparing relative targets in banking is quite straightforward, as all banks must report in the same way. It might be more difficult in other industries, but as far as I can see the obstacles are not insurmountable. You can also compare results with the last quarter or the same quarter a year earlier. There are many ways to construct relative targets. The best thing would be to make these comparisons every day, but of course this is not practicable so you have to be content with every month or every quarter. The comparisons will tell you if you are doing well or not so well. In the latter case you should do something about it and formulate plans for action. What you need to do is to constantly observe how your unit or company is doing and discuss and formulate plans for action as the performance indicators tell you that something needs to be done."

Fixed targets agreed upon in advance make no sense at all. How can anyone know what will happen during the following 12 or 18 months? In volatile markets targets are often re-set many times and usually lead to disruptive actions as managers try to "fix" the results. This undermines longer-term strategies and derails action plans. But if targets are not agreed, how does the board maintain control? And how do managers know what they have to do? These two questions are repeated many times whenever we raise these issues. The answers are that fixed targets have never given the board control. And managers just need to do their best because that's what the firm employs them to do. "Knowing the number" is seductive, but it too often leads to underperformance as a significant amount of potential value creation is left on the negotiating table.

The best approach is to consign fixed performance contracts to the Frederick Winslow Taylor museum of industrial age management and give managers the confidence to stretch and grow without the fear of failure hanging over their heads.

Promote a culture of truth, transparency and trust

Why do some leaders step over the ethical line when the chances of being found out are so high and the rewards so low (relative to their wealth)? Why would Martha Stewart, a millionaire many times over, risk her fortune and her company's reputation for a mere $45,000, the amount she allegedly made through insider trading? Why would Richard Strong allegedly engage in improper, short-term trading of his firm's mutual funds, netting (only) $600,000 in profits for himself and others over several years when he is worth hundreds of millions? Why can't these (and many other) business leaders see that being anything less than totally honest will only land them in trouble and possibly lead to the loss of their reputations and, in some cases, their freedom? What drives them to take such risks when the chances of being caught are now so high and the consequences so great?

In some cases, the abuse of power in the name of amassing more wealth is less to do with the amount of money gained and more to do with hubris, image and greed or even perhaps simply a means of keeping score. For some, worrying about your position on the next published list of the country's richest people might keep you awake at night and lead to irrational decisions. Some leaders see themselves as movie stars who should be highly visible and even more highly paid. For these people "business ethics" is an oxymoron. But most causes of unethical behavior are more rational. Indeed, how people think and behave is influenced by the prevailing organization culture (e.g. whether profit always comes before values/ethics; whether people are micromanaged or trusted; whether information is closed or open; and whether compensation and rewards are seen to be divisive or fair) and by the drivers of the management system (e.g. whether people are "contracted" to deliver short-term targets or free to meet aspirational goals; whether people act as though they have a "license to spend" the corporation's money or treat it responsibly; and whether control systems assume guilt before innocence).

Regulations: beyond compliance

The scale of corporate governance failures over recent years has caused government regulators to intervene in many countries around the world. The best known is the Sarbanes-Oxley (SOX) legislation enacted in the US in 2002. It made CEOs and CFOs take responsibility for the accuracy of financial statements and for establishing and maintaining an adequate internal control structure (this has to be accompanied by an external audit report). But nine years after SOX, many leaders are concerned about the total cost of compliance and how much time it takes. In the financial services industries, for example, some estimates have put the cost at up to four percent of revenue as they have to deal with not only SOX but also Basel II, the Bank Secrecy Act and other regulations.[31] They also worry that it diverts attention from key business improvement goals such as innovation and growth. Some senior executives are looking at the trade-off between compliance and cost and many are trying "to do compliance on a budget."

While many leaders agree that some sort of reaction was necessary, it has failed to change the management culture in most organizations. The reality is that rules and regulations only provide a basic framework of good practice. But rules, regulations, inspections and audits do not win hearts and minds. Instead they breed an "inspection" culture within which people "check the boxes" and meet the audit tests. But this approach only papers over the cracks of the problem.

To root out unethical behavior, obsessive secrecy and outright dishonesty, leaders need to go beyond compliance and build a culture based on truth, trust and transparency (see Figure 2.1). This must be an all-or-nothing belief system that governs every thought, action and relationship. Never cheating or even being "economic with the truth" with fellow employees, customers, external partners or investors must be the guiding maxim throughout the organization. As Professor Kim Cameron explains, it means being "positively deviant" toward what he calls "virtuousness." In other words, people go out of their way to be truthful, trustworthy and transparent.

	Negative Deviance	Normal	Positive Deviance
Physiological	Illness	Health	Wellness
Psychological	Illness	Health	Flow
Ethics	Unethical	Compliance	Truth
Information	Secrecy	Compliance	Trust
Integrity	Dishonesty	Compliance	Transparency

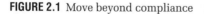

Adapted from: Kim Cameron *Ethics, Virtuousness and Constant Change* Paper for Noel Tichy and Andrew R. McGill (Eds) *The Ethical Challenge.* Jossey Bass, San Francisco, pp85-94

FIGURE 2.1 Move beyond compliance

Toward a virtuous organization

Cameron suggests that we think about the human body and points out that the large majority of medical research, and almost all of a physician's time, is spent trying to get people from the left point on the continuum (illness) to the middle (health). This middle point represents an absence of illness or injury. Very little is known about how to get people from the middle point to a state of wellness on the right. The same thing occurs psychologically. More than 95 percent of psychological research in the last 50 years has focused on closing the gap between the left point and the middle point – overcoming depression, anxiety, stress or emotional difficulties. Little is known about how to get people from a condition of health to a state of flourishing, vitality, or what's referred to as "flow" in psychology. Most of what we know about human physiology and psychology is how to overcome weakness or illness and reach a state of normality.

Ethics, information and integrity can be viewed in the same way. Unethical behavior, obsessive secrecy and outright dishonesty violate basic principles. We spend a lot of time – in our writing about ethics, in our legislation, in the popular press – addressing these types of behavior. The large majority of our attention is spent reminding leaders and organizations to comply with regulations. Hardly any attention is given, however, to the right side of the continuum – truth, transparency and trust. As Cameron notes, this "is not only a condition of not producing harm, but it is a condition of doing good, honoring others, taking a positive stance, or behaving in ways where self-interest is not the driving motivation."[32]

Virtuousness is also self-perpetuating. When people are exposed to virtuous acts, they are attracted to them. They are elevated by them. They tend to reproduce them. When we observe virtuousness, we are inspired by it. Just as these dynamics occur in individuals, similar dynamics occur in organizations. Organizational performance tends to improve when virtuousness is fostered and nurtured. When people see others behaving humanely, they tend to behave humanely as well. Integrity, compassion and trust, for example, create an environment where people are encouraged to be their best, where innovativeness, loyalty and quality are likely to be higher. That's the virtuous cycle. The amplifying nature of virtuousness causes it to reproduce itself and to improve organizational performance over time.

The implication according to Cameron is straightforward: not only must individuals and organizations avoid doing harm – that is, they must comply with ethical rules – but they must also act virtuously. Virtuousness is associated with positive outcomes, not just the absence of negative outcomes. It produces positive energy in systems, enables growth and vitality in people, and enhances the probability of extraordinarily positive performance. Doing good helps organizations do well. In conditions of turbulent change, virtuousness also serves both as a fixed point, a benchmark for making sense of ambiguity and as a source of resilience, protecting the system against harm.[33]

Virtuous organizations are high performers

When Cameron began measuring the performance of various kinds of organizations, he discovered that organizations with high scores on virtuousness significantly outperformed those with low scores (measures included profitability, productivity, innovation, quality, customer retention and employee loyalty). In other words, virtuous firms made more money than less virtuous firms. They also recovered from downsizing and retained customers and employees more than non-virtuous firms and were more creative and innovative than non-virtuous firms. Researchers Alistair R. Anderson and Carter Crockett confirmed these results within the oil and gas industry. They surveyed dozens of employees from five firms in the oil and gas industry and tracked the performance of each company from 1999 to 2004. In their admittedly small sample, the authors found that companies that valued the pursuit of virtuous "excellence" – putting such ideals as honesty, empathy and fulfillment ahead of short-term profits – tended to have more satisfied employees who were willing to make personal sacrifices for the company (for instance, taking a pay cut during a downturn to prevent layoffs). They also found that the companies were more profitable over the period of the study.[34]

Whole Foods Market CEO John Mackey has built a high-trust, virtuous organization. He explains what this means: "A very important measurement and condition of trust is transparency. If we want to optimize trust, then we must seek to optimize transparency. When we decide to keep something hidden the motivation is almost always a lack of trust. We are afraid that the information that we wish to hide would cause more harm than good if it were widely known. While some discretion is usually necessary to protect important organizational information from migrating to one's competitors or to outsiders who wish to harm the organization, such discretion can easily be overdone. Transparency is a very important supporting value for empowerment. Indeed, it is difficult for an organization to be empowered if it lacks transparency.

"Whole Foods Market strives to optimize transparency to all of our stakeholders," says Mackey. "Authentic communication with honesty and integrity are essential attributes of both transparency and trust. This is the exact opposite of what many organizations do, which is to try to 'spin' their messaging to tell people what they believe people want to hear so that people will think well of them. This lack of honest, authentic communication and transparency usually boomerangs, however, and undermines trust and creates cynicism. One of the main reasons why Americans don't trust many political leaders, including various presidents who have led us, is that we discover that they routinely lie to us. They don't tell us the truth and we come to understand that they don't trust us and feel that they need to manipulate us. We tell the truth to people we trust.

"The high-trust organization risks revealing too much information," notes Mackey. "We must be willing to take the risk that some valuable information may fall into the wrong hands because our commitment to empowerment and trust necessitates taking that risk. Creating transparency and authentic communication is an ongoing challenge that every organization faces. We must continually strive to remove the barriers that prevent them, knowing that we can't maintain high levels of organizational trust without transparency and authentic communication."[35]

Appoint inspirational leaders who empower rather than control

When asked what she thought a great leader should be like, Meg Wheatley, author of *Leadership and the New Science*, said this:

> *"The definition that I like best right now is by Mort Meyerson from Perot Industries. As CEO, he said, he realized everything he knew about leadership was wrong. Then he came up with these new definitions in which he said: the first task of a leader is to make sure the organization knows itself. We need to think of the leader as a mirror, or as a supporter of the processes by which we know our competencies and we know what interpretations of our history we're willing to enter into. We need to make sure we know our customers, we know one another and we know why we're in this business or in this public sector organization. There is so much that an organization needs to know about itself. But it needs to know it; it doesn't ever respond to being told what it is or what it's supposed to do. It's just not in our capacity as human beings to take direction. I don't actually think it's in the capacity of anything alive to take direction when it's trying to exercise its creativity in response to what you just asked it to do."[36]*

Great leaders tear up the rule book

Adaptive organizations do not cultivate hero worship. Their leaders prefer to be judged by their actions rather than their words. This was neatly put by Arne

Mårtensson, President of Handelsbanken, when he said that "Leadership is ten percent what you say and ninety percent what you do." In adaptive organizations, leaders are highly respected but not necessarily high-profile people. "Humility" is a word you hear many times if you ask about the qualities they see in themselves and seek in others. They believe in the purpose of the organization and assume that they will be leading it for some considerable time. They also "walk the talk" of their statements. For example, they really believe that their people are their greatest assets and they reinforce this belief by devolving authority and accountability to them at every level of the organization. In other words, they are not fixated on control. And they share information as they know that this is the key to devolved decision-making.

Leaders who truly believe in their people are not afraid to tear up the rule book. Just over 200 years ago, Rear Admiral Sir Horatio Nelson, one of Britain's greatest military leaders, did just this. He led his fleet to the battle of the Nile in 1798, the greatest naval victory in history up to that time. He carried a rule book that was meant to guide the actions of every British naval officer. First issued in 1653, it was called the "Fighting Instructions" – rigorous, strict and unforgiving, and by repute, a book that admirals ignored at their peril. Nelson ignored it almost completely. Even in the toughest boardroom battle, very few people today have to carry the level of responsibility Nelson bore in 1798. Yet the way he bore it could have come from a modern textbook: developing team work with defined roles and clear personal relationships; allowing the expression of different ideas; providing clear, shared and understandable goals; permitting participation in decision-making, fostering initiatives; promoting a sense of ownership and commitment – all today are at least recognized as valuable, and all figured in his conduct of the campaign. If Admiral Nelson had had time to write books, he could have advanced management theory by two centuries.[37]

Like Nelson, effective leaders influence what we do. They apply common-sense solutions to business problems. They act *on* the system rather than within it. They encourage everyone to challenge conventional wisdom. They enable people to "see" a better way. They don't rely on tools or techniques (or even IT systems). They define what success looks like and set a strategic direction to achieve that success. They set boundaries such as which businesses we are in (and not in). They help their teams to clarify the purpose of their work, measure against that purpose and take the right action to improve performance. They encourage the application of innovative thinking to business problems. They promote experimentation. And they remove barriers to change.

This type of leader is usually home-grown. They know the business and have credibility. They share the recognition and rewards with their teams, and team members will follow their direction and buy into their goals and plans. Most importantly, leaders see businesses as horizontal systems that connect and combine to deliver value for customers. Constantly taking waste out of these systems is the way to learn and improve. Serving and supporting customers, closing the books each month, paying a supplier, recruiting a new employee – these are examples of business systems that absorb time and costs. Some need challenging. What is their purpose? Do they add value? Are they necessary? Are they being performed with the least possible resources? Can we shorten the time taken? And failing everything else, should they be outsourced? In this way, leaders constantly act *on* the system.

Promote leaders from within

While there are many reasons why promoting senior executives from within the organization makes sense (it minimizes costs and sends the right signals about morale), it is especially critical in organizations that have changed their management models to emphasize empowerment and trust. In other words, if a company has spent much time and effort making these changes and then they appoint a traditional "command and control" leader, they shouldn't be surprised if people become confused and morale starts to dip. This happened a few years ago at Home Depot, one of America's largest retailers.

Founded by Bernie Marcus and Arthur Blank in 1979, Home Depot became the youngest-ever company to hit $40 billion of revenues, in just 20 years. But as sales stagnated in the late 1990s a new leader, Bob Nardelli, was recruited from General Electric (after losing out on the top job) in 2000. Nardelli, a total believer in command and control, made a point of recruiting large numbers of ex-military personnel for key positions. He also made some smart investments in new technology and expanded store openings that took advantage of an improving market. On the surface (in financial terms), the changes looked positive. But the shareholders marked the stock down and finally rejected Nardelli's management style, forcing him to resign in early 2007. The problem was that its main competitor, Lowe's, had done much better over the same period (Lowe's operates with a much softer empowerment model similar to Home Depot prior to Nardelli). Another problem, according to many employees who would only speak off the record, was that morale had slumped as a "management by fear" regime took over. Self-interest became the norm. Customer satisfaction ratings plummeted. By early 2006, the American Customer Satisfaction Index showed that Home Depot was at the bottom of the retailing list, 11 points behind Lowe's and three points below the much-maligned Kmart.[38]

It is perhaps no coincidence that most of the organizations we talk about positively in this book grow their own leaders. Companies such as Southwest Airlines, Whole Foods, Handelsbanken, W.L. Gore & Associates and many others promote from within and keep their leaders, in many cases for 20 years or more. They expect their leaders to be the guardians of the organization's values and culture and to pass them on to the next generation. They also know that it is *their* management model and *their* culture that represents their true competitive advantage.

Focus on the person, not the pay

While most CEOs are talented individuals with a range of qualities, do they really make as much difference as they are given credit for? And should they accept the lion's share of the blame if things go badly? Not according to the research done by Jim Collins. Indeed, few leaders are able to transform large organizations. Of the 1435 companies that have appeared in the Fortune 500 from 1965 to 1995, he found that only 11 executives had transformed their companies from "good" to "great."[39] Perhaps investors should heed the advice of the "Sage of Omaha," Warren Buffet, who once said that, "You should invest in a company that even a fool can run, because some day a fool will."[40] What most large organizations require today are leaders who can inspire people to raise their game and reach their potential, to harness their emotional commitment and to set the highest moral standards of personal and business behavior.

It matters how leaders are appointed and compensated

How leaders are appointed and compensated tells you most of what you need to know about their values. Henry Mintzberg is a cynic about executive pay. "It has been claimed," he notes, "that if you don't pay them, you don't get the right person in the CEO's chair. I believe that if you do pay bonuses, you get the wrong person in that chair. At the worst, you get a self-centered narcissist. At the best, you get someone who is willing to be singled out from everyone else by virtue of the compensation plan. Is this any way to build community within an enterprise, even to foster the very sense of enterprise that is so fundamental to economic strength? Accordingly, executive bonuses provide the perfect tool to screen candidates for the CEO job. Anyone who insists on them should be dismissed out of hand, because he or she has demonstrated an absence of the leadership attitude required for a sustainable enterprise. Of course, this might thin the roster of candidates. Good. Most need to be thinned, in order to be refilled with people who don't allow their own needs to take precedence over those of the community they wish to lead."[41]

According to Claudio Fernández-Aráoz of executive recruitment consultants Egon Zehnder International, the real aim should be not just to avoid public frustration and excess, but to aim for a much more ambitious objective: to ensure that CEOs and other leaders make the greatest potential contribution towards building lasting greatness.

The range of performance expands with the complexity of the job

He makes the point that people are very different when it comes to how they perform in complex jobs. Research shows that the difference in performance grows exponentially with the complexity of the job. While a star blue-collar worker on a traditional assembly line would be 40 percent more productive than a typical worker, that performance advantage can be 240 percent for a star insurance salesperson and more than 1000 percent for star workers in more complex jobs such as a computer programmer or an account manager of a professional service firm. Thus a CEO's performance, given the complexity of the job, will have a huge spread. Therefore, the key debate should not be about how much and how to pay the CEO, but rather about how to make sure that the best CEO is in place, and boards should focus much more, and much better, on that question.[42]

Exaggerated incentives encourage greed

Fernández-Aráoz goes on to note that recent research from neuroscience has demonstrated that our brain has an altruism center which is separate and quite distinct from the center aroused by financial incentives. Financial incentives trigger one of the most primitive parts of the brain, the *nucleus accumbens*, which has traditionally been associated with our "wild side." Scientists call this region the "pleasure center" because it is linked with the "high" that results from drugs, sex and gambling. Furthermore, research shows that the pleasure center and the altruism center cannot both function at the same time: one or the other is in control. Finally, it turns out that when the pleasure and altruism centers go head to head, the pleasure center seems to be able to hijack the altruism center. In other words, there is a neurophysiological reason why exaggerated financial incentives can override our altruistic motives. For this reason, companies should make sure that financial incentives are not exaggerated and are in any case properly aligned with the desirable objectives of building lasting greatness.

Fernández-Aráoz concludes that companies clearly need to pay reasonably well in order to attract and retain the right people in the first place. However, he believes that the purpose of compensation is *not to "motivate" the right behaviors from the wrong people.* Compensation should be reasonable because it is part of human nature to expect fair treatment when it comes to compensation, which should be somehow proportional to our efforts and/or results.[43]

Be careful with pay differentials

A recent study in the American baseball leagues suggests that the greater the difference between the pay of the stars and that of the rest of the team, the less impressive is the performance of the stars and the team as a whole.[44] Allowing the gap between executive and average worker compensation to grow provides fertile ground for what Professor Robert Simons calls rationalization. He suggests that this is an essential ingredient for turning the pressure of alienation into the opportunity of unethical behavior. In other words, if individuals can convince themselves that their contemplated behavior is not wrong – using excuses such as "Everybody does it," "The effect is immaterial," "No one is hurt" or "I'm doing it for the good of the company" – then there is little to prevent the type of behavior that puts both the individual and the organization at risk.[45]

One solution: use a multiple of average pay

For these reasons executives need to be more conscious about their levels of earnings compared with their employees. One idea is to limit executive pay to a multiple of average earnings. At Nucor Steel there are only four layers of management between the CEO and the floor worker, and only 66 people in the head office. Nucor's divisions are all independently run at the local level and employees work in teams that are largely self-directed. To remove barriers to communication, everyone is treated the same. There are no executive perks or privileges.[46] The pay of CEO Daniel Di Micco is also based on performance. In 2005 he collected a salary and bonus precisely 23 times that of his average steelworker. He gets few stock options, and most of his restricted stock and other longer-term bonuses don't materialize if the company doesn't beat the competition and outpace a sample group of other high-performing companies.[47]

CEO of Whole Foods Market John Mackey bemoans the trend that once a Fortune 500 CEO made about 25 times the average worker pay, and now that's climbed to 300 times average employee pay. He says this violates the principle of "internal equity – what your leadership is getting paid relative to everyone else in the organization." In 2006 the board of directors voted to raise the salary cap from 14 times the average pay to 19 times the average pay. Mackey explained that the reason was to make the compensation to his executives more competitive in the marketplace. "...Everyone on the Whole Foods leadership team (except for me) has been approached multiple times by 'headhunters' with job offers to leave Whole Foods and go to work for our competitors. Raising the salary cap has become necessary to help ensure the retention of our key leadership ..." This increase to 19 times the average pay remains far, far below what the typical *Fortune* 500 company pays its executives.[48]

The pay–performance link is unproven

What drives CEO pay to such high levels? According to Edgar Woolard, former CEO of Du Pont, the primary cause is that most boards want their CEO to be in the top half of the CEO peer group because they think it makes the company look strong. "So when Tom, Dick and Harry receive compensation increases in 2002, I get one too, even if I've had a bad year. We stopped doing that at Du Pont in 1990 ... Instead, we use the pay of the senior vice presidents – the people that actually run the businesses – as a benchmark and then decide how much more the CEO ought to get," notes Woolard.[49]

Stanford professor Jeffrey Pfeffer suggests that there is nothing in the process of setting CEO compensation that produces a pay-performance link. Companies and their compensation consultants choose a set of similar comparison firms, often on the basis of size and industry, and then compute the median pay for CEOs of these comparable companies. Setting aside the tendency to game the choice of comparisons, which is plentiful, what is most visible in the discussion of compensation is the median figure. Precious few companies take variables like company performance into account when determining compensation. So, what the compensation committee sees is not an equation relating pay to company-specific factors, but just the median. The tendency to pay at least at the median is overwhelming. And because the comparable firms have been picked partly on the basis of their similarity in size, it's not surprising that size looms large as a determinant of compensation. Moreover, because firms rely on comparables, if none of the comparison companies base pay on performance, neither will the focal company.[50]

A recent academic study in the UK supports these conclusions. While confirming that thousands of research studies on top management pay in public companies, using a variety of statistical and modeling techniques applied to different company samples, failed to find a relationship between pay and performance, the research did find a strong relationship between pay and company size: larger companies pay executives more. One meta-study concluded from US evidence that firm size accounts generally for more than 40 percent of the variance in total CEO pay, whereas firm performance accounts for less than 5 per cent of the variance.[51]

Firm size offers a better explanation of executive pay

Following their study Julie Froud *et al.* concluded that firm size explained more about executive pay than pay-for-performance. They went on to pose some interesting questions. For example, what if pay as fee is a more accurate characterization of market practice than pay for performance? What are the implications for our understanding of top management pay and why does this constitute a problem shift rather than a change of metaphor? The short answer they provide is that conceptualizing top management pay as a fee paid on the value of industrial capital managed reframes the whole issue of pay in three ways: first, it redefines the immediate problem of pay and pay incentive structures; second, it encourages divergent thinking about pay as an effort-focusing device rather than as an output-generating device for creating value; third, it opens the way for new thinking by investors about how to simplify top management pay.[52]

They raise other interesting questions. Can corporate executive compensation be comparable with other "fees" paid to professionals or government leaders? Thinking of executive compensation as a fee related to the size and complexity of an organization certainly has its merits. Of course, deciding on a formula for agreeing the fee would still be problematic. Should it be related to revenues, market capitalization, global spread and so forth? However, this has one particular strength – it takes the focus away from pay-for-performance that upsets so many people and might even satisfy Henry Mintzberg!

Conclusions

Governance embraces everything we will discuss in this book – from rethinking risk management, leadership, transparency, organization, accountability, trust, goal-setting, rewards, planning and control. Embedding good governance into the organization means tackling all these issues and *changing the natural drivers of risk*. The result will be a culture where people close to the action or to the customer have the scope and authority to take risk-based decisions that place safety and reputation before profit and bonuses. The drivers of risk are deeply embedded in the management model and therefore to change how the organization handles risk leaders need to change the management model itself.

KEY POINTS

- Create a climate of trust and candor; foster a culture of open dissent; utilize a fluid portfolio of roles; ensure individual accountability and evaluate the board's performance.

- The board should understand the bigger picture of risk and how one failure can trigger another. They should never countermand the advice of their risk officers. They should spell out their view of risk including "no-go" areas and risk limits (although attempting to define their "risk appetite" or "risk tolerance" is probably futile). They should also be aware of the key performance drivers of risk-taking behavior. In particular, aggressive targets and incentives are a common feature in those organizations that have failed.

- While organizations need to comply with legal requirements, leaders should be skeptical about the value of risk models, compliance rules, risk indicators and enterprise-wide risk management systems. Almost every failed bank had invested huge sums in these systems but few anticipated what happened in 2007–9. Leaders should also be aware of risks caused by a culture of failing to share bad news and whether or not their information systems keep managers and the board informed and in control at all times.

- The board needs to reframe success in terms of "continuous relative improvement" (this should be the primary definition of success at every level). This enables the organization and all its teams to break free from the tyranny of short-term fixed targets and set ambitious goals.

- Instead of spending so much time on compliance and control, make truth, transparency and trust your guiding principles. Make everyone aware that unethical behavior, obsessive secrecy and outright dishonesty violate basic principles.

- The best leaders empower rather than control people. They believe that their people truly are their greatest assets. If teams act within the values and other (strategic and behavioral) boundaries of the business they should be able to make decisions with confidence and the full support of their leaders.

- Develop your own leaders. It takes a long time to become an effective leader who understands the corporate culture in all its facets. So aim to recruit the right people, develop their capabilities and keep them for a long time.

- Recognize that whom you pay is much more important than how much you pay, and even *how* you pay. Companies need to pay executives reasonably well in order to attract and retain them in the first place. The purpose of compensation is not to "motivate" the right behaviors from the wrong people!

## CHAPTER 3

Principle #3 – Transparency
Make information open and transparent; don't restrict and control it

The two forces that we have placed in opposition to each other – freedom and order – turn out to be partners in generating healthy, well-ordered systems. Effective self-organization is supported by two critical elements: a clear sense of identity, and freedom. In organizations, if people are free to make their own decisions, guided by a clear organizational identity for them to reference, the whole system develops greater coherence and strength. The organization is less controlling, but more orderly.[1]

Margaret Wheatley

The power of radical transparency at Beth Israel Medical Center

When Paul Levy took over as CEO of Boston's Beth Israel Deaconess Medical Center in January 2002, the hospital faced severe financial difficulties. Levy had been given a short amount of time in which to turn the situation around; if he didn't, the renowned academic hospital would be sold to a for-profit corporation. Before noon on his first day, Levy sent an email to the entire staff, who knew about neither the hospital's dire finances nor the ultimatum. In it he wrote:

> *"This is a wonderful institution, representing the best in academic medicine: exemplary patient care, extraordinary research and fine teaching. However, the place is in serious trouble, and we are going to have to work very hard dur-ing the next few months if we are to secure our future as a non-profit academic medical center. I promise to have an open administration, sharing with you as much information as possible to help you be part of solving the problems of the medical center. Here is where things stand, as of today. Over the last several years, during one of the greatest economic booms in American history, hundreds of millions of dollars of the BIDMC's assets have gone toward paying the operating losses of the hospital. This was money that ordinarily would have been used as the source of funds for new facilities and equipment, for expansion of programs and as a cushion for hard economic times. For whatever set of reasons, there was a failure to act to stop this financial outflow. We now face our last chance to reverse this problem."*

In 2002 such radical corporate transparency had not yet become a trend, but to Levy it was simple common sense, and it soon became a fundamental part of the hospital's culture. After reading that only one CEO of a Fortune 500 firm had a blog, he started runningahospital.blogspot.com. When the Board of Trustees set the goal of eliminating preventable harm within four years, the hospital began posting data about clinical results and medical errors on its public website. Every month, an employee receives a "caller-outer award" for identifying "problems they see in the workplace, problems of safety, efficiency or anything else." When a surgeon accidentally operated on the wrong side of a patient's body, Levy discussed the mistake at length both in an email to the staff and on his blog. And in March 2010, faced with a potential $20 million operating loss, Levy wrote to his staff:

> *"Part of the solution to this problem will be to lay off people. I'm not sure how many yet, and I am hoping you can help me figure out how to minimize the number by using more creative and less disruptive ways to solve the problem. I am going to hold some town hall meetings in the next several days to get your thoughts about alternative concepts. I will lay out some ideas here, so you can be thinking about them. You can write back now, or you can tell me in person later. Perhaps you will want to discuss them with your colleagues. Perhaps you*

have better ideas to suggest. We'll soon set up an electronic chat room, too, to permit people to share their thoughts more broadly with the community."

At the first town hall meeting, employees quickly reached a consensus: those at higher pay grades would sacrifice more in order to protect the lowest-paid workers. Levy received about 3600 specific cost-cutting ideas and comments from the staff. And doctors affiliated with the hospital donated several hundreds of thousands of dollars to help offset staffing costs. Out of the 4861 facilities analyzed in compiling the 2009 edition of *America's Best Hospitals*, only 174 were ranked in any of 16 adult specialties. This hospital was one of them.[2]

The lesson is that if leaders are prepared to trust their people with information *and invite them into the problem-solving and decision-making process,* then amazing things can happen. But for many, the more likely reaction would be the same as Frank Borman, chairman of Eastern Airlines in the mid 1980s, when he is reported to have said, "I'm not going to have the monkeys running the zoo."[3]

Human networks thrive on openness and transparency

Unlike Paul Levy, most leaders preside over organizations that operate behind a cloak of secrecy and obfuscation. It seems that just because leaders have the authority to make decisions, they think they have the right neither to explain the reasons nor to accept the consequences. This leads to poor communication and decision-making and creates opportunities for misrepresentation and fraud. Dictating and directing information so that people only see "what they need to know" denies people the performance insights that come from seeing the bigger picture and prevents them from raising tough questions about the performance of their peers. "The risks of having a completely open system would be too great," they say. "Anyhow, how can we trust people with sensitive information? It would reach our competitors in no time at all." In such a culture, information is restricted, and with only one interpreter of that information the potential richness is lost and creativity is stifled. It is the synthesis of information in often unique ways that leads to insight and discovery. By denying this opportunity, command and control leaders do their best to destroy innovation.

While the problems of information sharing are endemic to command and control organizations, networks thrive on openness and transparency. The main advantages of open workplaces are the speed, responsiveness and learning capacity of their human networks. Knowledge, competence, value creation and the capacity to influence others create power in networks.

In the near future, leaders will have no choice but to accept complete transparency. In an increasingly digital world, information can no longer be hidden. In 2002 there were only 15,000 blogs, but this had grown to around 133 million by 2009.[4] But this sea change should be seen as an opportunity rather than a problem. Instead of trying to conceal information, leaders need to reveal it. This leads to more effective, consistent decisions being made by every team. Transparent information also breeds a collegiate, collaborative culture within which problems are immediately shared and dealt with before they get out of hand and lead to serious damage. Measurement becomes much more transparent. Trust is the outcome. Trust is inspiring. It is the cornerstone of an empowered and adaptive organization.

But total transparency is a step-change from where most companies are today. It requires changes in how leaders think about information and how the measurement and control process works. Information systems should provide front-line managers with the capability they need to "run their own business," to effectively manage project-based initiatives, and to share knowledge and best practices with colleagues across the company before taking important decisions. They enable managers to get answers to such questions as: "What do customers think about our products? What problems do they want us to fix? What new features do they want us to add? What problems do our distributors or resellers have and what needs to be done to correct them? Where and why are our competitors winning business from us? What are changing customer demands telling us about our core capabilities?" They also enable managers to synthesize apparently unconnected pieces of information and knit them together into flashes of insight. These "lightbulb" moments might be rare, but they are facilitated by having access to the whole panoply of information available rather than just seeing someone else's view of the world.

Without transparency, the adaptive organization will remain a pipe dream. We are not saying it is easy. But it is a critical part of the management mindset change that needs to occur if leaders want to break free from the suffocating controls of the command and control bureaucracy. Principle #3 tells us that openness and transparency is a core component of the empowered and adaptive organization and must be embraced by the leadership team.

Implementation guidelines

- Make information open and transparent.

- Publish the costs of everything.

- Teach people to understand the meaning of measures and reports.

- Share bad news immediately.

- Make hiding or manipulating information a firing offense.

- Ensure that data are clean and accurate.

- Operate with "one version of the truth."

Make information open and transparent

Too many leaders continue to manage the business through "remote-controlled" systems including targets, plans and budgets that local teams must follow or face the consequences. Neither the thinking behind chosen strategies nor the rationale for action plans and performance measures is shared with implementing teams. Thus leaders neither ask for nor receive any ideas or initiatives that may come from engaged and committed front-line teams. This separation of strategy and execution has other consequences. It often leads to teams failing to share information and ideas with other teams and failing to tell the full story about potential problems. Everyone keeps their head down and focuses on their own small piece of the action.

Meg Wheatley has been warning us against this approach for many years. She suggests that we "think of organizational data for a metaphoric moment as a quantum wave function, rich in potential interpretations. If this wave of potentials meets up with only one observer, it collapses into only one interpretation, responding to the expectations of that particular person. All other potentials disappear from view and are lost by that solo act of observation. This one interpretation is then passed down to others in the organization. Most often the interpretation is presented as objective, which it is not, and definitive, which is impossible."[5]

"If you don't have dissent, then you have a king"

Former CEO of Google Eric Schmidt believes that in the future corporations won't be able to be as controlling. As Schmidt explains, "They will need to let information out. So a more transparent company is a better organization. There is also a lot of evidence that groups make better decisions than individuals, especially when they are selected from among the smartest and most interesting people. The wisdom of crowds argument is that you can operate a company by consensus, which is, indeed, how Google operates. The role of a leader, in this case, is not to force an outcome, but to force execution – literally, by having a deadline. Either by having a real crisis or creating a crisis. You also need dissent. If you don't have dissent, then you have a king."[6]

Transparency enables empowerment

CEO of Indian IT Company HCL Technologies Vineet Nayar realized that it is hard to feel empowered if your manager has a lot of data you don't. With this in mind, HCLT's IT team created a simple widget that gave every employee a detailed set of financial metrics for their own team and other teams across the company. Suddenly, poorly performing teams had an incentive to improve, and high-performing ones to stay on top. Another benefit: employees now had positive proof that the company was willing to trust them with strategic information. "Need to know" had become "right to know."

Nayar has also encouraged open performance reviews. Today HCLT employees are able to rate the performance of *any* manager whose decisions affect their work lives, and to do so anonymously. These ratings are published online and can be viewed by anyone who has submitted a review. This visibility challenges managers to be more responsive and exercise their authority judiciously. The number and organizational scope of the reviews a manager receives are also a good indicator of an individual's zone of influence – is he or she adding value across a wide swath of the company, or only within a narrow sphere? Importantly, this "feed-forward" process isn't connected to compensation and promotion decisions. It is purely developmental. Nevertheless, there aren't many hiding places left at HCLT for mediocre managers.[7]

Ken Iverson, former CEO of Nucor Steel, was also a devout believer in sharing all information with employees. "Sharing information," said Iverson, "is another key to treating people as equals, building trust and destroying the hierarchy. I think there are really just two ways to go on the question of information sharing: tell employees everything, or tell them nothing. Otherwise, each time you choose to withhold information, they have reason to think you're up to something. We prefer to tell employees everything. We hold back nothing." Nucor president John

Corrcnti is aware that some of this information leaks to the media but, he notes, that, "the value of sharing everything with our employees is much greater than any downside there might be to some information getting out."[8]

What does real transparency mean?

Here are five key features:

*   *Everyone can see the organization's and their team's goals, strategies and plans.* This means that every team member has no excuse for not understanding goals, strategies and so forth and has every opportunity to engage in and contribute to these important processes.

*   *Everyone can see complete financial statements (apart from group forecasts) as well as key performance indicators (KPIs), trends and peer-to-peer comparisons.* Everyone can see how the business and their own team is performing.

*   *Everyone can see everyone's salary and bonus.* Salary and bonus differentials are a source of much employee concern and dissatisfaction. Make them open. Also open up the peer reviews of all managers.

*   *Everyone can see everyone's expenses.* Again, open up the books so everyone's expense account is available for scrutiny. This alone will probably cut expenses by 20 to 30 percent!

*   *Everyone can see the minutes of key meetings.* Open up the decision-making process so everyone can see how decisions were made, including which options were considered but discarded (and why).

Cutting red tape (and expenses) at Roche

Consider what happened recently at Roche, a $50bn Swiss pharmaceutical business. In April 2009 six Roche managers from different parts of the group met at London Business School. Their perception was that red tape was absorbing too much energy. "We needed to think of something to tackle bureaucracy that we as a group felt was getting a bit out of control," noted one manager.

The questions they asked were: Is it feasible to use radical transparency to dispense with bureaucracy without losing control? Is personal responsibility a substitute for external controls? These are big questions to which the Roche team believed the answer had to be "yes." Their intuition was that not only are there alternatives to bureaucracy, but there are simpler, more motivating ways of working that are more aligned with Roche's organizational values and (they hoped) neutral on costs.

After considering a number of options the team chose to examine travel expenses – Roche spends 450 million Swiss francs a year on travel and entertaining – to see what a change of management control might achieve. As one manager put it: "I'm responsible for €60m in sales but need approval to buy a cup of coffee."

So they set up two pairs of matched groups of 50 people each – one in Germany and one at the head office in Basel, Switzerland. In one group in each place there was no change in the travel policy. The other group was told that their travel would no longer require any prior approval provided they abided by the company's policies – *but* their expenses would be available on the Intranet for everyone to see.

The experiment was designed to test three things: Would people be more motivated by removal of the bureaucratic process of pre-authorization? Was the new process simpler than before? And what would be the consequences for costs?

The answer to the first question was that 45 percent were more motivated and 46 percent were neutral. Ninety-four percent were comfortable with full transparency and 83 percent said it was more in tune with Roche's values and wanted it to become permanent. On the second question, around 80 percent thought the system to be more efficient.

But the real surprise was the answer to the third question. While costs in the control groups remained the same, they went down in both groups operating under the new system – in one group substantially.[9]

Publish the costs of everything

It is no use empowering people to manage their own costs if they don't know what those costs are. And without this knowledge, there is every chance that they will take action that actually drives costs up rather than eliminates those that add no value. Every support services team needs to set out a menu of all its services and what each one costs. Front-line teams can then draw upon these services knowing what the impact will be on their cost statement. At Handelsbanken this happens through an "internal market" whereby buyers (branches) negotiate with sellers (support services) for which services they require and at what price they are prepared to pay. This has the effect of making all costs transparent and forcing central units to confront their excessive cost structures.

If everyone can see the costs of everything, then there is far more likelihood that people will look for imaginative ways to reduce them. This approach also harnesses the power of peer pressure. If one team can see that other teams are more cost efficient, they are likely to react by finding why this is so and taking action to bring their own costs into line. Also, they will have more opportunity to assess whether each item of cost adds value for the customer or just adds cost to the business. This is a key role for the finance team. Instead of spending so much time controlling costs from the corporate center, they might have a far better return on their time if they helped employees to understand which costs added value and which didn't.

Teach people to understand the meaning of measures and reports

The number-one complaint of most managers is that they don't know what's going on until it's too late. Few see the bigger picture and even fewer see what's happening even within their own team. Fast, frequent, relevant KPIs can help to overcome these problems. Using newsletters, websites, blogs, emails and any other forms of communication, the information system is capable of making sure that everyone can see what's happening everywhere at the same time. This needs to be a "pull" rather than a "push" system. In other words, managers can access information if they want to see it, rather than have it thrust upon them.

Southwest Airlines leaders know they can't fully empower front-line people unless they are trusted with information *they understand.* So that's what they provide. Southwest is known for saturating people with information and allowing each employee to analyze and interpret the key messages that have meaning for them. Access to information is especially critical for dealing with customers and for taking the right action.

The finance team has launched a "bizlit" campaign to educate people about the key numbers. This includes earnings debrief articles every quarter, scoreboard posters, other financial articles in intervening months, departmental newsletters aligned to the "knowing the score" message, and the "reel deal" initiative that turns "magic numbers" into animated characters.

They have also done an excellent job of communicating the key numbers to the workforce and helping them to understand what they mean. Posters are distributed throughout the field. They talk about "Four Magic Numbers" being the key to prosperity (and the "penalty" cost to employees if they are not achieved):

- Cost-per-available-seat-mile

- Net income

- Net income margin

- Return-on-invested-capital

The "individual profit-sharing penalty" is the difference between actual results and prosperity goals. For example, while the actual result for 2007 was net income of $471m, the baseline prosperity goal was $820m – that's a prosperity penalty of $850 per $25,000 of wages. This process was supported by extensive employee training. According to Southwest CFO Laura Wright, of the employees who completed the training, over 50 percent said they have an improved ability to identify and explain the company's strategy and that they can better explain what the magic numbers are, what they mean and what the goals are for their department. This is the essence of the Southwest approach of not only trusting employees with information but spending time educating them on how to interpret and respond to it.

Share bad news immediately

Though most senior executives today want to create an organization without boundaries in which knowledge, resources and best practices are shared, the management culture (underpinned by individual targets and bonuses) means that people fiercely protect their own parts of the business. It leads to an "I win/ you lose" approach where nothing is shared. People hide both good news and, far worse, bad news. This can lead to calamitous results as defective products, disaffected customers or environmental disasters are allowed to fester and grow as local people try to cover up their problems. How people are rewarded is a primary cause of this behavior.

What happened at Sears Roebuck in 2002 is a good example of how the suppression of bad news can have severe adverse consequences. Sears' credit card business was a major source of profitability: it was sometimes called a credit card company that dabbled in retail! While the recently introduced Sears MasterCard was successful, it was not achieving the planned growth levels – average user balances were well below forecasts. So, in early 2002, the company took steps to raise rates and fees to well above competitive offerings. But this move just pushed already rising delinquency rates even higher as few Sears customers could get credit elsewhere.

The problem erupted shortly afterwards as bad debts were increased by 50 percent in one quarter.

The problem was that Sears did not write off bad debts until they were 240 days old. So even though managers could see the trend of delayed payments and the likely write-offs, they were under pressure to make their numbers and were not obliged to report them until the due dates. Sears ultimately decided that the damage caused by inadequate monitoring and reporting on the credit portfolio had surprised the company too many times. In early 2003, Sears announced that it had sold its $29 billion receivables to Citigroup for $3 billion.[10]

Well-governed organizations assimilate bad news quickly and deal with it as a team. By doing this, local managers are not afraid of building the results of such bad news into their forecasts – the sting having already been taken out of them. Bill Gates, founder of Microsoft, offers some good advice: "A change in corporate attitude, encouraging and listening to bad news, has to come from the top. The CEO and the other senior executives have to insist on getting bad news, and they have to create an appetite for bad news throughout their organizations. The bearer of bad tidings should be rewarded, not punished. Business leaders have to want to listen to alerts from salespeople, product developers and customers. You can't just turn off the alarm and go back to sleep. Not if you want your company to survive."[11]

Make hiding or manipulating information a firing offense

Many leaders know that a few percent of people in every organization will abuse the freedom of information, but they judge that this risk is worth taking. Fast, open information is the glue that binds teams (at every level) together and enables fast, coordinated action. Everyone should get the same information at the same time (though in different degrees of aggregation). Peter Drucker likened this approach to the orchestra when he said that "the right model for the information-based organization is not the military, even in its modified form. It is the symphony orchestra, in which each player plays directly and without intermediary to the 'chief executive,' the conductor, and can do so because everybody has the same 'score,' that is, the same information."[12]

Hiding or manipulating information is endemic in many large bureaucracies. *In an organization that truly believes in its core values, this must be a firing offense.* On the other hand, no one should ever get fired for telling the truth, no matter how unpalatable it might be.

Organizations such as Handelsbanken, Southwest Airlines, Whole Foods Market and HCLT have promoted information flows to new levels of openness and transparency. They have given their people access to the sort of strategic, competitive and market-based information that was once the preserve of senior executives. And they have understood that all the numbers within the organization should stick to "one truth."

Ensure that data are clean and accurate

Operating with fast, transparent information is a laudable aim, but it will be a waste of time if the data in the system are unreliable. Dirty data are endemic to most management information systems and represent an increasing cost. Research shows that around 20 percent of all data is subject to error. Missing fields, wrong coding and duplicate entries make it difficult for managers to close the books with confidence.[13]

The Data Warehousing Institute estimates that data quality problems cost US businesses billions of dollars a year, yet most executives are oblivious to the data quality lacerations that are slowly bleeding their companies to death. More injurious than the unnecessary printing, postage and staffing costs is the slow but steady erosion of an organization's credibility among customers and suppliers, as well as its inability to make sound decisions based on accurate information.[14]

Leaders can learn from "lean" thinking. Take the example of a UK local government office that was in the dreadful position of having 7700 welfare claims waiting to be processed – 20 times the norm. The department was taking more than six months to pay a claim. When they examined the system they found that they weren't looking at the process from the claimant's point of view. There were two separate parts, inquiry and assessment, and no one was looking at it end to end, the way the customer experienced it; staff merely did what the system told them to do. When they were asked to study actual contacts and analyze what they meant, the results were a shock. Only around one-third of letters, phone calls and visits were new claims. All the rest were "waste" (demand resulting from a previous failure). Only three percent of claimants had their claim settled in one visit to the office. Most came in at least three times, some up to ten. It was no wonder that staff couldn't deal with the backlog. When scanning documents, the system was designed to sort them three times and check them eight times. As realization dawned, there was a turning point when one staff member confided: "We've forgotten our purpose. We're pushing paper to satisfy official specifications, not the claimants."

Once the whole team got clean information and was able to assess claims and pay them as quickly as possible to those entitled, redesigning the system was easy. As the call analysis had established, the real bottleneck was not the presumed culprit – assessing claims – but getting clean information in the first place. So staff formulated a bargain: if claimants provided all the right documents at the first point of contact, it promised to deal with the claim immediately or within days if it had to be referred elsewhere.

The team now uses measures that tell staff how well they are achieving things that matter to customers, not according to official specifications. Staff have "good" information that enables them to keep customers informed of progress at all times. They also know that customer claims will be dealt with on a "first-in, first-out" basis. The result is that because staff can confidently deal with customers, they are happier at work and therefore more caring and committed. After a three-week pilot it was clear that redesigning the system into a single flow allowed staff to cope with claims in days if not hours. Rolled out without fanfare to cover all 60 claims staff, it quickly began to reel in the backlog. Live claims came down to 300, and staff started coming to terms with unaccustomed gifts of flowers and cake instead of brickbats. Morale and quality were up, and extra capacity has been delivered to the front line at no extra cost.

The lesson is that all data should be entered correctly the first time. Batching, scanning, archiving and retrieving consume huge amounts of time and cost, as people need to reopen files many times.

Operate with "one version of the truth"

Effective leaders believe in only one set of numbers that is transparent throughout the whole organization. Maintaining one set of books, or "one truth," is the key to high levels of ethical practice. This is exactly what such firms as Handelsbanken and Southwest do. Gunnar Haglund, CFO at Swedish distributor Ahlsell, is a passionate believer in open information. During an interview with him a few years ago he expressed his view in the following way: "We established at the outset that one of our key principles was self-management and internal competition based on free access to information. We reduce all management reports to the simplest and most relevant content and format. Our reporting system has no 'middlemen' and thus there is only one 'truth.' This is really important. No one is 'treating' the information or giving it some particular 'spin.' Performance is transparent. We only use real numbers. There are no profits taken on transfer prices, for example.

Everyone can see relative success or failure. It drives knowledge sharing and the transfer of best practices."

Conclusions

As the 21st century unfolds, transparency and trust will become a prerequisite for attracting the right people, customers and investors. There will be nowhere to hide as organizations and their leaders are scrutinized as never before by employees, customers, environmentalists, regulators, 24/7 media and investors. The Internet enables and demands transparency. Leaders will be left with no option. The first step will be to realize that transparency and trust cannot be mandated from the center. It is not some new vision statement that everyone learns to follow; it has to be earned through action. Much of the agenda will be as much about stopping what we do now as about implementing new ways of working. That is the challenge and the opportunity.

KEY POINTS

- Be wary of a silo mentality toward information management. Recognize that transparency is the most powerful force for ethical behavior and management control. Decide what remains confidential and what is openly accessible. Accept that some sensitive information will leak. Enable everyone to see goals, strategies, complete financial statements (apart from group forecasts) as well as KPIs, trends and peer-to-peer comparisons. Open up salaries, bonuses and expenses for scrutiny. Open up minutes of key meetings. Use web portals to provide fast access to key information that supports strategy, planning, forecasting and decision-making.

- Make costs totally transparent. If each team knows all its cost components, then it is in a far better position to take action to reduce those costs that are not absolutely necessary. Also provide key cost benchmark indicators so that one team can compare its performance with another's. Each team will formulate their own peer group league table – they don't need a formal league table structure prepared centrally with senior management comments. This is the power of peer pressure. No manager wants to go to a meeting of their peers having underperformed the average and drained the bonus pool.

- The value of transparency will decline if people are unable to analyze, interpret and use information to make decisions. The role of the finance department is particularly important. Finance managers should devote more of their time to teaching their non-finance colleagues the meaning of profit, cost and cash flow statements and helping them to understand the root causes (i.e. "drivers") of costs. This investment will repay itself many times over (and relatively quickly).

- Be wary of a culture of resisting bad news. If senior managers only hear what managers want them to hear, then there is a disaster waiting to happen. Recognize people positively for sharing bad news immediately.

- Make hiding or manipulating information a firing offense, but never punish anyone for telling the truth.

- Make it a golden rule that data need to be complete and accurate at the original point of entry. Batching, scanning, archiving and retrieving documents consume huge amounts of time and cost as people need to reopen files many times.

- Use only "one truth" as far as the numbers are concerned.

## CHAPTER 4

Principle #4 – Teams
Organize around a seamless network of accountable teams, not centralized functions

To receive trust, it is usually necessary that we give trust. Organizing into small interlocking teams helps ensure that trust will flow in all directions within the organization – upwards, downwards, within the team, and across teams.[1]

John Mackey, CEO, Whole Foods Market

How accountable teams transformed Leyland Trucks

The transformation of Leyland Trucks is a remarkable story. Between 1986 and 1999 the UK truck industry had suffered a sharp decline (from an output of 69,000 to around 40,000 trucks). Although trucks had been manufactured at Leyland for over 100 years, few would have bet on its continued survival. The workforce had also been reduced from 14,000 in the 1970s to just 4000 in 1989, leaving deep scars and a lack of faith in the ability of management to secure their future employment.

The story since then has been one of consistent success. In June 2010 (for the second year running) Leyland Trucks was the overall winner in the annual UK Manufacturing Excellence Awards – the UK's premier recognition scheme for manufacturing companies run by the leading professional engineering body, the 160-year-old Institution of Mechanical Engineers (IMechE).[2]

The key to Leyland's transformation was the devolution of responsibility to self-managed teams down to plant level. Anyone old enough to remember the internecine warfare that raged between managers and workers at British Leyland in the 1970s will understand the extent of this transformation.

Management change is 70 percent about culture

In the mid 1980s Leyland Trucks was acquired by Dutch company DAF, and in 1989 John Oliver was persuaded to rejoin the company as CEO. He had previously been with the company from 1972 to 1986, so on his return he was pleasantly surprised at the strength of the management team but was equally dismayed that the old attitudes of "them and us" remained entrenched. He also joined the company at a critical time. Following the collapse in the market in 1989/90 something drastic had to be done. Various initiatives were tried. The total quality program was revived, but it was too procedural and bureaucratic. Improvements in manufacturing scheduling systems (MRP II) were made in an attempt to reduce production variability, but better programming and scheduling didn't improve productivity; re-engineering was proposed to improve process conformance, but again this didn't engage the workforce and produce the changes expected. In short, none of these initiatives presented a coherent or convincing program for change to hard-bitten employees who had the capability to wreck any new idea that came their way. As Oliver notes, "All the radical ideas and initiatives about organizational systems and structures in the world were going to be of no help at all if the underlying propensity to receive change was still negative. None of the eagerness, determination and urgency of the senior group had conveyed itself to the organization at large."[3]

HR director Charlie Poskett was equally dismissive of "technology" and "measurement" approaches. "We thought technology would drive the performance improvements we were seeking," he reflected. "But we soon realized that we had not devoted enough attention to culture. Management change is 30 percent about structure, processes, technology and measurement, and 70 percent about culture."

Though the cultural renaissance of the company was almost complete by 1993, problems were never far away. In February 1993 parent company DAF went into receivership, causing a similar result at Leyland Trucks. Most people thought this was the end of Leyland Trucks, but the management team thought differently. They eventually obtained venture capital to fund a management buy-out, although the capital base was still too tight to fund any future product development. Nevertheless, they continued to prosper for the next five years until the investment in new products became critical and they had to seek a business partner. US truck-maker PACCAR stepped in and acquired the company in 1998.

"Team Enterprise"

In 1989, Leyland's new management team under John Oliver realized that the only way to change the company was to create a "one team" organization in which everyone's interests were mutually dependent, so they came up with the definition of "Team Enterprise" as "empowered people working towards mutually beneficial objectives." Looking back, John Oliver is in no doubt of the benefits. "We are talking cash, we are talking profitability," he notes. "This is not some well-intentioned piece of social engineering conjured up by the human resources department. There are numerous and very welcome social spin-offs, but these are tangential. The whole justification for Team Enterprise is that it's the safest, quickest and most cost-effective means of improving your bottom line, long-term and permanently. And don't get hung up on the 'long-term.' Done correctly, Team Enterprise will start to pay back in months, not years."[4]

He backs up his beliefs with some compelling evidence. In the first two and a half years, from 1989 to 1991, the company turned in a remarkable performance including a return-on-sales of 10 percent, a reduction of 24 percent in operating costs, a halving of the break-even point, a 35 percent reduction in warranty costs, a more responsive and flexible organization and a step-change improvement in employee attitudes and satisfaction levels. A further benefit was the improvement in effectiveness of other initiatives. Many of the problems experienced with total quality, material requirements planning (MRP), Just-in-Time and Six Sigma programs disappeared once the work force could see the positive effects they could have on the business, and how these could contribute to better productivity and ultimately job security.

Team Enterprise embraced "lean" thinking. A key change was the switch from "make for stock" to "build to order." Thus there was a major change from a focus on cost and volume targets to satisfying customer needs profitably. Moving from a make-for-stock system with a typical lead-time of 12–14 weeks to a build-to-order system with a lead-time of 4–5 weeks was thought to be impossible. There was resistance everywhere. The sales force thought it was crazy, and the assembly plants thought it was an equally hare-brained idea. Oliver relates the impact of this change: "In 1989, this would have been impossible to contemplate. In those days, we still operated a monthly cycle where virtually nothing was delivered in the first three weeks, followed by an almighty crush in the last week before cut-off. The final weekend of the cycle was not one that any senior manager should witness, as it resembled sheer chaos. However, with the advent of Team Enterprise, we had not just moved to weekly controlled delivery, we were well on the way to daily predictability … The end result was that the Leyland plant pioneered the scheme and handled the change magnificently – so successfully in fact that ultimately a "fast-track" service was offered which turned urgent orders around in just two or three weeks."[5]

Fewer management layers

The principal change that produced these results was the devolution of responsibility to self-managed teams. Leyland moved from a traditional hierarchy with seven levels to a devolved organization with only three levels. However, it went through a steep learning curve. For example, managers learned that to be effective they had to empower teams rather than team leaders. Teams comprised 16 to 18 members. Every member of the team had to be paid the same. Equality was everything. Investing too much responsibility in team leaders was a mistake; spreading responsibilities around team members was the approach that worked. But, above all, Leyland's management learned that empowerment cannot be "given" to teams; it can only be "taken." In other words, teams must want to engage in the management process and accept responsibility. However, the realization (through surveys) that this is exactly what most of them did want took them by surprise.

But senior managers recognized that it was vital that authority and freedom were balanced by ability and responsibility. This balancing act is now generally carried out by a combination of the business unit manager and the business unit technician. Each business unit manager has around 120 direct operators working for them. With such limited scope to intervene, the role of the business unit technician becomes important. Their responsibilities are designed to generate a multifunctional support to the various teams in their domain. The ideal skills matrix would be a balance of quality, tooling, people management, method improvement and logistics.[6] The result of the new structure is that 85 per cent of day-to-day problems occurring on the tracks are addressed by line-based technicians with only the remaining 15 per cent necessitating the attention of a technical expert.[7]

Moving to a de-layered structured took out 42 percent of all senior and middle management positions within two years. Within four years, the figure had risen to 56 percent. In other words, as Oliver explains: "For the same deliverables, only 44 managers out of 100 remained after just four years."[8]

Teams now see themselves as part of a seamless network that serves the end customer. This also extends to the supply chain. This is vital because most of the key parts for trucks are built externally and must arrive at the appropriate time and to the exact specification. All information concerning performance and scheduling is open and shared with teams. Indeed, this was identified at the outset as a key part of the devolution process. Without fast and open information, how would teams be able to identify and deal with problems? How would they be able to adapt to "fast-track" orders entering the system?

Removing top-down targets and incentives

All piecework and other "payment-by-results" systems on the shop floor were eventually abandoned (despite resistance from the trade unions). The philosophy of Team Enterprise recognizes that people cannot be motivated solely by financial incentives (though they can be de-motivated by poor pay and conditions). Motivation is much more concerned with sharing common goals (e.g. maintaining job security) and being involved in the improvement efforts of the team. Recognition became particularly important. Simple thank-you cards for doing a good job and especially sending birthday cards to all employees have an impact far beyond the cost and effort involved. Using celebrities *and customers* to hand out certificates and awards is another powerful way of recognizing achievement.

One of the key lessons from the Leyland Trucks story is that radical devolution is only made possible and sustainable if it does not collide with top-down financially driven performance targets and incentives. Another is that the organization needs to fit the management model. In most traditional "command and control" firms, this means organizing around a few large divisions run by senior executives that report directly to the CEO. But in the adaptive organization it means creating many small self-managed teams and trusting them with information and decision-making.

Why haven't others followed the same approach?

Leyland took many of its "lean" ideas from Toyota (particularly, the legendary Toyota production system). You would have thought that many other manufacturers would have followed the Toyota and Leyland example. While many have tried to implement lean manufacturing using tools and practices such as "six sigma" and "just-in-time," few have understood (like John Oliver) that "lean" is much more than a set of tools. It is part of a broader management philosophy based around building-to-order rather than for stock and handing more accountability to self-managed teams. In other words, it is the cultural side of lean that is even more important than the tools.

You can't help thinking how different western economies such as the US and UK might have been had they understood and acted upon these insights. Would the car, motorcycle, shipbuilding, steel, electronics and many other manufacturing industries have performed so badly and, in some cases, disappeared altogether? Much of the blame was heaped upon the trade unions, but perhaps it was the reluctance by business leaders to admit that the command and control management model was at the root of the problem.

As we noted at Leyland Trucks, in the adaptive management model leaders aim to create a more entrepreneurial business climate, which requires multiple teams that give younger managers the opportunities to use their creativity and entrepreneurial skills. The benefits are considerable. Small autonomous units provide the potential for clarity and simplicity in setting the performance management framework. There is simply no hiding place; managers are exposed and must accept full accountability for their performance, or fail to survive. Performance comparisons are more easily made and peer pressure plays a major role in driving continuous improvement. Small independent units also stimulate entrepreneurial activity and give ambitious managers the opportunities they crave. This is a virtuous circle as the most talented managers look for companies that can give them these challenging roles.

Small teams that have the flexibility to react to unanticipated demands and focus on delivering value to their (internal or external) customers are the building blocks of the adaptive organization. Principle #4 advises leaders to create many small teams that naturally connect and combine with each other to deliver products and services to external customers.

Implementation guidelines

*   Turn the organization on its side to face the customer.
*   Create as many value centers as possible.

- Make the executive team accountable for becoming effective resource managers.

- Make support service teams accountable for becoming more efficient back-office managers and more effective business partners.

- Make value center teams accountable for satisfying customer needs at the lowest cost.

Turn the organization on its side to face the customer

Leaders in adaptive organizations go to great lengths to clear out stifling bureaucracy, central control systems, head-office empires and all the machinery that makes large company operations complex, costly and slow. And they create hundreds of small teams with profit- (or value-) creating accountability. At Handelsbanken, each branch team is a profit center with the scope and authority to run its own business (there are around 600 profit centers). At Whole Foods Market, each store is made up of multiple teams (e.g. fresh fruit) that are accountable for their results and that have the authority to appoint their own team members. At Southwest Airlines, each "route" and each airport "station" is a team. At Nucor Steel there are only four layers of management between the CEO and the floor worker and only 66 people in the head office. Nucor's divisions are all independently run at the local level and employees work in teams that are largely self-directed. To remove barriers to communication, everyone is treated the same. There are no executive perks or privileges.[9] Each Toyota plant is full of workstation teams that are responsible for continuously improving their performance.

In the new management model organizations operate through three kinds of team (see Figure 4.1):

1. *The executive team.* This is the C-level suite responsible for setting purpose, goals and strategic direction as well as challenging other units to maximize their performance.

2. *The support services team.* These teams are responsible for serving and supporting value centers teams. They include strategy, finance, human resources, marketing, legal, information technology, supply chain management, design, production, logistics, sales and service teams. They do not usually have profit and loss responsibility. They are primarily accountable for (internal or external) customer outcomes. In large organizations the work of these teams is increasingly centralized (and often moved to shared services centers) and, in

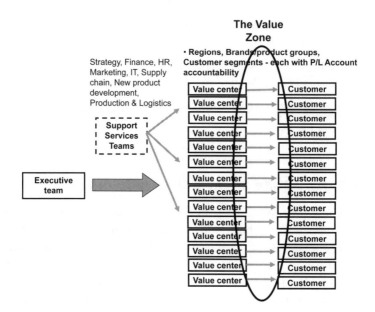

FIGURE 4.1 We need organizations with many small accountable teams

some cases, outsourced to third-party providers. Support service teams can either be an integral part of a value center or serve a number of value centers.

3. *The value center team.* These teams are responsible for formulating strategy and delivering value (or profit). They invariably have their own profit and loss accounts. They are typically created around lines of business, brands/product groups, regions/countries and plants/branches. They start at the lowest level possible (e.g. a small branch of a bank) but can be grouped into numbers of units (e.g. a country or region). The aim is to treat each value center as a stand-alone business.

Create as many value centers as possible

Leaders need to pay constant attention to the value center portfolio by adding new ventures and terminating underperforming units. Value centers are typically based on business segments such as product groups (or brands), customer segments and geographic territories. Managers focus on maximizing value as measured by some variant of profit (such as return-on-sales, return-on-capital or economic profit). The aim is that the team sees the value center as their own business and they are given maximum freedom to grow and improve it. They offer managers a more detailed, tangible way of gauging business value and economic activity and allow CEOs to spend more time on in-depth strategy discussions.

Vinnet Nayar, CEO of HCL Technologies, called the interface between the value center and the customer *the value zone*. "In traditional companies," notes Nayar, "the value zone is often buried deep inside the hierarchy and the people who create the most value in the company work there. Paradoxically, these value-creators are almost always accountable to bosses and managers – typically located at the top of the pyramid or in the so-called 'enabling functions' – who do not directly contribute to the value zone … To shift our focus to the value zone, we turned the organization upside down and made management and managers, including those enabling functions (such as human resources, finance, training and others) accountable to those who create value, not just the other way around. Without making these structural shifts, change is much more difficult, if not impossible. And only by making changes to the organizational structure does the change become sustainable and able to outlast the leader who initiated the transformation."[10]

The aim is to have as many direct costs *within* value centers and as few indirect costs supporting them as possible. If you are a Handelsbanken customer, you see your local branch as a complete business. Each branch has its own website and staff can make most decisions locally. Branches have full profit and loss account responsibility and can even make decisions on staff salaries. As well as Handelsbanken regions and branches, Southwest Airlines routes and Toyota product families are other examples of self-managed value centers. Each value center controls its own "value stream" that encompasses all income and expenditure. Expenditure also includes (where applicable) the cost of capital used thus enabling the reporting of economic profit (i.e. profit after charging the cost of capital[11]).

Another reason for creating many value centers is to encourage and enable innovation and growth. Leaders need to actively manage the value center portfolio in the same way as a venture capital company, diversifying their risk across a range of opportunities. This also means continuously prioritizing resources toward the best current opportunities, and this in turn means creating dynamic systems that enable fast decision-making.

Whole Foods CEO John Mackey is a devout believer in the power of self-managed teams. In a recent essay he made this point: "Human beings evolved in relatively small tribal bands. Many scientific studies indicate that our ability to maintain close trusting relationships with family, friends and co-workers is constrained to about 150 people. We can, of course, know many more people than this, but it is hard to know them well enough to develop close bonds of trust based on actual experiences. At Whole Foods Market we recognize the importance of smaller tribal groupings to maximize familiarity and trust. We organize our stores and company into a variety of interlocking teams. Most teams have between 6 and 100 members and the larger teams are divided further into a variety of sub-teams. The leaders of each team are also members of the Store Leadership Team and the Store Team Leaders are members of the Regional Leadership Team. This interlocking team structure continues all the way upwards to the Executive Team at the highest level of the company."

Mackey goes on: "It has been our experience at Whole Foods Market that trust is optimized in this type of smaller team organizational structure. This is because each person is a vital and important member of their team. The success of the team is dependent upon the invaluable contributions of everyone on the team. Trust is optimized when it flows between all levels within the organization. Many leaders make the mistake of believing that the key to increasing organizational trust is to somehow get the workforce to trust the leadership more. While it is very important that employees trust leadership, it is equally important that the leadership trust the workforce."[12]

Make the executive team accountable for becoming effective resource managers

In the adaptive organization, leaders reject secretive command and control structures in favor of open, collaborative networks. The executive team is no longer the central planner and coordinator of actions between one unit and another. Value centers and other teams aim to coordinate their plans dynamically to meet prevailing customer demand.

Some leaders have even challenged the role of the CEO's office. Early in his transformation program at HCL Technologies, Vineet Nayar and his leadership team set up an online forum and encouraged employees to ask tough questions and offer honest feedback. Nothing was censored on the "U&I" site; every post, however virulent, was displayed for the entire company to see. Nayar recalls that in the beginning, "virtually 100% of the questions were dirty questions. 'Why do you guys suck?' 'Why does your strategy suck?' 'Why aren't you living up to your values?'" While some managers bemoaned the fact that the all of the company's dirty laundry was now online, employees lauded the forum as a symbol of HCLT's commitment to transparency and as another way to hold top management accountable. The U&I portal had another value: it was also an early warning system for critical issues facing the company. In 2009, Nayar opened up a "My Problems" section on the U&I site where he could solicit advice on the crucial issues he was wrestling with. His logic: while he wanted managers to feel more accountable to the front lines, he also wanted employees to feel a sense of responsibility for tackling the big thorny issues that faced the top management team.[13]

Leaders see the investment portfolio through the lens of value centers and operate more like a venture capital provider than a central banker. They expect divisional leaders to constantly spawn new value streams. They also expect to engage in a dialogue about which value centers are creating value and which are struggling. Resource decisions are based on these reviews.

Leaders also involve themselves in the strategy development process, though their role becomes more one of challenger than developer. In other words, they must challenge the assumptions and risks implicit in any strategy presented to them and ensure that there are no better alternatives. This forces teams to think deeply about the business, especially about constraints, commitments, innovation, investment, competencies and risks. In other words, the knowledge and creativity of key managers (most of whom have been there for many years) is now being mined and used productively for the first time in achieving stretch goals that would otherwise be off the agenda.

But it is easy to allow command and control to return through the back door. Issuing memos, instructions and directives are all symptoms of centralizing forces and must be resisted. To support the new approach at Handelsbanken, a policy decision was made not to issue any more head office directives or reports. As former CEO Dr Wallander noted, "No one missed them. Many central staff were quite shocked when life carried on as normal." Devolution is unlikely to work unless leaders become coaches and mentors rather than commanders and controllers. Handelsbanken uses a coaching style of management. Even if senior managers can see at first hand that poor decisions are being made, all they will do is send an email or make a brief phone call to inquire as to the problem. It is up to the local manager to react. This discipline by leaders not to interfere is one of the toughest elements of the devolution process. As Handelsbanken president Arne Mårtensson has noted: "You have to learn to keep your hands down by your side even when you could intervene and help to solve a problem."

The result is a more purposeful executive suite within which senior executives have a clear understanding that they are there to serve value centers, so they must justify their time and cost in terms of how they add value. There is also less micro-management as leaders focus on supporting, teaching and mentoring rather than directing, dictating and controlling what their people should do. This

approach gives everyone more time to think about and reflect upon key performance issues.

Make support service teams accountable for becoming more efficient back-office managers and more effective business partners

Most organizations treat central service units as part of the corporate office reporting to senior executives rather than serving operating units. But in the opinion of
many value center managers, these units create costs rather than value. Take the
finance department. Over two-thirds of their time is spent on transaction processing and month-end routines. There are too many irrelevant measures, reports,
journals, spreadsheet errors and disconnected systems. The result of all these fail-
ings is increasing levels of detail and complexity and poor service to their internal
customers.[14]

Around half of the Fortune 500 companies have set up shared service centers to
improve the performance (i.e. reduce costs) of back-office functions. But moving
to shared services can destroy rather than add value, especially where there is no
"service relationship culture." In other words, if the relationship between shared
services units and internal customers is too top-down and contractual, then business teams will fail to embrace the changes. Moreover, the pressure to reduce costs
that comes from the need to meet "conditions of satisfaction" will be missing.

American Express is one organization that has got the balance right. Finance and
IT have worked together to deliver shared services with huge cost reductions, a
streamlined planning process with an emphasis on driver-based rolling forecasts
and an investment optimization process that lets senior managers prioritize new
investments on a monthly basis. The result is less "gaming" of resource requirements, more accountability for funds, better alignment of measures and actions
with strategy, improved compliance and control and annual cost savings of around
$200m.

Be wary of service level agreements

Service level agreements (SLAs) are a common feature of the change to shared
services centers. They are meant to be the outcome of a robust dialogue between
central services and business operations teams. However, if the power in this

relationship is with the functional head (as it often is), then this will be a one-way agreement with little change in the relationship. In other words, the SLA will simply codify what was happening before.

Despite these caveats, shared services centers can make sense provided the business partner relationship is properly fulfilled. To be successful it must be based on a long-term relationship and not be seen as a short-term cost-cutting exercise. The shared services center needs to continuously improve the transaction processing system and reduce costs to its customers as well as provide increasing levels of support in terms of insightful reports.

The switch from corporate function to business partner is crucial

In the new model functions such as finance, IT, HR and marketing become service providers (or business partners) to value centers. They agree which services to offer and how much to charge for them. But their role as business partner is becoming more important as value center teams take on more tasks such as planning, forecasting and control.

The transition from corporate function (or cost center) to business partner is crucial. For example, functional leaders need to liberate the organization from huge amounts of detail and the proliferation of complex systems that increase managers' workload and deny them time for reflection and analysis. This means purging their systems, measures and reports and eradicating work that adds little value (such as detailed planning processes, redundant systems and irrelevant reports). It also means being more wary of implementing new tools and IT systems that soak up valuable time and money but fail to provide reasonable value. Creating space and time for higher-value work is the crucial step that turns transformation rhetoric into practical reality.

Process owners are accountable for improving performance

In many support operations such as supply chain, production and some back-office functions such as accounts payable and receivable, "process owners" take charge of (and are accountable for) performance improvement. By reorganizing around key processes and activities, operating teams focus their attention on *how work is performed*. As a general rule, the fewer the steps involved in a process and the lower the error count, the more efficient is the process and the fewer costs it incurs. Well-managed processes generally require fewer people to carry out activities. For example, they don't need the chasers, inspectors, problem solvers, supervisors, reconcilers, counters, movers, stackers and the rework department. Perceptions of work are also changed – team members now work for customers (not for superiors) – and managers become "coaches" rather than bosses.

But, to make these changes, leaders must recombine fragmented tasks, review each activity within each new process and eliminate activities that add no value. As a general rule, the broader the work flow assigned to a process team, the more the scope for problem solving, innovation and the elimination of unnecessary work. The very act of remapping functional tasks into core processes can highlight significant areas where (often huge) cost savings can be made.

If support service teams see themselves as business partners instead of remote controllers, quality is likely to be improved as their partners demand better services. For the same reason, cost will be under constant pressure and start to reduce over time. And relationships will improve. Teams are not only accountable for their actions, they are also *held accountable for the consequences of their actions.* In other words, with freedom comes a higher level of accountability. If teams don't continuously improve their performance at a satisfactory rate, then they will be replaced.

Make value center teams accountable for satisfying customer needs at the lowest cost

Most businesses organize around a few large divisions split into profit centers accountable for meeting annual financial targets. While this has long been an effective way to prepare managers for the top jobs and to limit the number of direct reports the CEO has to manage, these large divisions make it difficult for managers to see clearly where value is actually created or destroyed. In these divisions, it is the division and functional heads that usually decide whether and where to place investment funds and how to make key trade-offs between innovative (but longer-term) growth opportunities and short-term demands to meet the numbers. But the evidence suggests a bias toward meeting short-term demands.[15] The outcome is a host of missed opportunities and a managerial blind spot where high-performing units mask the performance of poor-performing ones.

In the adaptive organization leaders aim to create as many value centers as possible and then focus managers on maximizing value as measured by some variant of profit (such as return-on-sales, return-on-invested-capital or economic profit). The aim is to transfer "ownership" of the value center to the local team and give them maximum freedom and higher levels of accountability to grow and improve it.

Customer-facing value centers take on the primary value-creating role, and it is up to each team to ensure they have the competences and capabilities to fulfill this role. This means knowing the business and its strategy and being able to hold their own with senior executives on these topics. They need to learn how to think and act as business owners running their own businesses. They need to learn to gather, analyze and interpret information quickly and make rapid decisions to avoid emerging threats and seize new opportunities. They need to learn how to use tools such as balanced scorecards and rolling forecasts. And they need to learn to balance short-term profit with long-term value creation.

Conclusions

Teams are at the center of the adaptive organization. Information flows to them and decisions are made by them. Moving from the traditional pyramid structure with the CEO at the top to a horizontal structure with the CEO on the left and the external customer on the right helps leaders to see more clearly how each team connects with their partners and how accountabilities should be framed. It also shows how many redundant layers of management there are and how many can be dispensed with. The result is a leaner and more adaptive organization as there are fewer people building empires and more transparency and accountability throughout the management system.

KEY POINTS

- To get real clarity about how to define and measure success, leaders need to turn the traditional vertically shaped organization on its side to face the customer. This means organizing around three types of team. The *executive team* is the C-level suite responsible for setting purpose, goals and strategy as well as challenging other units to maximize their performance. The *support service* team (including finance, HR, marketing, IT, design, production and customer service) is responsible for serving and supporting value centers. The *value center* team is responsible for satisfying its customers at the lowest cost. This is a "soft" restructuring. It is the *relationships* between teams that change (from "please the boss" to "please the customer") rather than the relocation of teams.

- Aim to create as many value center teams as possible by continuously sub-dividing them and adding new ventures. They should be based around a clear market niche and have a distinctive customer value proposition. And as they don't need much central control, their support costs should gradually reduce over time.

- Frame the role of the *executive team* in terms of acting more like venture capital providers than central bankers, always prioritizing resources to the best current opportunities and managing portfolio risk and reward. In other words, they should see their primary role as allocating resources to the best current opportunities and monitoring the performance of support centers and value centers ensuring that poorly performing units are either turned around or terminated.

- Recognize that *support service teams* such as design, production, supply chain, strategy, finance, human resources, marketing, legal, risk management and information technology have two roles. The first is the *efficiency role* – that is to manage routine transactions at the highest quality and lowest cost. The other is the *effectiveness role* – that is to act as a business (or strategic) partner to the value center team and provide performance insights on such topics as benchmarks, key performance indicators and cost drivers.

- Frame the role of *value center teams* in terms of formulating and executing strategy, improving customer outcomes and continuously improving performance against peers. They should have the freedom and capability to take action to improve their performance at any time. They are typically created around lines of business, brands and product groups and customer segments such as regions and countries. They act as stand-alone businesses and invariably have their own profit and loss accounts.

## CHAPTER 5

Principle #5 – Trust
Trust teams to regulate and improve their performance; don't micro-manage them

When constructing an organization, your outlook on the people who together make up the organization plays a vital role. The outlook on human nature that characterizes the organization of the Bank may be summed up in the words trust and respect.[1]

Dr Jan Wallander, former CEO, Handelsbanken

Devolution: the lessons from US public schools

Professor William Ouchi has spent most of his professional life trying to improve the US public schools system. After extensive research, his key recommendation is to devolve spending and decision-making authorities to individual school managers and away from office-bound bureaucrats. But getting the bureaucrats to agree has been a real struggle. As former Los Angeles mayor Richard Riordan said, "If you made a list of people's silver bullets for public education – smaller classes, better pay for teachers, more phonics, longer school years, no social promotions – the concept of changing governance structure would be near the bottom of the list." But as Ouchi maintains, none of these changes will work unless school principals are empowered.

Ouchi realized that no one cared how schools were organized. Even the academics who studied the field believed that parental background was the most important factor in a child's education. The only way that Ouchi could convince others was through rigorous research. By 1994 he found three districts in North America that had local school autonomy: Houston, Seattle and Edmonton (Canada). So he compared them with the three largest US districts – New York, Los Angeles and Chicago. His team interviewed many principals and went through all their budgets and found that, respectively, principals controlled 6.0, 6.7 and 19.3 percent of the money spent in their schools. In Seattle, Houston and Edmonton the comparative figures were 69, 80 and 92 percent. He also looked into the reporting standards of public schools and was shocked to find how much manipulation was going on to "make the numbers." The graduation rates in big cities like Chicago, New York and Los Angeles ran at about 50 percent, but they all reported around 88 percent. As he noted, "School districts commonly test only 60 to 70 percent of their students, the good test takers, and report that result as their performance.[2]

Professor Ouchi proved that those schools with local decision-making authority had much higher student achievement records. The reason is that local control over spending gives school principals control over three key school decisions: the staffing mixture, curriculum and schedule. He found that one key indicator was the most telling success factor: *total student load.* This is the number of classes a teacher takes multiplied by the number of students per class. The average daily figure was around 160 (5 classes times 32 students) compared with around 55 to 60 in the elite private schools.

Since then, more cities and hundreds more schools have followed his advice. In New York City, for example, Ouchi found some hardcore schools with load factors of 53. Each teacher handles two classes of 20 students each and a writing workshop of 13 more students. The teachers meet three times a week and discuss each student one by one because they know them well. Once principals have authority, the first thing they do is consult with other teachers and then invariably decide to distance themselves from the administrative overhead. When principals have autonomy they put their resources into the classroom. Everybody teaches. There is no registrar; a teacher handles the scheduling. There is no dean of discipline or guidance counselors. They also dump the seven-period, five-day-a-week schedule which nobody likes and which represents a poor use of teacher resources. Then they innovate. At one school, the math and science teachers set up a combined program. Both teachers geared up to teaching the other discipline. The result was to work slightly longer hours but with half the class size.[3]

Once school teams had the authority over their budgets they began to "see" opportunities for innovation and radical change that were previously invisible to them. They could see how teaching hours could be reorganized to benefit teachers and students. They could see how the key performance driver was not parental wealth but student load factor. They could see how reducing the back-office bureaucracy and transferring much needed resources to front-line teams would rapidly translate into positive results.

Accountability through targets doesn't work

Now contrast this story with what happened in the UK where different performance drivers were used to improve performance. While the UK treasury increased investment in the primary (age 4–11) and secondary (11–18) education systems between 1997 and 2010, it came with "strings" attached in terms of multiple performance targets. Examinations have always been part of the system, but schools are now ranked according to the results. Many people believe that these league tables often tell the wrong story and have an adverse impact on behavior as head teachers refuse to allow underperforming students to take exams or marginal students to progress to higher levels of education. The result has been huge investment but only marginal improvement in performance.

This alternative vision of "accountability through targets" fails to stretch and drive improvement. Instead, it stifles ambition and innovation and focuses school managers on meeting minimum standards (reinforced by school inspectors) rather than improving performance. Thus it failed to engage school principals or teachers in the improvement process. It was a "one-size-fits-all" approach straight out of the book of Industrial Age management. (Incidentally, leagues tables are not the problem – it depends how they are used. The call is for more emphasis on "value added" or "relative progress." In other words, if someone with high potential underperforms, then that is not success. But if someone expected to achieve nothing gets something, then that achievement should be recognized.)

Ouchi's work with schools has been an eye-opener not just in North America but all around the world. The lesson is that innovation and improvement are more likely to happen if front-line teams have more control over their planning, resources and decisions. This transfer of ownership and commitment occurred in Ouchi's schools, where district managers were prepared to trust local school teams, but not in the UK schools, where performance contracts were imposed from the center. [Following a change of government in 2010, the new ministers in charge are talking about scrapping the targets regime and handing more power back to schools.]

Empowerment is the product of freedom multiplied by capability

Most bureaucracies think like the old US schools districts and the UK Treasury. They use standards to control people, catch them breaking the rules and punish them to get back into line. Workers feel like part of a chain gang rather than a valued team. They are not trusted to use information to make decisions. In fact, decision-making is separated from the work. This creates a void that is filled with mixed messages and political behavior. To bridge this gap, firms spend huge sums on complex planning, budgeting, scheduling and control systems that program every action and activity on a daily basis at the front line. They tend to have a strict demarcation line between managerial and non-managerial work. Indeed, it is the essence of the command and control structure. The people who know the reasons for poor performance – especially the causes of non-value-adding work – are neither encouraged nor rewarded for suggesting or making improvements. In the traditional structure this is the role of management.

Margaret Wheatley, while agreeing that the vast majority of business leaders still remain addicted to the mechanistic view of their organizations, believes there is a way forward. "We have known for nearly half a century," she notes, "that self-managed teams are far more productive than any other form of organizing. There is a clear correlation between participation and productivity; in fact, productivity gains in truly self-managed work environments are at minimum 35 percent higher than in traditionally managed organizations. And in all forms of institutions, Americans are asking for more local autonomy, insisting that they, at their own level, can do it better than the huge structures of organizations now in place. There is both a desire to participate more and strong evidence that such participation leads to the effectiveness and productivity we crave."[4]

She then poses the critical question: With so much evidence supporting participation, why isn't everyone working in a self-managed environment right now? Wheatley's answer is that over the years leaders consistently have chosen control rather than productivity. She goes on: "Rather than rethinking our fundamental assumptions about organizational effectiveness, we have stayed preoccupied with charts and plans and designs. We have hoped they would yield the results we needed – but when they have failed consistently, we still haven't stopped to question whether such charts and plans are the real route to productive work. We just continue to adjust and tweak the various control measures, still hoping to find the one plan or design that will give us what we need."[5]

When asked, many leaders reply that they have tried "empowerment" and pulled back because it didn't work. Many empowerment programs failed in the past because people were not given the coaching and information they needed. Budgets stifled the very initiatives being promoted, and local managers were often "told" to share with others in the company but were reluctant to do so. Another problem was that middle managers who saw empowerment as a threat to their authority never allowed it to succeed.

Effective empowerment is the product of freedom multiplied by capability. In multiplication, if one of the variables is zero, the result will also be zero. This explains why so many attempts at empowerment ("devolution" is a better word) fail. Few leaders seem capable of supporting both variables at the same time. This is what distinguishes truly adaptive organizations from the rest of the pack. The result has been significant and sustainable success.

Trust has to start at the top

"Devolution" is an unfamiliar word to many business leaders. It means the transfer of power from the center to front-line managers, vesting in them the authority to use their intuition and initiative to achieve results *without being constrained by some specific plan or agreement*. It is about enabling and encouraging coordinated actions, not dictating and directing them. It also means allowing managers to make mistakes. One way to define devolution is in terms of "autonomy" – a Greek word meaning self-governance. Psychologist Edward Deci defines autonomy as "about acting volitionally, with a sense of choice, flexibility, and personal freedom. It is about feeling a true willingness to behave responsibly, in accord with your interests and values. The converse of being autonomous is being controlled, which means that you are pressured to behave, think, or feel some particular way."[6]

Trust is at the root of successful devolution. But trust is reciprocal and has to start at the top. When researchers examine trust in the workplace – for example, to determine how it affects productivity within groups – they often focus on whether subordinates trust their managers. Recent research, however, has focused on how a manager's trust in his or her employees affected employees' performance and loyalty to the job. The authors surveyed 172 employees of a hotel and resort company. Subordinates were asked to what extent they trusted their managers and whether they had intentions of quitting. Their bosses, meanwhile, rated each employee's performance and trustworthiness. The authors found that a higher level of trust felt by managers toward their employees had a significant positive effect on their subordinates' behavior (and more of an effect than the level of trust employees had in their bosses). The authors concluded that when managers have faith in their staff, employees tend to be more productive and dedicated to their companies.[7]

Author Charles Handy uses the following metaphor about "elephants and fleas" to compare slow and cumbersome large corporate bureaucracies with fast and nimble small companies and networks: "Elephants offer efficiency, resources for development, guarantees of reliability and employment for the bulk of the people. But elephants are cumbersome and slow to give birth to new ideas, and they can miss the niches of opportunity in their pursuit of bigger game. Fleas sit in those niches and on the backs of elephants. They are nimble and quick to change, providing the ideas and specialized skills that elephants often lack. Some fleas grow into elephants, but more often the elephants swallow the fleas if they seem interesting."[8]

Self-managed teams enable large bureaucratic organizations (elephants) to operate more like a network of small entrepreneurial firms (fleas). Without losing the benefits that only a large organization can provide (e.g. capital, brands, resources), leaders can turn the idea of the market-responsive organization into a reality by devolving accountability to self-managed teams. This does not mean that hierarchies disappear. But it does mean that they are much flatter, with far fewer layers required as teams take on the responsibility for strategy and decision-making.

Quite simply, if there is no trust there can be no empowerment and no adaptive organization. But trust has to be earned and it has to start at the top. Principle #5 shows us how leaders can transfer the scope and authority for planning and decision-making to front-line teams and build the essential trust that enables fast decisions at the front line.

Implementation guidelines

- Give teams real autonomy over decision-making and problem solving.
- Eliminate the bureaucracy.
- Provide strategic and operating boundaries.

- Provide the trust and confidence for empowerment to be "taken."

- Coach and support front-line teams.

- Integrate information in the work.

- Manage by exception.

Give teams real autonomy over decision-making and problem solving

There's a story about how Bill Gore (founder of W.L. Gore & Associates) dealt with a young supervisor who was trying to improve productivity. Back in the mid-1960s, when Les Lewis was a young leader, W.L. Gore & Associates was scraping by and still working out the kinks in its production of PTFE-coated cables – its only product at the time. When a batch went bad, Lewis came up with what he thought was an enterprising way to save money by stripping the bad cables so the materials could be reused. "So, I got these three associates in the back of the plant and I gave them a wire spool each to sit down on," Lewis explained. "And I put these spools of cable that had to be stripped there, and I gave them some kind of a knife or something to strip it, and they are sitting back there in the back of the plant, stripping this wire off." Needless to say, Lewis was pretty pleased with his economy and enterprise. Bill Gore, however, thought that Lewis needed some help.

"'Do you have a minute?' Gore said.

"And I said, 'Sure.' So we turn around and walk out of the shop and into the only office in the plant, where the only blackboard was in the whole plant, and he shut the door and said, 'Have a seat.'

"And I sat down, and he wrote up on the board, Formula for Failure, and underlined it.

"Underneath, Gore listed a series of bullet points:

- *Provide inadequate lighting*

- *Provide uncomfortable seats*

- *Provide tools that give blisters …*

"He listed about eight things. Honestly. And then he said, 'Are you responsible for that wire stripping in the back?'

"I said, 'Yes sir.'

"He opened the door and walked out."

Fairness means, above all, that human dignity is not subordinated to bottom-line considerations.

But there was an even deeper lesson for Lewis in Gore's "Formula for Failure." Lewis had a problem – how to save some money on the defective wire. And he imposed a solution on his employees. Lewis never asked whether they had any ideas for how to salvage the wire or what tools or conditions they'd need to get the job done. He never even asked himself whether the problem he was trying to solve was the right one. He never treated his fellow associates as intrinsically equal, as people who are paid to know how to do their jobs as well as he knows his.[9]

This story reminds us that particularly in today's fast-paced innovation economy the people best placed to see the changes taking place within processes, markets, competitors and customers are front-line teams. They are the ones who have to respond quickly to emerging events, and this means devolving to them the power and responsibility to take the necessary action.

At Toyota, problems are solved when and where they occur, at the level of the front-line team. Teruyuki Minoura, former president of Toyota North America, neatly summed up the paradoxical benefits of this process when he said that if some problem occurs in one-piece flow manufacturing, then the whole production line stops. In this sense it is a very bad system of manufacturing. But when production stops, everyone is forced to solve the problem immediately. So team members have to think, and through thinking they grow and become better team members and people.[10] Self-managed teams go some way to explaining why Toyota is so lean and efficient. Instead of hundreds of staff in white coats making remote-controlled decisions, all the key decisions are taken at the team level. The cost savings are huge.

Eric Schmidt, former CEO of Google, believes that organizations have to listen to customers because customers are talking to them. And if they don't, their competitors will. So there's a long list of reasons why a more transparent company is a better organization. Self-organization is a key part of Google's management model. As Schmidt explains, "One of the things that we've tried very hard to avoid at Google is the sort of divisional structure and the business unit structure that prevents collaboration across units. It's difficult. So, I understand why people want to build business units, and have their presidents. But by doing that you cut down the informal ties that, in an open culture, drive so much collaboration. If people in the organization understand the values of the company, they should be able to self-organize to work on the most interesting problems. And if they haven't, or are not able to do that, you haven't talked to them about what's important. You haven't built a shared value culture."[11]

Many management metaphors are borrowed from the military. Command and control and strategic planning are just a few. But trusting the team is often a better approach. An analogy from the world of sports serves to illustrate its power. Reflecting on how a resurgent English team beat their old enemy, Wales, with a stunning display of attacking rugby, one of the English coaches said this: "Players used to always be frightened of making a mistake. I hope the atmosphere has changed in this team. If you make a mistake six weeks running, that's one thing. But to make mistakes in a game when you are trying to play attacking rugby is inevitable ... We have to pass responsibility on to the players. Rather than insist on Plan A or Plan B, we set a framework in which they can operate themselves. It takes longer for this approach to become an integral part. It's easier to tell people what they must do in every situation; sometimes players are happier when they are being told. But, eventually, you get a more rounded, intelligent side."[12]

England's team went on to win the rugby world cup for the first time a few years later.

Eliminate the bureaucracy

Despite the best intentions of many leaders, empowerment initiatives are too often stifled by an unyielding bureaucracy underpinned by annual budgets. Leaders at US float glass manufacturer Guardian Industries are the exception. They have a pathological hatred of bureaucracy. So they cut management layers to the bare minimum. Instead they provide teams with the freedom and scope to make strategic decisions but hold them accountable for results. This builds commitment to success. One reason Guardian doesn't use top-down targets and budgets is a belief that they take away this freedom and authority. As Don Trofholz, Guardian Vice-President and Chief Accounting Officer, explains, each manager is told, "This is your kingdom, you are the king. You run the business the way you want." However, this freedom to act also carries responsibility and accountability for decisions. Guardian judges its people on the results achieved, not on good intentions.

As Trofholz notes, "We view good intentions as statements regarding next year's results such as projected sales, profits and production. Budgets are an example of good intentions. I don't want to hear about good intentions. I just want to see results."

Guardian empowers its managers by giving them control over their plants. This includes the freedom to make decisions such as hiring additional personnel, raising or lowering prices and reorganizing shift patterns. Like Toyota, line managers have the authority to stop the production line to solve a quality problem. The only substantial limitations on this discretion are a few big-ticket investment decisions.

Fewer layers = lower costs

Despite its size (19,000 people), Guardian operates with clean, simple lines of management and very few levels of authority. Examples of this mindset are seen in the eradication of formal mission statements, organizational charts and corporate policy manuals. The insistence on maintaining a small-company mindset encourages the empowerment of its employees and allows decisions to be made more quickly. This speed of response to changes in the market gives Guardian a competitive advantage over its rivals. The small-company attitude also fosters an entrepreneurial spirit throughout the organization. Guardian gives employees the freedom to make decisions but asks that they make these decisions as if they were the owner of the company and the money being spent was their own. This approach not only instils an entrepreneurial spirit but also helps create a sense of unity throughout the workforce. Though it was a public company for 15 years (in the 1960s and 70s), Guardian is now a private company. Its consistent growth and sustained profitability is, to a great extent, due to the leadership of William Davidson who successfully led Guardian for over 56 years until his death in 2009.

The whole point of devolution is to reduce management layers and make the organization more simple and transparent while operating with lower costs. Swedish bank Handelsbanken has only three management layers, compared with between five and nine for most other banks. Reducing layers means that the role of operating teams comes to the fore. The objective is to create a more innovative business climate and this requires multiple units that give younger managers the opportunities to use their creativity and entrepreneurial skills.

Design the organization around many small teams

Too many organizations focus on economies of scale and build large independent units rather than locating key units close to each other. At W.L. Gore & Associates there are a couple of practices that have served them well as CEO Terri Kelly explains:

> "We like to have the functions co-located because innovation depends on hav-ing research, manufacturing and sales all in the same place, where they can build off each other. This also helps us develop leaders.

> "Secondly, if a plant gets too big or a business gets too large – more than 250 or 300 people – you start to see a very different dynamic. The sense of ownership, the involvement in decision-making, the feeling that I can make an impact starts to get diluted. So we look for opportunities to divide a big business into smaller businesses. Bill Gore said that one of the most important responsibili-ties of the leader is to figure out how to divide so we can multiply. We look for opportunities where dividing a unit up and replicating some of its activities can accelerate growth.

> "In Gore, you'll see a lot of small plants with fewer than 300 associates, because this drives a different level of focus and ownership. Large businesses tend to stifle smaller businesses by hogging critical resources. When you split a business up, the smaller unit gets its own resources and can set its own priorities. Another bonus: new leaders emerge because you no longer have a single leadership team under one big roof, but now have two distinct leadership teams.

> "The last thing that's helped us in the current economic environment is that we co-locate different businesses together. If a particular industry has a downturn, you want to be able to move the associates to another opportunity. If our plants were all in isolated locations, this would be much more difficult. So we like the idea of campuses where a number of small factories are co-located within a 25-mile radius. This way, people don't fear moving on to something else, and are less hesitant to take on a new opportunity. This lessens the risk the associates will try to preserve a business or product area that may no longer be so promising to the company."[13]

Leaders of adaptive organizations know that decentralization founders on the rocks of bureaucracy. That's why they have eliminated top-down control systems that connect decisions made at the corporate center with actions taken at the front line. They don't have, for example, fixed targets, annual budgets, standard costing, batch scheduling or quality-control systems (quality is in the line – not inspected for) and all their associated costs. Teams have all the information they need to complete their work. They have plans, forecasts, key performance indicators and a stream of business intelligence flowing through their information systems.

When Dr Jan Wallander became CEO of Handelsbanken in the early 1970s one of his first actions was to eliminate the stifling bureaucracy. This is how he described the changes: "[Central] departments were forbidden to send out any more memos to the branch offices apart from those that were necessary for the daily work and reports to authorities. All activities connected with setting up a budget or following up a previous one were closed down. There were altogether 110 committees and working groups at the head office that were engaged in various development projects. These groups were told to stop their work at once and the secretaries were asked to submit a report on not more than one page describing what the work had resulted in so far. Several hundred people were working on a radically new data system. The work was stopped. Similarly, the department concerned with long-term planning and the formulation of visions and strategies was told to stop its work. At the time Handelsbanken was one of Sweden's largest advertisers. There was a marketing department of 40 people at the head office that prepared the major advertising campaigns and extensive advertising activities at the central and local levels. This work was stopped, and after a while the number of employees in that department fell from 40 to 1."[14]

Provide strategic and operating boundaries

Leaders cannot devolve decision-making to local teams and maintain an effective governance framework without providing some guidelines and boundaries that define their responsibilities and accountabilities. Essential boundaries include the strategic domain, codes of conduct and ethical and environmental considerations within which managers can operate, the time between reporting intervals, and the so-called "white spaces" between what managers must do and what they might do.

Charles Handy believes that unlimited trust is, in practice, unrealistic. "By trust," he notes, "organizations really mean confidence, a confidence in someone's competence and in his or her commitment to a goal. Define that goal, and the individual or the team can be left to get on with it. Control is then after the event, when the results are assessed. Freedom within boundaries works best, however, when the work unit is self-contained, having the capability within it to solve its own problems."[15]

Author Stephan Haeckel notes that if boundaries are unclear or non-existent, people will select their own. Coherence and the possibility of cooperation will decline.[16] One of the most important elements is what is called the "subsidiarity of time." In transparent organizations, people are "empowered to make mistakes" and equally "empowered to fix them." For example, a service engineer might have a reporting interval of one day (thus giving him or her 7 or 8 hours to "err and correct" as long as the outcome at the end of the day is within the limits of tolerance), a project manager one week, and a value center manager one month. In mature organizations, these standards are embedded in the culture. But in less mature organizations, they need to be clearly spelled out.

Provide the trust and confidence for empowerment to be "taken"

Whole Foods Market has built its future on self-managed teams. While other grocery chains have been slashing costs to compete with Wal-Mart, Whole Foods has grown steadily over the past 25 years. Everyone who joins Whole Foods quickly grasps the primacy of teamwork and the freedom that teams have to make decisions. That's because the basic organizational unit isn't the store but small teams that manage departments such as fresh produce, prepared foods and seafood. And only teams have the power to decide what to stock and who to hire for full-time jobs. Store leaders take great care not to recommend people they don't think the team will approve. Bonuses are paid to teams, not to individuals. The first prerequisite of effective teamwork is trust. At Whole Foods, building trust starts with the hiring vote. Another element involves salaries. Every employee can see the salary of every other employee.

CEO John Mackey tells us why you need to empower people to build trust. "While small teams are essential to optimizing the flow of organizational trust, equally important is the philosophy of empowerment. The effectiveness of teams is tremendously enhanced when they are fully empowered to do their work and to fulfill the organization's mission and values. Empowerment must be much, much more than a mere slogan, however. It should be within the very DNA of the organization. Empowerment unleashes creativity and innovation and rapidly accelerates the evolution of the organization. Empowered organizations have tremendous competitive advantage because they have tapped into levels of energy and commitment which their competitors usually have difficulty matching."

"Nothing holds back empowerment," notes Mackey, "more than the leadership philosophy of command and control. Command and control (C&C) is actually the opposite of empowerment and it greatly lessens trust. C&C usually involves detailed rules and bureaucratic structures to enforce the rules. Such detailed rules almost always inhibit innovation and creativity. People get ahead in the organization not through being innovative, but by following the rules and playing it safe. C&C may produce compliance from the workforce, but it seldom unleashes much energy or passion for the purpose of the organization. Empowerment = Trust. C&C = Lack of Trust."[17]

Coach and support front-line teams

As we noted earlier, freedom without capability means that empowerment will not work. One of the key duties of senior management is to ensure that front-line teams have the capability to evaluate information and take the right decisions. Thus their role becomes one of coach, teacher or mentor and their aim is to build decision-making capabilities throughout the firm.

At Nokia employees are coached, mentored and encouraged to experiment and "have fun" so they can grow as individuals and become more insightful. They are given rich opportunities to improve their competencies via lateral transfers. Everything of importance is done by self-organizing teams and a system of "distributed decision-making" that implicitly recognizes the value of those closest to the action. Nokia continually seeks employee feedback on important issues via surveys.

Toyota's workplace is also renowned for its culture of employee mentoring, trust and continual learning. Because employees feel valued, respected and vested in the company's success, they offer thousands of ideas each year for improving product quality and plant efficiency, most of which get adopted.[18]

Integrate information in the work

Transferring the responsibility for strategy, planning and decision-making to value-center teams needs to be supported with the right tools and information systems. In fact, one of the most common objections to building transparent organizations is the slow speed and high cost of communications and the lack of IT integration. Most organizations still operate with disparate "islands of knowledge." Each function or department has its own knowledge base that is not available to other teams, thus denying them access to the bigger performance picture. But technology (especially the Internet) has dealt leaders a new deck of cards. Communication is now instant and the costs are becoming negligible. Control can be everywhere at the same time.

To make timely and effective decisions, teams need access to fast, frequent and relevant information. This means providing open access to information, effective analysis, and performance insights based on KPIs, trends and forecasts. Integrated systems enable hundreds of people to participate in the planning process at any one time helping to build their strategic capabilities. Controls also change. Effective control depends on knowing where you are today, having good visibility into the short-term future and providing transparent information systems.

Manage by exception

Management "by exception" is hardly a new idea, but its application has been overlooked as the bandwidth of data has expanded over recent years. It is based on a simple operating principle: trust people to act within values and policies, and punish them if they abuse that trust. Some firms that operate this way take the view that if this trust is abused, then employees face the ultimate sanction – losing their jobs. Take employee expense claims. In many organizations, employees are treated like criminals when it comes to their expense accounts. In other words, there is a pervasive view that people are going to cheat on their travel and entertaining expenses. Judging by recent revelations in the Tyco and Hollinger cases, where CEOs spent hundreds of thousands of dollars of company funds on personal items, it is easy to understand why companies are keen to vet expenses carefully. But handling and approving expense submissions in detail is a time-consuming and costly exercise, and one that is annoying for employees who are waiting for the company to reimburse the expenses they've incurred on its behalf.

Adaptive leaders do not design their systems to catch the one percent of people who will abuse any system. They allow employees to submit expenses online and then pay them automatically straight into their bank accounts. But they randomly investigate a number of expense submissions thoroughly. Anyone caught cheating faces dismissal. Online processing reduces handling costs dramatically as there is little checking and keying into the general ledger to be done.

This type of random sampling should be designed to give senior managers the reassurance they need. But the same principle can also apply to internal management control. At Handelsbanken, senior managers go to every branch every year. Instead of having the agenda determined by the management of the branch, the meeting is an unstructured conversation about present and future performance, the environment and risk. That's also what an effective internal audit team should do.

Conclusions

While numerous studies show that empowerment brings significant benefits, it is also a minefield of misconceptions and contradictions. Harvard professor Chris Argyris has spent a lifetime studying it, and like other observers wonders why there has been little growth over the past 30 years. He notes that while managers love empowerment in theory, it is the command and control model that they know and trust. And employees also think it is great as long as they are not held personally accountable.[19]

But, according to Argyris, the real reason why empowerment is like the emperor's new clothes ("We praise it loudly in public, and ask ourselves privately why we can't see it") is that there are two kinds of commitment. First there is the *extrinsic* commitment that derives from external demands. This is the typical performance contract that must be achieved. Then there is the *intrinsic* commitment that comes from within the individual. This is derived from their participation in some plan or goal and leads to people taking risks and accepting responsibility for their actions. The problem is that many leaders preach about empowerment and *internal commitment*, but at the same time all goals, plans, reward and recognition systems send clear messages of *external commitment*.[20] Thus there is a massive collision of cultures with only one winner – the power of top-down measures will always be the primary determinant of behavior in a culture that values meeting fixed targets.

This is the challenge that leaders face. To build trust and empowerment they must dismantle the old systems based on annual budgets and targets that dictate and direct what people do. Otherwise, like most empowerment initiatives, trust and empowerment will fizzle and fade until a new management generation has to learn the same lessons all over again.

KEY POINTS

- Autonomy means much more than delegation. It means giving people the freedom *and* capability to make decisions and self-regulate their performance. What leaders hope for is that every employee is engaged in the thinking and planning process, each trying to improve the performance of their team. If thousands of people are thinking about improvement, it stands to reason that more creative ideas will be produced and a few of them will have a major impact.

- The rhetoric and the reality start to meet when front-line teams see that layers of management and all their control systems are shrinking in size and importance. Placing power in the hands of front-line teams is the only evidence that matters.

- Define your strategic and operating boundaries (for example, which strategies, products and businesses are core and which are not). This will enable managers to make key decisions without pre-authorization.

- Empowerment cannot be "given"; it can only be taken if managers truly believe they can make decisions (and make mistakes!) without getting blamed or punished. So building a "no blame" culture is essential.

- Giving teams the scope and authority to make decisions is useless without the support of supervisors and peers. Their role is to challenge strategic options, plans, forecast assumptions and risks so that there is an effective process of "pressure testing" and "buy-in" to the team's strategy. This dialogue and the subsequent sharing of responsibility is key to building trust and confidence.

- Self-managed teams cannot be effective unless they have fast, relevant feedback. For example, they need KPI dashboards that tell them where they are each day or week. They can then use this information to either stay on their existing course or take further action to raise their game. It also helps to provide an enterprise-wide information system that enables everyone to be on the same page at the same time.

- Leaders need to learn to interfere only when necessary. What they must *not* do is micro-manage.

## CHAPTER 6

Principle #6 – Accountability
Base accountability on holistic criteria and peer reviews, not on hierarchical relationships

A democracy requires accountability, and accountability requires transparency. As Justice Louis Brandeis wrote, "Sunlight is said to be the best of disinfectants." In our democracy, the Freedom of Information Act (FOIA), which encourages accountability through transparency, is the most prominent expression of a profound national commitment to ensuring an open Government. At the heart of that commitment is the idea that accountability is in the interest of the Government and the citizenry alike.

President Barack Obama, Memorandum, January 21, 2009

Why everyone is confused by "accountability"

The early-19th-century British military hero the Duke of Wellington, frustrated with the tiresome demands of his Government controllers in London, wrote this note back to England in 1812:

> *"Whilst marching from Portugal to a position which commands the approach to Madrid and the French forces, my officers have been diligently complying with your requests which have been sent by ship from London to Lisbon and thence by dispatch to our headquarters. We have enumerated our saddles, bridles, tents and tent poles, and all manner of sundry items for which His Majesty's Government holds me accountable. I have dispatched reports on the character, wit, and spleen of every officer. Each item and every farthing has been accounted for, with two regrettable exceptions for which I beg your indulgence. Unfortunately the sum of one shilling and ninepence remains unaccounted for in one infantry battalion's petty cash and there has been a hideous confusion as to the number of jars of raspberry jam issued to one cavalry regiment during a sandstorm in western Spain.*

> *"This reprehensible carelessness may be related to the pressure of circumstance, since we are at war with France, a fact which may come as a bit of a surprise to you gentlemen in Whitehall. This brings me to my present purpose, which is to request elucidation of my instructions from His Majesty's Government so that I may better understand why I am dragging an army over these barren plains. I construe that perforce it must be one of two alternative duties, as given below. I shall pursue either one with the best of my ability, but I cannot do both: To train an army of uniformed British clerks in Spain for the benefit of the accountants and copy-boys in London or perchance to see to it that the forces of Napoleon are driven out of Spain."*[1]

Wellington's anger and disdain at the government accountants is obvious, but what is equally obvious – and a lesson for every company today – is that their respective objectives and what they believe they are accountable for are completely different. The budgeting process is aimed at control while the strategy process is aimed at defeating the competition. The two processes and the people engaged in them talk a different language; thus it is hardly surprising that they fail to communicate easily or effectively.

Like Wellington 200 years ago, many of us have had bad experiences when dealing with large organizations (especially airlines, telcos, banks and utilities) that hide behind impenetrable layers of bureaucracy and whose "customer relationship management" systems seem designed to destroy rather than build relationships. While their web and telephone sales pitches are often finely honed, their customer service is, more often then not, abysmal. Unfathomable rules, policies and disclaimers written in small print on letters and websites are designed to protect the organization and, should anything go wrong, ensure that no one is accountable.

A customer service experience

This letter from a long-time customer of a UK bank encapsulates the feelings of many people as they deal with "computers" or "call centers" rather than real (and local) people.

"I am a 61-year-old retired teacher. In 1967 I left home and opened my first bank account, with A-Bank [name withheld]. I have banked with them ever since. When I married I persuaded my husband to change from his bank to A-Bank and, over the past 40 years, we have paid off personal loans of more than £20,000 and a mortgage. I have never gone overdrawn, missed a loan payment or failed to pay the full amount owing every month on my A-Bank Gold credit card.

"My son married an Australian girl 10 years ago and lives in Sydney. Every time we visit them I inform the A-Bank customer services line that I may be using my card abroad. Last year we returned on February 23. In plowing through three months of mail, somewhat jet-lagged, I was surprised to find four letters from A-Bank, all extremely impersonal, telling me I had failed to make the minimum monthly payment on the outstanding balance of £12 on my credit card, and threatening to take court action against me. I realized a demand on my account for £12 must have come in after I had paid at the beginning of December what I thought was a sum settling the full amount owing. I phoned A-Bank the following day to apologize, explaining what had happened and organizing payment of the £60.16 that I now owed.

"I was told my credit limit would be reduced from £4500 to £300 but that, if I banked responsibly for the next six months, I could apply to have it increased again gradually. My husband was so appalled at this treatment from an organization advertising itself as the bank with the 'personal' touch that he immediately cancelled his A-Bank credit card and moved his current account to B-Bank. I remained with A-Bank despite him pointing out to me that I could

earn interest on my current account with B-Bank. I was convinced that 42 years of dealing with the same organization must count for something.

"I was extremely careful over the next 11 months to bank more than responsibly, paying off my credit card balance early every month and keeping my current account well in credit. I could not buy my airline ticket to Australia with my card this year because of the £300 limit, but my husband was happy to put both on his B-Bank card. We leave on 14 March. Knowing I had gone well past the six-month period after which I could apply for an increase on my limit, I phoned to see how this might be actioned.

"This time I was truly appalled by the letter I received by way of response. Not only did it tell me that I could not have an increased limit, it also justified this by saying '... a number of factors are taken into consideration, including the operation of your card, credit reference agency information and affordability' and inviting me to pay £2 for a copy of my credit reference agency file.

"When I think of the irresponsibility of banking organizations – including AA-Bank, the owner of A-Bank – over the past couple of decades, handing out 125 percent mortgages and making 'fat cat' payments to directors who have helped land this country in the financial mess it's in, I am left totally speechless.

"... Although trivial, I believe my experience clearly illustrates how financial organizations like A-Bank have exploited the hard-working, responsible earner; abused the trust that was placed in them; creamed off the handsome profits that came as a result of their irresponsible lending; and now try to make themselves out to be 'responsible' at the expense of the people who have fed them."[2]

Who is accountable for this problem in this bank? Is it the designer of the customer relationship management system? Is it the head of customer relations? Is it the CIO or CEO? Clearly this bank has failed this woman and probably thousands of others like her.

Only people can have accountability

Stephan Haeckel defines accountability as the personal acceptance of the consequences of making a commitment. Only people can have accountability (processes, machines and systems cannot). Accountability is codified by specifying who owes what to whom.[3] The commitments between customer and supplier are sufficient to define and track the status of the interaction between them.[4]

It reflects a shift from being held accountable for one's actions to *being held accountable for the consequences of one's actions.*[5]

This is the point about the banking problem discussed above. The more that systems become automated, the less accountability there is. But the way that bank executives would likely rationalize the lady's credit card problem is to assume that the problem can be fixed at the next level of detail. Another set of policies is written, more documents designed and printed and more work procedures are specified. In other words, the system designer assumes that such a system can ultimately be "perfect." But in social systems (and even in physics), systems are never perfect. More analysis and detail cannot solve the problem. It needs someone or a team of people to be accountable to the customer and for that relationship to matter above and beyond anything else.

From the bank's perspective, using computers instead of people is a clear case of false economy. Like many large organizations, banks have built call centers and used "customer relationship management" systems to create many more customer contact opportunities at the lowest cost. But the real cost is hidden as customers take their business elsewhere. Unlike almost every other bank, Handelsbanken has not built call centers. It prefers to deal with customers on a personal contact basis through its extensive branch system – *yet it has lower costs than any of its peers.* How can this be? The reason is that Handelsbanken has fewer management layers, expensive IT systems and management controls.

It is no wonder that Handelsbanken is consistently voted one of the best places to work and has the highest levels of customer satisfaction in the countries it operates in. But in most large organizations accountability is ill-defined and wrongly measured. You only have to ask people what they think of the performance appraisal system to gauge how dissatisfied they are with this process.

Do you work for your boss or your customers?

Accountability and control are two sides of the same coin. Most people support the notion of clear accountability *as long as it applies to someone else.* "Passing the buck" or "pointing the finger" are common examples of dysfunctional behavior. In the traditional hierarchy, accountability goes with the position. If you can justifiably claim that you acted within your job description or met your management objectives, then you are in reasonably good shape. Indeed, management-by-objectives remains the accountability and performance appraisal system of choice in most organizations today. But, like fixed targets and rigid plans, the world has a nasty habit of not conforming to the plan, so while people may stick dutifully to their plans and objectives, the needs of customers (both internal and external) may well have changed.

"Who do you work for, your boss or your customer?" is a difficult question for most people. Haeckel believes that many people find it surprisingly difficult to think about their work in terms of outcomes and commitments rather than activities and plans. When asked to explain their work roles, they almost invariably describe one or more procedures, that is, a sequence of activities and a set of measurements for evaluating how well they carry out those procedures. Some other individuals, of course, do realize that if they cannot define the outcome produced by their activities and the customers for those outcomes, they should ask themselves why they do them. Nevertheless, because most people do not think this way about their jobs, many will resist redefining their roles in terms of outcomes owed to customers rather than their managers. Such people tend to be risk-averse. They want control over the variables that affect their rewards, and being responsible for executing well-defined activities gives them more control.[6]

In command and control organizations, most individuals are accountable for meeting their annual personal objectives and managers are accountable for meeting their budgets. However, in adaptive organizations, accountability is more holistic. Employees are accountable to their managers *and managers are accountable to their employees.* Individuals have obligations to the team and the team has agreed success factors for which they expect to be held accountable. Teams are accountable to their (internal or external) customers. Many teams have developed report scorecards that are designed to address the key performance issues under review. But they then *apply their judgment* rather than resort to simple (and simplistic) metrics. They recognize that metrics are an essential component of accountability but that they only provide evidence of performance (and some of it is very circumstantial).

As we noted earlier, another problem is that many organizations continue to operate with too many management layers, complex matrix structures and disconnected accounting systems that provide many opportunities for people to fudge accountabilities and hide ineffective performance.

Principle #6 provides guidelines as to how accountability can be changed from meeting a job description or a budget to being responsible for serving partners and meeting team-based success factors. These are the key changes that make accountability clear to all teams in the adaptive organization and align their performance with fair evaluation and rewards systems. But it is a mindset challenge that will test the resolve of even the best leaders.

Implementation guidelines

- Ensure that accountability naturally flows toward the customer.

- Hold teams accountable for meeting their agreed success criteria.

- Use peer reviews to evaluate accountability.

- Design jobs and projects to align flow and accountability.

- Ensure that accountability means full transparency and disclosure.

- Be wary about matrix management.

Ensure that accountability naturally flows toward the customer

While adaptive leaders see their organizations as communities comprising multiple teams that deliver customer value, this doesn't mean wholesale restructuring, nor does it mean the disappearance of the hierarchy (although there is a lot less of it). It is the *relationships and the information flows* between levels and across the business that change.

Figure 6.1 shows how accountability flows inside the adaptive organization. The dotted lines show support services teams are accountable for serving and supporting internal customers (value centers) and how value centers are accountable for meeting the needs of external customers at the lowest cost. These lines flow from left to right. The dashed lines show how teams are also accountable for continuously improving their performance against peers, best practices and prior periods. These lines flow from right to left.

Support services teams wear different hats for different purposes. They act as *process improvers* (improve quality and reduce costs) and *business partners* to value center teams. But the common thread is a sharp focus on customer outcomes. How these are monitored and measured is different for each purpose.

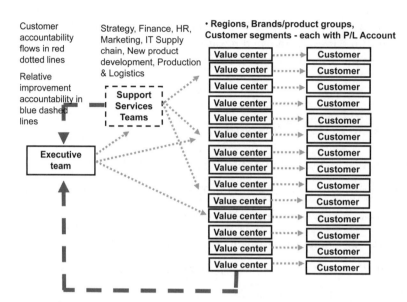

FIGURE 6.1 Teams are accountable for meeting customer outcomes and continuous relative improvement

Hold teams accountable for meeting their agreed success criteria

Accountability is primarily based on teams that have multiple stakeholders to serve and holistic success criteria to meet. Therefore it is important that each team agrees its success criteria against which they will be measured and held accountable.

Most teams have a reasonable idea of which measures are critical to their success. If they are given the scope and authority to find these measures, they often approach the task with enthusiasm and imagination. Trial and error is part of the process. They will develop complex multivariant formulae that might work for a while but get superseded by other more useful variants. And so the process goes on until it settles down. But the point is that these measures are *owned by the team*. They have not been imposed on them by a higher authority.

As we noted earlier, most organizations comprise three permanent teams (executives, support services and value centers). In most medium- to large-sized organizations value center teams will be grouped into geographic clusters such as regions or countries. It is around these three teams that measures and reports are based, together with management evaluation, recognition and rewards. So information systems designers need to ensure that all data gravitate to team-based accounts.

The implicit agreement is that executives will provide a challenging and open operating environment and that employees will deliver continuous performance improvement using their knowledge and judgment to adapt to changing conditions. It is based on mutual trust, but it is not a soft alternative to the fixed performance contract. Managers must perform to high levels of expectation or fail to survive.

Table 6.1 shows an example of an evaluation scorecard for a value center team. The performance criteria should cover the key elements of performance outcomes on which management will be evaluated. Column (a) enables these criteria to be "weighted" to lay greater emphasis on some criteria over others. Column (b) is the assessment score. The final column (a × b) reflects the weighted score and enables rewards to be paid based on the percentage score achieved.

The performance criteria for these scorecards will vary by type of team. For example, a support services team will want to emphasize efficiency (how well have they improved back-office processes) and effectiveness (how well have they satisfied the needs of their business partners). Underpinning each chosen evaluation criterion will be a number of points that judges will need to consider. These points provide some consistency across the evaluation process.

The relative improvement contract focuses managers on maximizing value at all times rather than playing games with the numbers, because there are no fixed targets that lead to irrational behavior. Performance is judged after the event rather than based on a fixed target. The logic is that it is only after the event that you can judge whether performance is good in the context of actual market conditions.

TABLE 6.1 Value center team evaluation scorecard

Performance criteria	Weighting (a)	Score (out of 100) (b)	Weighted average score (a × b)
How well are we doing relative to peers (based on a range of KPIs)?	30%	60	18.0
How well are we managing our strategic investment portfolio?	10%	50	5.0
How well are we innovating?	20%	60	12.0
How well are we managing our resources?	10%	60	6.0
How well are we satisfying our customers?	30%	80	24.0
TOTAL	100%		65%

Use peer reviews to evaluate accountability

In traditional organizations most managers spend two or three months each year negotiating targets and budgets which form a contract they have to meet. Accountability in the form of a fixed target is seductive. Managers "know what they have to achieve." Profit centers focus on profits and cost centers focus on costs. Though support services teams acknowledge that they need to serve their internal partners, they are not usually held to account for meeting this need. Value centers may be measured on customer satisfaction, but this is rarely measured in a timely way and the team is unlikely to be rewarded for excellent performance.

In adaptive organizations this "accountability by targets" culture is swept aside. Managers know that the best way to maximize performance potential is to set ambitious goals that are *not contracts* and then trust their people to do their best in the given circumstances. Managers are accountable for serving their partners and the whole team is accountable for continuously improving its results compared with its peers.

In-depth peer reviews: the hard edge of accountability

Some firms have developed peer review systems that achieve these objectives. Take W.L. Gore & Associates, a company that has a reputation for being radically decentralized with little or no hierarchy, few titles, and employees, called "associates," who are mentored by more senior people as they find the roles that best suit their talents.

But there is a hard edge to this model. In-depth peer reviews are used to rate leaders. Gore's CEO Terri Kelly explains how it works:

> *"Some days things are chaotic. I don't want to paint a picture of something that's perfect. You have teams coming together, storming and forming and building relationships. But there are some fundamental things that hold Gore together. One is the values to which we all subscribe, in terms of how we're going to treat each other – there's a huge trust element in the Gore culture. One of the more powerful things that creates discipline is that everyone in the organization knows that they will be ranked by their peers, and that their compensation will depend on this ranking. This peer pressure is much more powerful than top-down pressure.*

"Our associates get to choose what commitments to make. If they didn't know they're going to be evaluated by their peers, they might be tempted to take on an assignment that is personally interesting to them, a hobby, but one that's not important for the company. But instead, every associate is constantly thinking, 'I want to be viewed as making a big contribution to the enterprise,' so they're constantly looking for opportunities that will leverage their strengths and that they're passionate about. So there's a natural, built-in pressure: every associate wants to work on something impactful.

"Every associate knows that they won't be judged by one boss or superior, but by all their peers, by individuals who know what they've done and how they interact with others on a daily basis. Typically, an associate will be evaluated by 20 or 30 peers and will, in turn, evaluate 20–30 colleagues. You rank your peers from top to bottom. It's a forced ranking. You're asked to rank only people you know. What we find is that there's typically a lot of consistency in who people view as the top contributors, and who they view as the bottom of the list. We don't tell our associates what criteria to use, we simply ask them to base their ranking on who's making the greatest contribution to the success of the enterprise. You don't evaluate people solely on the basis of what they're doing within their team, but in terms of the broader impact they may be having across the company. And then beyond their contributions, are they behaving in ways that are collaborative? Are they living the values? Sometimes someone will get great results but at great expense to the organization. These are the issues associates think about when they're putting together their rankings.

"We have a cross-functional committee of individuals with leadership roles who look at all this input, debate it and then put together an overall ranking, from 1 to 20, of those particular associates. Then, in setting compensation, they ensure there's a nice slope to the pay curve so that the folks who are making the biggest contributions are also making the most money.

"The process is a bit brutal, but it ensures that real talent gets recognized. This system avoids the problem of paying someone more because of seniority or title. New associates joining the organization, the scientists who don't want to be people leaders – we want these people to feel highly valued, because the next invention may come from them. No system is perfect, but ours levels the playing field and allows real talent to emerge and get compensated accordingly.

"We don't need a bureaucratic system to hold people accountable. So you can deconstruct a lot of the typical bureaucratic processes that are typically used to measure and control performance. We've also found that by not having hard *and fast metrics of performance we can avoid a lot of unintended consequences. You get a lot of negative behavior when you have narrow metrics that really don't represent the complexity of the business. Instead, we ask our associates to view performance holistically, in terms of someone's total impact, versus focusing on a few specific variables."[7]*

In 2010, for the 13th consecutive year, Gore earned a position on Fortune's annual list of the US "100 Best Companies to Work For." For four years, Gore has been named by London's *Sunday Times* as the "Best Company to Work For" in the UK; Gore-Germany ranked second in the "50 Best Places to Work in Germany 2007" among mid-sized companies; and Gore-Italy ranked number 12 among the "35 Best Places to Work in Italy."[7]

Reverse accountability

HCL Technologies has also moved toward a peer review method of management accountability. CEO Vineet Nayar's idea was to "reverse" the traditional system of accountability whereby managers in the hierarchy were accountable to their bosses. However, he was careful to define what he meant by "reverse accountability": "We did not want to turn this into a discussion of individuals or specific positions. We were not talking about making executives accountable to front-line workers. We did not expect that our senior vice president of engineering would have to get his time sheet signed by the cafeteria worker. Reverse accountability simply meant that we wanted to get certain elements of the hierarchy to be more accountable to the value zone [teams working at the interface between the company and its customers]. In particular, we looked at three categories of positions: the enabling functions; the managerial chain of command all the way to the CEO; and the influencers who are not part of the hierarchy but are critical to achieving the desired wow in the value zone."

He started by looking at the support services teams. He found that accountability was the wrong way around – that front-line teams were usually more accountable to back-office units such as finance than the other way around. The solution was the "Smart Service Desk" concept, based on a problem management system that the company already had in place for its customers. Now, whenever an employee has a problem or needs information, he or she can open a ticket that is directed to the appropriate department for handling. Each ticket has a deadline for resolution. The system is transparent so that everyone can see the contents of the tickets and where they are in the process. And the employee who had opened the ticket is the one to determine whether the resolution has been satisfactory or the issue has been resolved at all.

As the idea was discussed, the support service teams were naturally resistant. They thought that such a transparent monitoring system would reflect badly upon them. They said they worked hardest of all and were the least appreciated. But then they changed their views. When they thought more about it, they realized that there would be real benefits, particularly as it gave them a recognized and robust system of measurement that would enable them to continuously improve.

Once an employee has filled out a ticket, the system automatically assigns it to a support executive in the appropriate team. He or she will then investigate the issue and take the necessary action to solve it. The support executive commits to a set of accountability metrics for each ticket based on a number of factors such as the complexity and urgency of the request. If the executive does not resolve the issue within the specified time, the ticket is automatically sent to the executive's manager, and so on up the line. Once the issue is resolved, the support executive closes the ticket. If, however, the employee who raised it is not satisfied with the resolution, he or she can refuse the closed status of the ticket. It will remain open and the clock will keep ticking. The employee can also rate the quality of service provided by the support executive.

What was the reaction? As Nayar explains, "It took time to settle in. People continued to pick up the phone rather than open a ticket until it was agreed that the support services teams would refuse to accept any request that did not come through the new channel. When people saw that it worked, the numbers rapidly escalated until at one point there were 30,000 requests *per month* (HCL has 66,000 employees). They didn't know whether to celebrate the success of the system or be worried at the volume of problems."

After the system had been in place for a few months, Nayar met with a group of people in the UK business. Out of the meeting came some further insights. While the system encouraged people to raise problems and rate how well they were resolved, it did not track or rate support services on whether they had fixed the problem for good. In other words, perhaps the real goal is *zero tickets*. When they analyzed the tickets they found three primary causes of problems: an unsatisfactory factory policy; inadequate or unclear communication; and poor execution or implementation of a satisfactory policy or process. So they asked the support services teams to address these issues. The goal for each team was to reach a zero-ticket week.

The result was that employee satisfaction rocketed as front-line employees felt they were now on the same level as back-office support people. Also the capacity of support service teams to carry out value-adding work (as opposed to problem-solving) escalated. It was a win-win for everyone.[9]

Design jobs and projects to align flow and accountability

How do team leaders get the best work from their team members? A number of researchers, most notably the psychologist Mihaly Csikszentmihalyi, have identified the value of "flow," the state in which people feel happy and fulfilled because they are completely absorbed in the work they do, as a key ingredient. In organizations, flow typically takes place when the challenges of a job fit naturally with the capabilities that people bring to it.

Csikszentmihalyi invites us to imagine skiing down a slope. Your full attention is focused on the movements of your body, the position of the skis, the air whistling past your face and the snow-shrouded trees running by. There is no room in your awareness for conflicts or contradictions; you know that a distracting thought or emotion might get you buried face down in the snow. The run is so perfect that you want it to last forever. If skiing does not mean much to you, this complete immersion in an experience could occur while you are singing in a choir, dancing, playing bridge or reading a good book. If you love your job, it could happen during a complicated surgical operation or a close business deal. It may occur in a social interaction, when talking with a good friend, or while playing with a baby. Moments such as these provide flashes of intense living against the dull background of everyday life.

Flow tends to occur when a person faces a clear set of goals that require appropriate responses (when flow and accountability are perfectly aligned). According to Csikszentmihalyi, flow happens when a person's skills are fully involved in overcoming a challenge that is just about manageable, so it acts as a magnet for learning new skills and increasing challenges. If challenges are too low, one gets back to flow by increasing them. If challenges are too great, one can return to the flow state by learning new skills.

Csikszentmihalyi tells us that there are many ways to make one's job produce flow. A supermarket clerk who pays genuine attention to customers, a physician concerned about the total well-being of patients or a news reporter who considers truth at least as important as sensational interest when writing a story can transform a routine job into one that makes a difference. Turning a dull job into one that satisfies our need for novelty and achievement involves paying close attention to each step involved and then asking: Is this step necessary? Can it be done better, faster, more efficiently? What additional steps could make my contribution more valuable? If, instead of spending a lot of effort trying to cut corners, one spent the same amount of attention trying to find ways to accomplish more on the job, one would enjoy working more and probably be more successful. When approached without too many cultural prejudices and with a determination to make it personally meaningful, even the most mundane job can produce flow.[8]

In hundreds of interviews at adaptive organizations we have found people who have been able to align challenge, flow and accountability. Employees at Handelsbanken, Toyota, Southwest Airlines, Gore and Whole Foods have the ability to improve their work (and the work of their team) and continuously challenge their performance and results. Empowerment leads to flow and flow leads to highly productive and satisfied people.

Ensure that accountability means full transparency and disclosure

Effective accountability is closely connected with transparency and disclosure. If everyone can see the performance of everyone else, then everyone feels the pressure of accountability. This also applies to disclosure outside the organization. As authors Epstein and Birchard note: "Disclosure energizes the accountability cycle ... It also cements stakeholder relationships more firmly in place ... In short, they need to create a communications strategy based upon greater transparency. However, keeping that high-level data secret today works just as often in the opposite way: It blocks the deepening of business relationships, staunches stakeholder commitment and suppresses feedback that promotes improvement. For years, most reporting has been based upon mistrust ... This legacy has led outsiders to lose faith in the key information managers provide."[9]

Many leaders fear that extra reporting will make a company a target for litigation. But according to Epstein and Birchard, the facts belie the fear. "The vast majority of disclosure-related lawsuits," they argue, "relate to 'failure to disclose' and 'inadequate disclosure.' Some relate to 'misleading disclosures.' For all practical purposes, companies cannot be held liable for disclosing too much, but they can be held liable for disclosing too little or disclosing in ways that do not present financial conditions fairly. The best defense against litigation is a documented, disciplined process for forthright disclosure of both leading and lagging indicators."[10]

Their view is that "accountable managers are rarer than they should be because most managers fail to grasp the opportunity before them. They interpret accountability as a tool from the dark side of management, as a noose of obligations. Too few comprehend accountability as a tool to empower the organization, as a lever for unparalleled performance."[11]

Some leaders have taken on this challenge and deal with the accountability problem by downplaying detailed rules and regulations (preferring "principles" to "rules") and eradicating fixed targets. But the key change is that accountability moves from the exclusivity of the executive suite to be shared with self-managed teams at every level. These teams have the scope and authority to fix what needs to be fixed. So they take responsibility for systems improvement as well as performance improvement. Accountability is the other side of the equation from empowerment. And empowerment can only be "taken" by managers who have trust and confidence in management systems and relationships. Not only that, they also need access to the information, resources and tools to take whatever action they believe is necessary.

Be wary about matrix management

A major barrier to achieving clear accountability is "matrix management." Many large firms use a form of matrix management to balance specialist functional roles (such as a service engineer) with operating roles. Thus the service engineer would report to his or her line manager as well as a functional manager, probably located in a different place. The point, as Haeckel explains, is that ambiguity about authority, priorities and who owes what to whom leaves people tethered to multiple bosses, any of whom might yank on the leash at any time with directives or requests that may or may not conflict with other priorities and responsibilities.[12]

Ambiguity is not just the opposite of clarity – it is its *enemy*. And ambiguity is most common in customer relationships. It is not untypical in large companies to find that all customers are "up for grabs," that is, any business unit has the right to fight for a customer's business. Even more common is dual responsibility for large customers where the global accounts team and the local sales team are both trying to maximize sales to the same customer and both receiving rewards for doing so. While this approach might inject a strong competitive element into the sales process, it neither fosters good customer relationships, nor does it help internal coordination. Who is responsible for satisfying the customer? To whom does the customer turn when problems arise? Nor do these issues just apply to external customers – they equally apply to internal customers. Clear accountability is seen as a positive (and essential) feature of the governance and control system. Most leaders fail to grasp this point.

Conclusions

In the adaptive organization teams need to know clearly to whom and for what they are accountable. The best way to achieve this clarity is to agree a performance (or "accountability") scorecard that spells out the success criteria for the team and how it will be evaluated and scored. Individual team members are accountable to the team, and the onus is on team leaders to communicate everyone's roles and responsibilities and how they are expected to support the team's goals.

KEY POINTS

- Whereas in traditional organizations accountability flows vertically up the hierarchy ("please the boss"), in adaptive organizations it flows horizontally across the organization toward the customer ("please the customer"). This means that team leaders are accountable to their team members and that one (upstream) team is accountable to another (downstream) team.

- Hold teams accountable for meeting their agreed success criteria. Define the success factors for each team. The discussion should involve the whole team so there is buy-in from all key people. The point is that these performance measures are owned by the team. They have not been imposed on them by a higher authority. Members will also know that they will be evaluated and held accountable for meeting these same success criteria.

- Each individual is a member of a team to whom they are accountable for their performance.

- A number of researchers have identified the value of "flow" (the state in which people feel happy and fulfilled because they are completely absorbed in their work). A critical component of achieving flow is accountability. If a job has its own discrete decision-making responsibilities, different from those in positions above and below, then the individual in that job feels accountable. The secret to determining the appropriate number of layers is to plot accountabilities from the customer back into the organization, to figure out which jobs are essential to providing customers with the best products and services.

- Effective accountability is closely connected with transparency and disclosure. If everyone can see the performance of everyone else, then everyone feels the pressure of accountability. This also applies to disclosure outside the organization.

- Be wary about matrix management. Accountability can easily fall down the cracks between different lines of reporting.

## CHAPTER 7

Principle #7 – Goals
Set ambitious medium-term goals, not short-term fixed targets

Our problem is not that we aim too high and miss, but that we aim too low and hit.

Aristotle

"Be the best": why Handelsbanken is consistently one of the best performing banks

In the late 1960s Swedish bank Svenska Handelsbanken was in crisis and near bankruptcy. Its strategy was to be the largest bank in Sweden and thus volume business was its declared aim. But this led to a reduction in the quality of loans and an increase in bad debts. The customer portfolio was becoming weaker, it was no longer profitable and shareholders were increasingly dissatisfied. Banking was highly regulated at that time, and the bank was also in trouble with the authorities. Though there was little competition in the sector, increasing calls for more deregulation were being voiced and tougher competition was anticipated. Handelsbanken was not well placed to deal with these pressures and senior managers and non-executive directors were becoming alarmed.

The bank also had internal problems. Its centralized bureaucracy meant that it carried a heavy cost burden and its decision-making was slow, reducing the ability of branch managers to respond adequately to customer needs. To support its strategy of becoming the biggest bank, Handelsbanken also wanted to be the first to introduce new ideas. These included the development of a sophisticated planning, budgeting and control system in the late 1960s. The staff union was strong and its members were demoralized. It was in these circumstances that Dr Jan Wallander was appointed CEO in 1970.

It did not take Dr Wallander long to realize the extent of the bank's problems. Its strategy was wrong and its management model focused on the centralized hierarchy rather than helping front-line managers deliver fast solutions to customers. The management model failed just about every test. It did not support the new strategy, it encouraged the wrong management behavior, it added little value and it emphasized centralized authority.

The aim: to be the best

Dr Wallander's arrival brought immediate changes, especially to the strategic direction of the bank. One of his first decisions was to replace the aim of being the biggest with one that read "*the best and most profitable bank in Sweden.*" Soon strategic plans and detailed forecasts based on assumptions of size and scale were dismantled and a new focus on profitability was created. This simple statement was enough to change many assumptions in the bank. Endless debates about acquisitions, divestments, expansion, contraction, reorganization and other strategic considerations were suddenly brought to a halt. Now every decision had to satisfy one question: Will it improve the profitability of the bank? Management roles, department costs and marketing activities were all questioned. A new focus on profit centers was crafted, and before too long, the radically decentralized management model and supporting management information system was taking shape.

Choosing profitability over scale meant selecting only good customers. This needed a whole new accounting system if branch managers were to know the profitability of their customers and indeed of their branches. Being able to keep customers required the bank to be more responsive, which in turn required that branch managers had more authority. So the core of Dr Wallander's vision was a decentralized model. He did not spend much time with the central departments and people at head office. He saw his own role very differently from the way his predecessors had seen the role of CEO. He would be the architect of the new model, a leader of the organization, not the leading banker.

Dr Wallander's approach to the scope of the project was influenced not so much by his intuition but by his rare depth of experience. His time as a professional economist and later as a non-executive director at L.M. Ericsson taught him that most planning and budgeting systems fall into two types. First there is the "*same weather tomorrow as today*" version, in which case "why bother to spend so much time making forecasts?" And secondly there is the "*different weather tomorrow from today*" version, in which case "you haven't a hope of making accurate budgets and forecasts." Phrased slightly differently, Dr Wallander noted that "either a budget will thus prove roughly right and then it will be trite, or it will be disastrously wrong and in that case it will be dangerous. My conclusion is thus: Scrap it!"

The new management model

The new management model was designed with these features in mind:

- *Clarity of strategic intent* – The strategic message must be clear and well understood and enable people's capabilities and actions to be closely aligned with customer needs. It must also enable decentralized decision-making to operate effectively within a well-defined framework.

- *Focus on the customer* – The bank must have a clear performance focus on customers rather than products and this will define the way the bank has chosen to compete, i.e. by attracting and keeping the right (profitable) customers. (This was – and still is – in stark contrast to most financial services companies, which use product targets or market share to dictate their performance ambitions.)

- *Radical decentralization* – Managers must be expected to "run their own business" – and maximize its profitability – within the framework of the bank's management policies. Well-trained and capable people acting on their own don't need much supervision and thus many of the costs associated with a large control-oriented organization will be unnecessary.

- *A simple model* – The new model must be simple to understand and operate. It will be firmly based on the link between managing people and serving customers. These two processes must be clearly welded together into a seamless operation with defined steps and key performance indicators.

* *Focus on profit centers* – The bank must develop an advanced accounting system that gives both senior executives and front-line managers a fast and comprehensive understanding of current performance in every profit center.

* *More controls, not less* – The new accounting system will give the group controller more controls than before. However, while head office can see management performance at every level, they must never use this knowledge to interfere and tell people what to do and what not to do. Instead they will pass careful messages down the (very short) line to suggest that this or that element of performance needs attention.

* *Relative targets and measures* – While the new system will provide many new performance indicators, it is important to focus everyone on just a few crucial indicators that determine competitive success. Thus the bank will measure its progress on three simple measures: return on capital employed, cost-to-income ratio and profit per employee. Every employee understands these measures, which are used to create internal competition between branches and a sense of common purpose across the bank.

* *Company-wide profit shares* – To build cooperative behavior across the bank and reward all employees for the success they have created, the bank will operate a company-wide profit-sharing scheme whereby all employees share equally in the allocated profit share.

Decentralization is the key

Dr Wallander's approach was to change the management model across the whole business. He believed that decentralization was the key, and this can only succeed with the total commitment of all senior managers and other key people. He equally knew that it would take time and resources and was not without risk – but he reckoned that the risk of not making the changes was much greater. There was never any doubt in his mind that these changes were right, and this conviction was to prove vital in making the radical changes that followed over the next few years. [Note: To place Dr Wallander's actions in context, in the early 1970s the command and control management model was rarely questioned in management books, and detailed budgetary control systems were the conventional wisdom in all large companies and in business schools.]

Relative performance drives continuous improvement

Wallander's vision was that beating the competition should pervade every aspect of performance management at Handelsbanken. As he explained: "We just communicate to people the average and a ranking that shows which branches are above and which are below. The system works on its own. Senior executives don't need to push people, they just advise. Managers know what is 'acceptable performance' – you can't linger in the depths of the league table for long! Of course it also relies on high levels of trust and motivation. Our managers can do anything to improve performance. Peer pressure plays an important part in this process. No branch manager wants to let down the regional team, and as they speak to each other all the time, there is both pressure to perform and a willingness to help each other. It is this tension between internal competition and cooperative support that enables us to keep improving."

He reinforced this competitive performance climate by introducing a series of "presidential visits" that occur throughout the year, in which the chief executive spends two days with a region and its branches. During this visit the CEO challenges regional and branch managers on their performance assumptions and how they can improve. This is an important part of the "stretch" thinking that the bank tries hard to encourage. But it is the sense of real competition that continues day in and day out between regional banks and between branches within a region that really drives improved performance. It works on its own and does not depend on any arbitrary targets to drive improvement.

Decentralization means abandoning budgets

Although Wallander's vision was to decentralize the business and empower front-line people, he realized from the outset that this could only be achieved by abandoning the top-down budgeting process. There is now no discernible company-wide goal-setting or budgeting process at Handelsbanken. Over the years the bank has used performance rankings based on a few key performance indicators (KPIs) to continuously improve performance relative to its peers. So successful has this approach been that the bank now sets the world-class standard. Its challenge is to stay there. Regions and branches in effect set their own goals, depending on the improvement step-change they want to make. But managers know that this is a moving target because every other branch and region is trying to do the same.

Relative improvement goals work at each level of the bank. At the group level, the bank aims to beat its rivals on its key measure of return on equity (ROE). At the regional bank level, regions compete with each other on ROE and on the cost-to-income ratio. And at the branch level, branches compete with each other on the cost-to-income ratio, profit per employee and total profit. The most intense competition is at the regional bank level, where a cup is awarded each year to the winner. There is also a system of handicapping. Each year, capital is allocated to regions according to the Bank of International Settlements (BIS) rules (i.e. standard lending-to-capital ratios set according to the risk profile of the investment portfolio) and based on results of the last three years. The most successful region receives the highest capital allocation, thus making it harder to make a return in the following year. Similarly, the poorest performer receives the lowest capital allocation, thus making it easier to catch up.

Many people struggle to understand how branches both compete and cooperate with each other at the same time. One of the secrets is that while they strive to be the best at achieving low costs and high profits, *they do not compete for customers*. Each customer belongs to a specific branch, and all transactions (no matter where they take place) are routed back to that branch's profit and loss account. Another of the secrets is the reward system.

The staff bonus scheme supports the delicate balance between internal competition and cooperation. Every year since 1973, the bank has allocated part of its profit to a profit-sharing scheme for employees. The funds are managed by the Oktogonen Foundation. The main condition for an allocation to be made is that the Handelsbanken Group must have a higher return on shareholders' equity after standard tax than the average for its chosen peer group. All employees receive the same allocated amount (paid into their personal pension plans). Disbursements can be made when the employee reaches the age of 60.

With a cost-to-income ratio of around 45 percent and customer satisfaction ratings that leave its rivals standing, Handelsbanken is consistently one of the most successful banks in Europe – a position it has maintained for over 35 years. It has been a public company since 1871. While its home base is Scandinavia, it has recently expanded in the highly competitive UK market with great success.

Why management models matter

Handelsbanken has also come through the credit crunch relatively unscathed. The reason is that the "casino banking" activities of other banks did not fit with its core values. But the real difference is its management model. Most banks spend months each year agreeing which products and services to sell and how much to spend on marketing them through various channels such as retail, corporate, wealth management and investment banking. The final budget defines what each team has to achieve, and promotions and bonuses depend on the outcomes. Cost efficiencies are gained through economies of scale such as replacing expensive branches with large call centers and acquiring or merging with other banks. It is an expensive model to operate.

We have heard how Dr Wallander's vision was different. There are no "channels." Apart from some investment banking, all business is conducted through the branch network. They have a saying that "the branch is the bank." There are no annual plans, budgets, targets or bonuses. Each branch runs its own business and can make nearly all decisions about location, staffing, salaries and so forth. Marketing is all local. Each branch sets its own goals and makes its own plans for how it will improve performance. The aim is to improve faster than other "peer" branches. Costs are much lower than other banks because there are few management layers, few central control systems and few marketing initiatives. And customer loyalty is high (customers are attracted by word of mouth).

Would Handelsbanken have been as successful if it had set annual stretch targets every year? Would its leaders have survived if they had failed to achieve them? The likely answer to both questions is "no." Nor would the bank have avoided takeover predators that are particularly aggressive in the banking world. It is not *aiming to beat the average* that's important. The absence of fixed targets has enabled the bank to pursue steady improvement with continuous innovation, organic growth and adaptation. Being measured against the average, and without the specter of a predetermined fixed target, has in fact enabled the company to be the *top performer* within its peer group in more years than not.

The point about relative measures is that you don't know if you have done well until all the other scores are known. Just like in a football league system, each team must set its course to improve its position and this means improving at a faster rate than others. But there is no "magic number" to aim for. You might set your goals at a certain number of wins, but ultimately you don't know how well you've done until the result of the final game is decided. This type of measurement system eradicates much of the gaming that goes on around meeting a predetermined "number." It means that every team must stretch and strive until the final day. And peer pressure drives performance. No team wants to be in fourth quartile, face relegation or, in some cases, be sold to the highest bidder.

But as Dr Wallander recognized, you need to balance competition with cooperation. Every football team in the league has a vested interest in making the whole league stronger, more viable and more enduring. Whether it be agreeing common platforms, standards or performance measures, every member in the business ecosystem needs to think about the impact of any action on the whole system before making a final commitment.

Short-term fixed targets are the nemesis of the adaptive organization. If you are looking for a reason why empowerment has not worked in the past, then look no further – fixed targets are likely to be the answer. Principle #7 tells leaders to steer clear of fixed targets and suggests alternative ways of setting goals without the undesirable side effects of dysfunctional behavior.

Implementation guidelines

- Abandon the obsession with shareholder value.

- Avoid giving specific earnings promises to analysts and investors.

- Set relative improvement goals.

- Enable teams to set their own goals.

- Use peer comparisons to challenge and stretch, not judge and blame.

- Be careful with league tables.

- Balance competition and cooperation.

Abandon the obsession with shareholder value

The former CEO of Coca-Cola, the late Roberto Goizueta, once said that: "I get paid to make the owners of the Coca-Cola Company increasingly wealthy with each passing day. Everything else is fluff."[1] Like Goizueta, many leaders in the past 20 years or so have become increasingly obsessed with creating "shareholder value."

Shareholder value represents a poor short-term target

While it might be a powerful measure of longer-term success, shareholder value represents a poor short-term target. There are too many dysfunctional ways in which even well meaning CEOs can manipulate messages to the market, providing a short-term thrill but ending in longer-term misery. Even Toyota has been seduced by shareholder value. According to long-time Toyota watcher Professor Tom Johnson, the cause of Toyota's recent problems (including numerous quality problems and product recalls) is found in its very recent surrender to Wall Street pressure to grow continuously – as virtually all large publicly traded American businesses, including those that pursue "lean" practices, have attempted to do for the past 30 years or more. Steady growth in size and scale presumably improves profitability by conferring increased control over market prices and decreased costs. Unfortunately, as Toyota has discovered, the strategy never works.

As Johnson notes, the flaw in this finance-oriented growth strategy is the belief that profitability improves by taking steps aimed at increasing revenue and cutting costs. While such steps embody impeccable arithmetic logic, they ignore the reality that long-term profitability results from satisfied customers and focused operations. However, boosting output as a means to increase revenue and cut costs invariably results in impaired quality, unhappy customers, higher overhead costs and diminished long-term profitability.[2]

As many leaders now realize, shareholder value is created as much by perceptions and promises as by actions and outcomes. Expectations of future performance are already factored into the share price, so the only way that it changes is if new information suggests that existing expectations need to be revised upwards or downwards. New information reaches the market in different ways. Sometimes it is provided through approved press releases concerning products, technologies, patents, strategies, acquisitions and alliances. But the most important information concerns earnings forecasts for the period ahead. Sometimes this is a public statement by the CEO, or it can reach the investment community through a series of "nods and winks" from business leaders to analysts. Once this forecast has been set, however, it becomes a contract to deliver results. Little happens if expectations are met, but if they fall short, then a heavy price is paid in terms of a (usually sharply) lower share price. The implicit "performance contract" with the market has been broken and leaders lose credibility, bonuses and even, in some cases, their jobs.

Shareholder value and profitability goals can lead to different results

Whether the board is pursuing "shareholder value" or "profitability" can make a huge difference to its decision-making and risk profile. (In the long run there should be no incompatibility, but in the short run there can be a significant divergence.)

For example, the share price can be impacted by announcements such as profit forecasts, acquisitions, new product releases and even job cuts. An aggressive board with large share options can be tempted to over-egg these announcements, sending "buy" signals to investors. But none of these announcements has a quantifiable impact on profitability. Leaders in less aggressive organizations prefer to let their results do the talking. They do not get themselves into a position of taking actions to protect the commitments they have made to investors.

Try this test. How would your board members react if they discovered that there was more shareholder value available if the organization was broken apart and sold off in pieces? And how would this view square with the words on the mission statement? Some boards see their organizations as no more than a portfolio of businesses that can be bought and sold rather like football players. The role of the CEO and, in some cases, the CFO is usurped by the role of the fund manager. "Chainsaw" Al Dunlap in America became a crusader for shareholder value as he closed down factories and cut product lines. Businesses didn't need to grow or satisfy customers, they only needed to "unlock underperforming assets." But his status soon turned from hero to villain as it dawned on shareholders that his actions ended up destroying value as employees and customers voted with their feet and order books respectively.

Pursuing shareholder value targets is "the dumbest idea in the world"

In a recent interview, legendary leader (and former CEO of General Electric) Jack Welch stated that shareholder value is "the dumbest idea in the world." He added: "Shareholder value is a result, not a strategy ... Your main constituencies are your employees, your customers and your products."[3] Paul Polman, chief executive of Unilever, has added his voice to the growing number of business leaders who argue that "shareholder value" is a misguided and potentially harmful goal for companies to pursue. He said shareholders had benefited as a result of his concentration on customers. "I drive this business model by focusing on the consumer and customer in a responsible way ... and I know that shareholder value can come."[4]

What Johnson understands, and Welch and Polman have come to realize, is that shareholder value is best seen as an outcome rather than a target. In other words, in a well-designed management model where customer needs and operating processes are perfectly aligned, employees will be highly motivated and productive, customers will feel the benefit in terms of high levels of satisfaction and shareholders will reap the rewards in terms of sustainable free cash flows and a high share price.

Avoid giving specific earnings promises to analysts and investors

Many leaders would like to stop giving specific targets to analysts, but they fear that share values and their reputation would suffer. However, this fear is not supported by the evidence. In a 2006 report McKinsey asked executives why they issued earnings guidance, and the answers were uniform: "higher valuations, lower share price volatility and improvements in liquidity." But in a review of around 4000 companies McKinsey found no evidence that issuing frequent earnings guidance affects valuation multiples, improves shareholder returns or reduces share price volatility. The only impact was the increase in trading volumes that only affects companies with illiquid shares. On the contrary, the only reason why companies continue the practice is to maintain good communications with analysts and investors.[5]

Great leaders know that it is only results that matter in the market. But making optimistic promises is not the way to achieve consistently good results. Aiming to be at the top of the peer-group league table is a much better goal. That's one of the reasons that increasing numbers of them are saying "no" to guidance. The overall percentage of US companies that give guidance has fallen from around 75 percent to 55 percent in recent years. In an SEC filing, Barry Diller, CEO of USA Networks, said he would no longer participate in a process he likened to a kabuki dance. Warren Buffett is a devout believer in not giving earnings guidance. That's why such companies as Coca-Cola, Gillette and The Washington Post Co. have stopped the practice.[6]

As the McKinsey report concluded: "The current trend – more and more companies discontinuing quarterly guidance and substituting thoughtful disclosures about their long-range strategy and business fundamentals – is a healthy one."[7] The ultimate test of any company's worth is how well it generates wealth compared with its peers. In other words, performance is relative to external peers rather than to self-determined targets.

The cessation of earnings guidance reduces the temptation to set a plethora of internal targets that, when aggregated, meet the group target. This gives leaders the opportunity to cease the target-setting practice at every level of the firm, thus going a long way toward eliminating the root causes of bad behavior, improving corporate governance and breaking away from an unhealthy focus on short-term performance. This, in turn, provides the necessary breathing space for experimentation and longer-term value creation. It also facilitates the realigning of executive rewards with longer-term success.

Many executives will worry about the reactions of analysts. In the end, the market will decide if less information is preferable to more. Doomsayers will point to companies such as AT&T whose shares plummeted 20 percent the day it announced that guidance would no longer be provided. However, the context is important. After all, AT&T also announced disappointing financial results at the same time. But when McKinsey analyzed 126 companies that discontinued guidance, they found that that they were as likely to see higher as lower total shareholder returns compared with the market.[8] But leaders can overcome the fear of analysts by building trust and delivering consistent results. Most leaders know that while performance promises might give the share price a short-term boost, their forecasts rely on a few key assumptions that are beyond their control.

The answer is that instead of taking the CEO's promises as the "contracted" number on which to base their performance expectations (and thus share price forecasts), analysts will make up the numbers themselves. But to do this they will have to find out how the company is performing to reach their conclusions. Analysts are invited into the company and executives share strategic information with them, but they must come to their own earnings predictions.

Breaking free from the fear of failing to meet analyst's expectations is the key step in removing the addiction to short-term targets.

Set relative improvement goals

While setting short-term targets such as "how much weight I need to lose" is natural to many people, targets in business invariably become fixed performance contracts between a manager and his or her subordinate, with the manager often separated from the work to be done. Targets are therefore set without intimate knowledge of the capability of the system or business. Quality legend Edwards Deming was vehemently against setting targets. In one of his many statements on the subject, he once said that goals are necessary for you and for me, but numerical goals set for other people, without a road map to reach the goal, have effects opposite to the effects sought.[9] He believed that targets are directed at the wrong people: "They arise from management's supposition that the production workers could, by putting their backs into the job, accomplish zero defects, improve quality, improve productivity and all else that is desirable. The charts and posters take no account of the fact that most of the trouble comes from the system."[10]

Abandoning short-term targets does not mean abandoning medium-term goals. But these goals should be aspirational and directional. They usually describe where a company wants to be in three or five years' time relative to its peers. For example, an Asian telecommunications company has set five three-year aspirational goals:

1. To become the number one Telco in the Asia Pacific Region based on EBITDA and ROIC.

2. To be in the top ten percent of its peers based on customer satisfaction and loyalty.

3. To be number one in terms of customer fulfillment (e.g. fastest broadband).

4. To be in the top three employers based on attracting and keeping the best talent.

5. To be in the top three based on an index of corporate social responsibility.

Goals framed in this way can be inspiring and motivating. They recognize that everything is connected and achieving any one goal depends on making good progress toward all the others.

Toyota, in addition to comparing performance against peers, sets three-year stretch goals such as: reduce packaging costs as a percentage of sales by 47 percent; reduce transportation costs as a percent of sales by 25 percent; reduce inventory by 50 percent and reduce parts per million defects by 75 percent.[11] These goals provide a context (but not a contract) for improvement and send a message to all teams that helps them to set their own goals.

Jack Welch was another champion of relativity. "For me," he said, "the idea is shun the incremental and go for the leap. Most bureaucracies – and ours is no exception – unfortunately still think in incremental terms rather than in terms of fundamental change. They think incrementally primarily because they think internally. Changing the culture – opening it up to the quantum change – means constantly asking not how fast am I going, how well am I doing versus how well I did a year or two before, but rather, how fast and how well am I doing versus the world outside. Are we moving faster, are we doing better against that external standard?"[12]

Once the relative performance goals are agreed upon, there is little need for nego-tiation. Performance is continuously evaluated based on progress toward them. Most companies set their sights on consistently being in the top quartile or decile of their peer group. In some industries, external peer comparisons are difficult to find, and even when they can be found there are often severe time lags. Most peer comparisons happen inside the organization as business units, branches, plants, brands, service teams and any business segment where there is more than one team are compared with each other. In these cases information is readily accessible.

Swedish distributor of plumbing and heating products Ahlsell is committed to relative improvement at every level. At company level, performance is measured relative to competitors, and at unit level, internal league tables are used. Together these provide a moving target and benchmark for driving continuous performance improvement.

Each month the performance of every unit is measured and league tables produced to identify the best and worst performers. The reporting system is fast and open. Everyone at every level in the company sees the results at the same time. Units are expected to use the information to govern themselves and control their own performance. There are no remote business controllers in Ahlsell who will do the job for the business teams. The exceptions where performance is not up to standard stand out clearly. There is no place to hide. At Ahlsell the culture is one of rewarding success (and learning from mistakes). Every month each staff member in the best-performing unit receives a bouquet of red roses delivered to their home. In addition the unit may be featured in the in-house journal that is published six times a year. "Why roses?" you may ask. Well, the Swedish word for rose is "ros," which is also the acronym for "return on sales" (RoS)!

Return on sales is the principal measure of performance in Ahlsell. Even the costs of central departments are expressed as percentage on sales and managed accordingly. In units that are achieving less than the "standard" RoS, only RoS is measured, but those achieving more than the "standard" are measured on the amounts of both profit and sales growth, using an index that combines the two factors. This underlines the policy that profit is the first priority and that it should be used to fund growth.

Enable teams to set their own goals

While group executives set high-level aspirational goals (e.g. to be number one in the region) within the organization, each team agrees its own relative goals (e.g.

to be in the first quartile of their peer group). When goal-setting responsibility is transferred to local teams, ownership and commitment is greatly strengthened. This doesn't mean that senior managers don't have a say. They do. Indeed, one of the key roles of senior executives is to set expectations and challenge (but not set) the strategies and goals that local managers propose. Stretch goals are not set down in detail but are based on broad-brush performance indicators such as cost-to-income ratios, stock-turns or cycle times. Managers usually know what their "baseline" performance needs to be to justify their existence (taking into account market movements). The outcome is that senior people have more time to engage in dialogue and debate about performance and goals. It is less a negotiation and more a positive conversation leading to action using all the experience of both parties.

Once leaders have abandoned negotiated (arbitrary) targets, they invariably begin to see performance improve way beyond the imagination of old-style target-setters. After all, what use is a negotiated cost increase of only 2 percent when the real potential is a *reduction* of 20 to 40 percent?

The context for success should be the team's view of best-in-class performance within its peer group and how long it will take to become number one. Managers are willing to accept (or propose) these stretch goals because their performance will not be evaluated and rewarded against them. They will subsequently be measured and rewarded using a range of relative indicators such as peer group performance, internal and external benchmarks and market movements. "Baseline" goals set a lower reference level of expectations.

Relative goals at Hilton Hotels

Hilton Hotels uses internal benchmarking to establish targets for its individual properties. It expects each property to close the gap each year between its current performance and that of one of Hilton's top-tier (or "green zone") hotels. This is how it works: Let's assume that a low-performing hotel has a current score of 50 on a particular metric such as customer satisfaction, whereas the best performance score for a comparable property is 90 – that's a difference of 40. Hilton would set a target for this property to close the gap by, say, 25 percent each year. So the target for next year would be 60 and the following year (assuming the best practice score doesn't move) of 67.5 and so on. This approach acknowledges that step-changes in performance take time. The Hilton approach to target-setting also recognizes that improvement becomes more incremental as properties approach performance "perfection."[13]

Stretching performance at a UK brewer

The CFO of a UK brewer describes what these changes meant for her managers. "The difference is that the old top-down controls have gone and we are now trusted to use our judgment to make sensible decisions based on the latest information we have. In effect, we don't have an agreement to achieve a certain fixed outcome. This gives us scope to make fast decisions. But the CEO is always challenging us. Are we beating the competition? Are we achieving world-class standards? The point is that he is not telling is to do it, he is challenging us to do it. There is a world of difference. We are responsible for our actions and accountable for our results. If we don't perform well enough against our peers, then our jobs are on the line. There are fewer hiding places in this style of management, but it's much more exciting."

One benefit is that the time this process takes is reduced dramatically. The experience with one sales team gets across the cultural change once managers have eradicated fixed targets. The goal-setting process now takes about one and a half days to agree, compared with three months before. This has freed up quality time for thinking about strategy rather than whether or not a particular number is right and how the team is going to achieve it. Managers had not been used to thinking like this before. In previous years, senior managers would say to the sales team that their target needed to be X and the sales team would say, "That's OK, we'll achieve it." Then, if they didn't achieve the target, senior managers would listen to their (very plausible) excuses that would point to ineffective marketing, poor service, lack of customer support and so forth. But now managers challenge them by requesting details of how they will achieve their improvement goals (which they have set) and what needs to be in place to ensure success. This means knowing how many new customers are required, what needs to be spent on marketing and how it is spent, and what actions production must take to ensure continuous and flexible supply. Instead of reams of numbers, senior people now need convincing answers. The point is that for the first time the sales team had to think deeply about their strategy and take accountability for achieving results. There is no hiding place. The result is much more focus on managing strategy and much less on managing the numbers.

Opening up the goal setting and planning process at HCL Technologies

CEO of HCL Technologies Vineet Nayar is renowned as a modern management innovator and has transformed HCL over recent years. The way he has changed the planning process is an example. Nayar explains his thinking: "So, what is the absolute power of the CEO? You come and make a presentation to me about what you're going to do, and I will sit in this chair God has given to me and tell you if I like the plan or not. The power of the hierarchy flows from the fact that I will comment on what you write. As my kids became teenagers, I started looking at Facebook a little more closely. It was a significant amount of collaboration. There was open understanding. They didn't have a problem sharing their status. Nothing seemed to be secret, and they were living their lives very openly, and friends were commenting on each other and it was working.

"Here is my generation, which is very security-conscious and privacy-conscious, and I thought, what are the differences? This is the generation coming to work for us. It's not my generation. So we started having people make their presentations and record them for our internal website. We open that for review to a 360-degree workshop, which means your subordinates will review it. Your managers will read it. Your peers will read it, and everybody will comment on it. I will be, or your manager will be, one of the many who read it. So, every presentation was reviewed by 300 to 400 people.

"What happened? There were three very interesting lessons that I learned. One, because your subordinates are going to see the plan, you cannot lie. You have to be honest. Two, because your peers are going to see it, you are going to put your best work into it. Third, you didn't learn from me. You learned by reviewing somebody else's presentation. You learned from the comments somebody else gave you. For the 8000 people who participated, there was a massive collaborative learning that took place."[14]

Use peer comparisons to challenge and stretch, not judge and blame

One way to challenge ambition is by showing managers that high performance has been achieved elsewhere. But how this process works determines its effectiveness. Benchmarks in the wrong hands can easily be seen as a "big stick" with which to beat managers into submitting to impossible targets and then judge and blame them if they don't perform. This problem is compounded if there is no culture in the organization of measuring success against the competition. Teams need to be given a reasonable period of time to make step-change improvements, and they need encouragement along the way.

Once external benchmarks are agreed, there is little need for "negotiation"; per-formance is continuously evaluated based on the progress made against them. Most teams set their sights on consistently being in the top quartile of their peer group. Typical goals include return on equity and cost-to-income ratio. The idea is for teams to make "step-changes" and thus be prepared to "think the unthinkable."

Once chosen, benchmarks can remain in place for years as businesses or processes improve against them. Remember, of course, that the benchmark figure itself is not static: it is, in effect, a moving target. Benchmarks can also be both external and *internal.* The power of ranking one business unit against another (providing you are comparing "apples" with "apples") should not be underestimated. Done well, it is a recipe for continuous improvement. Once again, it is the annual fixed performance contract that is the primary barrier. When removed, firms can begin to measure and reward progress toward a series of stretch goals that over time amount to a huge step-change in performance.

Be careful with league tables

No self-respecting manager wants to go to a meeting of his or her peers knowing that they have underperformed, let down the whole team and possibly drained the bonus pool. But peer pressure can be either positive or negative. Negative peer pressure leads to a "fortress" mentality. Local vested interests are paramount as managers seek to gain the maximum advantage (e.g. the most resources) from the corporate center. Other similar business units are seen as the "enemy." Positive peer pressure is about improving faster than rivals but within a climate of cooperation and sharing. Achieving a balance between competition and cooperation needs to be carefully managed. The defining difference is the rewards system. If rewards are set at the whole business level, then individual units have little need to act with a fortress mentality.

Peer comparisons can be inspiring if done well

Building "league tables" and using them to report performance can be a sensitive issue and can easily torpedo the implementation of relative measures. Ahlsell is an example of how to do it well. Ahlsell moved rapidly from only 14 profit centers to over 200 (including acquisitions). Each business area team (e.g. heating and plumbing) within each local unit is now a separate profit center. With so many profit centers, the system of using performance league tables (based on measures of return on sales and profits growth) to drive continuous improvement among front-line units has grown even stronger. The impact on performance can best be seen when new acquisitions are exposed to the league tables for the first time. Managers new to the culture who previously thought they were performing reasonably well are often shocked when they find they are so far behind existing Ahlsell units. This drives them forward. "If they can do it, then so can we" is their response. They are driven to find out what they need to do to improve and work their way up the league tables.

When former CFO Anton Stadelmann was asked how he encouraged people to share knowledge under a relative measurement system at Swiss Bank UBS Wealth Management, he replied that "we see internal benchmarking primarily as a basis from which to learn from each other, to institutionalize a learning organization. This means that we demand 'best practice' of ourselves, in the sense of sports, and that we are willing to learn from the best. This is inspiring. It releases power and energy. We will never measure bonuses by a formula. The bonus decision has always had soft components: Is someone willing to pass on his knowledge, to contribute to the development of others? This counts just as much as personal performance and is a very important part of cultural change … Our experience with the new platform shows us that it is all about giving and taking. We measure performance using several key performance indicators. No one is the best at everything, everyone can get better. If we help each other and learn from each other, in the end everyone wins. Anyone who misunderstands the internal benchmarks, along the lines of 'I have to keep secret what I do better than the others, so that I can stay number one' will never have a successful career in the bank and will feel it in their bonus. We live that and communicate that. We have institutionalized processes to foster the active sharing of experience. Employees can distinguish themselves here just as they do in their own performance."[15]

Ensure that league tables encourage the behavior you want

Designers of management information systems need to be wary of producing highly structured league tables or rankings lists. Choosing only one or even a few metrics can influence what teams focus on to the exclusion of other areas of work that can be equally (if not more) important. This was a real problem for the UK public sector when senior managers used league tables to spur improvements in National Health Service hospitals. They picked emergency-room units to make their point. Unfortunately, they committed their first mistake in selecting just one from a range of important indicators relating to a hospital's performance, thinking it could be isolated from what happened elsewhere. But Deming's law of "unknowable consequences" came into play as hospital managers pulled resources from trauma clinics and cancer wards in their efforts to reduce emergency-room waiting lists (the league table measure). Non-critical patients were left in ambulances and in corridors because the "waiting time" didn't officially start until they were registered. The UK press had a field day.

League tables, particularly in the public sector, should reflect the *rate of improvement* rather than just present a crude snapshot of different units at one moment. Thus the league table should not just compare one school's standardized test results or inspection reports against another but should also look at how well they improved with the inputs as their disposal. Done well, tables can create real peer pressure to perform and, in some cases, lead to the sharing of insights and knowledge.

Peer pressure is often at its most powerful when not "force-fed" in published league tables. The trick is just to publish *all* performance results – in other words, make them completely transparent so that every manager can see the performance of those teams they compare themselves with. The power of the system works on its own. Total transparency is the way forward.

Balance competition and cooperation

Most leaders want to create an organization without boundaries in which knowledge, resources and best practices are shared. The problem is that targets, incentives and budgets drive the opposite behavior. In fact, in most organizations, managers maximize their personal advantage (and bonuses) by *hoarding* rather than sharing knowledge. The real enemies appear to be other business units rather than external competitors. This is supported by recent research in the executive recruitment industry. The conclusions were that people rewarded for individual performance shared information least; those rewarded for team performance more; and those rewarded for company performance shared the most.[16]

Organizations that abandon fixed targets tend to experience high levels of knowledge-sharing primarily by removing the barriers such as targets, budgets, incentives and performance measures. Though they often compete in terms of results, teams see themselves as part of an integrated and interdependent organization that continuously connects and combines to produce results. One of the secrets of the Handelsbanken model is that while branches strive to be the best at achieving low costs and high profits, they *do not compete for customers*.

Egon Zehnder International (EZI) is a classic example of an organization with a strong culture of sharing. By 2009 EZI was the largest executive search firm in the world, with over 400 consultants in 36 countries. Since its foundation in Zurich in

1964, the firm has been a model of true collaboration: equality, collegiality, non-competitive internal sharing and non-hierarchical organizational structures. It operates with a single, firm-wide profit center. It selects employees whose interests dovetail with those of the firm. It develops people to foster deep collaboration. Its salaries are open for everyone to see. Clients are charged fixed fees and no bonuses are paid based on revenues earned. And EZI evaluates potential partners on how well they collaborate. The whole model is geared to putting clients' interests first, encouraging deep collaboration and the continuous development of the firm. It has been described as an "all for one, one for all" culture. In the executive search industry the average turnover rate among partners is 30 percent. EZI's attrition rate is dramatically lower, averaging only two to five percent annually.[17]

Conclusions

The dilemma that most leaders face is that they know the process of negotiating annual fixed targets rarely leads to innovative thinking or stretch goals, yet in the absence of any better ideas they are left with no choice but to continue with it. Goal-setting should be aspirational and medium-term, and the context for success should be set by the competition (either internal or external). Striving to be the best company in your industry or region or the best team in your company is highly motivating. It also enables the aspiring adaptive organization to finally ditch the annual budgeting process that takes so much time, costs far too much and drains the energy of managers to innovate and grow. All success is ultimately relative.

KEY POINTS

- Persuade all key influencers that increasing shareholder value is a long-term goal (the result of good management) rather than a short-term target (that can be manipulated)

- Stop being a slave to analysts. Most investors want to know if your performance is (a) reliable (steady improvements over time) and (b) better than peers (consistently near the top of the peer group). What merit is there in striving to meet a number promised a year earlier when the market has improved and competitors are showing much better results? The share price will only be marked down. Over time, it is only relative performance that matters.

- Support "continuous relative improvement" at every level. For example, a goal might be to move from third quartile to first quartile performance within three years. Organizations that have replaced fixed targets with relative goals and measures have experienced *better results* as their teams set ambitious goals without the fear of failing to meet them.

- Ensure that teams understand that their goals will not form the basis of a performance contract against which their performance will be evaluated. The idea is that ambitious goals above and beyond "business as usual" can only be achieved by encouraging innovation and step-changes in performance. Ensure that the executive team supports (but doesn't control) the goal-setting process. Its role is to challenge ambition, encourage innovation and engage in a dialogue about risks, rewards and resource requirements.

- Frame the success of teams in terms of internal peer-to-peer comparisons (top quartile, top decile or number one) based on a range of financial and non-financial indicators. Use peer comparisons to encourage teams to raise their game (if another team can do it, then why can't you?).

- Be wary of using league tables to make management judgments (peer pressure works best when it is understated – every team should know who they need to improve against).

- Balance internal competition and cooperation. Ensure that there is no competition for customers (for example, local versus national sales teams). Frame the success of support services teams in terms of performance benchmarks both against comparable external best practices and against internal peers.

## CHAPTER 8

Principle #8 – Rewards
Base rewards on relative performance, not fixed targets

You have to realize: if I had been paid 50 percent more, I would not have done it better. If I had been paid 50 percent less, then I would not have done it any worse.[1]

Jeroen van der Veer, former CEO, Royal Dutch Shell

To change mindsets, change rewards: the lessons from Groupe Bull

In the 1980s French computer company Groupe Bull was seen as a European challenger to IBM – a mainframe computer company that competed successfully for large IT contracts. But in the early 1990s the IBM comparison became too close for comfort as both companies misread the PC/server revolution that overtook the computer industry. By 1993 Bull was almost bankrupt, and in a desperate bid to turn it around, French government bureaucrats managed to persuade Jean-Marie Descarpentries to take over as chief executive.

Descarpentries' ideas and beliefs were formed while he was chief executive of the Franco-British company CMB Packaging (or Carnaud Metal Box). Before he arrived at Carnaud in 1982 it was a debt-laden French tin-can maker with a market value of $19m. By 1989 he had transformed the organization into a company worth $3bn – according to *Fortune* magazine, one of the best European corporate performances of the 1980s. In effect Descarpentries created a federation of entrepreneurs who successfully strived to multiply sales, profits and productivity.

Descarpentries repeated his rescue act at Bull. From losing FF5.1bn in 1993, the company recovered to make a profit of FF600m in 1997. In September 1997 Descarpentries and his CFO Camille de Montalivet decided to retire from business. Following their departure, profits plummeted to just FF17m in 1998. So what happened in the four years of Descarpentries' period in charge that was so effective yet so different?

Abandoning the negotiated budget

When Descarpentries arrived at Bull in 1993, managers thought he was a liquidator in disguise. Sales were declining, costs were too high and the company was laden with debt. If ever there was a "burning platform" that enabled radical changes to be made, this was it! But instead of slashing jobs and costs, he told people not to worry, to think positively, "be the best," but expect to be made accountable for performance.

The first casualty was the planning booklet – a 100-page document that was always far too optimistic and thus irrelevant as a managerial guide. He noted that in Bull, every department and business unit was earning money except the whole group! So he created a large number of profit centers and clear lines of performance accountability. He ensured that central departments were subjected to commercial pressures by charging their costs to profit centers. And he drove his message home by starting with head-office costs (he even moved his office from the 32nd to the 19th floor so that he would come into contact with most people in the building). His mantra on planning was that "speed is strategy." In other words, the budgeting process was an exercise in self-delusion. What he wanted were people at the front line who could weigh up threats and opportunities and use their judgment to make fast decisions without living in fear of budget variances. He also wanted regular forecasts that were fast and honest so that he could manage the expectations of shareholders.

Within a few years, Descarpentries had transformed the company. New shareholders (France Telecom, NEC and Motorola) were introduced, and by 1997 the government's holding was reduced to 17 percent. It was a textbook transformation not based on slash-and-burn downsizing, but on leadership qualities and faith in the capabilities of people that, given the right management climate, can achieve performance levels that the previous regime would have thought impossible. Simple monthly performance charts were displayed on notice boards and every team wanted to show how well they had done.

Rethinking performance evaluation and rewards

At the heart of the simple management model was the performance evaluation and appraisal system. This was based on the performance of business *teams*. Table 8.1 shows how a business unit's performance might be measured for a particular year. Both the corporate president and his executive committee would independently review performance. First they would examine growth versus last year and against the competition, bearing in mind all the competitive factors that pertained during the period. Secondly, they would examine profitability. Thirdly, they would look at debt. And finally they would look at certain operational factors such as employee turnover. This assessment sets the bonus levels of all managers and employees within that particular business unit. If a business unit team underperforms, they are given a second chance. But if they underperform again the following year they are likely to be moved elsewhere or face dismissal.

Maximum performance bonuses were set at 30–50 percent of salary at the executive level, 20–30 percent at the operating level and less (although not zero) at other

TABLE 8.1 Performance appraisal for business unit A

Measure	Weighting %	Total score*	Weighted score
Growth versus Previous Year	20	50	10
Growth versus Competition	20	40	8
Profit versus Previous Year	20	60	12
Profit versus Competition	20	50	10
Debt versus Previous Year	10	80	8
Quality Factors versus Previous Year	10	60	6
Executive Committee Evaluation			54%
President's Evaluation			60%
Final Evaluation			60%

* The total score (out of 100) is the average of all members of the executive committee including HR, manufacturing, R&D, finance, etc.

levels. But what was interesting was how the actual payout was calculated. If a business unit employee had a base salary of $50,000 and the maximum bonus was set at 30 percent or $15,000 and the formula set the payout at 60 percent of this, then the final payout would be $9000.

The key change: separating targets from rewards

According to former CFO Camille de Montalivet, "The whole point about the evaluation system is that it is seen to be fair and is *detached from both the target-setting and forecasting processes*. Stretch targets and the action plans and resources that they determine can be totally unrelated to the evaluation criteria, but the higher the level of achievement, the more likely is the team to receive the maximum payout. Also the components and weightings of the formula are cleverly thought out. With a strong bias towards growth, managers cannot simply 'make their target' by cutting discretionary expenditures such as training, marketing and satisfaction programs. And with the inclusion of qualitative factors (that can be any measures closely related to the needs of the business unit), there is a built-in assurance that managers will spend considerable effort on continuously improving the business. At senior levels of the organization, managers might have only part of their bonus linked to a business unit's performance and part linked to the group result. Share options have not been available due to the part government ownership and complications with other major shareholders."

The Bull story is a clear example of how targets and incentives influence how people think and behave. It tells us that disconnecting the management appraisal system from targets and budgets is the key to managing with an open and fair system in which people strive to do their best and senior managers enjoy unbiased information that helps them to make the right decisions. It also tells us that moving rewards from a few individuals to many small teams and then sharing the rewards fairly within the team is a key step in the right direction.

A debate is raging about the value of incentives

Since the Bull story happened in the mid-1990s, incentive compensation (especially at senior executive levels) has become a highly controversial subject. Indeed, it has been in the headlines recently for all the wrong reasons. In particular, at a time when many large organizations have suffered huge losses, the incentive element of total executive compensation has risen to extraordinary levels (especially in the US), often accounting for over 90 percent of the total compensation package. The "bonus culture" has been castigated by politicians, journalists and the general public. All have wondered how senior executives could walk away from failing companies with millions of dollars in their pockets when employees and shareholders received next to nothing. Jeroen van der Veer (until recently CEO of the giant Shell oil company) is one among many CEOs who have been criticized by shareholders – in his case for receiving a €1.36 million bonus even though the company failed to meet its performance targets.[2] Some commentators have even gone as far as blaming such excessive bonuses for unbounded risk-taking and even the credit crunch and subsequent recession.

Why Mintzberg believes incentives should be scrapped

Management guru Henry Mintzberg believes that executive bonuses should be scrapped altogether. "This may sound extreme," he notes, "but when you look at the way the compensation game is played – and the assumptions that are made by those who want to reform it – you can come to no other conclusion. The system simply can't be fixed. Executive bonuses – especially in the form of stock and option grants – represent the most prominent form of legal corruption that has been undermining our large corporations and bringing down the global economy. Get rid of them and we will all be better off for it."[3]

He lists five reasons why senior executives have failed their organizations.

1. They play with other people's money – the stockholders', not to mention the livelihoods of their employees and the sustainability of their institutions.

2. They collect not when they win so much as when it *appears* that they are winning – because their company's stock price has gone up and their bonuses have kicked in. In such a game, you make sure to have your best cards on the table, while you keep the rest hidden in your hand.

3. They also collect when they lose – it's called a "golden parachute." *Some gamblers!*

4. Some even collect just for drawing cards – for example, receiving a special bonus when they have signed a merger, before anyone can know if it will work out. Most mergers don't.

5. On top of all this, there are chief executives who collect merely for not leaving the table. This little trick is called a "retention bonus" – being paid for staying in the game![4]

Is Mintzberg right?

The evidence that incentives lead to higher profit performance is tenuous at best. Jensen and Murphy showed that there was virtually no link between how much CEOs were paid and how well their companies performed for shareholders.[5] Of the 12 companies employing the highest-paid CEOs in America in 2005, only four outperformed their peers in terms of shareholder return.[6] A study by McKinsey found an inverse correlation between top executives' pay and innovation. They suggest that the secret of persuading people to focus simultaneously on developing new businesses and managing current operations may be to rely less on pay for performance.[7]

Two schools of thought

The issue of "incentive compensation" (or "pay-for-performance") and its impact on management behavior has exercised the minds of academics and practitioners for decades. Broadly speaking, it is expected to achieve three aims: to attract, keep and motivate people. One school of thought believes passionately in the power of incentives to improve individual performance. They point to stories about Chinese peasants who, when allowed to keep a proportion of what they produced and sell it at market prices, saw their output rocket. They also point to the fact that those jockeys who are on commission win more races than those on retainers. Another school of thought believes that in a complex large organization that is well structured and aligned, such additional "bribes" are unnecessary – they are only needed to force people to do what they would not otherwise do naturally. So why do we need to (a) pay people for doing their job and (b) pay them again for doing it well? In other words, "incentives" – or bribes – are a poor and ineffective substitute for good management practices. This is backed up by dozens of studies over the past 75 years. A study by consultants William Mercer concluded that most individual merit or performance-based pay plans share two attributes: they absorb vast amounts of management time and resources, and they make everybody unhappy![8]

In an effort to reduce the complexity of these issues we will assume that incentives *can work* if people are paid more for producing more measurable output over a given period of time. Also, we can accept that owning a significant stake in a small-medium sized business can be highly motivating. But, in this chapter, these are not our primary concerns. We are more interested in the role that motivation, performance evaluation, recognition and rewards can play in maximizing the potential performance of a medium to large organization and its subunits.

Most rewards systems are designed to support a management model with short-term fixed targets at its core. To break free from command and control means tackling targets *and* rewards. There is no fudging the issue. It must be tackled head-on or the whole transformation will be in jeopardy. Principle #8 implores leaders to redesign their recognition and rewards systems to encourage ambition, team-working, collaboration and creativity. It is the seminal change along the road to the adaptive organization.

Implementation guidelines

- Assume that people are motivated by self-fulfillment, not financial incentives.
- Base rewards on teams rather than individuals.
- Evaluate and reward team performance "with hindsight."
- Give everyone a stake in success.
- Be wary of share options and restricted stock grants.
- Take employee recognition seriously.

Assume that people are motivated by self-fulfillment, not financial incentives

To many people, "motivation" and "rewards" go together like peaches and cream. They are inseparable. But if we just revisit Motivation 101 for a moment, we will recall that all the great social scientists of the past were careful to avoid this connection. In fact, if anything, there was almost a negative correlation. Herzberg's most telling point is often forgotten. He argued that the opposite of job dissatisfaction is *not job satisfaction*. In other words, if an employee is unhappy because of problems with pay, status or working conditions, he will not suddenly be motivated to greater effort and productivity by removing these problems. Motivation is intrinsic to the job. It is about responsibility, recognition, achievement and personal development, and no amount of pay on its own will drive a person to higher levels of achievement.

Theory X and Theory Y

In Douglas McGregor's terminology, adaptive leaders have rejected Theory X and embraced Theory Y management principles.[9] Just to remind you, Theory X states that people hate work, need to be told what to do, dislike responsibility and will do no more than the minimum stated in their employment contract unless driven to raise their performance by additional incentives. Theory Y assumes that people are motivated by self-esteem and personal development, and organizations produce better results by encouraging their people to be creative, to improve their skills and to derive satisfaction from their work. It is difficult to imagine how any business could succeed today without talented (and happy) people, satisfied (and profitable) customers and loyal (and trusted) investors. And it is equally hard to imagine any CEO voting for Theory X. They all have visions of being "team-based," "total quality," "knowledge-driven" and "customer-focused" organizations. *The problem is that they have Theory Y visions and Theory X systems.*

Why incentives switch off most people

When most people start a new job they are highly motivated to perform well. They want to prove that their new employer made a good decision in hiring them. They simply want to prove themselves. That's the *default state of motivation*. But what happens then is that these natural motivators are gradually switched off and the system (and worse, constantly tinkering with it) makes people think about incentives and what they need to do to achieve them. It diverts their attention from their main task (doing quality work for customers) to how to work "the system" to maximize their personal advantage. The challenge for most organizations, therefore, is not so much how to motivate people but how to *stop de-motivating them*.

The primary problem is that many leaders believe in the power of *individual rewards*. They see the organization as a machine whose parts can be manipulated to change power, speed and direction. People are an important part of this machine and their performance can be "fine-tuned" by changing *extrinsic* motivators such as fixed targets and financial inducements. These beliefs can be encapsulated in the expression "Do this and you'll get that." Its management origins come from piecework – the more repeatable tasks you perform, the you more you will earn. However, relating pay to performance when individual output can be precisely measured is one thing, but applying this approach to complex modern organizations where success is more dependent on design, innovation, quality and customer service is another.

It is hard to measure an individual's contribution

Another problem is that knowledge workers now form the vast majority of the workforce in most organizations today.[10] Whereas workers used to serve machines, machines now serve workers. While yesterday's car plants and textile factories employed few managers and thousands of "hands," today's banks and software companies employ many managers and thousands of "brains." Moreover, whereas industrial organizations were designed around separate functions, today's knowledge-based organizations (including most modern manufacturing firms) are designed around *interdependent parts*, so setting targets and incentives for each part doesn't make much sense. Nobel Prize-winning economist Herbert Simon makes this perceptive point: "If you could reliably and easily measure and reward individual contributions, you probably would not need an organization at all as everyone would enter markets solely as individuals."[11]

Do rewards work: what's the evidence?

The theoretical basis for individual incentives lies in experiments with dogs, rats and pigeons. With enough practice you can teach rats to ring a bell every time they want food. The step up to people is a small one. B.F. Skinner, an American who conducted many of these animal experiments, wrote the bible of the "behaviorist" school. He believed that people are nothing more than "repertoires of behaviors" and these can be explained by outside forces he called "environmental contingencies."[12]

In 1993 social scientist Alfie Kohn's article "Why Incentive Plans Cannot Work" in the *Harvard Business Review* generated more comment than just about any other article in the history of this famous journal. When asked, "Do rewards work?" Kohn replied that the answer depends on what we mean by "work." Research suggests that rewards succeed at securing one thing only: temporary compliance. When it comes to producing lasting change in attitudes and behavior, however, rewards, like punishment, are strikingly ineffective. Once rewards run out, people revert to their old behavior. They do not create an enduring commitment to any value or action. Rather incentives merely – and temporarily – change what we do.[13] When asked, "Do incentives build commitment?" Harvard professor Chris Argyris answered with a resounding "no." "In all my years as a change consultant," he noted, "I have repeatedly witnessed how offering employees the 'right' rewards creates dependency rather than empowerment."[14]

The point that Kohn and Argyris make is that various devices (including financial incentives) can be used to get people to do something they might not otherwise do, but this is a far cry from making people *want to do something*. It is the difference between what social scientists call "extrinsic motivation" (where the task is seen as a means to an end, a prerequisite for receiving a reward or avoiding a punishment) and "intrinsic motivation" (where the task itself is appealing). In other words, it is not the *amount* of motivation that matters, but its *type*. Kohn tells us that at least 70 studies have found that rewards tend to undermine interest in the task itself. "This is one of the most thoroughly replicated findings in the field of social psychology," he says. Psychologists tell us that people have a basic need to feel related and to belong, so the challenge is to create a workplace that is collaborative and feels like a community.[15] Table 8.2 shows the fault line between extrinsic and extrinsic theories of motivation.

"The desire of most people to do a good job is the most powerful asset a complex modern economy has," notes economist John Kay.[16] But despite hundreds of research studies over 50 years that tell us that extrinsic motivation doesn't work, most leaders remain convinced that financial incentives are the key to better performance. It remains one of the greatest barriers to transforming organizations from inflexible and expensive centrally controlled machines to adaptive and lean human networks.

TABLE 8.2 Two theories of motivation

	Extrinsic motivation	Intrinsic motivation
View of organization	**Organization is seen as a machine** whose parts can be managed by understanding their "cause-and-effect" relationships	**The organization is seen as a complex network of inter-dependent relationships** that requires the right leadership to release the untapped potential of human capital
Motivation theory	**Theory X**. People hate work, need to be told what to do, dislike responsibility, and will do no more than the minimum stated in their employment contract unless driven to raise their performance by additional incentives	**Theory Y**. People are motivated by self-esteem and personal development, and organizations produce better results by encouraging their people to be creative, to improve their skills, and to derive satisfaction from their work
Primary supporters	**Most "command and control" managers**	**Most "adaptive" managers, systems thinkers and social scientists** including Mayo, Maslow, McGregor, Argyris, Herzberg, Senge, Deming, etc.

Base rewards on teams rather than individuals

This may sound like a purely semantic point, but the language used in the organization to talk about rewards sets the tone for how people understand and internalize them. Most people, if told they will get a financial reward for doing task X instead of task Y, will choose task X. However, the incentive switch can be turned on and off in unpredictable ways. As we noted earlier, if employees feel that the target is too high or too low, it changes their behavior. The whole idea is dysfunctional. Now, if we turn around the discussion to talk about "teams," "rewards" and "sharing," the tone changes dramatically. People are no longer looking at what they can do to maximize their self-interest. They are now part of a team that if it performs well might provide some extra pay. But the reward is exactly that: something extra but not taken for granted.

Before Leyland Trucks implemented lean manufacturing, its performance culture was based on the "push" system of driving production to maximize volume and at odds with lean manufacturing principles based on the "pull" system of building to customer order. Leaders realized that here was a collision waiting to happen. So they scrapped decades of piecework-type incentives and introduced team-based rewards. The change in the language was crucial. Instead of talking about meeting volume targets, suddenly the conversation was about output quality, productivity, safety and customer delight.

The new language also touched another hotspot. Leaders knew that the primary concern of employees was not so much about pay and conditions but more about job security. So they told the workforce that the proposed changes were about meeting customer needs and that this was the best strategy to maintain their jobs. And the way to achieve this was to regulate production through the plant, focusing on high quality and waste reduction. Making thousands of trucks that they struggled to sell was no longer the way forward. A number of years later, Leyland Trucks won the "factory of the year" award and its employees have had a more secure future than in recent memory.

But the benefits didn't stop there. There is now a remarkable degree of cooperation between management and the shop floor. This even extends to smoothing production. For example, the company has introduced a scheme known as "Additional Vacation Days." This means that if there is a requirement to increase production, then employees accept the need to work longer hours *at no extra cost* and then receive those hours back in quieter times (usually tacked on to a public holiday or weekend). They receive around two to three weeks' notice. Workers don't like this arrangement, but they understand that it is all part of improving profitability and thus their own security of employment (the number-one objective of all managers and employees at the company). However, this agreement needs constant communication to remind employees of the benefits. This change alone contributed to a reduction in costs of 7.6 percent. Other seasonal fluctuations are managed through temporary workers.

"Star" performers often damage the team

The evidence on the impact of attracting "star performers" is sobering. When looking at what happened after "star" investment analysts moved from one company to another, Harvard professor Boris Groysberg found that bad things started to happen: "The star's performance plunges, there is a sharp decline in the functioning of the group or team the person works with, and the company's market value falls." In particular, "46 percent of the research analysts did poorly in the year after they left one company for another … their performance plummeted by an average of about 20 percent and had not climbed back to the old levels even five years later."[17] Contrast this with the experience at NUMMI (New United Motor Manufacturing)'s plant in Freemont, California in the 1980s, a joint venture between General Motors and Toyota (but managed by Toyota). The new management took a bunch of dysfunctional "F" players, retrained them and put them into a great system – and before long the plant was outperforming every other in the US. The lesson is that great systems are likely to be more important than great people.

In 2005, Nucor handed out more than $220 million in profit-sharing and bonuses to the workforce (the average Nucor steelworker took home nearly $79,000 in 2005). Add to that a $2000 one-time bonus to mark the company's record earnings and almost $18,000, on average, in profit sharing. Not only is good work rewarded, but bad work is also penalized. Bonuses are calculated on every order and paid out every week. If workers make a bad batch of steel and catch it before it has moved on, they lose the bonus they otherwise would have made on that shipment. But if it gets to the customer, they lose three times that.

Managers' pay is also at risk. Department managers typically get a base pay that's 75 percent to 90 percent of the market average. But in a great year that same manager might get a bonus of 75 percent or even 90 percent, based on the return on assets of the whole plant. Executive pay is geared toward team building. The bonus of a plant manager depends on the entire corporation's return on equity. So there's no glory in winning at your own plant if the others are failing. There's a healthy competition among plants and even among shifts, balanced with a long history of cooperation and idea-sharing. The pay of CEO Daniel Di Micco is also based on performance. In 2005, he collected a salary and bonus precisely 23 times that of his average steelworker. He gets few stock options, and most of his restricted stock and other longer-term bonuses don't materialize if the company doesn't beat the competition and outpace a sample group of other high-performing companies.[18]

In modern organizations, results are invariably due to the combined efforts of many people and teams. Even taking the example of a salesperson "winning" a major order, can anyone really say that they achieved that on their own? In most companies this is doubtful. There are usually back-up support teams involved in managing brands, designing solutions, preparing quotations, supporting demonstrations, doing cooperative marketing and so forth.

Even salespeople are part of a team

But abandoning individual sales incentives takes a leap of faith. One company that did this many years ago is Marshall Industries, a large US distributor of electronics (acquired by AvNet in 1999). In the early 1990s, CEO Rob Rodin decided to eradicate all incentives for the sales force including commissions, bonuses and other incentives. In the following six years productivity tripled. Distortions that used to mask real results – people shipping early to meet quotas, pushing costs from one quarter into the next to make the numbers and many other aspects of gaming – had disappeared. Rodin explained the effect: "Look at the trust that develops when everyone's on profit-sharing." But his colleagues remain unconvinced. "I have to explain the system to somebody every day," he said. "Except customers – they get it right away."[19]

According to John Seddon, a UK psychologist and business consultant, "in every case I know where the [sales] incentive scheme has been scrapped and replaced by salaries for the sales force, cooperation between salespeople has improved, customer service has improved and best of all sales have improved. Moreover, turnover of the sales force goes down. It is relevant to note that salespeople play the system by moving between organizations, taking their customers with them, as soon as the incentive system starts to work against them. Suppose you do find a salesperson whose sales are reliably better than others'. The reason will probably be *method* – what the salesperson does, how he or she spends his or her time. If and when this is the case, it is the leader's job to work on method: it is part of the system. In all organizational tasks, the major cause of differences in performance are beyond the attributes of individuals. It is the reason why people find appraisals so demotivating.[20]

MIT professor Edgar Schein, an acknowledged expert in the field of corporate culture, puts the problem of changing the incentive mindset down to the sacred cow of individual accountability. "No matter how much team-work is touted in theory," he notes, "it does not exist in practice until accountability itself is assigned to the whole team and until group pay and reward systems are instituted."[21]

Are team-based rewards a charter for free-riders?

Some people might argue that moving incentives away from individual perform-ance is a charter for "free riders" – those managers who keep out of the limelight yet produce little by way of results. The experience at Southwest and Handelsbanken, however, suggests that this is not as big a problem as feared. In a team-based organization driven by peer pressure, free riders are exposed very quickly and replaced by people more willing to commit themselves to team-based performance challenges.

Evaluate and reward team performance "with hindsight"

Many incentive compensation schemes are based on reaching an agreed financial target. Though they typically set the target at "100 percent," management bonuses usually begin at 80 percent of target and end at 120 percent of target (see Figure 8.1).

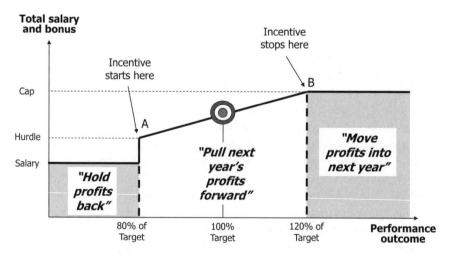

Adapted from HBR article "Corporate Budgeting is Broken – Let's Fix It" by Prof. Michael Jensen, November 2001.

FIGURE 8.1 Why traditional approaches fail

This can produce perverse effects. For example, if managers think they can't make the minimum target (at point A) then there is no incentive to maximize profits beyond that point. Nor does it matter if they miss it by a small or a large amount. They might as well ensure that next year is as good as possible (for example, by bringing spending plans forward), causing the current year to miss the target by a wide margin. Likewise, if the year has been exceptionally good and the maximum bonus is reached with something to spare (at point B), then again it is in their interest not to increase profits beyond that point, but instead to move that extra profit potential into the following year.

Only between points A and B does the incentive scheme encourage managers to maximize profits. But, in this case, the pressure is to hit the maximum bonus by fair means or foul. Booking next year's revenues in the current year and deferring current expenses into next year are just a few of the games that are commonly played. However, while all these games might be rational to managers, they are not so for shareholders, who would prefer to maximize performance in every year.

Most executives think targets motivate. They do – they motivate people to make the target. This is not the same as being motivated to do a better job or to improve the work. The targets regime often leads to a culture of fear and cheating. Many leaders maintain that the "cheats" are few and promise to find them out. But they miss the point. Cheating is an inevitable response to the targets regime; it is a systemic phenomenon, understandable and predictable.

One solution, according to Harvard professor Michael Jensen, is to provide an open linear relationship between results and rewards. He believes that leaders should "adopt a purely linear pay-for-performance system that rewards actual perform- ance, independent of targets. In other words, a manager receives the same bonus for a given level of performance whether the target happens to be set beneath that level (point A in Figure 8.1) or above it (point B). Removing the kinks eliminates the incentives to game the process."[22]

While this is undoubtedly a step in the right direction (and overcomes many of the "gaming" problems), the approaches that we have seen work best have different characteristics. Moving from absolute to relative targets and from individual to team-based rewards are perhaps the key differences.

Fixed performance contracts have become the *de facto* standard in most large organizations today. Some are explicit agreements (actually signed by the parties to them), but most are implicit. In other words, teams know what to expect if they fail to meet targets. Some leaders have rejected this approach. They have moved to something more akin to a "relative improvement contract" whereby teams are expected to improve their performance relative to others (these can be internal or external peers) or benchmarks.

Though freed from the fixed performance contract, managers must still perform to high levels of expectation. But performance needs to be evaluated *after the event* rather than based on a fixed target. Steve Morlidge, former change leader at Unilever, believes this is a critical change: "It is only after the event that you can judge whether performance is good in the context of actual market conditions, for example, how stretching the target *actually* was. 'What was the inflation rate? What impact did the floods have? What was the impact of our biggest customer going bankrupt?' It is only after the event that you can determine whether in achieving your goals you have beaten the competition or lost ground against them. 'Did we gain market share or lose it?' It is only after the event that you are able to judge whether performance in any one period has been achieved at the expense of the future. 'Did we cut marketing expenditure or launch a new product just before year end?' 'Was the year-end spike caused by responding to consumers or by forcing volume through sales channels?'"

The amount of subjectivity and judgment in this case is not to everyone's taste. But as Morlidge says, "While the process of calculating rewards is based on judgment, it is done using a rigorous process, one which is transparent and one which is immune to the exercise of prejudice or favoritism. It is, in effect, like the exercise of the law, using laws of evidence."[23]

Give everyone a stake in success

Share ownership and group-wide profit-sharing schemes are becoming increasingly popular, but many leaders understand that while their direct motivational powers are limited, it is an important part of building the right managerial culture. As Jeffrey Pfeffer notes: "Merely putting in ownership schemes without providing training, information sharing and delegation of responsibility will have little effect on performance because even if people are more motivated by their share ownership, they don't necessarily have the skills, information or power to do anything with that motivation."[24] However, except in rare cases such as the John Lewis Partnership in the UK and Whole Foods Market in America, share ownership has not been a part of the employee rewards agenda. But employee share-ownership plans that result from a crisis can lead to quite different outcomes from those that result from philosophical and cultural beliefs.

Get the timing right

In other words, the timing has to be right. Taking over a business in crisis can lead to bigger problems. Take the case of United Airlines. An employee buyout occurred in 1985 following the company's attempt to break a pilots' strike by replacing them with trainees. From that point on, an employee stock ownership plan began to acquire shares, but it wasn't until the mid-1990s that the investment community allowed it to happen. Employees agreed to swap wage concessions for stock, eventually acquiring 55 percent of the equity and gaining veto powers on the board of directors. For five years, employees agreed to hold wages below the industry average as a way to pay off the shares. From 1995 until 2000 it looked like a smart move. United's business (and share value) appeared to recover. But when the agreement came to an end and wages reverted to industry averages, the fortunes of the business and the share price tumbled. Morale collapsed. Trust in management evaporated. The company had three different executive teams in 18 months. United then filed for bankruptcy protection.

So what went wrong? It wasn't the principle of employee ownership that killed the company, which was in a parlous state before it happened. The problem was that by holding down their wages, the actions of employees masked the real problems of a bloated bureaucracy and heavy costs. They wouldn't vote to drastically reduce jobs. In other words, acquiring ownership doesn't make them think and act like shareholders.[25]

Get the design right

Group profit-sharing schemes also have a checkered history. How they are designed matters greatly. In 1990 Dupont pulled the plug on one of the most ambitious and closely watched incentive pay programs in American history – a plan in which the company's 20,000 fibers-division employees had a portion of their pay increases at risk. Employees received bigger increases if DuPont exceeded its profit goals, but smaller payouts or none at all if goals weren't met. Two years into a three-year trial, DuPont canceled the plan, partly in response to plummeting employee morale: the 1990 recession had made it almost certain that, for the first time, the company wouldn't reach its goals.[26] The problem is that employees feel good when they get rewards, but the moment the rewards stop, they feel resentful. This phenomenon, often known as entitlement creep, is a common problem with pay-for-performance schemes. "In a recent quarter I got 96 percent of the maximum bonus. Why was I docked the 4 percent?" is the typical question.

However, implementing a carefully crafted profit-sharing scheme can send a powerful message to employees. Handelsbanken and Southwest Airlines have both given all their employees a stake in success through their profit-sharing schemes. Southwest's Herb Kelleher is in no doubt of its success. "The profit sharing is an expense we'd like to be as big as possible so our people get a greater reward," he notes.[27] When the first Gulf War broke out, the cost of jet fuel rocketed. So Kelleher wrote a memo to his pilots saying that fuel needs to be cut back. "And in one week our costs went down, just like that. Now let me contrast that with the consultant who wanted to set up an incentive program whereby pilots' pay would be increased to the extent they conserved fuel. I kept telling the guy we didn't need to do that. Our pilots just did it on their own."[28]

The profit-sharing plan at Southwest started in 1973 and is at the heart of its compensation and benefits program. All employees qualify on January 1 following the commencement of their employment. Fifteen percent of pre-tax profits are paid into the profit-sharing pool and this is shared across all employees according to base salary. The payments go into a retirement fund for individual employees. While employees are free to increase that amount, 25 percent of the profit-sharing fund is used to purchase Southwest shares. Pilots and flight attendants have other stock option plans.

Like Southwest, Handelsbanken executives believe that its group-wide profit-sharing scheme is an important element in removing the "defend your own turf" mentality that pervades many organizations. It avoids the problem of rewards becoming entitlements that, if not received, lead to a disaffected and, in some cases, demoralized workforce. Another feature of the Handelsbanken/Southwest schemes is that they don't make an annual cash payment – they pay the bonus into an employee pension plan. This has the effect of minimizing any fallout from a poor year. In other words, employees are not planning to spend their bonus on "something special" and then become disappointed when it doesn't happen. The pension payment approach cushions poor years but also has the effect of relating performance to the share price (both pension schemes own a substantial element of company stock).

Be clear about the purpose of profit sharing

The profit-sharing system can only be understood in the context of its purpose. It is not intended to be an incentive for individuals to pursue financial targets; rather, it is intended as a reward for their collective efforts and competitive success. It might be called a "dividend" on their human capital. Many people find the lack of incentives hard to understand. Jan Wallander's answer is that "beating the competition or one's peers is a far more powerful weapon than financial incentives. Why do people need cash incentives to fulfill their work obligations to colleagues and customers? It is recognition of effort that is important. Managers will only strive to achieve ambitious goals if they know that their 'best efforts' will be recognized (and not punished) if they fail to get all the way."

Egon Zehnder International is another firm that pays its partners through a combination of salary, equity shares of the firm and annual profits. There is some variation in salaries to reflect different costs of living between, for example, New York and Kuala Lumpur. With regard to equity ownership, each partner has an equal number of shares no matter how long his or her tenure. When a partner leaves, the shares are sold back. Thus the longer they stay with the firm the more value they receive. Compensation is totally open. EZI reckons that money is simply a by-product of one's work. In order to be focused on the most appropriate goal – solving the client's problem – one has to be focused on doing the best work. EZI disdains the common professional service firm practice of compensating professionals on their individual performance (mainly the size of their client billings and selling prowess). Instead, compensation is seniority-based and transparent.[29]

In 2010 more than 70,000 staff at one of the UK's most successful retailers, the John Lewis Partnership have been handed a bonus equal to nearly eight weeks' pay after the group posted a near-10 percent rise in profits. The payout is equal to 15 percent of salary, and all permanent staff, from the mail room to the chairman, get the same level of reward.[30]

Be wary of share options and restricted stock grants

Most large companies pay their executives large amounts of stock options in addition to large salaries and cash bonuses. The average corporation in the United States distributes 75 percent of their total stock options to only five top executives. At Whole Foods Market, the exact opposite is true: the top 16 executives have received 7 percent of all the options granted, while the other 93 percent of the options have been distributed throughout the entire company.[31]

There is one major snag with fixed-price options. Around 70 percent of the stock price of individual companies is driven by market and industry factors and only 30 percent by individual company performance.[32] This means that executives could easily get a "free ride" when the market is improving and similarly suffer unfairly when the market is declining. Alfred Rappaport, one of the founding fathers of value-based management, believes this is wrong. "Fixed-priced options reward executives for any increase in the share price – even if the increase is well below that realized by competitors or by the market as a whole," he notes. He believes in the power of shareholder value measures to evaluate and reward executive performance, provided that such measures are based on returns equal to or better than those earned by the company's peer group or by broader market indexes.[33] Erik Stern of Stern Stewart also believes fixed options are flawed. He favors three types of relative measure. The first is beating peers based on exceeding the cost of capital. The second is based on an industry league table. And the third is based on a country league table. "The stellar performers are those that rank highly in all three over a five-year period," notes Stern.[34]

American Express is one company that has learned the lessons on executive pay and share options.[35] In early 2008 the Amex board gave CEO Ken Chenault options on 2,750,000 shares – a mega-grant by any definition. However, to receive the full grant, he must beat several goals over the next six years, an unusually distant time horizon. These include:

- Earnings per share must grow at least 15 percent a year on average

- Revenues must grow at least 10 percent a year

- Return on equity must average at least 36 percent per year

- Total return to shareholders must beat the S&P 500 average by at least 2.5 percent a year.

In recent years, companies have scaled back their interest in stock options. This has been caused by two practical considerations. The popping of the tech bubble rendered many options worthless, forcing companies to seek other ways to entice executives to stick around. Then came the Financial Accounting Standards Board's FAS 123R, which, by requiring the expensing of options, removed the cost advantage that options once held for US companies. Stock options can also lead to unethical behavior. One study of 435 companies comparing those that restated their earnings with those that didn't showed that those that restated them had a higher proportion of executives' compensation tied to share options.[36]

As they shopped for alternatives, directors first settled on time-vesting restricted stock. That pay form had lost much of its popularity in the era of stock-option mania. But the full-value shares remained attractive as executive compensation because, while the price may fall, the stock retains some value. To some companies, restricted stock also seemed a more shareholder-friendly choice, partly because it creates less dilution than options. Since one restricted share has more value than one stock option, companies need to issue fewer shares under a restricted-stock scheme. But investors don't like restricted stock either. Some call it "pay for stay," since executives need only avoid getting fired to earn their stock.[37]

Take employee recognition seriously

Respondents in a recent McKinsey survey viewed three non-cash motivators – praise from immediate managers, leadership attention (for example, one-on-one conversations) and a chance to lead projects or task forces – as no less or even more effective motivators than the three highest-rated financial incentives: cash bonuses, increased base pay and stock or stock options. The survey's top three non-financial motivators play critical roles in making employees feel that their companies value them, take their well-being seriously and strive to create opportunities for career growth. These themes recur constantly in most studies on ways to motivate and engage employees.[38]

Recognition (as opposed to rewards) is one of the most potent tools in the manager's toolbox, but it is rarely used to maximum effect. Going out of your way to praise someone's effort or performance can make their day. A birthday card, some flowers or a book voucher says that your work has been recognized – these are all simple expressions that say "thank you." And it's inexpensive!

Toyota's US plants have what they call a "perfect attendance" award each year. Attendance at Toyota is critical because associates are skilled members of a team and staffing is lean. Those who make the perfect attendance club are invited to a big banquet held at a major convention center. About a dozen brand-new Toyota vehicles are paraded on stage. A lottery picks the winners who take ownership of the vehicles. About 60–70 percent of employees make the club: that is, not a single day of missed work or lateness.[39]

Southwest Airlines takes employee recognition seriously. If you walk around Southwest's head office in Dallas you will see thousands of photographs and certificates on the walls concerned with employees and teams and what they have done for the organization. Kelleher has never believed that compensation was the primary motivator. "If somebody was working just to be compensated," he says, "we probably didn't want them at Southwest Airlines. We wanted them working in order to do something in an excellent way. And to serve people. So we said to our employees: This is a cause, this is a crusade. This isn't just an ordinary corporation, and you're doing a lot of good for everybody. We're proud of you, and we want you to have psychic satisfaction when you come to work. We get people who take a 25 percent cut in pay because they say: We just want to enjoy what we're doing. They've done pretty well with their 401(k) and stock options. But those are variable. People are willing to take that risk and take lower pay because they want to feel fulfilled in the workplace."

The important issue is not so much the financial payout but the recognition of the contribution that employees make to the organization's success. The cases of Toyota, Handelsbanken, Whole Foods and Southwest all reject the idea that financial incentives are necessary to reinforce performance improvement.

Conclusions

Nothing undermines the best intentions of an adaptive organization like a misaligned or ill-thought-out method of evaluating performance and rewarding people. Rewards should be disconnected from fixed targets and based on a fair, open, and agreed formula underpinned by relative performance measures. Many reward systems carry a great deal of "excess baggage" from a company's history. They are notoriously difficult to change. But change they must if an adaptive organization is to become a reality. The best approach is for a senior team to thrash out a set of common principles to which everyone can agree. A combination of group-wide and team-based rewards based on relative performance seems to be the way forward. Perhaps the secret of motivation is to make everyone believe that the job they do is important. As Herzberg once said: "If you want someone to do a good job, then give them a good job to do."[40]

KEY POINTS

- Base your assumptions about human motivation on Theory Y (people want to learn, develop and improve and will work hard if the task is appealing) rather than Theory X (people are lazy and will only stretch their performance if they receive extra financial incentives).

- Choose whether you want to implement a group-wide profit-sharing scheme or a team-based rewards scheme (or a combination of both) at each level. "Sell" the scheme on the basis of everyone sharing in the exceptional performance of the company or team.

- Breaking the direct connection between financial rewards and fixed targets is the crucial step if firms really expect managers to strive for exceptional performance. So evaluating performance with the benefit of hindsight is the way to go. However, this involves some judgment, usually based upon agreed success factors. Agreeing success criteria for each team is important to establishing fairness in the process.

- Spreading share ownership and implementing group-wide profit-sharing schemes are becoming increasingly popular, but many leaders understand that while their direct motivational powers are limited, it is an important part of building the right culture. With regard to profit shares, pay them into a deferred pension plan so that employees don't feel the demotivating "hit" of a poor year.

- Providing shares (in the form of options or restricted stock) as "benefits" should be examined very closely, as such benefits can lead to short-term actions aimed at influencing the short-term share price rather than longer-term success (there is evidence that accounting restatements are linked to the use of share options). Also, if offering options, spread them widely around the management team.

- Employee recognition is often a more powerful motivator than financial rewards. Simple ideas often work best, such as giving an employee an award directly from a customer he or she serves.

## CHAPTER 9

Principle #9 – Planning
Make planning a continuous and inclusive process, not a top-down annual event

Beyond budgeting is not merely a negative idea that trashes budgeting. Instead, it is a positive idea that uses the abandonment of budgeting as a trigger for improving the entire management control process. Budget abandonment forces deeper and broader examination of how organizations should be managed.

Charles Horngren , Foreword, *Beyond Budgeting*, 2003

Moving beyond budgeting at Tomkins

With sales of around £3 billion ($5bn) and 30,000 employees, Tomkins is a UK-based global engineering and manufacturing group that operates in three business segments: Industrial and Automotive; Air Systems Components; and Engineered and Construction Products. It has around 100 direct reporting units with average annual sales between $25m and $400m. Prior to 2002 the group's management model was based on detailed systems of planning, budgeting and control. Managers were accountable for meeting the plan, so most would attempt to negotiate low targets that would be loaded with contingencies in case performance was tougher than expected. The pressure to perform was based on the fear of a unit being sold if it failed to hit its targets. This severely restricted what managers would do. For example, they would be reluctant to make longer-term investments and would be hesitant about taking strategic risks. The result was that investors perceived the company as just a bundle of financial variables that didn't have a coherent or imaginative strategy, and consequently the share price traded at a discount.

Rethinking targets

The arrival of Jim Nicol as CEO in 2002 brought about a significant change. He wanted to free managers from top-down control and encourage them to improve their businesses rather than just meet the numbers. Instead of setting detailed targets, each manager now had a framework of performance expectations to work within. It was known as 10:10:10 (10 percent sales growth, 10 percent return-on-sales and 10 percent after-tax return on invested capital). However, managers' acceptance of this new freedom was patchy. Some used it to rapidly improve their businesses while others were slow to change their ways.

Though well run, Tomkins was an "old economy" company. Its businesses were either number one or two in their markets, but growth was too often pedestrian. According to CFO of global operations Dan Disser, one of the reasons was that the budgeting process was a disincentive and a barrier to growth. Budgets focused on internal negotiations instead of business improvement. As Disser explains, "The budget process created inertia to change. Managers were not short of good ideas but because they had already reached their targets they held their ideas back for the following year." The company's annual planning process was too detailed, protracted and expensive (it took four months to complete), leading to inflexibility and dysfunctional behavior. It was a "perform or go" culture based upon annual targets that people had to meet. Every six months managers would prepare a revised forecast that informed them about the year-end outlook and what action they should take to meet the numbers. Reporting was slow. The month-end books took five working days to close and reports weren't available to managers for a further five days (that's 10 days after the month-end). This meant that the company was flying blind for much of the time in the rapidly changing markets of many of its businesses. Compounding the problem was a system of capital allocations based more on whether a business had achieved its numbers the previous year than on the economic merits of a proposal. A project's value potential was rarely explored.

Focusing on continuous improvement

The initiative for change came from Dan Disser, CEO Jim Nicol and CFO Ken Lever. The previous regime had made much of the strategic planning process. But as Disser notes, there was nothing "strategic" about it. Soon after Nicol joined the company he attended one of these "budget negotiations dressed as a strategic plan presentations" and asked the presenting team shortly after the proceedings began, "Why am I here? Why is no one is talking about strategy or planning to talk about strategy?" From that point on, the focus has been on the present and future performance rather than the past. Over the next few years Nicol and the Tomkins finance team set out to design and implement an alternative management model based on a quarterly business review supported by fast-rolling forecasts and real-time capital spending authorizations. The aim was to improve response times in all business operations and focus on continuously improving business processes.

There is no longer any negotiation of targets. Businesses now set their own goals that are *no longer agreed to by head office*. In other words, there is *no longer a fixed performance contract between operating businesses and the corporate center*. Expectations are set by the 10:10:10 formula. If managers don't consistently get near these parameters (with the possible exception of the growth parameter) then their businesses are effectively in the portfolio danger zone. The focus now has switched to continuous improvement. This is based on achieving as much growth in *economic profit* (defined as EBITDA plus or minus net investment/divestment in sustaining working capital and capex, less tax paid, less a charge on capital at Tomkins' weighted average cost of capital applied to the total investment in the business unit, including any goodwill) over the prior year as possible. As Disser explained: "No one cuts the shareholder a break when the business doesn't perform in a tough year, so managers simply have to maximize economic profit in every circumstance. Even in a lousy market, managers still have options to improve. For example, they can shrink their capital base, improve their margins and reduce their costs. Economic profit makes them think like business owners."

In the old system managers produced what was called a financial digest. This was due on the eighth working day following the month end. It was geared to explaining variances from budget and whether any further action was needed to meet the agreed year-end targets. While six-quarterly rolling forecasts were part of this process, they were not taken seriously beyond the fiscal year-end. They were also the last thing to be done during the monthly closing process and usually by the finance people. In other words, they were neither taken seriously nor were they treated as a key part of the management process. Since the changes, however, the forecasting process is now *the key management tool* for managing the business at every level. As Disser notes, "there is now as much energy put into preparing the forecasts as closing the books."

While there is still an annual strategy formulation process where the big issues are discussed (e.g. Have we got the right products? Are we focused on the right markets? Have we got the right value proposition?), action planning is now a quarterly event. These quarterly business reviews together with supporting six-quarter rolling forecasts are completed around three weeks after the quarter end. Forecasts have been separated from performance measurement (and targets – there are no targets), thus taking much of the gaming out of the forecasting process. However, an annual financial plan remains, though it is simply the four quarterly forecasts that fall within the fiscal year. This is what is communicated to analysts.

Switching from annual budgets to rolling forecasts

Another important element of the forecasting process is the monthly "flash" forecast. These forecasts are now prepared in the middle of each month (when there is more time available) and look to the end of the current month and a further two months ahead. So Jim Nicol and other leaders at the center now receive monthly results and short-term forecasts for the following two months, the current quarter and the full year *four working days prior to the month-end*. Given that average organizations take six days to close the books, a further 11 days to finalize reports and 15 days (concurrently) to prepare forecasts, this is a real breakthrough in information management.

Forecasts are "bottom-up." As Disser notes, "I spend a lot of time helping business unit teams to improve their forecasting processes. Some are excellent and have coherent, integrated systems. They spend time talking to production and marketing. It is no longer an 11th-hour process done by finance. Others are hopeless. They have a long way to go. But overall it's improving and we're pleased with the results. We're getting much more visibility into the business. By separating forecasts from targets and measures, we've also taken the gaming out of the system. The serial optimists have gone. If anything, forecasts err on the low side, which is the right side to be on. More importantly, the businesses now see that forecasting is principally for them, a valuable tool in managing for value, not an academic exercise for the center."

Quarterly business reviews are not financially oriented. They focus on strategy and improvement initiatives rather than the numbers. Group CFO Ken Lever and Dan

Disser meet with operating business CFOs the week before the business reviews each quarter to address the "numbers issues."

Tomkins maintains a comprehensive reporting and control system. As Disser explains, "We have robust grass roots, 'meat and potato' controls – like periodic, line-by-line balance sheet reviews with our business unit CFOs and their staff. We will comply fully with the spirit of Sarbanes-Oxley but we think it goes over the top and do not intend to alter our pragmatic approach to life." As noted earlier, at monthly intervals managers provide "flash" month-end forecasts 4 working days *prior to the month-end* based on local business modeling, key value drivers and exceptions analysis. The books are then closed six days after the month-end.

The company reaped significant benefits from the new management model including faster, more relevant information, the elimination of gaming, a transition to managing the future rather than the past, the ability of front-line teams to manage the business rather than be stifled by head-office management and a stronger and more efficient finance function. Finance has now more time to focus on supporting key decision makers and provide more insightful analysis.

By 2005 Nicol, Lever and Disser had injected new energy into Tomkins and transformed its fortunes. The organization became much more entrepreneurial and the changed management model helped to build a more adaptive organization. In 2008–9 the company was hit hard by the global collapse in the automotive and construction industries but was able to take swift action to avoid a total calamity. In 2010 it recovered well as markets improved. In September 2010 its share price rocketed as private equity companies took an interest and it was sold for around £3bn.

Continuous change means continuous planning

Most organizations are stuck in the same place that Tomkins was in 2003. Given today's levels of uncertainty and turbulence, isn't it astonishing that most firms still spend three to six months each year hammering out a detailed plan and budget for the year ahead? This process not only takes too long and costs too much, but it also adds little value as key assumptions remain valid for a few weeks or months if you're lucky and drive the kind of "meet-the-numbers" behavior (greed and self-interest) that would embarrass most self-respecting CEOs.

So how has this process survived intact for so long? The likely answer is that it is the core management process in most organizations as it ties together annual targets, management incentives, resource allocations and performance measures, and leaders are reluctant to replace it. In other words, the perceived risks of change are too high. Besides it is not clear what they would replace it with. What is the alternative and how does it work?

As we noted in the Tomkins case, the emerging process is based on leaders setting medium-term high-level goals based on clear strategic directions and local teams setting their own aspirational goals. These are underpinned by carefully aligned metrics and action plans that they believe will take them toward their goals. In this way, the organization operates as a team rather like an orchestra, with the conductor providing strategic direction, harmonizing and coordinating activities, and setting and upholding values and standards.

These organizations do less (or no) annual budgeting but a lot more planning. However, the key change is that these plans remain flexible (more akin to "playbooks" or "scenarios"). Teams respond to prevailing demand rather than a fixed plan. Also, goals are not a "fixed performance contract." They are reset to reflect the latest market conditions and peer-group comparisons. As we've stated earlier, the aim is to consistently beat your peers rather than meet a fixed target.

Annual budgets are the glue that holds the command and control organization together. They need to be eliminated and replaced. Principle #9 outlines alternative steering mechanisms such as rolling plans and forecasts that enable organizations to break free from the annual budget cycle and move toward a truly adaptive organization.

Implementation guidelines

- Make planning an inclusive process.
- Make corporate strategy more responsive.
- Make business strategy a continuous process.
- Use rolling forecasts to guide actions.
- Use scenario planning to respond rapidly to unpredictable events.
- Use an integrated planning system.

Make planning an Inclusive process

Many CEOs complain about lack of visibility and poor response times when the unexpected event happens. None of this is surprising when you consider that most of them have a fixation with meeting a predetermined target and realigning strategy, structure and systems to cope with unanticipated change. This not only drains management energy and upsets morale, but it also increases complexity and cost. It's a high price to pay for being "strategy-focused." Marching the organization to the drumbeat of a fixed strategy without the flexibility to respond to emerging threats and opportunities can be a recipe for disaster.

Think about how the process works. Most organizations follow a formal strategic planning process that takes many months to complete. MOST (mission, objectives, strategy, tactics) is an acronym used in many companies to describe this step-by-step process. The mission is followed by strategic objectives (or strategic "themes") that will move the organization along a pathway toward the mission. Then a strategy can be developed that meets these objectives and this can be handed down to "implementers" who decide on the tactics needed to meet the strategy. In this process, planning is seen as a hypothesis for getting from A to B. Thus the planning process is highly centralized and deterministic.

Adaptive leaders recognize that the best ideas and strategies do not necessarily come from the senior executive team. In a fast-changing world in which new business opportunities and process improvements often rely on deep knowledge of information technology, it is more likely that front-line teams and younger people will have the best ideas. But how can leaders take advantage of this pool of talent and creativity?

The answer is to transfer the responsibility for strategy and innovation to front-line teams and open up channels so that younger people can present their ideas. Take US steelmaker Nucor Steel. The spontaneous flow of ideas off the floor of a typical Nucor Steel mill is prodigious. Virtually every process improvement the company has made, from finding simple ways to save money to designing whole systems, has come from the people doing the work.[1] Employee health and safety constitute a vitally important indicator of caring, particularly in manufacturing where there is often exposure to injury and harmful substances. Nucor serves employees by giving them a sense of empowerment over their work lives, creating a team environment in which people freely exchange ideas and coaching, and maintaining an open-door policy to division leaders. At Nucor steel mills there are no employee time clocks – there is only a work ethic that arises from within each individual team as it strives to surpass its production goals. Employees write their own job descriptions and are given wide latitude to self-organize around tasks as they see fit. The presumption behind this system is that plant workers closest to the action care about collective welfare of their teams, are intelligent, and can therefore be trusted to do the right thing. What makes the system work is a culture of account-ability. People understand that their teams and divisions will stand or fall on their own merits. In the words of former CEO Ken Iverson, "There's no cavalry waiting to ride to the rescue ... There's just you and the people working with you."[2]

W.L. Gore attributes its astounding product diversity and rate of innovation not only to its polymers and patents but also to a unique corporate culture that eschews hierarchy and encourages teamwork and hands-on innovation. For example, there are no chains of command or predetermined channels of communication. Associates (not "employees") are hired for general work areas, are assigned no titles and work under the guidance of sponsors (not "bosses") on projects that match their skills and career objectives.

The result is an egalitarian work atmosphere that minimizes bureaucratic delays and fosters rapid decision-making and product development. The company encourages hands-on innovation, involving those closest to a project in decision-making. Teams organize around opportunities and leaders emerge based on the needs and priorities of a particular business unit. Employees communicate directly with each other and are accountable to fellow members of multi-disci-plinary teams. The associate benefit plans include an Associate Stock Ownership Plan that allows associates to share in the risks and rewards of the enterprise by acquiring ownership in it. In nearly 50 years of business, the company has developed hundreds of unique products that reflect an underlying commitment to innovative technologies.[3]

Make corporate strategy more responsive

Many leaders responsible for developing strategies are often resistant to signs that these may not be working. When asked, fully two-thirds of corporate strategists admitted that they were surprised by as many as three high-impact events over the previous five years, and 97 percent had no early warning systems.[4] Part of the problem is that in two-thirds of companies the strategy process is annual *and focused on individual business units*. Yet all executives say that strategic decisions are made without regard to the calendar and 70 percent say that they are focused on "issues" (strategic questions such as Should we enter China? Should we out-source manufacturing?) rather than business units. Recent research shows that most companies with annual strategy processes make only 2.5 major decisions a year (3.5 if focused on issues), whereas companies moving to continuous strategy planning can cope with 4.1 decisions focused on business units and 6.1 decisions focused on issues.[5]

Adaptive leaders believe that discontinuous change is now the norm. They see planning as a continuous process driven by events (such as the launch of a new product or a competitive threat) and emerging knowledge, not constrained by the current financial year. Mintzberg uses the term *natural continuous improvement* to describe this approach to strategy making. He also calls this management style "quiet management," encapsulating the typical actions of adaptive leaders. Quiet management, he notes is, "not about drinking champagne in business class; it is about rolling up sleeves and finding out what is going on. And that is not parachuted down on the organization; it rises up from the base."[6]

Mintzberg seems to capture the whole flavor of strategy making in adaptive organizations. It doesn't need sophisticated tools. It relies on fast, relevant (actionable) information and responsible people who know what is expected of them and what to do in any given situation.

Corporate strategy is about setting the right strategic direction and medium-term goals and ensuring that resources support the best business opportunities. But too often the executive team is operating in the dark. For example, they don't know which project initiatives are strategic and they don't know which business segments, product lines, customers or markets add value greater than the costs of funds used.

How much to invest in one business or another, how much to invest in new products or new ventures, and how to evaluate performance across the strategic portfolio are questions that go to the core of effective strategy management. This is the province of the board. These are truly strategic choices that are *difficult or costly to reverse once made.* Such hard-to-reverse commitments might include entering a new market, making an acquisition, and investing in a particular brand position. The level of commitment distinguishes strategic from tactical decisions. For example, a price cut might be a tactical decision if it is easy to reverse.[6]

Corporate strategy should be reviewed at least once a year, more often in fast-changing markets. It is during this review that the "big" questions are addressed. Have the needs of our customers changed? Are our products and services still appropriate? Is our value proposition still valid? Do our chosen value drivers and key performance indicators still reflect the way that value is driven in the business? Do our core competences still support the value proposition?

When changes occur, effective communication is essential. There are many ways to do this including "town hall" meetings, websites, bulletin boards, scorecards and newsletters. It also needs to be a continuous "drip-feed" process with continuous feedback so that strategy is updated as and when necessary.

Make business strategy a continuous process

Business strategy (as opposed to corporate strategy) is about how front-line teams (value centers or business units) compete in the market place. In the traditional organization this is invariably an annual process that can take months to complete and then mutate into an equally long budgeting process. Strategies and improvement plans are submitted by each business unit and debated until some negotiated settlement is made.

In adaptive organizations, senior executives set strategic direction but planning happens within front-line teams who are better able to respond to customer needs and competitor actions. But as author Michael Goold has rightly noted, "Decentralization can only work well if two conditions are fulfilled: [First] the center must be able to determine whether the business is on track with its strategy. Unless the center knows when to intervene, decentralization becomes abdication of responsibility. [Second], the business heads must know what will be counted as good performance. Without clear goals, the whole concept of decentralized responsibility suffers, since the conditions under which a business head can expect to operate free from central intervention are ill-defined."[7]

But the devolution of planning and control cannot take place unless senior people are prepared to let go. That doesn't mean they are excluded. They still have an important role to play. For example, they challenge business unit managers to justify key assumptions, forecasts and risks. This is the process at General Electric, where group executives demand from their business unit managers one-page answers to five strategic questions:

1. What does your global competition look like over the next several years?

2. What have your competitors done in the last three years to upset those global dynamics?

3. What have you done to them in the last three years to affect those dynamics?

4. How might your competitors attack you in the future?

5. What are your plans to leapfrog the competition?

What isn't required is a detailed business plan with 50 pages of numbers and charts.[8] It is broad-brush and fast. There are no detailed submissions and presentations.

Leaders need to remember that while there is every reason to report annually to stakeholders such as investors and bankers, there is no reason to *manage annually* to achieve some target or forecast. They need to break free from these artificial cycles and manage strategy. The real goal is continuous improvement rather than meeting a negotiated target. Despite increased volatility, most organizations continue to use a protracted budgeting process that involves target setting, planning and budgeting that is *annual, negotiated and fixed* (see Figure 9.1). This process not only takes too long, it is also too detailed, too expensive, too rigid and too political. It was designed to support a bureaucratic command and control organization that moves at a snail's pace. But using the rear-view mirror of budgets and variances to manage performance when the market is changing rapidly is a recipe for disaster. Managers need early warning of changes that impact their business, particularly if they spell trouble ahead. And they need the scope and authority to act on any new information.

The key change is to move to a more continuous or "event-driven" planning cycle. Many leaders choose a quarterly business review cycle, always looking five quarters ahead (see Figure 9.2). This is how it works. Let's assume we are just approaching the end of quarter one. The management team gets the rough figures for that quarter and starts to review the next four quarters ahead. Three of those

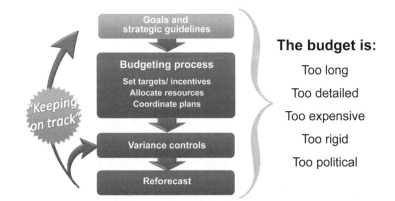

FIGURE 9.1 The budgeting process is annual, negotiated and fixed

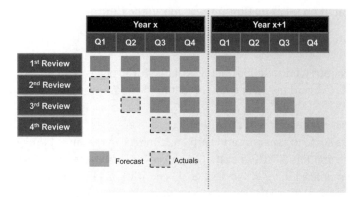

FIGURE 9.2 A five-quarterly rolling planning review process with rolling forecasts

quarters are already in the previous forecast, so they just need updating. A further quarter, however, needs to be added. More time will be spent on the earlier quarters than the later ones, using as much relevant knowledge and business intelligence as can be gathered. The fiscal year-end always appears on the 12- or 18-month rolling forecast radar screen so leaders are always in a good position to deal with market expectations. Some firms use the four quarters that fit the fiscal year as the annual plan to be approved by the board. There is no need for a separate annual budgeting process.

Performance reviews follow a standard process that has three steps: check, plan, and act[9] (see Figure 9.3).

- *Check.* The cycle starts with *check* – How are we doing against our strategy? Where are we right now? What does the short-term future look like?

- *Plan.* The second step is *plan* – What actions do we need to take to improve our performance? What impact will these actions have on our performance?

- *Act.* The third step is *act* – How should we execute the plans?

You will note that nowhere in this check–plan–act cycle has the team made a commitment to a higher authority to reach a specific target. In other words, there is no fixed performance contract. All the commitment to improve is within the local team. This taps the power of intrinsic motivation. It is the team that sets the goals and plans, and it is the team that has the drive to make them succeed. This check–plan–act cycle is typical of these organizations. But the key to its success is that it is driven locally by people who want to improve their relative performance.

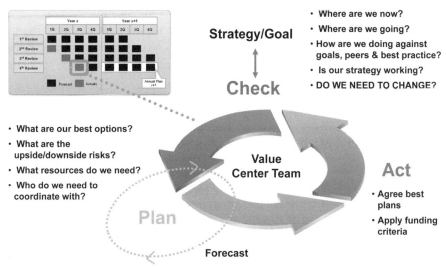

FIGURE 9.3 A rolling performance review process

Use rolling forecasts to guide actions

Most companies use forecasts to see if they are on track for meeting their annual targets. Forecasts usually occur every quarter and the horizon narrows as the fiscal year-end approaches. Thus there is little visibility into the following year. Not only is there a lack of foresight but there is also an inherent fear of providing forecasts that break the trend or surprise superiors. The common mistake is assuming that forecasts are about "predicting and controlling" future outcomes. The only certainty about a forecast is that it will be wrong. The only question is by how much. Narrowing that variation comes from learning, experience and reducing bias. The purpose of a forecast is not so much to provide an accurate view of the future but to provide some insights about how strategic options and future events will combine to produce the best financial outcomes. If forecasts are used as controls (like budgets), then don't rely on the numbers to provide a realistic view!

Adaptive leaders know that the more practice managers have at preparing short-term forecasts, the better they become. That's why their focus is less on annual budgets or long-term views and more on rolling views – usually a monthly or quarterly rolling plan and forecast that always looks four to eight quarters ahead. These forecasts are an integral part of the check–plan–act review process and help managers to make decisions. They also enable senior executives to manage shareholder expectations; they enable finance managers to consolidate and manage cash requirements; they help value center managers to make the right decisions; and they help operational managers to plan future capacity. But while adopting rolling forecasts is a major step forward, it is how these forecasts are prepared that is crucial to successful management. Forecasts must be seen as a tool for better decision-making, not for tighter control.

A fast, light-touch process

It is important to understand that the forecasting process is light-touch and fast (a few days rather than many weeks). Without exception, rolling forecasts cover only the important figures such as revenue, operating costs, working capital and capex. In effect they are the aggregate of "business as usual" forecasts (extrapolations of existing trends), all the action plans in progress and all new plans in the pipeline. In other words, forecasts should be "baseline" plus anticipated "events" with the effort being focused on "events."

Forecasts must not be seen by senior managers as a tool for questioning or reassessing performance targets. Nor must they be used to demand changes or improvements. If forecasts are used to micro-manage or demand immediate action, then trust and confidence will rapidly evaporate. The only time such questions can fairly be asked is if forecasts show a significant change and such a change has not been explained beforehand. Managers should be responsible for dealing with problems and reflecting any corrective actions that they have taken in their revised forecasts. Again, if managers see that forecasts have an impact on their investment plans, they will be reluctant to present an unbiased picture. This was borne out at Danish petrochemicals company Borealis. When rolling forecasts were introduced, the initial response of managers was to include – indeed inflate – their capital expenditure forecasts, thinking it would influence their approval ratings; but when they realized that this had no affect (these investment decisions were taken over by a quarterly review committee), they gradually adjusted their forecasts to reflect a more realistic view of essential project expenditure.

Separate forecasts from targets and rewards

A senior manager at a large French company made a similar point: "Forecasts and targets must be independent if we want to obtain both relevant action plans and reliable forecasts allowing risks and opportunities to be identified and relevant corrective actions to be taken. They must not be produced for control purposes. Action plans must be focused on the 'battlefields' where we can really act. There should be no 'wishful thinking.' It is also important to be realistic. Forecasts should reflect the fact that some businesses are cyclical and thus cannot always grow, even if this is 'politically incorrect.'"

Gary Crittenden, former CFO of American Express, captured the change of emphasis in the planning and control system when he said that "an ideal finance function spends very little time on reconciliations and a minimal amount of time reporting on what has happened. Instead, a great organization spends the majority of its time trying to anticipate what's going to happen in the future, making sure the company's resources are allocated to the most important opportunities that it has, and to ensuring that the company operates with tight controls and great processes."[10]

Ten implementation insights

Here are ten insights that will guide you to a successful implementation of rolling forecasts:

1. *Stop forecasting to the wall.* You need to move forecasts from budget revisions aimed at meeting the annual target to a framework for continuous planning and improvement.

2. *Stop confusing forecasts with budgets.* Budgets are intended to be contracts and commitments to meet a fixed target. A fixed target represents where we want to be at the year-end. A budget is also a basis for evaluation and reward as well as a basis for resource allocation. Forecasts, on the other hand, are intended to be a best guess of future outcomes – they must not be seen as commitments or contracts. They are a rolling series of estimates aimed at addressing the question "Where will we be in the future?" Most important of all, they are a framework for decision-making. They address the question: "What actions do we need to take to change future outcomes?" And they are a basis for dynamically allocating resources according to the best current opportunities available.

3. *Choose time horizons and forecasting intervals that are appropriate to the business.* There are no fixed rules as far as time horizon is concerned. In a rapidly changing market, intervals need to be regular (weekly/monthly), whereas in a more stable market (such as in a capital-intensive business) they are likely to be quarterly. One low-cost airline uses only a few key variables to drive its forecasting process. It maintains a schedule that reflects each variable's economic importance (that is, what proportion of the income statement or

balance sheet is affected?). It also shows variability (how often does the value change and how significant are the changes?). And finally it shows the speed of response to change (how quickly can we change the operating plan and how important is a fast response?). The answers to these questions determine the update frequency and forecast horizon. Note that while these variables are updated at different times, they remain part of one integrated forecast.

4. *Focus on only a few key drivers rather than hundreds of lines of data.* If there's one thing we've learned over the years, it is that more detail does not deliver more accuracy! So ensure that managers spend their time acting on the drivers, not compiling detailed numbers. Value drivers must be defined at a level of detail consistent with the decision variables that are directly under the control of management. At the value center level, variables such as number of sales prospects, order size and conversion rate drive sales growth, and customer satisfaction and loyalty drive customer churn rates. And at the operating process level key drivers will likely be based around cycle times, quality levels and process improvements. Examples include the speed and quality of completing a loan in a bank, which directly impacts capacity and customer satisfaction; the turnaround time of an airplane, which directly affects asset utilization and costs; the speed of finalizing an insurance claim, which directly affects costs and customer satisfaction and the number of defects for a car manufacturer, which directly affects costs, customer satisfaction and loyalty.

5. *Focus on the sales forecast.* The basic building block of any forecast is the sales or income line. Most other variables are related to sales. However, getting sales forecasts, according to many finance managers, is "like pulling teeth." No one wants to commit themselves. It is perhaps because managers see little personal advantage in preparing forecasts that they are so unhelpful and have so little interest in whether the outcomes are right or wrong. In other words, they don't own the numbers. This leads to other departments second-guessing what the sales forecast will be and making up their forecasts based on this number. Then, when backed into corner, sales simply gives up and says, "Just tell us the number you want." A well-prepared sales forecast should take account of marketing and promotion and new product launches. It should consider market share, production capacity and competitive actions. And it should examine customer behavior patterns.

6. *Move from single point forecasts to ranges and scenarios.* Many business leaders demand single-point forecasts but these can lead to short-term gap-filling decisions and undermine longer-term strategy. They also lead to minimal targets and sub-optimal performance. Some firms have overcome this problem by moving to ranges and scenarios whereby managers set expectations

across a range of outcomes and of course always aim for the best options. At each quarterly review, new action plans are submitted and the best ones are funded. The aim is always to maximize the performance potential of the team. This removes the target ceiling and much of the dysfunctional behavior that is often a feature of poor forecasting. Quarterly business reviews enable each team to propose new action plans always based on maximizing their profit potential

7. *Remove bias*. This is perhaps the greatest forecasting challenge – to produce a forecast that is genuinely objective (that is, with no systemic errors). Forecast error is made up of *variation* based on external volatility and *bias* or consistent, internal systematic error. The problem is that many people confuse bias with variation. Variation can't be avoided. By definition, it is beyond anyone's control. It is caused, for example, by volatile markets and unpredictable events and is almost impossible to correct. However, the degree of volatility can be estimated and control or "tolerance" ranges can be provided that if exceeded will alert managers to investigate whether there is bias in the system. Bias is the real enemy of effective forecasting and is endemic in many companies. The most common problem is "second-guessing" that can lead to shock profit warnings as forecasts repeatedly tell senior executives what they want to hear rather than the unpleasant reality. Once a forecast becomes a target or a commitment, it ceases to be an effective forecast. That's the nub of the problem. Managers avoid attention if they provide forecasts that fit prevailing expectations. In other words, chronic bias is driven by the system. Whether it is intended or not, the prevailing culture is one of providing forecasts that are treated as fixed targets or commitments, and if these forecasts change, then explanations are necessary and can sometimes lead to unpleasant confrontations. Needless to say, few managers want to go through this ordeal (at least not more than once a year). The lesson is that implementing rolling forecasts within an existing regime of fixed targets often leads to spurious outcomes and a devalued process.

8. *Use dedicated models rather than spreadsheets*. While spreadsheets are fine for small local requirements, they can cause problems when they need to be aggregated across and up the organization. In most large organizations, different units use different assumptions, algorithms and software. This makes it difficult to combine and consolidate forecasts. Consider using dedicated models. The IT industry is now offering sophisticated models to enable large organizations to prepare forecasts quickly and consolidate reports. Teams can build business rules and structures, then modify the model as their business evolves, easily accommodating changes such as additional locations, new or discontinued product lines or restructured cost centers. Many have powerful

modeling capabilities that enable teams to flexibly devise, compare and assess alternative business scenarios.

9. *Ensure that forecasts are integrated across the business.* Executive leaders want an enterprise-wide view that provides the essential visibility that many of them now complain about.

10. *Transfer the ownership of forecasts from the corporate center to the front-line team.* Value center teams based around product lines or customer segments such as regions need to start using forecasts for their own decisions rather than just producing the numbers for "corporate." These are the teams that generate revenue and profit, and it is the aggregate of these forecasts that should provide the consolidated picture. We are often asked whether forecasts should be top-down or bottom-up. The answer is bottom-up, but there should always be a dialogue with more senior people who have the right to challenge key assumptions. However, once agreed they should not be changed.

Rolling forecasts, if well prepared, form the backbone of a new and much more useful information system that connects all the pieces of the organization and gives senior management a continuous picture both of the current position and the short-term outlook. An honest view has no bias, so managers should expect half of their forecasts to be on the high side of actual outcomes and half on the low side. The ideal forecast has "clean" data that enables managers to improve decision-making. Forecasts must not be seen as commitments, otherwise bias and distortion (dirty data) will be inevitable. That's why implementing rolling forecasts under the umbrella of fixed targets rarely works.

Use scenario planning to respond rapidly to unpredictable events

Another use of the forecasting model is scenario planning. In a highly uncertain environment, the advantages of scenario planning are clear: since no one base case can be regarded as probable, it's necessary to develop plans on the assumption that several different futures are possible and to focus attention on the underlying drivers of uncertainty.

Scenario plans are usually based on driver-based models. The revenue forecast, for example, will be based on a range of variables such as customer demand, price, customer acquisitions and retention levels, market share, brand marketing and capacity utilization. In other words, the idea is to simulate the business with a relational model. Many drivers are non-financial. Managers can then play the "what if?" game many times as they look at the various ways that the future might unfold and what the implications of different outcomes might be. Southwest Airlines' leaders believe in strategic and scenario planning. The company's executive planning committee meets periodically to create future scenarios in which the airline might find itself. For example, if it is considering opening up a new city to fly to, it will look at what the competition might do, how many more planes it will need (and where they will get them from) and so forth. "Future scenario generation" (as the company calls it) enables Southwest to prepare for the future in a way that provides direction yet allows it to maneuver on many fronts.[11]

Today's pervasive uncertainty complicates scenario-planning efforts: the number of variables at play – and the range of plausible outcomes – have exploded in recent years. Consider, for example, the predicament of an industrial supplier that is not only heavily exposed to commercial and residential real estate but also has many government customers. For this company, the critical uncertainties include the direction of the commercial-credit and mortgage markets, house prices, tax revenues and government stimulus spending. Different outcomes for each of these uncertainties produce vastly different paths for the business. Since the heart of scenario planning – crafting a number of strategies for different outcomes – has become significantly more complex, strategists should prepare for a more demanding process of gathering information, exploring possibilities, and plain old hard thinking.[12]

Senior executives outside the strategic-planning group – even those accustomed to developing scenarios – may find the diversity and complexity of today's scenarios bewildering. It's critical to bring such executives into the process early: for example, by kicking off the planning process with a scenario-development exercise involving the full senior team. Similarly, as the process of reviewing business units gets under way, a company can inculcate an appreciation of the threats it faces and of its collective strategic response by inviting executives from a number of divisions to participate in the proceedings – rather than hold one-off events between the senior team and the leader of each individual unit.[13]

Use an integrated planning system

The unique infrastructure at one financial services company required extra security within the data center to protect against applications interacting in authorized ways. Choosing the right software vendor to support a project of this magnitude was critical to the ultimate success. The software's requirements included the robust modeling of scenarios, sufficient flexibility to meet multiple needs, self-servicing, integration with Excel and a secure and user-friendly interface.

The selection process lasted nine months. By walking through the steps required, the team created a proof of concept with 14 test cases. These cases mimicked the company's multiple products across a wide number of regions. The cases also dealt in multiple currencies. Using a weighted scoring system, the team evaluated their options. One of the weighted criteria was that the software vendor appeared to stay out in front of the competition by continuing to put development behind the forecasting tool. The company did not want to have to go through the software selection again in a few short years.

The key to providing this new process was a fast, web-based business intelligence (BI) system using a single enterprise-wide database. But how it is used is critical. Research shows that the top two reasons (by a long way) why CFOs choose BI is for better visibility into current results and a better understanding of future perform-ance trends. It is not about incremental improvements to the existing planning and budgeting system; BI is about gaining new performance insights based on key drivers, trends and relative performance and responding rapidly to them.

Conclusions

Many organizations are turning away from protracted annual plans and budgets and moving toward rolling plans and forecasts. Done well, these rolling plans and forecasts can become the "sensors" of the adaptive organization, enabling managers to operate more effectively at a tactical level. But to be effective, rolling forecasts need to be prepared honestly and openly, without fear of blame or recrimination. Of course, the assumptions can be challenged by higher-level managers and a robust dialogue should be part of the compilation process. But if forecasts are prepared on the basis of providing senior managers with "what they want to see" rather than current reality, then they will be worse than useless.

Effective forecasting is the key to managing the future and keeping "in control." It is also a change that is uncontroversial and can be made without fanfare and directives. Most importantly, it is a key step in convincing CFOs to let go of the old annual planning and budgeting system with its time-consuming preparation and revisions. It fills the gap between the coordination elements of budgeting and the more dynamic elements of fast-response management. Rolling forecasts also enable executives to finally kick the addiction to "managing the year-end." Rather than focus all their efforts on making the target commitment, managers are now able both to see the year-end on their radar screens and to focus on managing future outcomes. Alignment is another benefit, as forecasts done speedily by different value centers can quickly be assembled and consolidated to enable executives to see what's happening across the whole organization. The potential benefits are huge.

KEY POINTS

- Too many organizations continue to separate strategy from execution. We are now in an age when the best ideas are more likely to come from front-line teams. While high-level goals and strategic directions are set at the board level, most strategic thinking and action planning takes place in teams closer to the front line. It is important that everyone is engaged in the performance improvement process. Leaders need to open channels (usually through the web) that give everyone the chance to understand goals, plans and results and participate in the strategy process.

- The board should set longer-term directional goals and strategic aims that are reviewed at least annually (and more often in fast-changing markets). It is during this review that the "big" questions are addressed: Have the needs of our customers changed? Are our products and services still appropriate? Do our chosen value drivers and KPIs still reflect the way that value is driven in the business?

- In organizations subject to continuous change, it might be appropriate to set regular (monthly or quarterly) business reviews, or to make a review dependent on some significant event. These reviews typically start by looking at the latest performance information and then reviewing whether "business as usual" will take the company or team to where it needs to be (for example, top quartile in its peer group). If not, then the team will need to think about which new initiatives are appropriate and act upon them.

- You need to move forecasts from budget revisions aimed at meeting the annual target to a framework for continuous planning and improvement. This means implementing some form of "rolling" forecast that typically rolls beyond the next fiscal year-end. Avoid turning forecasts into "commitments." Ensure that forecasts are separated from target setting and performance measurement. Also ensure that forecasts are "light-touch" and take no longer than a few days to compile. Identify (and base forecasts on) 10 to 20 variables (each underpinned by driver-based models). Make the forecasting horizon appropriate to the business needs (taking into account the degree of market volatility and organizational change).

- Given the likelihood of disruptive change, it makes less sense to spend time on long-term planning and more sense to focus on scenario planning (which assumes that several different futures are possible). With a "relational" model, managers can play the "what if?" game many times over as they look at the various ways that the future might unfold and what the implications of different outcomes might be.

- Depending on the degree of size and complexity, it may be necessary to use a dedicated enterprise-wide planning and forecasting system that enables common methods of working and encompasses version controls.

## CHAPTER 10

Principle #10 – Coordination
Coordinate interactions dynamically, not through annual budgets

Instead of more control, what companies need is more coordination.[1]

Mike Hugos

From "make-and-sell" to "sense-and-respond"

The overarching philosophy of most manufacturers might be described as "bigger is better." In other words, the way to cut costs and maximize profitability is to increase volumes. While this was clearly understood by early business leaders such as Henry Ford and Andrew Carnegie, they also realized that quality mattered, and that the way to achieve higher quality was to train workers, pay them well and balance processes so that work flowed according to customer demand. Henry Ford introduced the Model T in 1908 and the first moving assembly line in 1913.

Assembly-line workers were responsible for simple repetitive tasks, leaving the design, product engineering and quality to functional specialists. Ford's strategy was, in contemporary language, one of operational excellence. He designed for manufacturability; increased his production speed by controlling his supply chain (mostly by acquisition); and questioned every aspect of the work performed to ensure that it added value to the product. In the 1920s, Ford's total business cycle from mining the ore to shipping the car was three and a half days. By the 1960s, with the added complexity of multiple products, no American auto company could manage this same cycle within five or six weeks.[2]

Ford's primary competition was to come from General Motors, which, recognizing that competing on cost was too difficult, began to offer customers a variety of products "to fit every purse." But competing on the basis of more variety also increased production complexity and, with the need to maintain low unit costs, GM began to decouple its processes, leading to a patchwork quilt of disparate and unbalanced production processes. GM managers reasoned that the only way to reduce unit costs was to run each separate process at its maximum speed and capacity, which in turn led to the need to maintain essential buffers between processes to ensure coordination and continuity of production.

This "decoupled" batch production approach to mass-producing variety featured uninterrupted work only in each separate operation, followed by transit to a central staging area, or warehouse, where material waited until a schedule directed it to flow (in varieties) to a final assembly plant.[3] Thus production was made for inventory rather than for customers, a position that led to waste, write-offs and poor quality. The task of the marketing department was to persuade customers to buy (often unwanted) products at discounted prices while at the same time ensuring that a "contribution" was made to fixed costs.

Making all the pieces in this complicated flow come together in the right places at the right times required people and equipment not employed in the actual making of the products themselves. These resources ("overheads" or "indirect costs") were employed in activities such as scheduling, controlling, expediting, storing, inspecting, transporting and reworking. And so IT companies designed and manufacturers bought expensive production planning and programming systems ("MRP systems") to manage this process. Miller and Vollmann described all these resources as a "hidden factory" within the more obvious physical production setting. Eventually, this hidden factory would employ more workers than the real factory would employ to transform material into finished products.[4]

This rise in indirect costs focused accountants on how to "recover" them through volume production. Their models of competitiveness focused on the relationship between costs, volume and profits. Students learned from break-even analysis and capacity planning how to compute the "optimal" production volume and mix or "economic order quantity." Even more insidious was the "contribution margin" approach, which invited managers to increase the range of products and extend the list of channels and customers on the basis that each additional sales unit would contribute to the ever-growing pool of indirect costs.

The lessons from Toyota

While American and European firms were pursuing strategies based on "economies of scale," Toyota was concentrating on "economies of flow." One of the stories told about Taaichi Ohno, the architect of the Toyota Production System (TPS), is that when he returned from America in 1956 (having studied their manufacturing methods) to set up a new plant in Japan, he didn't have much capital so he had to manage with a few small machines. So his primary task was to reduce changeover times. Within a few months he had reduced the time it took the Americans from ten days to *ten minutes.* He then had a counterintuitive moment – *his costs went down.* He, like others, assumed that smaller batch sizes would lead to higher costs, but he soon realized that his costs had reduced because he had less inventory to hold and fewer quality problems to correct.[5]

Ohno's great idea was to re-think how work should be organized and thus to design and manage flexible "pull" processes to satisfy customer needs rather than to "push" output through rigid processes to meet cost and volume targets. As Johnson and Bröms explain, Ohno reckoned that if every step in a continuous flow *works at the same rate*, then at any moment each step consumes only the resources required to advance one customer's order one step closer to completion. This means that costs will be *as low as they can possibly be* (as long as the process and the work are well-designed). With all the steps linked in a balanced flow, no worker need do more than prepare the work called for by the next step, and then pass it on. Moreover, Toyota people perceived that if each worker could design and control the steps he or she performed, then workers could perform *different steps* on each unit that passed by them in every time interval. Thus, *variety could be achieved at no greater cost than if all units were identical.*[6]

The success of the new system depended on the ability of the company to reduce changeover times to a rate faster than the rate at which output flows off the end of the line. This took the effort and imagination of everyone on the line. Toyota recognized that it is more profitable to invest in capable, responsible people on the front line than to invest in expensive machinery and computerized manufacturing systems.

From "push" to "pull"

A key feature of the system is the use of customer order information to *pull* material through the plant. Whereas Toyota produces to the *end-customer order*, most other car manufacturers produce to the *dealer order*. At hundreds of workstations along both sides of the line, team members attach and install parts which they pull from line-side conveyance racks that are replenished every hour or so by "kanban" (signboard). This was typically a piece of paper in a rectangular vinyl envelope. It contained three pieces of information: pickup information, transfer information and production information.[7]

The only information from outside the system itself is the external customer order. Otherwise, all the information is in the flow. *There are no targets, budgets, standard costing systems or other accounting or production controls that drive the system at Toyota.* This is not to say that it doesn't have comprehensive planning and control systems at a higher level. It does. But these are in advance of operations. It is just that they are *not used to manage or control operations*.

The whole TPS is one seamless process starting from the customer order. Every worker is connected to every other in a supplier–customer relationship that ensures that the highest quality standards are maintained. However, the TPS balances the work that teams do to maintain the rhythm or "pulse rate" through the plant. Ohno gives an example of a rowing team to illustrate this. "Imagine a boat rowed by eight men, four on the left and four on the right. If they do not row correctly, the boat will zig-zag erratically. One rower might feel he is stronger than the next and row twice as hard. But this extra effort upsets the boat's progress and moves it off course. The best way to propel the boat faster is for everyone to distribute force equally, rowing evenly and at the same depth."[8]

It is important to emphasize that workers are not working to a predetermined computerized schedule. There is no plan. What's important is that the "handover" from one workstation to the next goes smoothly and without any problem. Ohno compares the "handover" from one process to another with passing the baton within a track relay team. "There is always an area where the baton may be passed. If the baton is passed well, the total final time can be better than the individual times of the four runners."[9]

The collision of management and measurement systems

When Western firms tried to copy the TPS, their accounting and reward systems often went haywire. Initiatives such as just-in-time production and quality programs didn't show up well in standard costing variance reports and, in many cases, caused these new ideas to be disregarded. Standard cost-efficiency variances, for example, encourage the recovery of all direct labor hours, no matter what the consequences might be for quality or other hidden costs (such as high or unsaleable inventories) of the finished output. They encourage long production runs and large batch sizes, whereas just-in-time and total quality management emphasize production to demand and high quality. The result is invariably more waste, more indirect labor costs needed to patch-up poor quality, higher inventories and a mad scramble at the end of each accounting period in an effort to hit volume and efficiency targets, all of which leads to *higher costs* and *fewer satisfied customers*.

The genius of Ohno was to build an adaptive organization within perhaps the most complex manufacturing operation (i.e. car manufacturing) in the world. But too many observers only saw tools and techniques such as "quality circles" and "just-in-time" inventory management. They didn't (and still don't) understand the fundamental changes in the whole management model. All the pieces of the traditional command and control model have to be taken apart and rebuilt to achieve the degree of responsiveness that Toyota is able to achieve. It is only now (more than 50 years after Ohno's insights) that other business leaders are realizing how expensive the existing model based on central planning, coordination and control really is and that they must look for alternative approaches.

Principle #10 tells us that organizations, like adaptive systems in nature, don't need a central coordinator and controller. While this might have sounded interesting but dismissed as impractical a few years ago, the advent of the latest communications technologies means that it is now both practical and a key element in the design of the adaptive organization.

Implementation guidelines

- Design coordination into the system.
- Switch the management model from "make-and-sell" (or build to plan) to "sense-and-respond" (or build to order).
- Use front-line teams and IT to improve efficiency and responsiveness.

- Use ad hoc agreements to enable real-time coordination.
- Work in partnership with strategic suppliers.

Design coordination into the system

According to a recent study, the most successful collaborations between multiple business units within firms occur not when they are mandated by management, but when self-interested managers spot opportunities to collaborate and share resources with one another. One reason is that managers at individual business units understand their immediate needs better than executives who take a higher-level view. Another is that business unit managers will pursue joint projects only when they believe those projects will benefit their own department.

The study focused on six software firms, examining one successful and one unsuccessful collaborative project at each company. The key finding was that effective collaborations bubble up from small events within individual units – for example, when one engineer finds out that an engineer at another business unit is trying to solve a similar problem – and are polished and expanded by self-interested business unit managers at that level who realize they can extend the value from the collaboration.

This conclusion contrasts with the commonly held view that top executives make the best decisions because they have the highest vantage point in the organization and can use firm-wide incentives to increase motivation for unit general managers to work together. In one example from the study debunking that notion, a manager decided to bundle a group of products from different business units into one piece of packaged software because he couldn't afford the marketing costs of promoting each product individually. Corporate executives were against the idea, fearing that overall revenue would fall. But the bundled product was a hit with consumers, generating $100 million in sales and giving the business units that originated the programs near-monopoly status in their markets.

The authors conclude that executives are most effective at removing barriers to collaboration and coordination among individual business units and can eliminate incentives for managers to work against one another.[10]

Adaptive leaders design coordination into the system rather than impose it on the system. They recognize that what teams need is the flexible use of resources based on dynamic supplier–customer relationships and the sharing of ideas, information, and best practices. A business should be designed for one purpose only – to deliver the highest customer value at the lowest cost – and this requires each working part to contribute value within a coherent and coordinated system.

Switch the management model from "make-and-sell" (or build to plan) to "sense-and-respond" (or build to order)

In the annual budgeting process, the "master" budget defines the financial commitments that one unit makes to another through the year. The firm first decides what to make and sell, then the production department follows the production plan, then stock enters the warehouse, and finally (and concurrently with the production process) the sales team uses all the powers at their disposal to persuade the customer to buy their products and services. Under this "make-and-sell" approach (see the left-hand side of Figure 10.1), the annual budget determines what each unit in the value delivery process must produce and sell. But by the time the plan is executed the market may well have changed, making it harder to sell the products currently being made at the margins assumed in the budget. The result is that stock builds up in the warehouse, leaving the sales team with little option but to resort to discounts and other "special deals" to move the stock. The final outcome is that the profit target is missed and customers are dissatisfied.

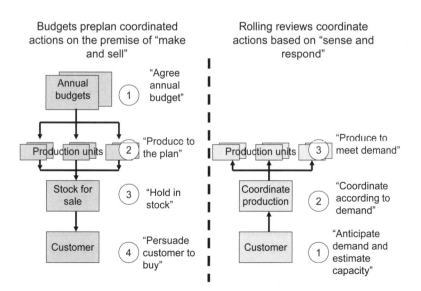

FIGURE 10.1 "Make-and-sell" vs "sense-and-respond"

In organizations that manage without such predetermined plans and budgets, however, managers tend to coordinate these commitments according to the pace of market demand (see right side of Figure 10.1). This means that capacity is not fixed in advance and products are not made for stock according to an annual production plan. Nor are materials purchased to support this plan. Instead, firms either build to order (as at Toyota) or anticipate customer demand on, say, a rolling 90-day cycle (depending on the customer order cycle and using rolling forecasts to anticipate demand), and then schedule production runs accordingly. The benefits are reduced waste and fewer products that are subject to special offers and write-downs. This is the approach adopted in a UK brewery. Salespeople are now geared to selling in 90-day promotional cycles and production units are similarly geared to supporting them.

To support this "sense-and-respond" process, relationships are established between internal suppliers and customers with all the disciplines of the external market. The ultimate objective is to satisfy the needs of external customers profitably. This might involve one or more business units together with one or more service providers – and some of these providers can be external suppliers. Thus these companies are operating more like consultancies, listening to customer requests, deciding if those requests can be fulfilled profitably and then combining their internal and external resources in the fastest and most efficient way to satisfy those requests.

Use front-line teams and IT to improve efficiency and responsiveness

In fast-changing markets a company's survival often depends on its ability to use intelligent IT systems to sense what's happening earlier than competitors and respond faster to unpredictable events. The OODA loop (observe, orient, decide and act) is a term often used to describe this process (Loop 1 in Figure 10.2). Another term sometimes used is *managing by wire* – an expression meant to draw an analogy to modern aviation's fly-by-wire systems. As author Stephan Haeckel explains, "When jet engine technology arrived, airplanes became so fast that un-assisted human pilots could no longer sense, interpret and act on information quickly enough to fly them. So computer systems were developed to present pilots with concise displays of essential information and then translate pilot responses into the myriad actions needed to execute the pilot's decisions. This technology mediated and accelerated the pilot's adaptive loop, making it possible to fly a plane traveling at several times the speed of sound. Managers needing to 'fly' modern,

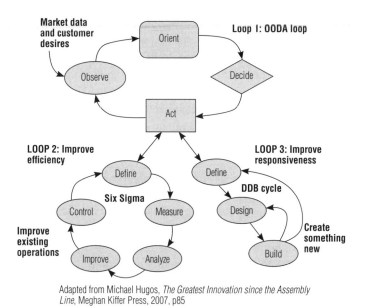

Adapted from Michael Hugos, *The Greatest Innovation since the Assembly Line*, Meghan Kiffer Press, 2007, p85

FIGURE 10.2 Process model of responsive organization

fast-moving businesses will increasingly find similar systems both technically feasible and necessary."[11]

But *how* managers react is crucial. There are two approaches depending on the situation. The first is to improve existing processes to respond more rapidly (Loop 2). People in this loop find and fix root causes or errors that create non-standard input. This is what delivers *efficiency*. The second is to create a new process (Loop 3) that might be needed to support a new strategy or product that responds to external threats and opportunities. People here develop new procedures and systems to deal with the appearance of something new (a new threat or a new opportunity). This is what delivers *responsiveness*.[12]

Through the combination of these three loops an agile, real-time organization senses and responds to change in a way that is both efficient and effective. While the role of the executive team is to set strategic direction and medium-term goals the (the "what" and "where"), the role of local teams is to take the right decisions to maximize performance (the "how").

IT expert Mike Hugos believes that the effect of a thousand small adjustments in the operating processes of a company as business conditions change day to day is analogous to the effect of compound interest. An agile organization constantly makes many small adjustments to better respond to its changing environment, and in doing so it reduces costs and increases revenues every day. No single adjustment by itself may be all that significant, but the cumulative effect over time is enormous. "Compared to companies that do not make these small adjustments," notes Hugos, "the results are amazing. An agile company in any industry can consistently earn an additional gross margin beyond that of its non-agile competitors. This additional margin is equal to the average compound rate of interest – about two to four percent (and sometimes more)."[13]

Constant real-time coordination was impossible before the advent of modern communications technologies. This technology enables what Hugos calls "swarming behavior." He notes: "Think like a kid and write down all the cool things you could do in your organization if everybody had a current-generation mobile phone … In other words, think about how the business could operate differently and more profitably if everyone had instantaneous voice, data and video communication as well as Web access, e-mail and instant messaging … an organization whose members all have current-generation mobile phones can now create a single big picture view or map of their world that is created from the eyes of all the people in the organization … as long as people all have a common understanding of what they are trying to accomplish, everyone will act with a common purpose without needing to be told what to do. This is *swarming* behavior … The very existence of the agile, real-time organization is based on everyone having the same big-picture view of their world. Everyone does not need access to all the detail but everyone does need access to meaningful summaries and indicators of business activity and performance in each area of the company. And this information needs to be kept current, hour by hour and day to day."[14]

Hugos also has some advice for how managers prioritize and handle IT work. "Most activities in any business are 80 to 95 percent routine and those are the activities that you standardize and automate as much as possible. This is where you focus relentlessly on efficiency and low cost. But resist the temptation to create complex systems to handle the unique or non-routine activities, because that complexity will become expensive and will bog you down … Instead, empower people to handle the unique and non-routine situations. You want people in the loop when something unexpected happens – you don't want artificial intelligence, you want real intelligence.[15] It is this blend of efficiency and responsiveness that will enable you to outperform your competition.[16]

Hugos's message is clear. In a fast-changing world in which many profit-making opportunities are based on digital products and services and web-based marketing, no organization can wait for a central coordinator and controller to make decisions. Of course, this assumes that local teams have the scope and authority to formulate plans and launch new actions whenever appropriate without, in many cases, obtaining approval from a higher authority.

Use ad hoc agreements to enable real-time coordination

Adaptive leaders enable teams to coordinate their plans and actions across the business through ad hoc agreements that cover different time periods or specific projects. These can vary from dealing with individual customized requests to anticipating and managing the periodic demand of whole customer segments.

In adaptive organizations, it is the supply *network* (rather than the supply *chain*) that continuously connects and combines to meet changing demand. In fact, the pace of change is often so fast that traditionally managed, sequential corporate supply chains are becoming obsolete. The knowledge of a few decision-makers at the top is no match for the collective wisdom of thousands of people who daily connect with customers, work on factory floors, manage distribution centers and service customers.

Finnish company Nokia is in every way an open, inclusive and vibrantly interactive network. Nokia continually seeks the best ideas of strategic partners through its "value net" – an open, interactive IT network. And it engages customers by constantly asking them what they would want in an ideal world and then delivering it to them quickly.[17] Nokia's "value net" strategy is a classic example of its capacity to achieve continual improvement via networking. Its idea is to move goods to customers quickly and seamlessly "through one Nokia window" by electronically linking everybody on the supply chain into a single net. This means they have to be very transparent to suppliers and share a wide spectrum of information about goals and processes. In adopting this strategy, Nokia is less concerned about exposing some of its best ideas to competitors than it is about failing to adapt quickly enough in a market that is evolving at lightning speed. This collaborative strategy has enabled Nokia to be the innovation leader in its industry.[18]

Work in partnership with strategic suppliers

Toyota does not believe in bullying suppliers: it knows that its best long-term interests are served by developing their capabilities and potential. Toyota helps its key suppliers cut their lead-times and costs.[19] In the US market, Toyota's suppliers need to hold less than half the inventory that they hold for their other US customers.[20]

Many other organizations are copying Toyota's model. UK retailer Tesco, for example, is now the world leader in applying these principles and is now achieving a level of service of more than 96 percent. By replenishing every store continuously over a 24-hour day to eliminate the need to hold stock either at the back of the store (like Wal-Mart) or in highbay storage (like Home Depot), Tesco reorders from key suppliers that produce – in a matter of hours – items that have just been purchased. What's more, Tesco picks up directly from suppliers' shipping docks at precise times and takes the goods to regional distribution centers where fresh products and fast-moving items are cross-docked onto vehicles delivering to stores. In a further lean innovation, Tesco satisfies online shopping orders by having store personnel fulfill orders from the shelves during lulls. This process has reduced personnel costs, avoided the cost of separate warehouses for internet orders and made Tesco the world's largest online grocer.

These techniques have helped Tesco to grow its share rapidly and become the UK's market leader in groceries, as well as fueling its global expansion in Eastern Europe and East Asia. They have also allowed the retailer to increase customer satisfaction and loyalty by giving shoppers what they want without wasting their time.[21]

Conclusions

Convincing others that you don't need tight coordination and control from the center is a tough challenge. So don't bother. What holds the organization together is not a plan, but a commitment to a clear purpose and to a set of clearly articulated principles and values. It is these that provide the framework for coordinated actions. If everyone knows their part in the value delivery system and plays it well, then the result is satisfied and profitable customers. Customers can sense the power of such a system. They know if processes are working in harmony and front-line people have the power to deal with their requirements. They can feel the experience. And because it is so rare, they will return again and again. Building adaptive organizations is about setting people free: free from stifling bureaucracies, free from the restrictions of predetermined plans, free from the fear of failing to meet fixed targets and free from the forced cross-company actions designed by central planners. It is likely to be a key competitive advantage in the years ahead.

KEY POINTS

- Adaptive leaders design coordination into the system rather than impose it on the system. They recognize that what teams need is the flexible use of resources based on dynamic supplier–customer relationships and the sharing of ideas, information and best practices. A business should be designed for one purpose only – to deliver the highest customer value at the lowest cost – and this requires each working part to contribute value within a coherent and coordinated system.

- Most management models are based on the assumption that managers can anticipate which products and services consumers and businesses want to buy and then formulate strategies and plans that deliver those products and services. This often results in high inventories, heavy discounts and expensive write-offs. So design your systems from the outside in and respond to prevailing demand rather than be a slave to a fixed plan.

- Enable local teams to use IT to improve efficiency and responsiveness. Provide the requisite tools and technologies to enable fast, coordinated actions.

- Enable teams to coordinate their plans and actions across the business through ad hoc agreements that cover different time periods or specific projects. These can vary from dealing with individual customized requests to anticipating and managing the periodic demand of whole customer segments. The knowledge of a few decision-makers at the top is no match for the collective wisdom of thousands of people who daily connect with customers, work on factory floors, manage distribution centers and service customers.

- Don't try to bully suppliers. Your best long-term interests are served by developing their capabilities and potential.

## CHAPTER 11

Principle #11 – Resources
Make resources available just-in-time, not just-in-case

All we are doing is looking at the time line from the moment the customer gives us an order to the point when we collect the cash. And we are reducing that time line by removing the non-value-added wastes.[1]

Taiichi Ohno

Rethinking cost management at Sydney Water

Sydney Water Corporation provides drinking water, wastewater services and some storm water services to four million customers in the communities around Sydney. It is the fifth largest water utility in the world. Since deregulation it now operates on a commercial basis. But its activities are governed by a regulatory authority. Every four years the company must agree a "price path" with the regulator. This sets the agenda for improvement projects, capital spending and consumer prices. The company works from a target return on investment that governs its allowable expenditure. The asset management division (AMD) is the largest of six divisions, spending over two-thirds of the company's operating costs. In 2000 the AMD's budget was cut by around 7 percent – a reduction of $35m. It was this sharp reduction that triggered the division's innovative approach to cost reduction.

Until 2000, the whole of Sydney Water's planning and budgeting process was run in a very traditional way. Every division and department would put in its budget, hoping to get as much of the available resources as possible. Working to a June year-end, the budgeting process started in December of the previous year with managers following a recipe to calculate their expected yearly costs. Financial controller Aubrey Joachim and his finance team then compiled the divisional budget, which was sent up the line to the corporate finance division.

"This is how ridiculous it got," says Joachim. "Our budget was being compiled from 1400 accounts. I remember one of these line items was an amount of $6198 for parking and another for postage of $3250 made 18 months in advance. Yet once managers were given those dollars no one really monitored what happened afterwards." Training is another example. "A manager would include an amount in his budget but would have no idea who he was going to train and what the training was for. It would just lie there until someone asked to go on a course. The control was not 'Do you really need to go to that course and will it add value to your work?' Rather, the question was directed to the accountant: 'How much money is there left in the training budget?'"

Following the reduction in the budget number for the year 2000, Joachim tried the usual method of asking operating managers to identify where cuts could be made, but this approach had virtually no effect. "Try as they might, the divisional managers wouldn't, or couldn't, accept more than a total of two or three million to be cut from the budget," says Joachim. Part of the problem was that, as much as they hated the budgeting process, managers had no guidelines at all on what they were trying to achieve. "Today, with e-commerce, prices often change hourly. How can you match that to a yearly budget which might have been compiled up to 18 months earlier?" asks Joachim. He goes on: "The traditional budget approach wasn't working. It was time to try something new. We looked for an innovative approach to solving this problem, rather than going mad at budget time like everyone else."

Avoiding the "spend it or lose it" problem

It was around this time that he attended a seminar on "Beyond Budgeting." "I looked at our costs and identified around $80 million (around 16 percent of the total budget) that could be classified as "discretionary." If I could somehow influence management not to spend some of this discretionary amount then we could achieve this reduction," says Joachim. He told the division's general manager that a change in mindset was needed. "Throw away the budget," said Joachim. He went on to explain that "we will keep all the discretionary costs at a divisional level, and tell each of the managers to go and run their business the way they think they should best be run."

The divisional manager supported the idea from the start. Joachim then told operating managers, "There are no budgets, and I'm not telling you what the numbers are." Once the split between "mandatory" and "discretionary" costs was agreed, Joachim told managers that their core spending would be funded but their discretionary spending would not. "Give someone a budget and they won't give it back," says Joachim. They had to manage their overall spending patterns while always trying to minimize costs. So there are no specific targets though the rough spending parameters are clearly known.

Focusing on rolling forecasts and cost drivers

The six-month planning and budgeting cycle has now disappeared. Instead there is a continuous focus on cost and investment management. Quarterly rolling forecasts that project eight quarters ahead are now in place. The discretionary funds – around $40 million – are now kept in a pool and each business area manager is required to justify to his or her peers why they need these extra funds (but below a threshold figure they can access these funds without prior approval, provided they follow agreed criteria including setting out a compelling reason why the funds are required). Joachim described the reaction: "I told them to spend what was required and I'd monitor. Everyone, from top executives to the plant managers, went crazy. The group accountant asked me, 'How the hell will you be able to tell me what the variances are?' I said, 'Don't worry – I won't tell you.' And he hasn't asked me since."

The process has required Joachim to look at costs differently. Re-categorizing them into discretionary and non-discretionary makes managers think about the true purpose of their expenditures. "We have reduced core cost categories to the 22 that really matter," says Joachim. These include chemicals, energy, administration, asset improvement and asset maintenance. While the initial focus was on driving out unnecessary discretionary costs, more recently managers have been examining core costs as well.

With the extra time now available (not doing detailing planning and budgeting!), they are now able to use activity-based costing (ABC) to better understand their cost drivers. "Managers now receive meaningful answers to such questions as 'Why are my operators spending 40 percent of their hands-on time operating a plant, another 10 percent on raising purchase orders and so much on safety training and other administrative tasks?' In short, they can now identify product and service delivery costs, process costs and capital and operating costs of infrastructure assets. And for any of its activities, Sydney Water can pose 'what-if' scenarios that can model costs. "No one had ever figured out exactly what the cost of operating each of our assets was. ABC does just that," notes Joachim.

The result: significant cost reductions with no redundancies

The AMD replaced its planners with only four business analysts. Perhaps Joachim's biggest success, however, has been in changing management mindsets. Managers now focus on achieving outcomes rather than matching costs with budgets. Another major benefit has been to remove the 'silo effect' which encouraged managers to build 'fat' into their budgets. The result was that the AMD met its cost-reduction goals without any compulsory redundancies – an outcome that was thought impossible at the outset.

This case just shows what can be done with imaginative solutions even within a tightly regulated and controlled public sector organization. By challenging decades of accepted practice Aubrey Joachim had been able to make radical changes in the performance management process, leading to millions of dollars of savings.

The opportunity for cost reduction is huge

Unlike Sydney Water, and despite many years of cost reduction programs, most organizations still operate with much higher levels of cost and capital expenditure than is warranted by their size, scale or profit potential. As we observed at Sydney Water, the annual budgeting process has much to answer for, as it almost guarantees that costs and capital will increase over the previous period and that all the money allocated in the budget will be spent (whether justified or not) by the end of the year.

The result is that most organizations are adding costs faster than value. They fail to understand a simple fact of business life: while revenues relate to individual customer orders, costs are related to a host of activities and transactions, many of which have nothing to do with customer orders – so the more activities that people do and the more transactions they handle, the more costs they incur.

The adaptive organization depends on a more dynamic deployment of resources so that they support the best current opportunities. Principle #11 suggests ways this can be achieved as well as offering alternative methods of controlling resources without the need for an annual budget.

Implementation guidelines

- Align investments with the best current business opportunities.

- Design and use a standardized decision process.

- Give teams more accountability for cost management.

- Use an internal market to enable teams to acquire products and services when needed.

- Manage cost drivers rather than cost centers.

Align investments with the best current business opportunities

One of the primary responsibilities of the executive team is to align investments with the best current business opportunities. They act like a venture capital

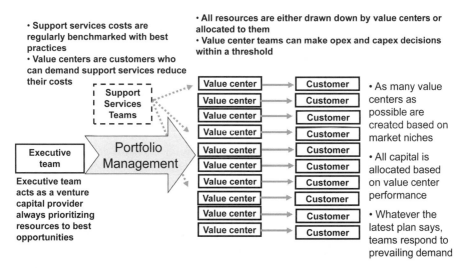

FIGURE 11.1 The head office role is to ensure that resources follow the best current opportunities

provider always prioritizing resources to best opportunities (see Figure 11.1). Value center teams can make operational (opex) and capital expenditure (capex) decisions within a threshold. Above this level, all plans needing capex decisions need (fast) approval.

Few companies have control over their investment portfolios. In some cases, these can include hundreds of initiatives with an aggregate investment cost of billions of dollars. Even fewer firms have clearly defined processes for reviewing project proposals. Bad projects squeeze out good ones and there is little visibility throughout the organization. A recent report by AMR Research contends that as many as 75 percent of IT organizations have little oversight over their project portfolios and employ non-repeatable, chaotic planning processes.[2]

But excellent portfolio management processes can save companies huge amounts. One insurance company claims that portfolio management has reduced their company's overall IT applications expenditures by 20 percent and that, within that spending reduction, maintenance costs have gone from 30 percent to 18 percent.[3] Effective portfolio management begins with gathering a detailed inventory of all your investment projects, ideally in a single database (including name, length, estimated cost, business objective, return-on-investment and business benefits).

Dynamic resource management at American Express

A number of years ago American Express didn't have much of a clue how much of its discretionary spending was on worthwhile projects. Nor did it know if it was optimizing risk across its portfolio. Its investment initiatives were tracked on thousands of spreadsheets, but no one could collate the whole picture. Each of its ten business units had its own funding projections for technology, sales, operations and marketing projects. Cost estimates for these projects were then compiled by each unit's finance department which submitted the proposals. With around 7000 investment initiatives in play at any one time and a total spend of $5 billion (representing around 30 percent of the total operating expense base), the potential wastage in the system was huge.

The problem was that business units didn't use the same methods to calculate returns. The Global Corporate Services group, which handles corporate card and travel customers, might use a 12 percent discount rate to calculate net present value on a project, while the Consumer and Small Business Services unit might use 6 percent. Other complications included unregulated version control, little accountability for financial projections and no easy way to get a corporate-wide view of projects and their finances.

The International Payment Services group was the first unit in American Express to take the initiative and built a prototype for what would eventually become the parent company's Investment Optimization System (IOS). This system puts American Express's global business units on an equal financial footing with standardized models and assumptions, tighter version control and better analytics. Since it went online a number of years ago the system has reallocated tens of millions of dollars between business units for more optimal investments. Because of the new system, when American Express detects an opportunity and they have funding, they can quickly move forward. In one year the company was able to invest 20 percent more funding over their base plan, which led to an 8 percent rise in new cards.

Resource decisions have moved to front-line teams with the board (or an appointed subcommittee) in control of the strategic project portfolio and the prioritization of resources. This committee is constantly looking at rolling forecasts and releasing funds on the basis of capacity plans and strategic initiatives. This process tells them what funds they have available, how many funds are already committed and what is left to release into the system. This approach has cut costs dramatically as capacity is not fixed months in advance based on unrealistic assumptions.

The investment optimization system includes all discretionary investments whether based on "capital" or "revenue." The IOS is an ongoing process that utilizes data on financial returns, risk and strategic importance. It is a way of doing business and a way of thinking about investment decisions. It addresses the question: "How do we use available resources to improve future performance?" In essence, IOS is the process of allocating resources among various projects, functional groups (e.g. marketing, IT, operations, R&D, etc.) and/or business units. It's a way to increase enterprise flexibility by showing which items to fund if more resources become available and which items should be sacrificed if total funding must be reduced. Above all, it enables executives to focus on value creation rather than budget variances.

Adaptive organizations see the investment portfolio through the lens of value centers and operate more like a venture capital company than a central banker. Leaders expect business leaders to constantly experiment and spawn new value streams. They also expect to engage in a dialogue about which value centers are creating value and which are struggling. Resource decisions are based on these reviews.

Like American Express, some adaptive organizations have also designed standardized investment approvals processes that apply at every level. These approvals processes include a number of criteria such as strategic impact, risk assessment, net present value, timeframe, investment cost, sustainability and so forth. Some companies then apply a "weighting" to each criterion to reflect its importance for the business or project. While approving small-ticket items is a fast process, they spend much more time on larger-ticket items obtaining "buy-in" from colleagues and peers. The aim is to research all the facts and prepare a thorough case, then implement the project quickly and get it right first time.

Design and use a standardized decision process

Most organizations use tried and tested capital approval processes with a number of "gates" that each project must pass through as it works its way through the system towards approval and execution. However, where the risk assessment comes in the process is critical. More often than not, risk is included in a subsection of the proposal marked "project risk." The problem, as author Matthew Leitch points out, is that it's too little too late: "By the time we write that part of the document we are already committed to our ideas and approach. We've probably defended it verbally in more than one meeting. We identify the approval of the proposal with our personal success."[4] His advice is that leaders should promote techniques where uncertainty gets identified early, before people are personally committed. Risk thinking needs to be part of the way ideas develop, not just part of how they are evaluated.

Some organizations have designed standardized processes that can be applied to every investment at every level of the organization. This means that below agreed thresholds, project decisions can be delegated to local teams. American Express has done this successfully. Its "investment optimization system" enables managers at every level to evaluate new projects within a common set of rules and guidelines. The process is fully transparent and subject to compliance audits after the event. It has led to a faster and more effective decision process and has enabled the company to make many more decisions in shorter timeframes.

Give teams more local accountability for cost management

Many finance teams add more and more cost centers in the belief that this provides more control over spending and makes business managers more accountable for that spending. But does this cat-and-mouse game really produce results? The likely answer is "no," as business managers use their creativity to describe and analyze their spending to fit what's available in the budget account codes.

Some finance leaders have moved in the opposite direction, reducing up to 95 percent of cost centers and budget lines and giving managers much more scope and authority to spend within larger cost "buckets." This cuts out huge amounts of detail and cost as well as changing the perverse behavior of playing the system. It also makes managers more accountable for their spending. Providing larger spending buckets gives managers much more flexibility as to how those funds are spent and saves time on cost allocations and variance analysis. It also helps to educate employees as to which costs add value and which don't.

Show people which costs add value

In 2008 Cisco Systems slashed annual travel expenses from around $750 million to a run rate of approximately $350 million. In April 2008 Cisco revised its travel policy to eliminate a pre-trip approvals process. Now, only policy exceptions are forwarded for manager approval. The self-booking tool was reconfigured to ask employees to identify a reason for travel: customer travel, external travel, internal travel, emergency travel or training. Depending on the response, employees are directed to the appropriate tool. For example, those who identify the travel as customer or external travel land on the self-book tool site. Provided travel is booked within Cisco's "lowest available preferred" policy, the reservation is booked. Employees who select internal travel are redirected to a booking site for WebEx, TelePresence, audio- or videoconferencing. Cisco found that 49 percent of travel was for internal reasons. Now when you click on internal meetings as a reason for a trip in the self-booking tool, you stop. It won't let you go further. Only a senior vice-president can approve internal travel. Travel expenses have gone from around $7900 per employee down to a run rate of $3400.[5]

Set directional cost goals

While senior executives may well accept that managers should be accountable for managing total cost (as opposed to line-by-line budgets), they may still want to set overall cost targets and manage performance against them. This can be done by setting ratios (e.g. cost-to-income), or moving averages (e.g. a 2 percent decrease over a period) and then managing cost center performance by exception. At Borealis in the late 1990s, accountability was devolved to operating managers who monitored trends within a medium-term goal. No specific targets were set

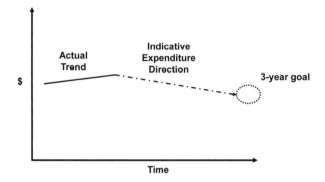

FIGURE 11.2 Setting directional spending guidelines

for costs (except for a "default" reduction level of between zero and two percent) *unless there was a step-change required.* In the absence of such a step-change, costs were simply tracked on a monthly moving average (year-on-year) basis. This is an important part of the reporting system. Again there is no "micro" picture, just the broad-brush view of cost trends. Nor does it require an annual review. It is a rolling system of cost management. The moving average picture is sufficient for most purposes. It answers the broad questions such as: "Are costs under control?" and "Are they moving in the right direction?" Borealis used this approach successfully to reduce its fixed costs by 30 percent over 3 years.

Moving averages can also be used to set "directional" levels of spending, usually in the form of expenditure directions (for example, over three years) set in relation to the latest 12 months' actual expenditure. The message is this: "Your current spending level is following this trend. Over the next three years you should manage your resources so that the level of spend moves in this direction." The direction is usually expressed as a percentage change in the level of spending on a rolling 12-month basis, *measured over any 12-month period* (see Figure 11.2). The value of expressing the directional goal as a percentage change is that actual performance can be assessed against the medium-term goal. Thus the control lever is relevant over any set of 12 consecutive months. It is important to contrast this approach with using absolute dollar targets that are changed every year (or more often depending on performance), encouraging every type of gaming behavior. The indicative spending trend line is a ballpark destination in terms of both size and timing. There is deliberate imprecision in the goal on both axes – timing (x axis) and spending level (y axis). This approach also negates the importance of the fiscal year-end and the "spend it or lose it" mentality. The message from senior management is this: "We want spending by the unit to be at an approximate level at an approximate time. The degree of satisfaction at the actual level of spending and what has been achieved using those resources is assessed retrospectively, whenever appropriate, with the benefit of hindsight."

Value center leaders make their plans on the understanding that resources will be made available to the level indicated when they need them to implement agreed strategies. This approach transfers the responsibility for resource management from the corporate center to the front-line team. This transfer of "ownership" changes the spending mindset. Instead of local units spending "corporate" funds (which they are entitled to spend following the budget negotiation) they start to see these funds as their own money to be spent with more care and attention. They also know that they can overspend and underspend as long as they keep within agreed parameters over time. At Handelsbanken these parameters are defined by the cost-to-income ratio.

Unit benchmarks to drive down costs

Focusing on unit cost benchmarks (such as IT cost per employee) is another alternative cost-control mechanism. Placing the unit cost in the context of a league table instead of a ratio neutralizes changes in assumptions (such as changes in demand or in raw material prices), which affect all teams in the league table. It also uses peer pressure as a powerful driver of lower costs. Cost benchmarking is now an accepted part of cost management but it critically depends on comparing the right processes and costs.

One major benefit is that "sandbagging" associated with negotiated budgets will disappear. Managers are well known for including contingencies in their budget estimates. These amounts will vary according to the level of uncertainty, ranging from 10–20 percent up to 50–70 percent of the total cost. The nature of a contingency means that it may or may not be needed depending on unpredictable outcomes. But it is not available for the rest of the organization to spend (by definition, it's hidden!). Suppose that the contingency amount is 50 percent and the probability of not being met is 40 percent. This means that 20 percent of the budgeted amount is excess and *will probably be spent toward the end of the year to protect the budget for the following year.* While the accountants know this goes on, they try to cut the budgets back. Managers pre-empt this tactic by increasing the contingency amount. Whatever the outcome, the result is wasted expenditure in one part of the business while other parts are starved of much needed resources. This is a classic problem of traditional budgeting and is particularly prevalent in the public sector.

Use an internal market to enable teams to acquire products and services when needed

One way of making resources available "on demand" is through an *internal market*. Former CFO of Handelsbanken Lennart Francke tells us how the "internal market" works in practice. "The internal market is a system designed to put central services under the same sort of market pressures that customer-facing teams operate under. Where possible, market rates (or lower) are determined using benchmarks for the prices of the outputs of the central service departments. Under my supervision as well as the group controller, four representatives of 'sellers' (central service functions) and four representatives of 'buyers' (profit centers such as regions and branches) meet to hammer out a price for each possible process or transaction (around 500 prices in total).

"Each transaction within the internal market is charged to the branch immediately through a 'shadow' accounting system. This means that branch and profit center managers have a fairly good view on a continuous basis of what is happening. This is one of the really great advantages from having a decentralized organization like ours. Managers can always act on their own numbers, they don't have to sit and wait for management to make any important strategic decisions. Every transaction in a branch has either an income or a cost or both. All central and regional costs are roughly cleared to branches each month, so that if you add up all the branch income statements they will give you the total figures for the whole bank (although there are some head-office costs like directors salaries that are not charged)."[6]

By transferring authority to internal customers, the internal market enables Handelsbanken to coordinate new actions in hours and days and exert continuous cost pressure on its central services units. That goes some way to explaining why Handelsbanken is so adaptive and has such low costs.

Manage cost drivers rather than cost centers

The focus of cost management is usually upon (sometimes thousands) of cost centers including sub-analyses of functions, departments and lines of business. Knowing how many blue pens were consumed in branch X compared with the previous year is often the level of cost analysis done to maintain tight control. But little learning comes from this type of analysis. Columns of figures month- and year-to-date show actual spending compared with the budget, but these budgets actually prevent managers from seeing the full extent of their costs (many of which are hidden in the joins between multiple lines of business). Budgets focus on cost account codes within the general ledger, whereas costs are caused by the work that people do usually within business processes such as processing an order, paying a supplier or recruiting an employee.

If managers switch their attention from a general ledger view of cost to a business process view, they can begin to see the root causes of costs (or the cost "drivers"). They will see, for example, that some processes have too many steps (or "activities") and too many transactions (some of which are caused by processing errors and other work not done right first time). Cutting unnecessary activities and reducing the volume of transactions offer significant opportunities for cost reduction. Table 11.1 shows more examples of these drivers (some of which need to be reduced and some of which need to be eliminated altogether). One idea is to do an inventory of these cost drivers and work out a plan for eliminating those that add no value.

Leaders in adaptive organizations adopt a process-based management structure to align their operations with the needs of the customer. Professor Tom Davenport has defined a process as "a specific ordering of work activities across time and place, with a beginning, an end, and clearly identified inputs and outputs: a structure for action."[7] Process teams are constantly looking for ways of eliminating work that adds no value and then doing the value-adding work more quickly, with higher quality and, as a result, lower cost. Some firms are using statistical control techniques such as variation analysis to understand whether or not processes are stable. It is well known that unstable processes (those that suffer wide variations in activity flow) incur higher costs.

TABLE 11.1 Examples of cost drivers

Reduce	Eliminate
# of products	# of production defects
# of customers	# of warranty returns
# of purchase orders	# of stockouts
# of sales orders/orderlines	# of supplier late deliveries
# of machine set-ups	# of supplier defects
# of schedule changes	# of order entry errors
# of SKUs	# of customer claims
# of schedule changes	# of refunds
# of goods-in inspections	# of customer returns
# of in-line inspections	# of customer complaints
# of invoices processed	# of repeat telephone calls
# of customer visits	# of late payments
# of checks processed	# of irrelevant reports
# of reports	# of data errors
# of journals	# of unnecessary meetings

Managing cost drivers rather than cost centers: a procurement example

Budgets tell teams leaders little about the drivers of costs. Let's consider a simple process – procurement. In this example, all that's required is for the purchasing department to order supplies to ensure that sufficient parts are available to meet current orders. There are three steps in the process. The first is planning and purchase order processing; the second is quality assurance; and the third is warehousing management. You are the manager in charge of this process and you have been called into the CFO's office to discuss this year's results and next year's budget (see Table 11.2). The CFO starts the meeting by telling you that the company is facing a difficult period ahead and that we all have to tighten our belts. Besides, you have overspent last year's budget by $80,000. He then asks you for your comments. You say that you've struggled to keep costs as low as they are, particularly as transaction levels have increased by 20 percent and it would make life extremely difficult if the budget even remained the same as the actual, never mind if there were any cuts. The CFO points out that warehousing costs have caused most of the increase and finally you agree to cut costs in this area. The final outcome is that you accept a new budget of $2,050,000 – a reduction of $40,000 on last year's actuals.

Now let's replay this meeting but with different information. As the manager in charge, you have been persuaded to prepare a process map (see Figure 11.3). You can now see a completely different picture, which prompts different questions. For example, you want to know why so much time is spent on planning when the lead times within the supply chain are now so fast (within 24 hours for most products). Why can't we just replenish the products on a just-in-time basis? In fact, why do we need to spend any time and cost on planning at all? The next question is on "certifying vendors." Why do we need to do this at all and why is there a 24-hour

TABLE 11.2 Procurement and goods received example – what does this report tell us?

	Actual ($000s)	Budget ($000s)	Variance ($000s)
Purchasing			
Salaries	290	270	20
Expenses	110	100	10
Quality assurance			
Salaries	420	440	−20
Expenses	170	160	10
Warehousing costs			
Salaries	700	660	40
Expenses	400	380	20
	2090	2010	80

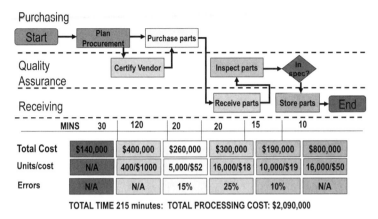

MINS	30	120	20	20	15	10
Total Cost	$140,000	$400,000	$260,000	$300,000	$190,000	$800,000
Units/cost	N/A	400/$1000	5,000/$52	16,000/$18	10,000/$19	16,000/$50
Errors	N/A	N/A	15%	25%	10%	N/A

TOTAL TIME 215 minutes: TOTAL PROCESSING COST: $2,090,000

FIGURE 11.3 Now let's look at the same costs through the lens of a "process map"

delay? Why can't we pre-certify vendors and extend the certification to quality assurance? And why do we have so many vendors? The next question is about purchase ordering. Why do we stock so many products and why are there so many processing errors? Why can't we move to electronic ordering or get suppliers to manage their own inventories? And how can we eliminate the errors? You move on to receiving and inspection. Why do we need a separate quality assurance department? Why can't the warehouse people also be trained to do inspection, and why are there delays in inspection and storage? Why are warehousing costs so high? Is there overcapacity or redundant assets? And how many transactions are caused by errors as a result of earlier problems?

As a result of these questions, you reassess the cost position. You decide to cut planning completely; reduce the number of vendors and arrange certification including quality assurance at the vendor's premises (and if their deliveries fail to match purchase orders, they take them back immediately at their cost); remove the quality assurance department (placing inspection with the warehouse team); remove the causes of the delays; and most important of all, reduce the number of transactions, eliminate the errors and improve the flow. The overall result is to reduce the budget by around 40 to 50 percent over the next few years. And, just for a change, the meeting with the CFO will be rather pleasant!

Now also think about this. The first scenario resulted in a "stretch" target reduction of about 2 percent, yet in the second scenario the reduction was over 40 percent. What does this tell you about the value of negotiated targets based on annual budgets?

Capacity = work + waste

Ohno once described capacity as work plus waste. The aim is to eliminate the waste and thus increase the capacity. This is why adaptive managers spend time "mapping" their key processes to understand where the non-value work is taking place and thus find ways to remove waste from their systems. None of these insights can be seen from the chart of accounts perspective. Their aim is to make every employee conscious of good and bad transactions and involve them in the removal of waste.

Managing costs through (usually negotiated) budget variances tells managers nothing about how much cost should have been incurred to execute a particular activity or process. Nor do they point managers to activities that need to be eliminated. How many non-value costs in one year are budgeted for in the next? The lessons for forecasting are also apparent. Stable processes lead to more reliable forecasts than unstable processes with wide variations. Another lesson is for target-setting.

Conclusions

Adaptive organizations are, more often than not, also lean. They focus on horizontal processes rather than vertical budgets. Budgets not only act as a ceiling for costs, they also act as a floor. As a mechanism for understanding and reducing costs they are remarkably ineffective. They act to protect costs rather than help to reduce them. Understanding processes offers many more insights and helps managers to find much deeper (and more sustainable) cost reduction opportunities.

KEY POINTS

- The executive team needs to act more like a venture capitalist than a central banker and ensure that resources follow the best current opportunities. They need to see value centers as a portfolio of businesses that balance risk and return.

- Capital expenditure decisions should be subjected to well-crafted, standardized processes that provide a disciplined framework to guide managers through the process. Preparing a compelling business case, evaluating risk for all the options considered, assessing strategic impact and evaluating return-on-investment are all part of the process. Such a process makes it easier to set thresholds and devolve decisions.

- Don't try to control costs through hundreds of cost center codes (this too often leads to "sandbagging," "spend it or lose it" behavior and "last year plus 5 percent"-type negotiations). Give teams more local accountability for cost management within larger account-code "buckets." For example, use directional cost guidelines such as ratios and moving averages to set cost goals and then monitor the trend line (e.g. cost-to-income ratio). Another option is to use unit cost benchmarks. While senior executives may well accept that managers should be accountable for managing total cost (as opposed to line-by-line budgets), they may still want to set medium-term cost targets and manage performance against them. This can be done by setting ratios (e.g. cost-to-income) or moving averages (e.g. a 30 percent decrease over 3 years) and then managing the trend line by exception.

- One way of making resources available "on demand" is through an *internal market*. By transferring authority to internal customers, the internal market enables firms to coordinate new actions in hours and days and exert continuous cost pressure on central services units.

- Instead of managing costs through hundreds of account codes in the general ledger, focus managers on understanding the root causes of costs (or the cost "drivers") that can only be seen through a process lens. What they will quickly find is that some transactions are caused by errors and work not done right the first time. Cutting unnecessary activities and reducing the volume of transactions are the real opportunities for cost reduction.

## CHAPTER 12

Principle #12 – Controls
Base controls on fast, frequent feedback, not on budget variances

Management by results creates "needs" goals that we feel we must achieve for our survival or for personal gain. Management by means nurtures aspirations, aims that we pursue because they matter to us.[1]

H. Thomas Johnson

Ambition to action : performance management at Statoil

Statoil is the largest company in Scandinavia, with 20,000 employees in 34 countries. It has a strong collegiate culture and hundreds of empowered teams. Over 1100 units use the company's version of the balanced scorecard known as "Ambition to Action" that drives growth and innovation.

Ambition to Action is more than a scorecard. It is the name of the company's integrated performance management process, which runs all the way from strategy

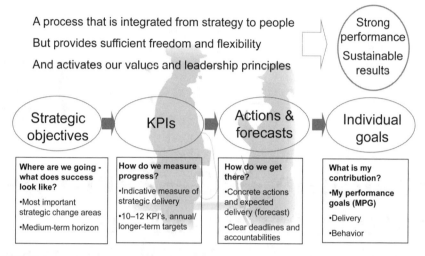

FIGURE 12.1 Ambition to Action at Statoil

to business management and into individual goals, evaluation and rewards (see Figure 12.1). But the company did not just overlay Ambition to Action on top of what it already had. It also took something away. The budget is a serious competitor that almost always wins when two steering mechanisms collide. When budgets were eliminated, it was a strong signal to the organization that leaders were serious about Ambition to Action because that was all they had. Project leader Bjarte Bogsnes' comment was that "by eliminating the budget we turbo-charged the scorecard."

Bogsnes recalls one story that typifies the budgeting problem. "One year the Global Exploration unit announced that they were 'giving money back to the company.' The budget they had fought so hard for had not been spent. At that time we had introduced balanced scorecards. These were very much KPI-dominated. An important metric on the Global Exploration scorecard was 'Exploration costs versus budget.' Even I, who struggle with colors, especially separating red and green, was able to see that this KPI was shining green. The scorecard was also connected with the incentive system, so the greener the KPI, the higher the bonus. But it was not difficult to understand why the exploration budget had not been spent. It was about not entering new exploration areas as planned (which are expensive) and about delays in exploration drilling. None of the two is about good performance. But we managed to turn it into good performance through a very misleading metric called cost versus budget."

But this is not the only reason for the change. According to Bogsnes, "The most important reason for moving away from the budget was the mismatch between today's dynamic and unpredictable business environment and the static budget concept. The modern business environment is also more demanding on performance and results. The response to these fundamental changes cannot be more command and control from the top. It has to be the opposite. You need to give managers and teams more freedom and responsibility. This must be combined with a more transparent and meaningful performance language and more continuous and dynamic performance management processes."

Translating strategy into goals, measures and action plans

The purpose of the Ambition to Action "document" is simple. The starting point is an established strategy where the necessary situation analysis, ambitions, strategic choices and overall direction are established. Ambition to Action helps managers *execute* the strategy by *translating* it into something more concrete by addressing such questions as: where are we going, how do we get there and how do we know that we are moving in the right direction? This is expressed through four standard balanced scorecard perspectives: Finance; Market; Operations; and People and Organization. Statoil has, however, added a fifth – Health, Safety and Environment (HSE) – due to its extreme importance in the oil industry. The conventional order of these perspectives is also changed. While most reporting against scorecards starts with the Finance perspective, Statoil starts with People & Organization perspective, followed by HSE, and ending with Finance. Finance now comes last as a consequence of the actions and deliveries on the other perspectives. Figure 12.2 shows an Ambition to Action document in practice.

This process is subject to challenge by senior people. In other words, the role of senior managers is to challenge ambition, strategic options, forecasts and risks so that everyone is comfortable with goals and actions. At group level it is either continuous and issue driven or it takes place at two executive committee sessions each year. Key outcomes are ambition statements and strategic objectives. Once established these remain relatively stable unless there are major changes in strategic direction.

A strategic objective has a medium-term horizon whose length varies depending on the type and rhythm of the actual business. The objective should describe "what success looks like" when the team has achieved its aims. As Bogsnes explains, many teams get impatient when working with strategic objectives. They want to move on to the KPIs and actions because these appear to be more relevant. It is,

FIGURE 12.2 Example of Ambition to Action at Statoil

however, critically important that each team spends sufficient time developing their strategy together. The discussion itself has value because it often brings out different views about goals and direction that otherwise might not be properly addressed.

From a group perspective, strategic objectives become more operational the closer they get to the front line. Front-line teams still see their own objectives as strategic because they provide guidance and direction.

Using KPIs to set goals and "pressure-test" results

KPIs are derived from the agreed success factors, and then action plans are formulated that the team believe with take them toward their goals. These goals also form the basis for the individual goals of team members. Goals are not fixed to performance measures and rewards. Through a holistic performance evaluation process, team goals are evaluated through a "pressure testing" of KPI results against KPI goals. Results are now the *starting point* for an evaluation, not the end point. These five questions are used to pressure test the results:

1. *Did the KPI result contribute towards meeting the strategic objectives*? With the benefit of hindsight, if we look at what the KPI was unable to pick up,

how does it then look? The answer might confirm what the KPI indicated or provide a more positive or negative picture.

2. *How ambitious were the goals?* Did you stretch yourself or not? This is often much more visible with hindsight than at the outset. The assessment provides a more level playing field and offers a fairer basis for performance comparisons.

3. *Are there changes in assumptions* that should be taken into account? Did you have a tailwind or headwind that had nothing to do with performance?

4. *Were agreed or necessary actions taken?* Did you take action to deal with threats and meet new opportunities?

5. *Are the results sustainable?* Or have you taken action you shouldn't have done to lift your results?

Moving toward relative measures

In this way Statoil is using KPIs as evidence of performance but then looking at the context and other factors before making a final (more holistic) evaluation. While linking accountability to measurement remains imperfect, the system aims to be as fair as possible. Statoil is also replacing fixed goals and measures with relative ones. This peer ranking of team performance is building a more fair and equitable evaluation and accountability framework.

According to Bogsnes, the most challenging part is finding good *relative* KPIs, especially peers to compare with, inside and outside the company. However, in his experience there are many options when you use your imagination. If direct benchmarking doesn't work, indirect benchmarking is always an alternative. This compares a team's *own* relative improvement compensating for different conditions and starting points. However, it is critical that teams feel comfortable with (and therefore own) the peer comparison. It must be seen as relevant and sensible.

The two financial KPIs on the group's Ambition to Action are now both relative. The first one, "Relative Return on Capital Employed," used to be an absolute KPI expressed as a percentage figure. Instead, Statoil now uses a league table of 14 other reasonably similar oil companies and compares the company's return on capital employed performance with this peer group. They have done the same with the other financial KPI, "Relative Shareholder Return." Again, they use a league table and measure against a targeted position. These two KPI targets are the only financial targets the board approves as part of its overall Ambition to

Action goals. More relative KPIs are underway, including benchmarking based on production, oil reserves replacement and project execution.

Devolving decisions within a flexible control system

KPIs are only one part of the control framework at Statoil. Its leaders believe that decisions are best when made close to the situation. This requires sufficient authority and responsibility at the front line. People need room to think and act. This is why they have made the room to move much bigger, but the room still has four walls. This is not freedom without boundaries.

The first "wall" in the bigger room is the Statoil handbook, which sets out its leadership principles and ethical values. Though it spells out how people should act in the company, it is not a telephone-book-sized manual that provides micro-instructions. The second wall is each team's Ambition to Action, which provides specific guidance and direction through agreed strategic objectives, KPIs and action plans. The third wall is the common set of decision criteria and processes for larger projects and major new activities. This is nothing new. What is new is that the company has eliminated the competing decision-making processes set by the budget. In addition, Statoil has well-established decision thresholds. The last wall is sound business judgment. Instead of spending money on marketing or other expenses "because we have a budget," managers now have to ask themselves, "What is the compelling reason for spending this money?"

Managing costs within boundaries (but without budgets)

Within this framework, resources are available in principle for running operations. Different types of cost KPI regulate these costs, including unit cost targets, overall cost frames and also EBIT (earnings before interest and tax) targets as an indirect way of managing cost. For larger projects and major new activities, leaders still "hand out bags of money," but they do this *when* the funding is needed, not during the annual budget allocation process. The funding bank is now open 12 months a year, not just during the four weeks in October when the budget negotiations take place. But your "loan application" can still be turned down. "We shall be just as good at saying no as yes," says Bogsnes. "But why make all those decisions in the autumn? Why not make them as late as possible when we have better information (not just about the project itself but also about our ability to fund it or staff it?")

Statoil now has more than 1100 Ambition to Actions and the number is still grow-ing. As Bogsnes says: "We are constantly asked by front-line managers if they should use Ambition to Action in their own units. Our answer is simple. There is no 'corporate instruction' imposing its use on such teams. We absolutely recom-mend that these managers try it out, but making your own Ambition to Action should be driven by a wish to use it because it works and makes sense for the team itself. If someone established an Ambition to Action because they were told to, they might be better off without it."

Moving beyond the annual reporting cycle

The company has recently decided on the next step on their Beyond Budgeting journey. The calendar year will disappear wherever possible. There will no longer be annual versions of Ambition to Action. "You will have an Ambition to Action until you have another one," says Bogsnes. This does not mean a completely new one, but changed where it needs to change, driven by business events and not by the calendar. The definition of an event is simply "big enough for you." Forecasts will be updated locally on a rhythm and with time horizons which reflect the variety of business realities across the company. For some units three months is a long time, for others two years is a short time. KPIs and targets can be revised when necessary (major changes can be approved one level up; minor changes are just communicated). The unit initiating change is also responsible for informing any other affected unit. Local coordination is not a corporate responsibility. The control mechanism is transparency.

Performance evaluation and appraisal still take place on an annual basis, but in some cases it will review performance in the context of changes to the Ambition to Action. Statutory accounting and other external reporting will still follow an annual cycle.

"We still have a number of questions about how this will work in practice but we are very confident that this is right direction for us. Instead of spending two years on planning, we have decided to jump, and sort out the issues as they arise." Even if this is new and unexplored territory for the company the risk is viewed as minimal. "If it doesn't work, we can go back to the calendar year overnight. Nobody will have forgotten how the process works," says Bogsnes.

The Statoil story is explained in far greater depth in Bjarte Bogsnes' book, *Implementing Beyond Budgeting* (Wiley, 2009).

The control system today: drowning in data yet thirsty for knowledge

Unlike Statoil, most organizations suffer from measurement mania. "Drowning in data and thirsting for knowledge" is one of the pithier phrases sometimes used to describe what's wrong with measurement today. The root of the problem is that measurers are often detached from the performance activity they are trying to measure. The result is that they tend to measure what's easy to measure, that is, "inputs" such as time, costs and activities. What they don't measure are value "outputs" such as the customer relationship experience. Budget variances tell managers very little about what they should do differently tomorrow.

The problem is that accounting numbers show only a one-dimensional view of performance. Like an iceberg, most reports show us only the one-tenth of information that we can easily see (i.e. above the surface). The real performance insights – the other nine-tenths – remain below the surface. We need to use a lot more imagination as well as good systems to find and report upon them. In other words, financial numbers tell you the score but don't help you to play and win the game.

These are not the only problems concerned with the management information system. The volume of data and the level of detail are escalating out of control. Until a few years ago business leaders were shielded from much of the detail flowing through the organization. Now technology has delivered greater power, speed and capacity, and the dataflow is not only overwhelming but can also be accessed instantly by senior people at increasing levels of detail. But for many senior managers the "information overload" problems have outweighed the "control" benefits. And these problems have got worse since the introduction of mandatory compliance procedures that require organizations to keep just about every document that flows through the organization every day (including emails). According to one expert, between 10 and 30 percent of this data is inaccurate, inconsistent or incorrectly formatted.[2]

It's often said that "what you measure is what you get" or "what gets measured gets done." This should concern every business leader, because measures based on short-term (usually negotiated) fixed targets (often reinforced by aggressive incentives) can cause a range of unbalanced (and often undesirable) behaviors, as well as high levels of stress and burn-out as managers strive and strain to meet them. Few of these behavioral problems are caused by mischievous managers or salespeople. Nor are they isolated examples. The problems are *systemic*. They are all examples of Goodhart's law: when a measure becomes a target, it ceases to be a good measure.[3] Goodhart's law is a sociological analog of Heisenberg's uncertainty principle in quantum mechanics. In essence, it states that measuring a system usually disturbs it. And the more precise the measurement, and the shorter its timescale, the greater the energy of the disturbance and the greater the unpredictability of the outcome.

In a budget-driven system the behavior expected of managers is compliance rather than creativity. But, as many organizations are now discovering, this is not enough. They need far more from their people. They need more initiative, creativity, collaboration and leadership. But to switch on these behavioral drivers takes not only new rhetoric but, more importantly, a change to the measurement system.

Principle #12 guides leaders toward designing measurement, control and reporting systems that enable teams to continuously learn, adapt and improve. It means paying more attention to "soft" feedback rather than to "hard" numbers.

Implementation guidelines

- Enable each team to regulate its performance.

- Know your values and boundaries.

- Know where you are, where you're going, why the trend is changing and what action to take.

- Turn dumb KPIs into intelligent analytics.

- Know how you're doing against peers, best practices and market movements.

- Know if your strategy is working.

- Open up information to peer scrutiny and review.

- Maintain a healthy skepticism about measurement.

Enable each team to regulate its performance

As we noted earlier, most organizations consist of three permanent teams (executives, support services and value centers) plus a number of temporary project management teams (see Figure 12.3). It is around these four teams that measures and reports, together with management evaluation, recognition and rewards, are

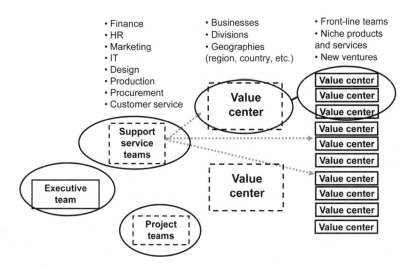

FIGURE 12.3 Identify teams and define success criteria

based. So information systems designers need to ensure that all data gravitate to team-based accounts.

Agree team-based success factors

To start the process of what to measure and report upon, each team needs to agree its success criteria. Take an *executive* team. They might want to know: How well are we improving our financials? How well are we satisfying our customers? How well are we improving our operations? How well are we managing our people? How well are we innovating and growing? How well are we managing risk?

A *value center team* might want to know: How well are we improving our financials? How well are we satisfying our customers? How well are we managing our operations? How well are we managing our people? A value center team is primarily responsible for executing its strategy successfully.

A *support services team* aims to be both efficient and effective. Thus it needs to manage routine back-office transactions at the highest quality and lowest cost, and it needs to provide an effective service to its value center partners. Its success factors might therefore be: How well are we managing our costs? How well are we improving our competences? How well are we improving our systems and processes? How well are we managing our people? And how well are we satisfying our business partners?

A *project management team* might want to know: How well are we managing our major projects? How well are we meeting our cost goals? How well are we meeting our project milestones? And how well are we managing our resources?

These success criteria are examples of what teams will likely want to know. But they should emerge from a "brainstorming" discussion about what success looks like for each type of team.

Deriving the best KPIs

At this stage the success criteria are couched in high-level terms. Keeping the criteria for each team to a range between four and six is important, otherwise the measurement and reporting system will become overloaded. The real challenge comes next. How do you choose the right KPIs that enable you to measure and report upon these high-level performance criteria?

Individual KPIs are important, but they rarely capture enough information about what's happening to tell managers whether one or another success factor is being achieved. You wouldn't know, for example, if customer relationships were in good or bad shape just from looking at customer complaints (many unhappy customers don't complain – they just never return or repurchase). This KPI would give you some clues but it would not tell the full story. So we need a minimum of three KPIs to support each success factor.

Take customer relationships. How many metrics would you need to be confident that you know whether these are strong and improving or weak and deteriorating? You might want to start by breaking down customer relationships into three key issues:

1. How good are we at attracting new customers?

2. How good are we at satisfying our existing customers?

3. How good are we at improving the profitability of our customers?

Think of the metrics you might use for the first issue (attracting new customers). You might think about the number of seminars, one-to-one contacts, demonstrations, brochures, leads, prospects, proposals and percentage of proposals that are closed. These are all quantifiable factors that can be counted, and some might provide a useful correlation with actual sales. You can then move on to customer satisfaction and customer profitability and think of another 10 to 20 possible metrics. You could easily end up with over 50 metrics that in one way or another help you to measure customer relationships.

The aim is to choose only three to five KPIs for each success factor. As far as customer relationship management is concerned, some managers might choose "willingness to recommend," "number of complaints" and "customer retention." What managers are looking for is a "triangulation" effect. In other words, do all KPIs relating to one success factor tell the same story? If so, the confidence level that the story is right (and therefore any action plan based on it will also be right) will be much higher.

10 tests for effective KPIs

1. Are they derived from business purpose or strategy?

2. Do they provide clear direction and guidance about what's important?

3. Do they encourage the right behavior?

4. Are they understandable (are they written in a language that doesn't use too many buzzwords)?

5. Do they include both leading and lagging indicators?

6. Do they lead to fast action if the trend line changes?

7. Can data be collected in an accurate and timely way?

8. Are they "owned" by the team?

9. Do they enable managers to set appropriate goals and show relative results?

10. Do they help to evaluate and reward teams fairly?

While each team should be engaged in thinking about the right KPIs, it is important to remember that if you are using KPIs as the basis for peer comparisons, then each team within the same peer group must use the same set of KPIs.

Know your values and boundaries

It is highly unlikely that leaders will feel comfortable with empowering people unless they are convinced that the new control system will be at least as effective as the old. Front-line teams not only need clear values, they also need some guidelines to strategic direction and to know the broad boundaries within which they can operate.

Harvard professor Robert Simons sets out a number of "belief" and "boundary" systems that help to guide managers when formulating their strategies and action plans (see Table 12.1).[4] He also notes, however, that setting strategic boundaries within which front-line managers can work can have both positive and negative effects. In other words, such guidelines can either be too loose or too tight, leaving the whole process subject to trial and error. This approach, however, is probably an inevitable compromise (at least in the early part of the transition to an adaptive organization) if senior executives really want to devolve responsibility for strategy formulation yet retain some written guidelines.

Front-line managers should formulate alternative strategic options; select those that they believe best meet competitive needs; and then subject them to vigorous challenge by senior executives and peers to ensure they "fit" with the broad strategic direction of the organization. This process of *challenge* is an important part of the new relationship between senior and local managers. Managers must have the self-confidence to think and act locally, but expect their strategic choices to be subject to vigorous challenge. In many cases, however, such challenge is not so much directed at excessive risk as at *too little risk and ambition*.

TABLE 12.1 Beliefs and boundary systems (see Robert Simons, *Levers of Control*, p178)

	Belief Systems	Boundary Systems
What?	Explicit set of beliefs that define basic values, purpose, and direction, including how value is created; level of desired performance; and human relationships	Formally stated rules, limits and proscriptions tied to defined sanctions and credible threat of punishment
Why?	To provide momentum and guidance to opportunity-seeking behaviors	To allow individual creativity within limits of freedom
How?	Mission statements Vision statements Credos Statements of purpose	Codes of business conduct Strategic planning systems Decision authorities Operational guidelines
When?	Opportunities expand dramatically Top managers desire to change strategic direction Top managers desire to energize the workforce	Business conduct boundaries: when reputation costs are high Strategic boundaries: when excessive search and experimentation risk dissipating the resources of the firm
Who?	Senior managers personally write substantive drafts Staff groups facilitate communication, feedback and awareness surveys	Senior managers formulate with the technical assistance of staff experts (e.g. lawyers) and personally mete out punishment Staff groups monitor compliance

Know where you are, where you're going, why the trend is changing and what action to take

Managers can only respond to the information they receive. If this is slow and unhelpful, then they are unlikely to be able to assess the situation and take the right action. If, however, it is fast, frequent and insightful, there is a fair chance they will respond rapidly with the right decisions. How reports are prepared and presented is critical to success, but this has been a neglected part of management improvement for too long.

Relevance is the most important attribute of any report. In other words, if it shows a variation from the trend line it should indicate that some action is required either to correct the deviation or to rethink the strategy or purpose. But nine out of ten reports are focused on accounting cycles rather than strategic demands or management needs.[5] Most organizations have twice as many reports as they need. Many should be either consolidated or eliminated. What remains should be those reports that provide real insight and early warnings of changes in the management landscape. Just as the fuel gauge in a car forewarns drivers that they have only 30 to 40 miles to go before they run out, so management indicators should act as early warning systems that tell managers to sit up and take action. But, contrary to providing more control, most reporting systems are a primary cause of why companies are *out of control*.

Design reports to "fit on a page"

Here are five features of a reporting system that would provide managers with the information they need to make a reasonable assessment of what is happening and what (if any) action to take. Reports should tell us about *context* – for a report to be meaningful, the reader needs to know how success is defined (do we compare results with fixed targets or relative goals based on, for example, peers, best practices or prior periods?); *level* (what is going on today and is there cause for review?); *trend* (what is the trend and what will be the outcomes over the next 6–12 months?); *analysis* (why is the trend moving up or down?) and *action* (what action, if any, should we take?). An important principle is to use only one page for a report where possible (see Figure 12.4). This forces the person preparing the report to be brief yet capture the key pieces of information that the reader needs. Further depth can be found should the report reader require it.

Level

Failure calls this week

		# Calls	% Failure
Agent	1	270	60%
Agent	2	220	45%
Agent	3	280	62%
Agent	4	300	40%
Agent	5	240	30%
Agent	6	190	70%
Agent	7	310	35%
Average		259	49%

Trends

% Failure calls

Moving average

Context

Best practice

Weeks

Analysis

Despite previous actions, failure calls continue to run at unacceptable levels. We need to urgently rethink how we tackle these problems as our costs remain at far higher levels than best practice competitors

Action Plan

Goal: To reduce failure calls by 80% over 2 years

Action: To engage a lean consultant to investigate the problem and recommend improvements

FIGURE 12.4 Report on a page

Design reports that show KPI trends and forecasts

The best organizations produce reports that focus on KPIs, trends, forecasts and peer performance gaps rather than on the "rear-view mirror" of budget variances (see Figure 12.5). In other words, they know where they're going and whether

	History								Forecast					GOAL
	Q0	Q1	Q2	Q3	Q4	Q5	Q6	Q7	Q8	Q9	Q10	Q11	Q12	BP
KEY FINANCIALS														
Orders	290	300	312	324	290	302	314	326	339	353	367	382	397	500
Sales	280	290	300	312	324	290	302	314	326	339	353	367	382	500
Gross profits	84	81	90	87	97	84	90	91	98	102	106	110	114	175
Gross margin	0.30	0.28	0.30	0.28	0.30	0.29	0.30	0.29	0.30	0.30	0.30	0.30	0.30	0.33
SG&A costs	50	55	57	56	58	52	51	56	59	58	60	59	61	75
Net profit	34	26	33	31	39	32	39	35	39	44	46	51	53	100
Cash flow	44	37	44	42	51	42	49	46	51	56	58	63	66	115
KEY COST KPIs (% sales)														
SG&A costs (% sales)	0.18	0.19	0.19	0.18	0.18	0.18	0.17	0.18	0.18	0.17	0.17	0.16	0.16	0.15
Packaging costs (% sales)	0.06	0.06	0.05	0.05	0.05	0.05	0.05	0.05	0.05	0.05	0.04	0.04	0.04	0.03
Transportation costs (% sales)	0.04	0.04	0.04	0.04	0.04	0.04	0.04	0.04	0.04	0.04	0.04	0.04	0.03	0.03
IT costs (K per employee)	3.6	3.6	3.6	3.3	3.3	3.3	3.3	3.3	3.0	3.0	3.0	3.0	3.6	2.4
KEY OPERATIONAL KPIs														
First time through rate	86%	86%	84%	85%	84%	85%	87%	87%	88%	88%	90%	90%	92%	96%
On-time delivery	87%	87%	88%	85%	88%	89%	90%	88%	89%	90%	91%	92%	94%	98%
Customer retention	66%	67%	70%	68%	72%	74%	75%	75%	77%	80%	82%	84%	84%	80%
Inventory (number of days)	65.0	66.0	66.0	64.0	62.0	62.0	60.0	60.0	55.0	50.0	45.0	40.0	35.0	30.0
Accounts receivable days	92.0	90.0	90.0	88.0	82.0	82.0	84.0	84.0	82.0	80.0	78.0	76.0	75.0	60.0

FIGURE 12.5 Move from budget variances to KPI dashboards, forecasts, trends and best-practice goals. BP = best practice

or not to take further action. In this example, the team is looking at a 12-quarter moving-performance window showing seven quarters of actuals, five quarters of forecast and a medium-term goal. This goal provides the context for the report (and it doesn't remain static – it is updated as best-in-class performance improves). It tells the reader what success should look like and how far away the business is from achieving that result. The executive team can see (usually for the first time) a more complete view of performance, including both financial metrics and non-financial KPIs. These prompt different questions from those usually asked about budget variances, such as "Why are we not improving against our peers?" "What actions have we taken and what more do we need to do?" and "Why are our forecasts consistently too optimistic/pessimistic?" They focus on performance improvement issues and relate directly to strategy. Now compare this review with the typical budget meeting where line-by-line variances are discussed. What do we learn from such a review? Not much.

Ken Lever, former CFO of UK manufacturer Tomkins, was a believer in this type of control report. "We can see patterns and pictures of how things are changing and this enables us to ask a lot more relevant questions about performance. One of the things I track is moving annual totals on operating profit and cash flow for each of the businesses. If I see the two moving out of line, I then ask what's happening. And that triggers a constructive dialogue with the business unit team. It might, for example, mean that a business is over-investing, in which case we need to pull back. We also do some scenario planning exercises and we use the forecast information to support them," noted Lever.[6]

The aim is to create a real-time, forward-looking organization. Most companies will tell you it takes months – even up to a year – to get an up-to-date full view of their business today. But this is no way to compete in today's tough, dynamic environment. Managers need fast, high-quality actual numbers and equally fast and high-quality forecasts. Then they will be in control. Then they can make fast and effective decisions. Teams are expected to learn as they go and improve their work processes when appropriate.

Turn dumb KPIs into intelligent analytics

Despite the increased use of non-financial KPIs and the success of the balanced scorecard, problems remain with measurement and reporting. For example, within most "standard" balanced scorecard reporting systems:

- Measures are usually single-point (with no ranges or trends), and too many measures can easily be manipulated to meet agreed targets (for example, surveys show that working capital ratios fall significantly at corporate year-ends but rise rapidly in the first few months of the following year).

- There are too many financial and lagging measures (managers don't know where they are now, what the trends are and what went right or wrong).

- The only context for good/bad performance is the annual target, which is negotiated and fixed (there is no relative context and no rate of improvement).

- Measurement bases are varied (for example, some are in dollars, some in absolute numbers and some in percentages).

- There is no weighting that reflects the relative importance of different measures.

- There are rarely any measures related to ethics, risk or external (e.g. environmental) factors.

Consider grouping KPIs into "analytics"

We need to find a better way to achieve simplicity and depth. This is where we need to move to what's becoming known as "analytics." To understand how analytics work, think of how you measure your health. You might think of a number of key measures such as body weight, blood pressure, exercise level, sleep and so forth. You can probably think of 10 to 15 measures that are important. But wouldn't just a few measures and one composite "index" be helpful? You might think of three distinct measurement categories including lifestyle, body fitness and medical history. Then you might consider the relative importance of each one. While most people are aware of their diet, exercise and sleep patterns, they are not usually good at measuring them accurately. On the other hand, blood pressure, cholesterol and weight are precise measures often taken by professional medical people. Rating your own medical history is also an exercise in judgment rather than precise measurement. Thus you might want to give body fitness a much higher "weighting" in the overall health index than the other two.

By converting all the measures of health into one common scale (score out of 100) and forming one health index underpinned by 10 to 15 KPIs, you can more easily monitor whether your overall health is improving or declining. An analytic focuses on a particular aspect of performance, not just more detail. Each team should have three to six high-level analytics, each with two to three sub-analytics (each with around three KPIs attached) to measure its performance. This can result in around 30 to 50 individual KPIs, but you only need to drill down to them when there is a problem.

Analytics are always shown as scores out of 100. This is a scale that everyone understands and allows you to combine unlike units of measurement. For example, customer complaints are an absolute number, customer retention is a ratio and customer satisfaction is usually a survey. Using software to convert these different measurement bases into a common index simplifies understanding and enables KPIs to be combined into a higher analytic. Analytics should be "weighted" according to importance, data integrity and credibility. Analytics provide managers with reports direct from the system rather than translating information onto spreadsheets and PowerPoint slides so that key people can monitor performance on a daily basis. The next step is to "brainstorm" the analytics and KPIs. Analytics are high-level alerts while KPIs provide the depth.

Take the customer experience. Most of us can think of more than 20 KPIs that can inform us about the customer experience, from "willingness to recommend" and "number of referrals" to "average speed to answer a call" to "average wait and hold time on the interactive voice-recording system."

Let's assume that a customer service team has decided on two sub-analytics for "customer experience" (see Figure 12.6) – customer satisfaction and customer aggravation (that is, what really annoys customers). They have also decided that

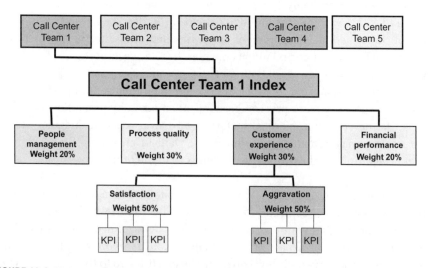

FIGURE 12.6 Using analytics to monitor performance

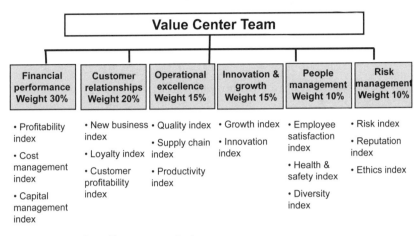

FIGURE 12.7 Examples of business analytics

they are equally important and thus have equal weightings. For customer satisfaction they have chosen three KPIs: customer retention, willingness to recommend and satisfaction of top 20 percent of customers, with "willingness to recommend" having 50 percent of the weighting. For customer aggravation they have chosen percentage of failure calls, percentage of complaints solved first time and number of complaints. In this case the percentage of failure calls is the most important and takes half of the weighting. In this way, managers can keep the metrics they track and respond to down to manageable levels, but also have the ability to drill down to lower levels if the higher-level indicators suggest there is a reason to do so.

A well-designed analytics system enables managers to monitor performance every day, week and month. Unlike most balanced scorecard or KPI reports, analytics not only enable managers to monitor performance in realtime but also find out what is happening and *why*. The *why* is the critical advantage, enabling managers to take swift action to deal with problems before they fester and become major issues that affect the bottom line. Figure 12.7 shows how an executive team might see the performance of the whole business through the lens of six analytics and 17 sub-analytics.

Nine steps to an analytics-based scorecard

As *Beyond the Balanced Scorecard* author Mark Graham Brown suggests, you can build an analytics scorecard using nine steps:[7]

1. Identify a dimension of performance for focus.

2. List all current metrics and brainstorm possible metrics to be tracked. Think of past, present and future metrics. Also think about the integrity of the data.

3. Narrow down the list to a vital few metrics.

4. Assign weights to the submetrics that will make up the analytic. Give the more important metrics a higher weighting.

5. Complete metric definition sheets for each individual metric and analytic that make up the high-level analytic.

6. Develop data collection plans, instruments and procedures. You need to work out how to gather the data. For example, this might involve designing a survey.

7. Collect baseline data or gather historical data on all individual metrics that make up the analytic. Ideally you will be able to go back in time and build up some historic data to provide a baseline for current performance.

8. Establish red, yellow and green targets or ranges. Beware of arbitrary fixed targets. Use best practice ranges where possible.

9. Establish values for expected ranges of performance on all submetrics.

The use of analytics is a recent innovation and often takes managers some time to assimilate and master.

Know how you're doing against peers, best practices and market movements

Traditional organizations set short-term targets and focus all their energies on meeting them. But meeting a target (especially if recognition and rewards depend on this outcome) is often a recipe for gaming and other dysfunctional behavior as managers "fix the numbers." Adaptive organizations focus performance measurement on relative improvement, as they reckon this is the only result that matters. Though no measure or measurement system is perfect, relative measures offer fewer dysfunctional side effects and are grounded in competitive reality rather than internal negotiations.

As Handelsbanken has proved, being the "best" at something is highly motivational and can also be measured over time (Handelsbanken's declared aim is to be the "best and most profitable bank in the Nordic countries"). The bank reports the results of each region and branch every month. Each team can see how it has performed against peers (though no comments are made on performance by senior managers). Comparisons cover cost-to-income ratio, return on equity, customer satisfaction (and complaints) and credit ratings. To improve faster than the competition, Handelsbanken invested not in achieving greater scale and market share but in changing its business model and introducing innovative management practices. With no quotas or short-term targets to reach, managers are free to set medium-term improvement goals and take the appropriate actions to improve faster than others. Of course, even at Handelsbanken 25 percent of branches will be in the fourth quartile! The difference is that the performance of these branches is likely to be higher than top quartile branches in rival banks.

Many publicly listed organizations show their share price performance relative to an index (for example, the S&P 500 in America or the FTSE in the UK). The index can be broad (e.g. all equities) or narrow (e.g. sector performance). Perhaps the best-known measure of "shareholder value" performance is *total shareholder return* (or TSR). Many institutional investors are looking at TSR as their primary measure of managerial performance. Their message to company executives is clear: create value for your shareholders, or your shareholders will find another management team who will.

Employee and customer satisfaction indices offer other ways to track relative performance. The American Customer Satisfaction Index (ACSI) was established in 1994 to provide a new economic indicator tracking the quality of products and services from the perspective of the customer. Research is showing the ACSI to be a leading economic indicator and a predictor of financial performance at the firm level.[8] Individual sectors also have their measurement compilers. One of the best known is in the auto industry, where the JD Power charts track the relative performance of cars in many countries across the world. In the employee satisfaction field, *The Great Place to Work Institute* has been tracking satisfaction levels for over 20 years.[9]

The overall effect of these changes is a management process based on a *relative improvement contract* rather than a fixed performance contract. The implicit agreement is that executives provide a challenging and open operating environment and that employees deliver continuous performance improvement using their knowledge and judgment to adapt to changing conditions. It is based on mutual trust. But it is not a soft alternative to the fixed performance contract. High visibility of individual and team performance offers no hiding place. Managers must perform to high levels of expectation. Otherwise they will fail to survive.

Know if your strategy is working

Value center teams know their strategies (or *customer value propositions*) and use fast KPIs to monitor whether their strategies are working. There are three classic value propositions (see Table 12.2): *product leadership* (best product), *operational excellence* (best value-for-money products and services) and *customer intimacy* (best customer solution). Every strategic position looks for ways of bonding with the customer, thus making it costly or difficult for the customer to switch to other products, services or suppliers. Determining your core value proposition is not easy. Most senior managers like to think their company is good at all of them. However, while this might be true, at least to some extent, the point to remember is that to achieve competitive advantage you need to be *exceptionally* good at one of them, and it is this one that distinguishes you from the competition. It is important to recognize that the value proposition is what distinguishes the business from its competitors in the eyes of the customer, but that managers *must meet industry standards* in all other elements.

It is important that leaders align their metrics with their chosen value proposition. Some product leaders track organic growth and the percentage of sales that come from products released in the past three or four years as a measure of innovation. Operational excellence exemplar Toyota looks at a range of operational KPIs daily

TABLE 12.2 Derive metrics from strategy

	Product leadership	Operational excellence	Customer intimacy
Customer value proposition	• Best products • State of the art products/services • Feel-good brands	• Best total cost • No hassle, speedy service • Reliability, availability	• Best total solution • Customized product or service • Expert knowledge
Core processes	• Talent recruitment • New product development • Commercializing products • Brand management	• Demand management • Supply chain management • Production and distribution • Integrated logistics • Service and support	• Customer service • Customer knowledge gathering • Solutions development • Relationship management
Key metrics	• Organic growth • % sales from new products • Talent recruitment metrics • # of patents filed	• Supply chain metrics • Process cycle times • Quality metrics • Asset utilization metrics • Working capital turn	• Customer acquisitions and defections • Customer retention • Customer complaints • Complaints resolved first time

and weekly, including the percentage of vehicles (or components) produced with no defects (indicator of quality), percentage of items produced to *takt* time (indicator of productivity) and percentage of part numbers running with more *kanban* in circulation than planned (indicator of inventory management). Customer intimacy companies such as Handelsbanken monitor customer acquisitions, retention levels, defection rates and transaction volumes as measures of customer relationships.

In each value proposition there are key metrics that tell managers whether their strategies are working or veering off course. In the latter case they need to either take swift action or, if the problems relate to key underlying assumptions, they should change their strategy.

Adaptive organizations have occasionally used balanced scorecards in parts of their businesses to enable self-managed teams to better see their connections in the network and provide guidance on how to provide more value. But they are not treated as annual performance contracts that are relentlessly measured like monthly budget variances. The wiring is soft and flexible. As demand changes, so do the connections.

Open up information to peer scrutiny and review

Many organizations invest huge amounts of time and expense on improving their management information systems – especially implementing KPIs – but then blow the benefits by tightening the coils of central control rather than empowering their people. The opportunity to use KPIs to improve transparency and communication is now beckoning. Control can now be at the front line *and* at the corporate center at the same time. In other words, control and empowerment are no longer trade-offs that leaders need to make.

In the adaptive organization *transparency is the new control system*. Think about travel and entertaining expenses. Why do so many companies spend huge sums on managing these when just opening every manager's expenses up to scrutiny by everyone else would be the cheapest and most effective control system available? What many leaders fail to realize is that control is not only about complying with agreed processes and procedures but also about building a cohesive management culture. It is difficult for one (or even two or more) people to commit a fraudulent act if their decisions are open for others to see. Of course, no one expects to spend hours poking around in other people's files, but just the fact that they *could* is enough disincentive to nip any bad thoughts in the bud. There is, of course, a trade-off between open information and leakage to undesirables. But in an age of instant copying, your most sensitive information is probably already sitting on some personal storage device ready for when people might leave the organization. That's why the option of full transparency is the best one to take. Could an Enron or WorldCom have happened with fully open systems? Unlikely.

Despite these developments, too many organizations continue to operate in a gray area between what's right or wrong and too often step over the wrong side of the ethical line. But in a world of constant digital surveillance, 24/7 media and web-based social networks, any of which can turn an error of judgment or hidden truth into a reputation melt-down in an instant, operating in the twilight world of balancing cost/profit against what's ethically right/wrong makes no sense at all. The ethical decision is the only one to make.

But total transparency is a step-change from where most companies are today. It requires changes in how leaders think about information and how the measurement and control process works. Information systems should provide front-line managers with the capability they need to "run their own business," to effectively manage project-based initiatives, and enable them to share knowledge and best practices with colleagues across the company before making important decisions. They enable managers to synthesize apparently unconnected pieces of information and knit them together into flashes of insight. These "lightbulb" moments might be rare, but they are facilitated by having access to the whole panoply of information available rather than just seeing someone else's view of the world.

Transparent information systems give leaders confidence that effective, consistent decisions will be made by every team. They also breed a collegiate, collaborative culture within which problems are immediately shared and dealt with before they get out of hand and lead to serious damage. Measurement at Toyota is based on learning and improvement at the front line. That's why Toyota, despite having an excellent accounting system that allows it to comply with regulatory authorities, actually has no standard cost-accounting system. The only measures inside the plant are visual ones. They don't drive operations with the numbers. They don't measure to check where they are against some target. They follow a different logic, a deeper logic. They measure only to enhance awareness of how the work is flowing.[10]

Maintain a healthy skepticism about measurement

Leaders of adaptive organizations recognize that a business is a complex system operating in a changing world. Therefore a range of measurement tools or perspectives is required to determine how the business is performing, whether intervention is required and what form it should take.

But some leaders rely too much on measurement and not enough on judgment. Deming, for one, was a skeptic. He once observed that over 97 percent of the circumstances that affect a company's results are unmeasurable, while less than 3 percent of what influences final results can be measured. Nevertheless, American managers, according to Deming, tend to spend over 97 percent of their time analyzing measures. Less than 3 percent of their time is spent on what really matters – the unmeasurable.[11] He also believed that answering the question "How do you know?" is crucial. People would talk about performance in terms of numbers and he would ask, "How do you know? How can you possibly assess things with the minuscule little elements you're looking at here? How do you know?"[12] This is a disturbing question for all those involved in performance measurement.

Conclusions

The primary role of traditional measurement systems, which are still used in most companies, is to pull "good information" up so that senior managers can make "good decisions" that flow down. However, information is much more useful if it is available in realtime and action can be taken immediately by the team doing the work. This is the role of KPIs. They enable front-line teams in the adaptive organization to regulate their own performance and thus continuously improve. But it is *how* you derive and implement KPIs that is the key to success. Most of us gain some advantage from using KPIs, but few of us really get what we're looking for: a system that tells us where we are now, what the trends are and whether they are moving up or down and what action to take to execute our strategy effectively and meet our longer-term goals.

KEY POINTS

- Control starts with a clear understanding of who you are as an organization and what you stand for. Thus core values and boundaries set the decision-making parameters. Producing a handbook setting these out can be helpful.

- Defining success is the cornerstone of management control (if you don't know where you want to go, how can you monitor progress?) Switching from fixed targets to relative goals changes what managers need to measure and control from budget variances to peer comparisons.

- Every organization is vulnerable to short-term twists and turns and thus needs to manage the short term effectively. You need to ensure that information is fast, open and transparent and sits on a common IT platform that enables all managers to see the same information at the same time. A few well-chosen key performance indicators available at every level act like a radar screen to enable managers to avoid threats and seize opportunities. But it is hard to strike the right balance between using only a few simple KPIs and providing relevant, actionable measures and reports. For these reasons, some companies are combining a number of KPIs into what is becoming known as "analytics." An analytic focuses on a particular aspect of performance (for example, customer relationships or employee satisfaction) and is made up of a series of sub-analytics, each of which tracks a different dimension of performance (not just more detail). A scorecard that includes three to six high-level analytics each with two to three sub-analytics and two to three KPIs per sub-analytic is likely to have more than 50 KPIs. However, with well-designed software (an essential ingredient of the analytics system) you only need to drill down to them when there is a problem.

- Not only do most organizations suffer from slow information (often lacking relevance), but they also have little visibility into the near-term future (i.e. three to 18 months ahead). Needless to say, this is a critical handicap in turbulent times, thus rolling forecasts become a key part of the control system. They inform leaders about future cash flows and capacity needs. And they give them extra time to deal with demand changes.

- Start the process of what to measure and report upon by agreeing the strategic goals or key success criteria for each team. "Brainstorm" the potential KPIs. Choose three to five for each success factor that, when taken together, provide a robust view of its performance. The metrics to choose are those that have high data integrity and help managers to learn and improve. Consider using a "balanced scorecard" to derive KPIs.

- Keep reports brief (preferably on one page) showing level (where are we now?), trend (where are we going?), analysis (why is the trend moving up or down?) and action (what action should we take?)

- An emerging part of the control system is the checks and balances that come from transparency and peer scrutiny. There is evidence to suggest that when information is open and transparent people are more careful what they plan and what they spend!

## CHAPTER 13

Implementation insights

Culture changes only after you have altered people's actions, after the new behavior produces some group benefit for a period of time, and after people see the connection between the new actions and the performance improvement.[1]

John Kotter

How do you change management mindsets?

Our key message in this book is that the management culture of too many organizations is trapped in a time warp of Industrial Age management thinking. Just like the problems of environmental climate change, most business leaders have inherited a cultural legacy from Industrial Age management that is as toxic as fossil fuels and just as damaging as global warming. And just as the planet is being overwhelmed by carbon emissions and melting icecaps, our businesses are being misdirected by over-aggressive targets and suffocating controls. And, to continue the analogy, most business leaders are in denial about their impact. What's needed is a deep cultural climate change.

But, unlike the challenges of tackling global warming, business leaders can transform their organizations reasonably quickly if they replace the greed-induced, "win-at-all costs" management culture with one that promotes accountability, transparency, trust, collaboration and fairness. But how do you change a management culture? For sure, culture does not exist in a vacuum. Nor can you buy a new "culture" from a consulting firm or even change it easily with the introduction of a new CEO. For the most part, culture is a combination of standards and behavioral norms underpinned by a management model composed of leadership principles and management processes. It is notoriously difficult (but not impossible) to change. The trouble is that most leaders attempt to fix parts of the model rather than ensure that the changes are holistic and coherent.

While there is no "blueprint," "recipe" or "roadmap" that you can implement, there are a few experts who can act as our guides as we lay out a number of steps that should help you to move along the transformation path. These include John Kotter, Professor of Leadership at Harvard Business School, and Rosabeth Moss Kanter, also a professor at Harvard Business School. However, the experience of even these leading thinkers was before the advent of new technologies such as YouTube and Facebook that have provided aspiring change leaders with many more options for galvanizing opinion and driving change. Judging by the HCL case, once people are invited into the change discussion and debate, many become advocates and are capable of rapidly building an unstoppable force for change. So our messages will be a mix of old and new experiences. We leave it to you to decide which are most appropriate.

One thing is certain. Cultural change is difficult. Indeed, the landscape of cultural change is littered with good intentions and abject failures. A classic problem is the disconnection between leadership visions and process designs. A well-functioning management model is a highly delicate and complex system. Like every great orchestra, each part has to operate in harmony. Only then can the organization minimize conflict and maximize potential. Simply selecting some parts of the model and omitting others will guarantee failure. If the model loses coherence at any stage it will fail to deliver its full potential. The danger of a reversion to command and control management is high. Thus implementation requires revolutionary thinking supported by evolutionary change.

In particular, a successful management model based on transparency and trust depends on the coherence between leadership principles (with the CEO as cheerleader) and management processes (with the CFO as chief sponsor). In other words, the CEO and CFO need to act in harmony. But this is easier said than done. Typical CEOs want to exceed shareholder expectations by responding rapidly to opportunities, threats and customer needs; launching innovative products, services and business models; driving top-line growth; and of course producing better shareholder returns than their peers. They also want to unleash ambition and encourage risk taking while improving customer satisfaction, making sustainable investments and reducing costs. And they are prepared to trust people to think on their own and make the right decisions, provided they are accountable for results. While CFOs might agree with this vision, they are more skeptical about its execution. In their minds, words such as ambition, innovation, growth, trust and transparency spell one word: *risk.* The fear of losing control is their recurring nightmare. That's why they are more comfortable maintaining tight control over decision-making and spending. They want to bind managers to short-term performance contracts and tie them to detailed budgets. While the CEO is the accelerator, the CFO is the brake.

While introducing new systems and tools need take only a few years, changing management behavior can take much longer. Vineet Nayar believes that transforming an organization takes you on an interesting journey without a map. There are wrong turns, surprising discoveries and moments of both exhilaration and discouragement. Not everyone agrees on the destination – at least in the beginning – much less on how to get there. When you reach an important milestone, you risk mistaking it for your goal. Instead of stopping at that point, you need to review what you've collectively learned – some of it the result of passionate debate – and continue on the quest to make your organization far better than ever seemed possible.[2]

Implementation insights

The problems facing every company are different. They largely depend on history, culture, capabilities and information technology. The importance of vision and communication cannot be overestimated. A clear vision of the task ahead and good communication skills will enable you to navigate around the most difficult obstacles and prevent the organization sliding back into its old habits. The following insights will guide you toward a successful transformation:

- Think like a revolutionary.

- Build an urgent case for change and convince the board.

- Establish a "guiding coalition."

- Create a compelling and coherent vision for change.

- Communicate the vision.

- Enable and encourage people to change.

- Look for quick wins.

- Work around the resistors.

- Consolidate the gains and maintain the momentum.

Think like a revolutionary

Gary Hamel believes that you can't shuffle your way onto the next S-curve. You have to leap. You have to vault over your preconceived notions, over everyone else's best practices, over the advice of all the experts, and over your own doubts.[3]

Revolutionary thinking can start anywhere in the organization. Typically, one person goes to a seminar or reads a book and recognizes the problems in their own organization. They then have three choices. The first is to moan to their colleagues but generally do nothing. The second is to realize that the current management regime is highly unlikely to be receptive to these ideas and to leave, instead joining a company that either operates with the new model now or is receptive to change. And the third is to act the part of a revolutionary and begin the transformation journey within their own organization.

Revolutionaries are people with open minds who can see how new ideas and models can radically reshape and revitalize their organizations and *want to be part of that change program*. Of course, it helps if they happen to be the CEO or the CFO, but change agents can also appear in finance, human resources, operations, IT or, in fact, any part of the business.

Revolutionaries infect their organizations with a change idea almost like a "positive" virus that becomes contagious and gets people talking. Above all, revolutionaries challenge conventional wisdom. They think the unthinkable and discuss the unmentionable. For example, they are prepared to argue that:

- Growth is being stymied through lack of creativity and innovation. The problem is that there are no channels that enable ideas to move from the front line to the corporate center.

- The center of power in the organization needs to be switched from back-office functions to front-line teams.

- Creating many small teams and then devolving accountability to them is the key to driving performance improvement.

- Short-term "stretch" targets don't maximize performance potential (20 to 30 percent of improvement potential is sacrificed in the negotiation process). Subjecting managers and teams to peer comparisons and reviews might be far less dysfunction, and far more powerful.

- The organization is wasting its time and money agreeing complex incentive schemes that drive people to meet targets but fail to improve the business.

- Annual budgets take too much time, cost too much, add too little value and reward the best negotiators rather than the best value creators.

- The obsession with managing earnings is taking management's eyes off the real problems: reducing the huge amounts of waste in operating and back-office processes and unleashing the potential for innovation and improvement. Growing the free cash-flow pie is what really matters.

The challenge for revolutionaries is to make their voices heard. In large organizations it takes time, courage, patience and perseverance. Of course, for every revolutionary there are a hundred experienced executives who have mastered the art of command and control management. They will say, "Okay, we accept the need for change, but why don't we do it in an incremental way?" Revolutionaries do not accept this as a valid answer. They know that an incremental approach doesn't change what's wrong. It only means doing less of the bad stuff. It doesn't challenge the old mental models that are at the root of the problem. That's why revolutionaries take every opportunity to challenge this thinking and convince senior people that they will become corporate dinosaurs unless they face the current reality. That's why revolutionaries are the real heroes of management transformation.

Build an urgent case for change and convince the board

While revolutionaries rattle cages and raise awareness, senior executives want to be presented with a clear, compelling and urgent case for change. They have many calls on their time and have limited attention spans. So why should this idea take precedence over others such as reorganizations and mergers/acquisitions (often promoted by senior people and supported by "command and control" consultants)? The answer is that this is not another "initiative" or "project." It is about how the company is to be managed and how value will be created in the future. The reputation (and longevity) of senior executives is at stake.

The case for change should be both a clear statement of the "current pain" experienced with the command and control model as well as the benefits to be gained by transforming it. Some of this pain comes from the external environment (such as global competition) and some from self-inflicted pressures inside the business (such as lack of growth or falling profits). Some factors are likely to be more urgent than others.

While the case for change might appear to be compelling to you, it can seem too vague and "in the future" to others. So you need to think hard about how you *sell the case.* Hard-pressed managers need more organizational change like a hole in the head. So the reasons must be compelling and the case well prepared and presented. There are many questions to be answered. What will it involve? What are the costs and benefits? Which parts of the business are affected? Is this the only option? What evidence do we have that it will work? What are the risks? How long will it take? How will we know if we have succeeded or failed? Most of these are difficult questions that cannot be answered with any certainty. But addressing them objectively will add to your credibility and increase your chances of success.

It is particularly important to deal with the problem of risk. It would be convenient if we could explain risk using a simple numerical equation, but we can't. However, we can tackle a few of the important factors. For example, although there is always some extra cost involved in any program of management change, there are also cost savings, and this particularly applies to the issue of removing the control bureaucracy. How do you value the time you "give back" to operating managers (often up to 30 percent)? There is also the issue of cost avoidance. Consider, for example, the huge investments that many firms make in trying to fine-tune the existing management system. Millions are spent every year on re-engineering, restructuring and team-building. Most of this expenditure is destined for oblivion because of the constraining power of the command and control model. How do you factor this "hidden benefit" into the equation? "With difficulty" is the answer.

The notion of risk also presents us with a problem. Some managers are genuinely worried that anarchy will break out unless they have the discipline and tight cost controls provided by the top-down budgeting system. However, we have found no evidence whatsoever that any of our cases suffered from loss of control. Nor is it irreversible. This issue was neatly put in perspective by Bjarte Bogsnes when he said that he neither felt exposed nor isolated during the implementation period. In his very pragmatic way he noted that "there is no easy option. The only way is to go for it. However, if it doesn't work you can quite quickly reintroduce the old system. You don't have to burn the budgeting manuals, nor do you forget how to do traditional budgeting in a few months. So the actual downside risk is pretty low."

Finally, the case needs to be "sold" to the people that matter. Who are the key "influencers" that you need to convince? In most companies the two primary persons to convince will be the CEO and CFO. However, engaging the whole organization is now feasible using the latest communication tools and technology as we discovered in the HCL case.

Establish a "guiding coalition"

Attempting a change program on this scale demands that you establish a "guiding coalition" of around 12–15 (usually senior) people who will oversee the whole transformation process. Its responsibilities include:

- Agreeing the case and vision for change.

- Generating a sense of urgency.

- Supervising (but not controlling) the teams responsible for the changes. It is important to understand that this transformation is *not project-driven* from the corporate center.

- Agreeing the principles that will guide implementation.

- Removing any barriers to change.

- Deciding upon the priorities for implementation.

- Deciding upon any investment proposals.

- Maintaining the momentum.

There are four keys to creating such a guiding coalition:

1. *Engage the right people.* Coalition building is not just about reaching out to whomsoever happens to be "in charge" of a department or business. It is about assembling the necessary skills, experience and chemistry as well. Kotter believes there are four key characteristics to building effective guiding coalitions:[4]

    - Position power. Are enough key players on board, especially main line managers, so that those left out cannot easily block progress?

- Expertise. Are the various points of view – in terms of discipline, experience and nationality – represented so that informed decisions can be made?

- Credibility. Does the group have enough people with good reputations so that its pronouncements will be taken seriously by others?

- Leadership. Does the group have enough proven leaders to be able to drive the change process?

Like Kotter, Rosabeth Moss Kanter believes that change leaders need the involvement of people who have the resources, the knowledge and the political clout to make things happen. As she notes: "You want the opinion shapers, the experts in the field, the values leaders. That sounds obvious, but coalition building is probably the most neglected step in the change process. In the early stages of planning change, leaders must identify key supporters and sell their dream with the same passion and deliberation as the entrepreneur. Coalition building requires an understanding of the politics of change, and in any organization those politics are formidable."[5]

2. *Grow the coalition strategically.* Like a good board of directors, an effective guiding coalition needs a diversity of views and voices. Once a core group coalesces, the challenge is how to expand the scope and complexity of the coalition. It often means working with people outside your organization – even for an internal change effort.

3. *Work as a team, not just a collection of individuals.* Leaders often say they have a team when in fact they have a committee or a small hierarchy. The more you do to support team performance, the healthier will be the guiding coalition and the more able it will be to achieve its goals. Especially during the stress of change, leaders throughout the enterprise need to draw on reserves of energy, expertise and, most of all, trust.

4. *Influence, but don't control.* It is important that the program is not seen as a "solution" rolled out from the corporate center. Everyone has to have a voice and be part of the transformation. When asked if a transformation program can work if the CEO is not leading the change, Vineet Nayar gave this reply: "Yes, the original seed of the idea came from me, but it has been developed, detailed and put into practice by a large number of people throughout the company, starting with HCL's 300 most senior managers, and then involving almost everyone. EFCS [Employees First, Customers Second – the name given to the transformation program] was not a top-down program, complete with directives and criteria and all of that; there was no traditional roll-out level by level; I did not present myself as the ultimate judge of whether or not we had succeeded. The transformation eventually has come to have the quality of a

'movement' to it, rather than of a top-down campaign. So, yes, this particular transformation had a leader and that leader was the CEO. However, one of the goals of the EFCS approach is, as I have mentioned, to transfer the responsibility for change away from the office of the CEO and to the employees. That means that, ultimately, leaders can and will emerge who have the ability and the will to create change."[6]

Gary Hamel suggests that you get 30 or 40 of your colleagues together and divide them into four or five teams. Have each of them pick a central management process to focus on (planning, budgeting, recruiting and training are particularly good candidates for this exercise). Now ask each group to outline the primary characteristics and features of their chosen process. Specifically, they should ask:

- Who "owns" this process? Who has the power to change it?

- What purpose does this process serve? What contribution is it supposed to make to business performance?

- Who gets to participate in this process? What voices are heard?

- What are the inputs to this process? What data get considered?

- Whose opinions get weighted the most heavily? Who has final decision-making authority?

- What decision tools are used? What kind of analysis gets done?

- What are the criteria for decision-making? How are decisions justified?

- What events or milestones drive this process? Is it calendar-driven or real-time?

- Who are the "customers" of this process? Whose work does it most directly impact?

The goal is to develop a relatively detailed "as is" description of each team-nominated process. Once they've mapped their particular process, ask the team members to imagine how that process might be redesigned to reflect the new management principles that have been discussed.[7]

Create a compelling and coherent vision for change

While building an urgent case for change is an important step in the change process, it is not sufficient to galvanize people into action. You also need to explain to your people how the organization will look and feel if you successfully navigate your way along the transformation journey. In other words, you also require a compelling and coherent vision for change. This is the first task for the guiding coalition and it can take months to complete.

There are many pitfalls. "Because it relates to the future," says Kotter, "people assume that vision building should resemble the long-term planning process: design, organize, implement. I have never seen it work that way. Defining a vision of the future does not happen according to a timetable or flowchart. It is more emotional than rational. It demands a tolerance for messiness, ambiguity, and setbacks, an acceptance of the half-step back that usually accompanies every step forward." Kotter believes that leaders must convey a vision of the future that is clear in intention, appealing to stakeholders, and ambitious yet attainable. Effective visions are focused enough to guide decision-making yet are flexible enough to accommodate individual initiatives and changing circumstances.[8]

Leaders need to articulate a vision that "grabs" people. It needs to paint a picture in people's minds of what the organization will look like when the transformation is complete. They need to believe, as you do, that the benefits are worth the risk and the sacrifice. Just imagine for a few moments that you could wave a magic wand, take advantage of every piece of new technology, change the mindsets of your people and generally replace your management model. Where would your imagination take you? Try this wish list for size.

- Imagine that your people are suddenly free from the burdens of bureaucracy and stifling controls and have 30 to 50 percent more time to add value as well as improve their work/life balance. How would they spend this extra time? Growing the business? Developing their people? Improving their business processes? Finding and satisfying the right customers? What would be the impact on staff morale and business improvement?

- Imagine that everyone thought your business was a great place to work, with high levels of trust, integrity and knowledge sharing. Imagine that your people have the capability (training, information, tools and support) to assimilate, evaluate and act on information as it emerges in real time and take the best decision available. What would be the impact on staff morale, employee participation and customer service? What would be the impact on productivity and value creation?

- Imagine that your people have the capability, scope and authority to constantly think about strategy, innovation and improvement. Imagine that these people are constantly watching dashboards of key predictive indicators and forecasting the near-term future (without the bias and "second-guessing" that make most forecasts useless), enabling them (and you) to take the right actions to favorably influence future outcomes. Imagine that new plans are conceived, coordinated and executed in days rather than months. How much faster would you respond to threats and opportunities? How many more improvement ideas would you implement? How much more control would they (and you) have?

- Imagine that information about supply chains, production processes, product problems, competitor actions, order shortfalls and customer problems is shared around the organization in a matter of minutes instead of days. Imagine that your managers can tell day by day or week by week whether your customers are profitable and satisfied. Imagine that everyone can see the performance of everyone else? What would be the impact on the sharing of knowledge and best practices? How much more open and transparent would your organization be? What would be the impact on ethical behavior?

- Imagine that your managers are able to spend time experimenting with new products and processes with the prospect of a small percentage of them becoming winners. Imagine that your resources are dynamically prioritized to follow the best current opportunities. Imagine that all your projects represent the best strategic options and were closely tracked to ensure they met their objectives. What would be the impact on the quality of your investment portfolio? How much wasted investment would you avoid? How many more innovative projects would you sponsor?

- Imagine that your teams set realistic goals without the need for annual negotiations (and these goals are far more "aspirational" than before). Imagine that accountability and rewards are shared around the organization and are seen to be fair and consistent and support the value-creating behavior you desire. How self-motivated would your people be? What would be the impact on commitment, growth and profitability?

The vision of this hypothetical organization is of course just a pipe dream for most of us. But there are some organizations (some of them described in this book) where most of these dreams have come true. They have succeeded in building great places to work, do business with and invest in. So what is holding you back? Is it lack of ambition, courage or perhaps the fear of letting go? Think about this. Transforming your management model is probably the greatest service you can provide to your organization. It will provide a platform for future growth and renewal. And, given time, it will leave your competitors standing.

Communicate the vision

While agreeing that the vision is an essential platform for transformation, communicating the vision is even more important. "You cannot sell change, or anything else," says Rosabeth Moss Kanter, "without genuine conviction, because there are so many sources of resistance to overcome: 'We've never done it before; we tried it before and it didn't work.' 'Things are OK now, so why should we change?' Especially when you are pursuing a true innovation as opposed to responding to a crisis, you've got to make a compelling case. Leaders talk about communicating a vision as an instrument of change, but I prefer the notion of communicating an *aspiration*. It's not just a picture of what could be; it is an appeal to our better selves, a call to become something more. It reminds us that the future does not just descend like a stage set; we construct the future from our own history, desires, and decisions."[9]

Kotter has seven key elements for effectively communicating a vision statement:[10]

- *Simplicity*. All jargon and technobabble must be eliminated.

- *Metaphor, analogy and example*. A verbal picture is worth a thousand words.

- *Multiple forums*. Big meetings and small, memos and newspapers, formal and informal interaction – all are effective for spreading the word.

- *Repetition*. Ideas sink in deeply only after they have been heard many times.

- *Leadership by example*. Behavior from important people that is inconsistent with the vision overwhelms other forms of communication.

- *Explanation of seeming inconsistencies*. Unaddressed inconsistencies undermine the credibility of all communication.

- *Give-and-take*. Two-way communication is always more powerful than one-way communication.

Communicating the vision will enable all participants in the change process to agree and subsequently access a store of information that will guide the whole implementation program. There are typically three stages:

1. *Awareness*. The process of awareness and understanding usually starts with a one-day workshop involving all key people. This will be supplemented with other reading materials such as websites, books, interviews, blogs and so forth.

The purpose of this stage is for key people to gain a clear understanding of the new model and some of its key features. In particular, they should begin to realize that this is not a short-term "fix" to a particular problem but a journey toward replacing the whole management model.

2. *Engagement.* The guiding coalition will agree to start a number of initiatives and engage many people in agreeing the best path to follow. Should the change be company-wide or a pilot in one division? One approach is for the guiding coalition to "post" a number of questions such as:

- How should we redefine our "reason for being?"

- How should we define success?

- How do we remap team-based relationships so that accountability flows toward the customer?

- How should team roles and accountabilities be defined?

- What training and tools do teams need to take over planning and decision-making?

- How do we motivate, evaluate, recognize and reward people without using fixed targets?

- What planning mechanisms and tools (e.g. rolling forecasts, balanced scorecards and risk models) do we need and how will they support the continuous planning process?

- How do we give teams more freedom to manage (and reduce) operating costs (what methods should they use)?

- How (and to what extent) should we make our information open and transparent?

The engagement process is really about "sketching the vision." If the HCL experience is anything to go by questions such as these will provoke hundreds of responses and a treasure trove of new ideas for transforming the business. Even better, because these ideas have not emanated from a only few senior executives, people throughout the organizations are more likely to embrace them.

3. *Team-building.* To the extent that there are physical (as opposed to relationship) changes in the make-up of teams the guiding coalition needs to ensure that teams get to know each other and how their roles and responsibilities will change. Each team should start with its own case and vision for change.

The guiding coalition must sell the vision to managers and employees who work in each type of team (executive, support service and value center). They need to be comfortable that they have the information flows and management processes that enable them to effectively manage the business. But do not underestimate how much effort it takes to communicate the key messages. There is often a problem of definition or a common language. Spell out the meaning of words such as strategy, plan, budget, target, forecast, process and control. How you present the changes is also crucial. Employees want to hear that it's about a better management system to improve customer value rather than just another top-down accounting system that they must learn and conform to.

Enable and encourage people to change

Like empowerment, change cannot be mandated from the corporate center. People must want to become involved. Key influencers have an important role to play in this process. It often takes leaders by surprise how involved some people become and how many good ideas they have. In practice we have found that instead of trying to be too proscriptive it is better just to set out a list of guiding principles that people can use to design new processes. These principles are set out in the preceding 12 chapters. Also you can use the chapter summaries as a more detailed set of guidelines.

Vineet Nayar believes that employees at all levels need to be not only responsive to organizational change but also responsible for it. "For example," he notes, "our annual planning process for FY 2010 included a review of business plans for HCL customer accounts not only by top management but by 8000 people throughout the organization. Under the program, dubbed My Blueprint, the plans were available on a portal where customer-facing employees, who would be charged with implementing those plans, could comment on them. This produced a flood of feedback and prompted the re-engineering of several plans. I truly believe that, as in a democracy, those at the grassroots of an organization are as much the harbingers of change as leaders at the top. Everyone isn't always in complete agreement about the need for change or how to carry it out. But, again like a democracy, they're charged with being active participants in the process."[11]

When the recession started to bite in 2008 Nayar turned to his employees and said, "What can we do to get through this? Give us ideas about how to cut costs, increase revenue and retain customers." He received thousands of suggestions from employees, and from those suggestions came a number of initiatives that were shared and executed on. Uncertainty and fear were reduced by transparency.

And though some unproductive employees were laid off, the company increased overall headcount, including in the US and Europe.[12]

Look for quick wins

Demonstrating short-term wins is important to keep the resistors at bay. There will always be people looking for the first signs of failure, so there is nothing better than to show them hard evidence of success. Early wins were important at American Express, as former CFO Gary Crittenden explains: "Early wins are really important because they help to build credibility in the organization. Delivering significant cost savings and better information sent clear messages to all the businesses that these changes meant something. Another lesson is that at American Express, you get more done with partners. Even when people don't have direct responsibility for an activity, they often feel that they have a stake in the outcome and therefore want to be involved. None of this was done in a vacuum. All of the thinking and execution has taken place in consultation with our business leaders. We've involved them every step of the way. We would always listen to their concerns and even when we took action they might not agree with, they at least understood what we were trying to accomplish and why. I can't say we've had 100 percent agreement all the way through, but we've had a good understanding most of the way. That is one of the prerequisites of effective change. With that, I think the two main lessons are to deliver clear benefits and communicate continuously and effectively with all of your key people."[13]

Short-term wins should have three characteristics: They should be visible (people can see the results for themselves), unambiguous and clearly related to the changes. Whereas the "big wins" come from behavioral changes (and are difficult to relate to specific financial results), there are some benefits that can appear relatively quickly. Here are a few:

- *Cost savings.* Companies such as Southwest Airlines and Handelsbanken that have dismantled the management control factory have reduced costs by 10 to 30 percent. Self-managed teams go a long way to explaining why these organizations are so lean and efficient. Instead of hundreds of staff in white coats making remote-controlled decisions, most key decisions are made at the team level. The cost savings from not producing (often irrelevant) management reports was one of the surprises. One example concerned a production manager who maintained his own detailed reports that evidently provided little strategic value yet cost over $100,000 to produce! The payback on the changes – both tangible and intangible – has therefore been quickly in evidence.

- *Attracts the best people.* It is no coincidence that most of the organizations featured in this book regularly appear in the lists of "best companies to work for" (at least those that take part). In 2008, Google was number one in the US and the UK. W.L. Gore & Associates, Southwest Airlines, Handelsbanken, Toyota and many others also regularly appear in the top echelons of these surveys. And employee satisfaction levels are among the highest in their peer groups. These companies are inundated with job applications. At Southwest, Whole Foods and Google it can take weeks and many interviews before an applicant gets through the system – such is the time and value these organizations place on attracting and keeping the *right people*. The reasons are obvious. From the employee perspective, talented people want to learn and develop; they value time to think, reflect and try new ideas (Google and others give them that time); they want decision-making responsibility and they want a friendly, collegiate culture. From the employer perspective, they want people who have the right attitude, have ideas, want to participate in decision-making, are good team players and have the talent to become leaders at any level.

- *More entrepreneurial energy, innovation and growth.* Large business units are seductive to leaders as they promise cost savings through economies of scale. But such savings can be illusory as the energy and enterprise is snuffed out. In the new model it is small teams that provide the dynamism and energy for value creation and growth. It is no coincidence that organizations such as Toyota, Southwest, Whole Foods and Handelsbanken have all grown organically rather than by acquisition. Every team is accountable for delivering competitive results compared with internal or external benchmarks. Handelsbanken managers at every level are accountable for competitive results and are free to decide what action is needed to achieve them. They know that if they are not performing well there is no hiding place. They cannot make excuses with the numbers.

- *A more agile and responsive business.* Freed from the constraints of top-down plans and fixed contracts, managers have the scope and authority to make decisions and thus respond more rapidly to emerging threats and opportunities and meet the changing needs of customers.

According to Vineet Nayar, there is no doubt that HCL recorded strong financial results during the five years from 2005 to 2010 – the same timeframe during which they transformed the organization. He noted that while it is always difficult to prove correlation and causality, "I would say that EFCS is largely responsible for our surge in revenue and profit growth since 2005, which transformed HCL from a laggard compared to others into a leader. The other factors that point in this direction are results of independent surveys on both employee and customer satisfaction. From being nowhere in the 'Best Employer' survey ranking in 2005 we were rated among the best employers in various parts of the world by various agencies, including No. 1 in Employee Satisfaction across all industries in India in 2009 by Hewitt. Our customer satisfaction index, based on factors such as loyalty and value received for money spent, rose 43 percent between 2008 and 2009 and an additional 21 percent in 2010, based on an independent survey done by Feedback Consulting. HCL was also rated as the Number 1 outsourcer in a survey produced by The Black Book of Outsourcing."

However, the strongest indicator of the power of EFCS is the company's performance during the economic downturn. One of Nayar's proudest achievements is that HCL was among the very few IT services providers in the world that continued to grow throughout the years of the recession. HCL grew 17 percent and 24 percent in FY09 and FY10 respectively.[14]

Work around the resistors

If the benefits of going beyond compliance and building adaptive organizations are so compelling, why isn't every leader adopting this model? This is a difficult question to answer. Maybe it's because most leaders prefer to stick with the existing command and control model that they know so well rather than face a cultural climate change. After all, that's the culture that most of them have grown up with and understand. It is this myopic and self-interested view that is the hardest to shift. Here are some of the comments that are frequently expressed:

- *"We'll lose control."* Many senior executives who have only ever worked in command and control organizations believe they can "predict and control" future outcomes through a performance management system that includes targets, budgets and incentives. They have little faith in the capabilities of their people to achieve outstanding results without these mechanisms. They believe that devolving planning and decision-making and releasing key information is a recipe for chaos and anarchy. All organizations make mistakes (why else is the average life of a Fortune 500 company less than 40 years?) and transparent, high-trust organizations are by no means immune from them. Indeed, failure is as essential to the learning process as success. But the evidence tells us that these organizations have excellent control systems. What's different is that they are not based on top-down systems of control but on systems of self-regulation supported by fast, relevant financial and non-financial key performance indicators (KPIs), forecasts and trends, and a continuous process of benchmarking against peers and best practices.

- *"It's too expensive."* If you look at the many exemplars of transparent organizations including Toyota, Southwest Airlines and Handelsbanken, you will find that they are the lowest-cost competitors in their industries. The reality is that their transparent models enable leaders to scrap layers of control-oriented bureaucracy and rely more on open checks and balances. The result is often a reduction in fixed costs of up to 40 percent.

- *"It's too risky."* Many leaders will be concerned that more transparency will provide their competitors with sensitive information that will give away their competitive advantage. Of course, we are not suggesting that you lay open the "secret recipe of Coca-Cola" or your company's innermost know-how and strategies, and certainly not their high-level financial forecasts, but we are suggesting that all current information is openly shared with employees and investors *and explained to them*. Employees and investors need to be treated the same with regard to information access, and both should be subject to insider dealing rules. Bill Gates, Chairman of Microsoft, is one who believes that leaders would be better advised to stop trying to control information and open it up to broader scrutiny. "The value of having everybody get the complete picture and trusting each person with it far outweighs the risk involved," notes Gates.[15]

- *"It will constrain risk-taking."* Many believe that too much transparency will stop people from responding rapidly and taking risks. This is a valid objection *if decision-making and risk remain the prerogative of a few senior executives.* This is the point. In transparent organizations, the opportunity is to open up decision-making and risk-taking to many more people. For the first time, these people will have the information they need to make the right decisions and experiment with new ideas. Transparency builds confidence at every level.

- *"The regulators and internal auditors won't wear it."* Many regulators and auditors understandably focus on process rather than culture. Agreeing and following a plan leaves an audit trail that can be followed and checked. But it is based on the wrong model. Having said that, regulators also have a strong interest in truth and transparency, though many finance leaders overlook this aspect of compliance.

- *"It's not the real world."* Some people believe that words such as trust and transparency belong in Sunday school classes or philosophy seminars and not in the "real" cut-throat world of business. "We live in a dog-eat-dog world and if we don't operate this way then we won't win orders and satisfy our shareholders," is a typical comment. But as various studies have shown, the evidence does not support this view. If the perpetrators of unethical behavior such as Bernie Ebbers (ex-CEO of WorldCom) and Dennis Koslowski (ex-CEO of Tyco) could do it all over again, it is doubtful that any would have chosen the actions that led to their demise. None would now take the view that mis-representing the truth was the best option, even in the precarious situations they found themselves. Of course it is easy to be wise after the event. But this is the point. It is *never worth it.*

- *"But we need command and control when times get rough."* This might be true, and leaders need to explain to people that some tough centralized decisions need to be taken to protect the long-term future of the business. But, again, the evidence suggests that even after serious downsizing, an organization based on principles of trust and transparency comes through in better shape than those that operate with command and control systems.

After making many mistakes in the transformation program at Leyland Trucks, John Oliver had this advice for dealing with people who failed to understand or support the initiative program: "Management needs to maximize their attention to the 'good guys,' that top 80 percent who conform to the idea of positive corporate citizenship … We need to lead by example in marginalizing those who are inher-ently at odds with both the company and, perhaps, even the world of work … The culture of any organization is largely created by what we as managers pay attention to, what we care about and what we reward. We may not intend to convey that impression when we devote a disproportionate amount of time with that bottom 20 percent, but we most certainly do."

When Vineet Nayar was asked if the transformation at HCL was an unqualified success, this was his reply: "Does every single person buy in to a change of this magnitude? That's never going to happen, particularly in a global organization of 64,000 employees which added 8000 new people in just the last 3 months. There will always be an array of responses to change, from people who seize the op-portunities change presents to those who focus on its shortcomings. In the case of the change around EFCS, some people, who I call transformers, 'got it' early. They saw the logic of the approach and the power in the realization that the company's performance and future aren't in the hands of managers but of employees.

"Then there were those – people I call the fence-sitters – who began to see that EFCS was yielding positive results for the company and for individual employees and so joined the transformers in supporting it. But a few employees – say, the last two to five percent of the workforce – will never see the logic or the benefits. They have a different point of view and will never get on board ... Transformation doesn't happen overnight. But initial results make me confident that EFCS is a process worth our patiently pursuing. We are not in pursuit of perfection; our focus is simply to get better with each passing day."[16]

Another way to overcome the resistors is to promote those people who embrace the new values and forge ahead. The real test is when the new culture creates leaders instead of leaders creating the culture. It is no accident that the most successful cases we studied have had stable executive teams at the top for many years. They have also had chief executives who have been promoted from within and who are well versed in the empowerment philosophy. Conversely, there are some cases in which new chief executives have been parachuted in from outside, with disastrous results.

Consolidate the gains and maintain the momentum

It is vitally important to maintain the momentum of change. There will always be people who block and resist. This resistance group will soon start to undermine confidence unless the guiding coalition can demonstrate that the transformation is achieving its objectives. Periodic reviews are essential to give people a chance to assess their achievements and deal with any outstanding problems.

One certainty is that there will be problems. Leaving them unattended will sow the seeds of discontent and potentially ruin what otherwise could be a significant change in people's attitudes. It may be that more training and education are needed, so project leaders shouldn't hesitate to provide them. Kotter offers some good advice: "Irrational and political resistance to change never fully dissipates," he notes. "Even if you're successful in the early stages of a transformation, you often don't win over the self-centered manager who is appalled when a reorganization encroaches on his turf, or the narrowly focused engineer who can't fathom why you want to spend so much time worrying about customers, or the stone-hearted financial executive who thinks empowering employees is ridiculous. You can drive these people underground or into the tall grass. But instead of changing or leaving, they will often sit there waiting for an opportunity to make a comeback. In celebrating short-term wins change agents can give the opposition just that opportunity. I'm confident of one cardinal rule: Whenever you let up before the job is done, critical momentum can be lost and regression will follow."[17]

Vineet Nayar offers this message on the progress of change: "Change management is a complex and evolving topic. You don't want to make the mistake of getting married to one idea or declare victory too early – simply because you've outgrown your competitors or garnered a few rewards. Conversely, though, you don't want to make the mistake of prematurely declaring failure and giving up, just because some people do not agree with you or have not seen the full impact of the changes yet. As I said, EFCS is evolving and maturing. A transformation initiative of this kind isn't a one-time exercise – it requires constant care and feeding and courage to walk the path which you believe to be right. I believe that when you sit back and think about it, you'll agree with me that this is the right path to walk."[18]

Conclusions

It is relatively easy to grow and make profits (provided you have good products and services) when the business climate is set fair and you can predict and control short-term outcomes (at least within a few percent). Many leaders have built management models based on the "same weather as today" assumption. They have agreed strategies, targets and plans (and underpinned them with aggressive incentives) and then marched their people to the drumbeat of the budget. But with such a rigid model, when the recent credit crunch rocked the boat they were unprepared and unable to change direction. Many have hit the rocks, with disastrous consequences.

The question you have to ask is whether the current turmoil is a temporary blip in the economic climate or whether we have entered an era of continuous turbulence and increased uncertainty. If you believe, as we do, that turbulence and uncertainty are now the norm, then you need to think seriously about redesigning your management model to cope with these different assumptions. In other words, you need to design a boat capable of surviving in all possible weather systems.

We believe that in the wake of the credit crunch and recession *now* is the best opportunity in a generation for leaders to convince their people that they need to rethink their management models and the mindsets that underpin them and build a more adaptive organization. How information is used is crucial. If it is seen as a weapon of control, then the transformation process will be stillborn. If it is seen as a liberating tool for front-line managers to use their knowledge and judgment to respond responsibly and quickly, then a new opportunity beckons. We urge you to take it.

KEY POINTS

- Start a debate about performance. Talk to all stakeholders. Organize a survey and hold some workshops. Build a case for change around a clear consensus of opinion.

- Gather together a core group of people to act as a "guiding coalition." Include people from different functions and backgrounds. Give them the scope and authority to supervise the key changes (but be careful not to "project-manage" the changes from the center).

- Don't waste too much time on detailed visions. Agree an outline vision, set some directional goals and get started. Act *on* the system (the "whole"), rather than within the system (the "parts"). Learn as you go.

- Post a number of challenging questions and invite transformational ideas from anyone, anywhere. Select the best ones and try them out.

- Don't alienate managers most impacted by the changes. Involve them in the change process. They often have the best (and most practical) ideas for improvement.

- Whatever you do, don't make management life more complex! Avoid complex systems. Aim to simplify everything at every level.

- Build confidence by showing some early wins. Don't assume they will be self-evident. Point them out and celebrate your success.

- Recognize at the outset that this is a long-term journey. You need perseverance and patience. So take your time but maintain the momentum.

- Don't waste time trying to persuade the blockers. Work around them. They will follow once they see that others are embracing the changes.

- Don't declare victory too soon. This is a long-term journey.

## CHAPTER 14

Make management change your legacy

American management has missed the point – the point is management itself.[1]

W. Edwards Deming

Most organizations don't endure for very long. Even so-called "excellent" companies have a poor longevity record. Of the original 36 companies listed in Peters and Waterman's best-selling book *In Search of Excellence* (1982), only two remained in the *Forbes* top 100 companies in 2002 based on similar criteria: Wal-Mart and IBM.[2] So what have the long-term survivors done that others haven't?

Arie de Geus, award-winning author of *The Living Company*, provides the answer. He believes that firms that base all their beliefs on an economic model that focuses on central control and short-term profits to the exclusion of everything else usually fail to learn or survive.[3] In his research into what distinguished long-term survivors, he discovered one major distinction: "The long-term survivors did not see themselves as primarily economic units to produce profits and value for the entrepreneur and the shareholder. They saw themselves as living systems composed of other living systems – the people who worked for them and thus belonged to them."[4]

The late Bill O'Brien, former CEO of Hanover Insurance, believed that organizations should develop measures that encourage a legacy mentality at the top. "I think most of us buy into what I call a 'chopping wood' syndrome in our early life," he suggested. "We see ourselves as piling up wood from our direct efforts, and equate our effectiveness with how much wood we piled up each day. That's a normal and healthy work approach in one's 20s and 30s. But it is a mistake when managers continue this attitude long after they rise to the top level of organizations. Instead, a maturing transition that senior management teams must go through is to begin seeing themselves as building something to leave for the next generation. This is a little like the transition between being a parent and being a grandparent. You love your grandchildren, but you take your responsibility a little bit differently. You worry a bit less about what they did today and look instead at their development over time. Unfortunately, there are too many executives who are still piling up wood, and this interferes with their ability to develop a legacy mentality."[5]

Robert McCurry, former Executive VP at Toyota Motor Sales, put the importance of the long-term view this way: "The most important factors for success are patience, a focus on long-term rather than short-term results, reinvestment in people, product and plant. And an unforgiving commitment to quality."[6]

These comments by O'Brien and McCurry seem to encapsulate the beliefs of successive leaders at adaptive organizations. Instead of looking for short-term gains to feed their egos and satisfy analysts' short-term cravings for good news, leaders use their knowledge and experience to guide and support their younger managers and help them grow and mature. Like a relay baton in a marathon lasting many years, leaders should be around to hand on a stronger and fitter company than they inherited. That is the true legacy of leaders. While this will reflect in the financial strength of the business, this is not the sole measure. Building capable people and a culture of common sense decision-making at all levels of the organization is an even better measure of the inheritance handed on to the next generation.

Many leaders of large corporations spend their time addressing issues of strategy and performance improvement. They rarely spend time thinking about management and even less time thinking about *management innovation*. While new strategies and improvement initiatives come and go, the impact of management change can last a long time and its impact can be far greater as competitors find it difficult to copy. This could be your opportunity to really make a difference. It could be your greatest gift to the organization.

If you are interested in building a better management model, then why not join the Beyond Budgeting movement? The Beyond Budgeting Round Table (www.

bbrt.org) is a diverse group of people and organizations that are sharing ideas and experiences in their pursuit of a management model that is more empowered and adaptive as well as lean and ethical.

This book is a milestone along the journey. It represents our collective thinking at one point in time. But we all know it is a work in progress. New practices are emerging all the time and adding to the richness of our knowledge. Vineet Nayar's management innovations at HCL Technologies are a case in point.

Members of the BBRT passionately believe not only in improving their own organizations but also in a greater purpose of improving management standards across the world. Raising these standards has the potential not only to sustainably improve the bottom line of individual organizations but also to increase wealth creation with all that implies for jobs and families. The opportunity is that we are starting from a low point on the graph. In other words, management standards are universally poor and the opportunity to raise them is unlimited. Our aim is to unleash the energy, creativity and productivity of people who are too often stifled and frustrated within the command and control organization.

So join us on our journey as we continue to transform management thinking. Everyone is welcome. Everyone has a voice. Everyone can make a difference.

Notes

A note about notes

In many instances throughout this book we have drawn upon references from case studies, interviews and company materials used within the Beyond Budgeting Round Table. In some instances these have not been subjected to specific references.

Preface

1   See Gary Hamel. *The Future of Management.* Harvard Business School Press, Boston, 2007, x.

Introduction: The organization as an adaptive system

1   Gary Hamel. *The Future of Management.* Harvard Business School Press, Boston, 2007, x.

2   William A. Sahlman. Management and the financial crisis (We have met the enemy and he is us…). Working Paper 10-033, Harvard Business School, 2009. In studying the financial crisis as it unfolded over the past couple of years, Harvard Professor of Business Administration William S. Sahlman in his excellent paper *Management and the Financial Crisis* concludes that management is at the core of the crisis. "I believe that the root cause of bad decision-making," notes Sahlman, "resides in the nexus of culture, incentives, control and measurement, accounting and human capital. When those elements are aligned, good things happen and bad things don't happen. When they are out of alignment, particularly in competitive industries, really bad things happen."

3   John Lanchester. It's finished. *The London Review of Books*, Vol. 31 No. 10, May 28, 2009, pp3-13. www.lrb.co.uk/v31/n10/john-lanchester/its-finished

4   Fixed targets are a relatively recent feature of the management model. According to Professor Tom Johnson (one of America's greatest accounting historians), it wasn't until the 1960s that annual budgets began to mutate from a method of planning and coordinating actions to a nexus of targets and contracts that were used to drive performance improvement. By the early 1970s, notes Johnson, accounting results dominated most managers' attention to the point where they no longer knew, or cared, about the production, technological and marketing determinants of competitiveness.

5   W. Edwards Deming, perhaps the greatest management mind of the 20th century, saw the writing on the wall when he said that "management by results is not the way to get good results. It is action on outcome, as if the outcome came from a special cause. It is important to work on the causes of results – i.e., on the system." Those who manage by results focus on the bottom-line target and consider that achieving financial goals justifies inherently destructive practices. W. Edwards Deming. *The New Economics.* MIT Press, Cambridge, 2000, pp31-33.

6   William A. Sahlman. Management and the financial crisis (We have met the enemy and he is us…). Working Paper 10-033, Harvard Business School, 2009.

7   The number and amount of settlements made by corporations with the SEC for accounting mis-statements is on a rising trend and in 2010 the third largest ever settlement was made with The State Street Bank for $314m – See SEC Settlement Trends 1H10 Update 14 May 2010. www.nera.com/67_6589.htm

8   Marie Leone. SEC Charges Former Citi CFO. CFO.com, July 30, 2010, www.cfo.com/article.cfm/14514146

9   Accounting Web press release, July 21, 2010. http://www.accountingweb.co.uk/topic/practice/accountants-failing-clients-record-fraud-losses-announced/439264

10 Though they vary with each particular study, it is rare that figures of less than 20 percent of total costs are quoted. A recent McKinsey report noted that "no company can sustain a long-term program [of cost reduction] without tackling overhead functions, including finance, human resources, IT, and legal, *whose costs typically match the profit margins of most of today's corporations and are often growing faster than revenues.*" *McKinsey Quarterly*, 2005, Number 2.

11 Sheila M.J. Bonini, Kerrin McKillop and Lenny T. Mendonca. The trust gap between consumers and corporations. *McKinsey Quarterly,* 2007, Number 2. www.mckinsey-quarterly.com/article_print.aspx?L2=39&L3=0&ar=1985

12 Towers Perrin study finds significant "engagement gap" among global workforce towers. Perrin press release, October 22, 2007. www.towersperrin.com/tp/showdctmdoc.jsp?url=HR_Services/United_States/Press_Releases/2007/20071022/2007_10_22.htm&country=global

13 Christopher A. Bartlett and Sumantra Ghoshal. Beyond the M-form: toward a managerial theory of the firm. www.gsia.cmu.edu/bosch/bart.html

14 Barry Jaruzelski, Kevin Dehoff and Rakesh Bordia. Smart spenders – the global innovation 1,000. *Strategy & Business*, 2005, www.strategy-business.com/resilience/rr00039

15 Sumantra Ghoshal. Bad management theories are destroying good management practices. *Academy of Management Learning and Education*, 2005, Vol. 4/1, pp75–91.

16 Sumantra Ghoshal. Bad management theories are destroying good management practices. *Academy of Management Learning and Education*, 2005, Vol. 4/1, pp75–91.

17 Sumantra Ghoshal. Bad management theories are destroying good management practices. *Academy of Management Learning and Education*, 2005, Vol. 4/1, pp75–91.

18 Sumantra Ghoshal. Bad management theories are destroying good management practices. *Academy of Management Learning and Education*, 2005, Vol. 4/1, pp75–91.

19 Eric D. Beinhocker. *The Origin of Wealth.* Random House, London, 2006, pp17–18.

20 Eric D. Beinhocker. *The Origin of Wealth.* Random House, London, 2006, p55.

21 Eric D. Beinhocker. *The Origin of Wealth.* Random House, London, 2006, p47.

22   Margaret Wheatley. Goodbye command and control. *Leader to Leader*, No. 5, Summer 1997.

23   Eric D. Beinhocker. *The Origin of Wealth*. Random House, London, 2006, p323.

24   Eric D. Beinhocker. *The Origin of Wealth*. Random House, London, 2006, p52.

25   Eric D. Beinhocker. *The Origin of Wealth*. Random House, London, 2006, p18.

26   Fritjof Capra. *The Web of Life*. Flamingo Books, London, 1997, pp29-30.

27   Fritjof Capra. *The Web of Life*. Flamingo Books, London, 1997, p36.

28   Fritjof Capra. *The Web of Life*. Flamingo Books, London, 1997, p81.

29   Fritjof Capra. *The Web of Life*. Flamingo Books, London, 1997, p27.

30   Margaret Wheatley. *Leadership and the New Science*. Berret-Koehler Publishers, San Francisco, 1999, pp10-11.

31   Interview with Steve Morlidge, January 26, 2005.

32   Interview with Steve Morlidge, July 14, 2009.

33   Kevin Freiberg and Jackie Freiberg. *Nuts!* Bard Press, Inc., Austin, 1996, p311.

34   Sumantra Ghoshal. Bad management theories are destroying good management practices. *Academy of Management Learning and Education*, 2005, Vol. 4/1, pp75–91.

35   Margaret Wheatley, *Leadership and the New Science*. Berret-Koehler Publishers, San Francisco, 1999, p145

36   Sumantra Ghoshal. Bad management theories are destroying good management practices. *Academy of Management Learning and Education*, 2005, Vol. 4/1, pp75–91.

37   Joseph H. Bragdon. Profit for life. *Society for Organizational Learning*, Cambridge, 2006, p241.

38   Edwin Locke *et al. Goal setting theory: A Theory of Goal Setting and Task Performance*. Prentice-Hall, 1990.

39   Lisa D. Ordóñez, Maurice E. Schweitzer, Adam D. Galinsky and Max H. Bazerman. Goals gone wild: the systematic side effects of over-prescribing goal setting. Harvard Business School Working Paper 09-083. www.exed.hbs.edu/assets/goal-setting.pdf

40   Lisa D. Ordóñez, Maurice E. Schweitzer, Adam D. Galinsky and Max H. Bazerman. Goals gone wild: the systematic side effects of over-prescribing goal setting. Harvard Business School Working Paper 09-083. www.exed.hbs.edu/assets/goal-setting.pdf

41   Sean Silverthorne. When goal setting goes bad. *Harvard Working Knowledge*, March 2, 2009.

42   Mitchel Resnick. Changing the centralized mind. *Technology Review*, July 1994.

43   Stafford Beer. *The Brain of The Firm*. John Wiley, Chichester, 1981.

1   Principle #1 – Values

1   Joseph H. Bragdon. *Profit for Life*. Society for Organizational Learning, Cambridge, MA, 2006, p41.

2   Southwest Airlines website. www.southwest.com/about_swa/airborne.html

3   Mark Morrison. Herb Kelleher on the record part II. *Business Week*. December 23, 2003. www.businessweek.com/bwdaily/dnflash/dec2003/nf20031223_5702_db062.htm

4   Rob Meyer. Southwest's Kelly emphasizes integrity in Lyceum Presentation. McCombs School of Business. November 13, 2006. http://www.mccombs.utexas.edu/news/press-releases/kelly06.asp

5   Christine Negroni. Interview with Gary Kelly. December 17, 2009. http://christinenegroni.blogspot.com/2009/12/interview-with-gary-kelly-ceo-southwest.html

6   Kate McCann. Gary Kelly Southwest Airlines CEO on the business of building trust. 2005 Lyceum Speaker Series: Integrity. October 11, 2005. http://www.mccombs.utexas.edu/news/pressreleases/lyceum05_kelly_wrap05.asp

7   Ulla K. Bunz and Jeanne D. Maes. Learning excellence: Southwest Airlines' approach. *Managing Service Quality* Volume 8, Number 3, 1998, p165.

8   Kevin Freiberg and Jackie Freiberg. *Nuts!* Bard Press, Inc., Austin, TX, 1996, p289.

9   Rob Meyer. Southwest's Kelly emphasizes integrity in Lyceum presentation. *McCombs Weekly*, University of Texas, Nov. 13, 2006. http://www.mccombs.utexas.edu/e-news/mccombsweekly/issues/vol08no11.html

10 Herb Kelleher. A Culture of commitment. *Leader to Leader*, No 4, Spring 1997.

11 A number of US states have already passed laws mandating various levels of transparency such as posting all contracts, grants and even all state expenditures on the web. Governor Matt Brunt of Missouri has gone the furthest and fastest. He has established the Missouri Accountability Portal ("Map Your Taxes") website, which posts a wide range of government expenditures. Opponents said it would cost millions of dollars to achieve transparency but Blunt demolished their arguments by achieving his aims without a single additional appropriation (i.e. just using existing staff and resources). The popularity of these websites has astounded even their most ardent fans. In the first two months there were over one million visitors to the Missouri portal. Grover Norquist. Accountable transparency is the new democracy. *Financial Times*, August 9, 2007, p13.

12 Jeffrey Abrahams. *The Mission Statement Book – 301 Corporate Mission Statements from America's Top Companies*. Ten Speed Press, Berkeley, 1999.

13 Stephan Haeckel. *Adaptive Enterprise*. Harvard Business School Press, Boston, 1999, p106-107.

14 Heather Stewart. Shareholders and targets won't do the business. *The Observer*, 14 March 2010. www.guardian.co.uk/business/2010/mar/14/shareholder-value-comment.

15 Heather Stewart. Shareholders and targets won't do the business. *The Observer*, 14 March 2010. www.guardian.co.uk/business/2010/mar/14/shareholder-value-comment.

16 Heather Stewart. Shareholders and targets won't do the business. *The Observer*, 14 March 2010. www.guardian.co.uk/business/2010/mar/14/shareholder-value-comment.

17 Henry Mintzberg. The fall and rise of strategic planning. *Harvard Business Review*, January-February 1994, pp107–114.

18 Stephen Moore. The conscience of a capitalist. http://online.wsj.com/article/SB10001424052748704471504574447114058870676.html

19 Julian Birkenshaw. *Reinventing Management*. John Wiley, Chichester, 2010, p138.

20 Sheridan Prasso. Saving the world with a cup of yogurt. *Fortune*, February 5, 2007, pp41–5.

21 Nathan T. Washburn. Why profit shouldn't be your top goal. *Harvard Business Review*, December 2009. http://hbr.org/2009/12/why-profit-shouldnt-be-your-top-goal/ar/1

22 Joseph H. Bragdon. Profit for life. *Society for Organizational Learning*, Cambridge, MA, 2006, p41.

23 Joseph H. Bragdon. Profit for life. *Society for Organizational Learning*, Cambridge, MA, 2006, p41.

24 Stephan Haeckel. *Adaptive Enterprise*. Harvard Business School Press, Boston, 1999, p126.

25 The Constitution of the John Lewis Partnership Introduction, Principles and Rules.

26 John Mackey. Creating the high-trust organization. Whole Foods Market CEO Blog, March 9, 2010. http://www2.wholefoodsmarket.com/blogs/jmackey/2010/03/09/creating-the-high-trust-organization/#more-155

27 Joseph H. Bragdon. Profit for life. *Society for Organizational Learning*, Cambridge, MA, 2006, pp130-131.

28 Joseph H. Bragdon. Profit for life. *Society for Organizational Learning*, Cambridge, MA, 2006, p131.

29   Joseph H. Bragdon. Profit for life. *Society for Organizational Learning*, Cambridge, MA, 2006, pp132-133.

30   Tim Stevens. Follow the leader. *Industry Week*, November 18, 1996

31   Taking away Dell's cookie jar. The Economist online, July 23,2010. http://www.economist.com/blogs/newsbook/2010/07/dells_sec_settlement

32   Michael J. de la Merced and Julia Werdigier. The origins of Lehman's "Repo 105". Deal-Book, *New York Times*, March 12, 2010 http://dealbook.blogs.nytimes.com/2010/03/12/the-british-origins-of-lehmans-accounting-gimmick/

33   David S. Hilzenbath and Carrie Johnson. SEC tells Fannie Mae to restate earnings. *The Washington Post*, December 16, 2004, A1 and A13.

34   John Mackey. Creating the high-trust organization. Whole Foods Market CEO Blog, March   9,   2010.   http://www2.wholefoodsmarket.com/blogs/jmackey/2010/03/09/creating-the-high-trust-organization/#more-155

35   Kurt April. The morality of business: It's time for our global leaders to show some moral courage. *Business Report South Africa*, March 2, 2010. www.busrep.co.za/index.php?fArticleId=5373113&fSectionId=2515&fSetId=662

2   Principle #2 – Governance

1   Herb Kelleher. A culture of commitment. *Leader to Leader*, No 4, Spring 1997.

2   Guy Chazan, Benoit Faucon and Ben Casselman. As CEO Hayward remade BP, safety, cost drives clashed. *The Wall Street Journal*, June 29, 2010. http://online.wsj.com/article/SB10001424052748703964104575335154126721876.html

3   Pete Engardio, Kerry Capell, John Carry and Kenji Hall. Beyond the green corporation. *Business Week*, January 29, 2007. www.businessweek.com/magazine/content/07_05/b4019001.htm?chan=search

4   Ed Crooks. BP: the inside story. *Financial Times*, July 2, 2010. http://www.ft.com/cms/s/0/4e228e56-84ae-11df-9cbb-00144feabdc0.html

5   Richard M. Steinberg. How did BP's risk management lead to failure? *Compliance Week*, July 20, 2010. www.complianceweek.com/article/6033/how-did-bps-risk-management-lead-to-failure-

6   Sylvia Pfeifer. BP links bonuses to safety performance. *Financial Times*, October 18, 2010. www.ft.com/cms/s/ca170960-dadf-11df-a5bb-00144feabdc0,dwp_uuid=2592a208-a4fb-11dd-b4f5-000077b07658,print=yes.html

7   Michael Power. *The Risk Management of Everything*. Demos, 2004. http://www.demos.co.uk/files/riskmanagementofeverything.pdf?1240939425

8   Michael Power. *The Risk Management of Everything*. Demos, 2004. http://www.demos.co.uk/files/riskmanagementofeverything.pdf?1240939425

9   Michael Power. *The Risk Management of Everything*. Demos, 2004. http://www.demos.co.uk/files/riskmanagementofeverything.pdf?1240939425

10   John Seddon Death to ISO9000 – An Economic Disease. www.lean-service.com/6-22.asp

11   Michael Power. The Risk Management of Everything Demos, 2004. http://www.demos.co.uk/files/riskmanagementofeverything.pdf?1240939425

12   Dan Roberts, *Financial Times*, March 3, 2004, p30.

13   Jeffrey A. Sonnenfeld. What makes great boards. *Harvard Business Review*, September 2002, p110.

14   Paul Coombes and Mark Watson. Three surveys on corporate governance. *McKinsey Quarterly* 2000, Number 4, pp74-77.

15 David A. Nadler. Building better boards. *Harvard Business Review*, May 2004, p103.

16 Patrick Hosking. HBOS sacked and gagged bank risk whistleblower. *The Times*, February 10, 2009. http://business.timesonline.co.uk/tol/business/industry_sectors/banking_and_finance/article5701380.ece

17 Eric Dash and Julie Creswell. Citigroup saw no red flags even as it made bolder bets. *The New York Times*, November 23, 2008. http://www.nytimes.com/2008/11/23/business/23citi.html

18 Michael Schrage. Boards of prevention. Strategy + Business, June 14, 2010. http://www.strategy-business.com/article/00037?gko=67f92

19 Bruce Caplain. Risk management: why it failed, how to fix it. Internal Auditor. http://www.theiia.org/intAuditor/free-feature/2008/risk-management-why-it-failed-how-to-fix-it-ii/

20 Michael Schrage. Boards of prevention. Strategy + Business, June 14, 2010. http://www.strategy-business.com/article/00037?gko=67f92

21 Matthew Leitch. Control of decentralized risk taking using 'risk appetite' rules. BBRT White Paper, 12 June 2008.

22 Michael Schrage. Boards of prevention. Strategy + Business, June 14, 2010. http://www.strategy-business.com/article/00037?gko=67f92

23 Bruce Caplain. Risk management: why it failed, how to fix it. Internal Auditor. http://www.theiia.org/intAuditor/free-feature/2008/risk-management-why-it-failed-how-to-fix-it-ii/

24 Michael Schrage. Boards of prevention. Strategy + Business, June 14, 2010. http://www.strategy-business.com/article/00037?gko=67f92

25 Michael Schrage. Boards of prevention. Strategy + Business, June 14, 2010. http://www.strategy-business.com/article/00037?gko=67f92

26 Yuri Mishina, Bernadine J. Dykes, Emily S. Block and Timothy G. Pollock. Why "good" firms do bad things: the effects of high aspirations, high expectations and prominence on the incidence of corporate illegality. *Academy of Management Journal*, August 2010, vol. 53, no. 4.

27 Clifton Leaf. Temptation is all around us. *Fortune*, November 18, 2002, pp67-71.

28 Robert Simons. How risky is your company? *Harvard Business Review*, May-June 1999, pp85-94.

29 Enterprise governance – getting the balance right. IFAC, 2003.

30 Stanley Pignal. Philips in rethink on target setting. *Financial Times*, September 15, 2010, p17.

31 Quoted by Andrew Wilson, partner with Accenture, in Beyond compliance, FST (US Edition). www.usfst.com/pastissue/article.asp?art=26019&issue=153

32 Kim Cameron. Ethics, virtuousness and constant change. Paper for Noel Tichy and Andrew R. McGill (eds.), *The Ethical Challenge*, Jossey Bass, San Francisco, pp85-94. http://64.233.183.104/search?q=cache:Z5r8tcM9EF0J:www.competingvalues.com/pdf/ethics.pdf+kim+cameron+vituous&hl=en&ct=clnk&cd=1

33 Kim Cameron. Ethics, virtuousness and constant change. Paper for Noel Tichy and Andrew R. McGill (eds.), *The Ethical Challenge*, Jossey Bass, San Francisco, pp85-94. http://64.233.183.104/search?q=cache:Z5r8tcM9EF0J:www.competingvalues.com/pdf/ethics.pdf+kim+cameron+vituous&hl=en&ct=clnk&cd=1

34 Alistair R. Anderson and Carter Crockett. Excellence: capturing aristotelian notions of meaning and purpose. *International Journal of Business Excellence*, April 2008, vol. 1, no. 3.

35 John Mackey. Creating the high trust organization. Whole Foods Market CEO Blog, March 9, 2010. http://www2.wholefoodsmarket.com/blogs/jmackey/2010/03/09/creating-the-high-trust-organization/#more-155

36 Scott London. The new science of leadership: an interview with Margaret Wheatley. Insight & Outlook. www.scottlondon.com/interviews/wheatley.html

37 Stephen Howarth. Leadership – fleets ahead of its time. *Financial Times*, August 1-2, 1998, Weekend IV.

38 Brian Grow. Renovating Home Depot. *Business Week*, March 6, 2006, pp50-58.

39 Simon Patterson and Peter Jauhal. Rewarding with shares rather than options is more fair. *Sunday Times*, July 15, 2001, Business Section 3.11.

40 Bill Gates. What I learned from Warren Buffett. *Harvard Business Review*, Jan-Feb 1996, p148.

41 Henry Mintzberg. No more executive bonuses. *Sloan Management Review*, November 2009. http://sloanreview.mit.edu/business-insight/articles/2009/5/5151/no-moreexecutive-bonuses/

42 Claudio Fernández-Aráoz. Getting the right people at the top. *Sloan Management Review*, July 15, 2005. sloanreview.mit.edu/the-agazine/articles/2005/summer/46412/getting-the-right-people-at-the-top/

43 Claudio Fernández-Aráoz. Whom to pay is more important than how much or how. July 2, 2009. http://blogs.hbr.org/hbr/how-to-fix-executive-pay/2009/07/whom-to-pay-is-more-important-than-how-much-or-how.html

44 John W. Hunt. Reward systems and disincentives. *Financial Times*, April 21, 1999, p21.

45 Robert Simons. *Levers of organizational design*. Harvard Business School Press, 2005, p111.

46 Joseph H. Bragdon. Profit for life. *Society for Organizational Learning*, Cambridge, MA, 2006, pp59-60.

47 Nanette Byrnes, with Michael Arndt. The art of motivation. Business Week Online, May 1, 2006. www.businessweek.com/magazine/content/06_18/b3982075.htm

48 Stephen Moore. The conscience of a capitalist. http://online.wsj.com/article/SB10001424052748704471504574447114058870676.html

49 Charles Elson. What's wrong with executive compensation. *Harvard Business Review*, January 2003, pp68-77.

50 Jeffrey Pfeffer. An insider's look at CEO pay. The Corner Office, 8 March 2010. http://blogs.bnet.com/ceo/?p=4059.

51 Julie Froud, Adam Leaver, Siobhan McAndrew *et al.* Rethinking top management pay: from pay for performance to pay as fee working. Paper No. 56, CRESC, University of Manchester, August 2008.

52 Julie Froud, Adam Leaver, Siobhan McAndrew *et al.* Rethinking top management pay: from pay for performance to pay as fee working. Paper No. 56, CRESC, University of Manchester, August 2008.

3 Principle #3 – Transparency

1 Margaret Wheatley. *Leadership and the New Science*. Berret-Koehler Pulishers, San Francisco, 1999, p87.

2 Katherine Bell. *Is transparency always the best policy?* Blog April 6, 2009. http://blogs.hbr.org/cs/2009/04/the_value_of_transparency_an_i.html

3 Quoted in Tom Peters: *Thriving on Chaos*. Macmillan, London, 1987, p285.

4 http://thefuturebuzz.com/2009/01/12/social-media-web-20-internet-numbers-stats/

5 Margaret Wheatley. *Leadership and the New Science*. Berret-Koehler Pulishers, San Francisco, 1999, pp67–68.

6 Eric Schmidt. Collaborate or perish. McKinseyDigital.com, February 26, 2009. http://whatmatters.mckinseydigital.com/organization/collaborate-or-perish

7   Gary Hamel. Blog *HCL: Extreme management makeover. Wall Street Journal*, July 6, 2010. http://blogs.wsj.com/management/2010/07/06/hcl-extreme-management-makeover/tab/print/

8   Ken Iverson. *Plain Talk*. John Wiley, New York, 1998, p67.

9   Simon Caulkin. Roche: from oversight to insight. MLab Notes, London Business School, July 16, 2010. http://www.managementlab.org/files/site/publications/labnotes/mlab-labnotes-016.pdf

10 Kenneth G. McGee. *Heads Up*. Harvard Business School Press, Boston, 2004, pp101–103.

11 Bill Gates. *Business @ The Speed of Thought*. Penguin Books, London, 1999, p179.

12 Peter Drucker. *Post-Capitalist Society*. Butterworth Heinemann, Oxford, 1993, p97.

13 John Goff. Drowning in data. CFO.com www.cfo.com/printable/article.cfm/3010723

14 TDWI's Data Quality Report "Executive Summary." http://www.webdedication.com/perfectdata/NewFiles/articles.html

4   Principle #4 – Teams

1   John Mackey. Creating the high trust organization. Whole Foods Market CEO Blog, March 9, 2010. http://www2.wholefoodsmarket.com/blogs/jmackey/2010/03/09/creating-the-high-trust-organization/#more-155

2   Leyland Trucks website. http://www.leylandtrucksltd.co.uk/news20100728.asp

3   John Oliver. *The Team Enterprise Solution*. Oak Tree Press, Cork, 2001, p48.

4   John Oliver. *The Team Enterprise Solution*. Oak Tree Press, Cork, 2001, p10.

5   John Oliver. *The Team Enterprise Solution*. Oak Tree Press, Cork, 2001, pp55–56.

6   John Oliver. *The Team Enterprise Solution*. Oak Tree Press, Cork, 2001, pp194–195.

7   John Oliver. *The Team Enterprise Solution*. Oak Tree Press, Cork, 2001, p195.

8   John Oliver. *The Team Enterprise Solution*. Oak Tree Press, Cork, 2001, p145.

9   Joseph H. Bragdon. Profit for life. *Society for Organizational Learning*, Cambridge, MA, 2006, pp59–60.

10 Vineet Nayar. *Employees First, Customers Second*. Harvard Business Press, 2010, pp11–12.

11 Economic profit (a.k.a. "Economic value-added" or EVA) is usually defined as the (adjusted) after tax profit for the period less the (weighted average) cost of capital. Thus if a company has after tax profits of $20m, shareholders funds of $100m (with a cost of capital of 12%), borrowings of $50m (with a net of tax interest cost of 4%), its EVA™ would be $6m (profit of $20m less equity cost of $12m and debt cost of $2m).

12 John Mackey. Creating the high trust organization. Whole Foods Market CEO Blog, March 9, 2010. http://www2.wholefoodsmarket.com/blogs/jmackey/2010/03/09/creating-the-high-trust-organization/#more-155

13 Gary Hamel. Blog HCL: Extreme Management Makeover. *Wall Street Journal*, July 6, 2010. http://blogs.wsj.com/management/2010/07/06/hcl-extreme-management-makeover/tab/print/

14 See Jeremy Hope: *Reinventing the CFO*, Harvard Business School Press, Boston, 2006, for a more detailed exposition of the finance role.

15 McKinsey concluded that only 59 percent of financial executives say they would pursue a *positive* net present value if it meant missing quarterly earnings targets. Even worse, 78 percent said they would sacrifice value – in some cases a lot of value – in order to smooth earnings. See Judith Samuelson, A critical mass for the long term, *Harvard Business Review*, February 2006, pp62–63.

5 Principle #5 – Trust

1   Dr Jan Wallander. *Decentralization – When and How to Make it Work.* SNS Förlag, Stockholm, 2003, p136.
2   Art Kleiner. William G. Ouchi: The Thought Leader Interview. *Strategy + Business*, 2006, Issue 43.
3   Art Kleiner. William G. Ouchi: The Thought Leader Interview. *Strategy + Business*, 2006, Issue 43.
4   Margaret Wheatley. Goodbye, Command and Control. *Leader to Leader*, No. 5, Summer 1997.
5   Margaret Wheatley. Goodbye, Command and Control. Leader to Leader, No. 5, Summer 1997.
6   E.L. Deci and R. Flaste. *Why We Do What We Do: Understanding Self-Motivation.* Penguin Books, New York, 1995, pp134–135.
7   Holly H. Brower, Scott W. Lester, M. Audrey Korsgaard and Brian R. Dineen. A closer look at trust between managers and subordinates: understanding the effects of both trusting and being trusted on subordinate outcomes. *Journal of Management*, March 2009, vol. 35, no. 2.
8   Charles Handy. Tocqueville Revisited. *Harvard Business Review*, January 2001, p61.
9   Brian M. Carney and Isaac Getz. Freedom, Inc: Bill Gore's Formula for Failure. Editor's Choice, *Strategy + Business*, Autumn 2010, Issue 60. August 24, 2010. www.strategy-business.com/article/10315?gko=f6dff
10 Quoted in Jeffrey K. Liker. *The Toyota Way.* McGraw-Hill, New York, 2004, p87.
11 James Manyika. Google's view on the future of business: An interview with CEO Eric Schmidt. *McKinsey Quarterly*, 2009, Number 1, pp143–145.
12 Stephen Jones. England back on fast track to glory. *Sunday Times*, February 11, 2001, Section 2, p14.
13 Gary Hamel. W.L. Gore: lessons from a management revolutionary. *Wall Street Journal*, Blog, April 2, 2010. http://blogs.wsj.com/management/2010/04/02/wl-gore-lessons-from-a-management-revolutionary-part-2/
14 Dr Jan Wallander. *Decentralization – When and How to Make it Work.* SNS Förlag, Stockholm, 2003, p49.
15 Charles Handy. Trust and the virtual organization. *Harvard Business Review*, May-June 1995. http://hbr.org/1995/05/trust-and-the-virtual-organization/ib
16 Stephan Haeckel. *Adaptive Enterprise.* Harvard Business School Press, Boston, 1999, p108.
17 John Mackey. Creating the high trust organization. Whole Foods Market CEO Blog, March 9, 2010. http://www2.wholefoodsmarket.com/blogs/jmackey/2010/03/09/creating-the-high-trust-organization/#more-155
18 Joseph H. Bragdon. Profit for life. *Society for Organizational Learning*, Cambridge, MA, 2006, p17.
19 Chris Argyris. Empowerment: the emperor's new clothes. *Harvard Business Review*, May-June 1998, p98.
20 Chris Argyris. Empowerment: the emperor's new clothes. *Harvard Business Review*, May-June 1998, pp98–99.

6 Principle #6 – Accountability

1   Anecdotes of Wellington. www.wellsoc.org/Anecdotes.htm

2   Guardian Money. NatWest and Aviva, is this really the way to treat people? February 13, 2010, p6.
3   Stephan Haeckel. *Adaptive Enterprise.* Harvard Business School Press, Boston, 1999, p273.
4   Stephan Haeckel. *Adaptive Enterprise.* Harvard Business School Press, Boston, 1999, p148.
5   Stephan Haeckel. *Adaptive Enterprise.* Harvard Business School Press, Boston, 1999, p152.
6   Stephan Haeckel. *Adaptive Enterprise.* Harvard Business School Press, Boston, 1999, p143.
7   W.L. Gore website. www.gore.com/en_xx/aboutus/timeline/index.html
8   Mihaly Csikszentmihalyi. Finding flow. *Psychology Today*, July 1, 1997. http://www. psychologytoday.com/articles/199707/finding-flow
9   Marc J. Epstein and Bill Birchard. *Counting What Counts: Turning Corporate Accountability to Competitive Advantage.* Perseus Books, New York, 1999, pp156-157.
10 Marc J. Epstein and Bill Birchard. *Counting What Counts: Turning Corporate Accountability to Competitive Advantage.* Perseus Books, New York, 1999, p160.
11 Marc J. Epstein and Bill Birchard. *Counting What Counts: Turning Corporate Accountability to Competitive Advantage.* Perseus Books, New York, 1999, p245.
12 Stephan Haeckel. *Adaptive Enterprise.* Harvard Business School Press, Boston, 1999, p109.

7   Principle #7 – Goals

1   Brian Singleton-Green. What do shareholders want? *Accountancy,* May 1995, p44.
2   H. Thomas Johnson. Financial results such as revenue, cost and profit are by-products of well-run human-focused organizations. *The Leading Edge,* February 18, 2010. http:// theleanedge.org/?p=462
3   Michael Skapinker. Replacing the 'dumbest idea in the world'. *Financial Times*, April 10, 2010. www.ft.com/cms/s/0/98e020d0-4664-11df-9713-00144feab49a.html
4   Stefan Stern. Unilever warning on 'shareholder value'. *Financial Times,* April 4, 2010. www.ft.com/cms/s/0/72d68b60-4009-11df-8d23-00144feabdc0.html
5   Peggy Hsieh, Timothy Koller and S.R. Rajan. The misguided practice of earnings guidance. *McKinsey on Finance*, Number 19, Spring 2006.
6   Peggy Hsieh, Timothy Koller and S.R. Rajan. The misguided practice of earnings guidance. *McKinsey on Finance*, Number 19, Spring 2006.
7   Peggy Hsieh, Timothy Koller and S.R. Rajan. The misguided practice of earnings guidance. *McKinsey on Finance*, Number 19, Spring 2006.
8   Peggy Hsieh, Timothy Koller and S.R. Rajan. The misguided practice of earnings guidance. *McKinsey on Finance*, Number 19, Spring 2006.
9   W. Edwards Deming. *Out of Crisis.* MIT, Boston, 1982 (26th Edition 1998), p69.
10 W. Edwards Deming. *Out of Crisis.* MIT, Boston, 1982 (26th Edition 1998), p66.
11 Jeffrey K. Liker. *The Toyota Way.* McGraw-Hill, London, 2004, p263.
12 Joseph L. Bower. Jack Welch: General Electric's revolutionary. Harvard Business School Case 9-394-065, April 1994.
13 Robert S. Kaplan. Target setting. Balanced Scorecard Report, May-June 2006. http:// www.nationalcollege.lmmattersonline.com/courses/hmm10/goal_setting/resources/ B0605C.pdf

14   Adam Bryant. He's not Bill Gates, or Fred Astaire. Interview with *New York Times*, February 14, 2010. http://www.nytimes.com/2010/02/14/business/14cornerweb.html?_r=1 &pagewanted=print

15   Leadership instead of budgeting. Translation by Franz Röösli of an interview held by Prof. Gaitanides with Mr Stadelmann, CFO, UBS WM&BB in *ZFO* 06/05.

16   Marshall W. Van Alstyne. Create colleagues, not competitors. *Harvard Business Review*, September 2005, p24.

17   Egon Zehnder website. http://www.egonzehnder.com/site/id/83700001

8   Principle #8 – Rewards

1   Carola Hoyos and Michael Steen. Outgoing Shell chief calls for reform of salaries. *Financial Times*, June 9, 2009, p1.

2   Carola Hoyos and Michael Steen. Outgoing Shell chief calls for reform of salaries. *Financial Times*, June 9, 2009, p1.

3   Henry Mintzberg. No more executive bonuses. *Sloan Management Review*, November 2009. http://sloanreview.mit.edu/business-insight/articles/2009/5/5151/no-moreexecutive-bonuses/

4   Henry Mintzberg. No more executive bonuses. *Sloan Management Review*, November 2009. http://sloanreview.mit.edu/business-insight/articles/2009/5/5151/no-more-executive-bonuses/

5   Quoted in Alfred Rappaport: How to link executive pay with performance. *Harvard Business Review*, March-April, 1999, p92.

6   Don Durfee. Pay daze – linking pay to performance is harder than it looks. *CFO Magazine*, December 1, 2006. www.cfo.com/article.cfm/8191567/c_8341296

7   Jonathan D. Day, Paul Y. Mang, Ansgar Richter and John Roberts. Has pay for performance had its day? *Mckinsey Quarterly*, 2002, Number 4.

8   Jeffrey Pfeffer. Six dangerous myths about pay. *Harvard Business Review*, May-June 1998, pp109–119.

9   Douglas McGregor. *The Human Side of Enterprise*. McGraw-Hill, 1960.

10   Peter F. Drucker. They're not employees, they're people. *Harvard Business Review*, February 2002, pp71–77.

11   Quoted in Jeffrey Pfeffer: Six dangerous myths about pay. *Harvard Business Review*, May-June 1998, p117.

12   B.F. Skinner. *Beyond Freedom and Dignity*. Bantam/Vintage, New York, 1971.

13   Alfie Kohn. Why incentive plans cannot work. *Harvard Business Review*, September-October 1993, pp54–63.

14   Chris Argyris. The Emperor's new clothes. *Harvard Business Review*, May-June 1998, p103.

15   Alfie Kohn. Challenging behaviorist dogma: myths about money and motivation. *Compensation & Benefits Review*, March/April 1998. www.alfiekohn.org/managing/cbdmamam.htm

16   Quoted in Simon Caulkin. Keep it simple – not stupid. *Observer*, February 23, 2003, p8.

17   Quoted in Jeffrey Pfeffer and Robert I. Sutton. *Hard Facts, Dangerous Half-Truths & Total Nonsense*. Harvard Business School Press, Boston, 2006, p99.

18   Nanette Byrnes, with Michael Arndt. The art of motivation. *Business Week Online*, May 1, 2006. www.businessweek.com/magazine/content/06_18/b3982075.htm

19   Geoffrey Colvin. What money makes you do. *Fortune,* August 17, 1999, p79.

20   John Seddon. *Freedom from command and control – a better way to make the work work.* Vanguard Education, Buckingham, 2003, p124.

21   Edgar Schein. *Corporate Culture.* Jossey-Bass, San Francisco, 1999, p53.

22   Michael C. Jensen. Corporate budgeting is broken – let's fix it. *Harvard Business Review,* November 2001, pp95–101.

23   Steve Morlidge. *Dynamic Performance Management.* An MTP and Unilever publication, 2004, p99.

24   Jeffrey Pfeffer. *The Human Equation.* Harvard Business School Press, Boston, 1998, p82.

25   Peter Cappelli. The workers clip United's wings. *Financial Times,* December 11, 2003.

26   Lynn Brenner. The myth of incentive pay. *CFO Magazine,* July 1995.

27   Kevin Freiberg and Jackie Freiberg. *Nuts!* Bard Press, Inc., Austin, 1996, p100.

28   Kevin Freiberg and Jackie Freiberg. *Nuts!* Bard Press, Inc., Austin, 1996, p102.

29   Excerpt from Marketplace Master, 2004 by Suzanne Lowe. www.egonzehnderknowledge. com/knowledge/content/ourfirm/publications.php

30   Julia Finch and Zoe Wood, Guardian.co.uk, March 11, 2010. http://www.guardian. co.uk/business/2010/mar/11/john-lewis-staff-share-151m-in-bonuses

31   *Fast Company* staff. I no longer want to work for money. February 1, 2007. http://www. fastcompany.com/magazine/112/final-word.html

32   J.C. De Swann and Neil W.C. Harper. Getting what you pay for with stock options. *McKinsey Quarterly,* 2003, Number 1.

33   Alfred Rappaport. How to link executive pay with performance. *Harvard Business Review,* March-April, 1999, p93.

34   Erik Stern. Putting the boss's achievements into context. *Financial Times,* March 6, 2001, p16.

35   Geoff Colvin. Amex gets CEO pay right. *Fortune,* January 6, 2008, http://money.cnn. com/magazines/fortune/fortune_archive/2008/01/21/102659595/index.htm

36   Floyd Norris. Stock options: do they make bosses cheat? *New York Times,* August 3, 2005.

37   Don Durfee. Pay daze – linking pay to performance is harder than it looks. *CFO Magazine,* December 1, 2006. www.cfo.com/article.cfm/8191567/c_8341296

38   Martin Dewhurst, Matthew Guthridge and Elizabeth Mohr. Motivating people: getting beyond money. *McKinsey Quarterly,* 2010, Number 1, p12.

39   Jeffrey K. Liker. *The Toyota Way.* McGraw-Hill, New York, 2004, p197.

40   Frederick Herzberg. One more time: How do you motivate employees? *Harvard Business Review Business Classics,* pp13–22.

9   Principle #9 – Planning

1   Joseph H. Bragdon. Profit for life. *Society for Organizational Learning,* Cambridge, MA, 2006, p62.

2   Joseph H. Bragdon. Profit for life. *Society for Organizational Learning,* Cambridge, MA, 2006, pp132–133.

3   A case study by Cyndy Payne, Communications Manager, Foundation for Enterprise Development. www.beysterinstitute.org/onlinemag/june98/briefcase.html

4   Leonard Fuld. Be prepared. *Harvard Business Review,* November 2003, p20.

5   Michael C. Mankins and Richard Steele. Stop making plans and start making decisions. *Harvard Business Review,* January 2006, pp76–84.

6   Eric D. Beinhocker. *The Origin of Wealth*. Random House, London, 2006, p325.

7   Michael Goold. Strategic control in the decentralized firm. *Sloan Management Review*, Winter 1991, p69.

8   Speed, simplicity, self-confidence: an interview with Jack Welch. *Harvard Business Review*, Sept–Oct 1989.

9   This sounds similar to Dr Deming's Plan-Do-Check-Act (PDCA) cycle. In fact, it's quite different. Deming was talking about a manufacturing system or subsystem, whereas we are referring to a business planning system. For example, when Deming talked about "plan," he meant have an idea for improving the system; check was "see if the idea works"; "do" was put it in the line and "act" was "go live."

10 *CFO Magazine* Research Series 2002. CFOs: driving finance transformation for the 21st century. www.cfoenterprises.com/research.shtml, p8.

11 Kevin Freiberg and Jackie Freiberg. *Nuts!* Bard Press Inc., Austin, 1996, p86.

12 Renée Dye, Olivier Sibony and S. Patrick Viguerie. Strategic planning: three tips for 2009. *McKinsey Quarterly* April 2009. www.mckinseyquarterly.com/Strategic_planning_Three_tips_for_2009_2340

13 Renée Dye, Olivier Sibony and S. Patrick Viguerie. Strategic planning: Three tips for 2009. *McKinsey Quarterly*, April 2009. www.mckinseyquarterly.com/Strategic_planning_Three_tips_for_2009_2340

10   Principle #10 – Coordination

1   Michael Hugos. *The Greatest Innovation Since the Assembly Line*. Meghan-Kiffer Press, Tampa, 2007, p40.

2   H. Thomas Johnson. *Relevance Regained*. The Free Press, New York, 1992, p51.

3   H. Thomas Johnson and Anders Bröms. *Profit Beyond Measure*. Nicholas Brealey Publishing, London, 2000, p20.

4   Jeffrey G. Miller and Thomas E. Vollmann. The hidden factory. *Harvard Business Review*, September-October 1985, pp142–151.

5   James P. Womack, Daniel T. Jones and Daniel Roos. *The Machine that changed the World*. Rawson Associates, New York, 1990.

6   H. Thomas Johnson and Anders Bröms, *Profit Beyond Measure*. Nicholas Brealey Publishing, London, 2000, p28.

7   Taiichi Ohno. *Toyota Production System*. Productivity Press, New York, 1988, p30.

8   Taiichi Ohno. *Toyota Production System*. Productivity Press, New York, 1988, p24.

9   Taiichi Ohno. *Toyota Production System*. Productivity Press, New York, 1988, p25.

10 A. Martin and Kathleen M. Eisenhardt. Rewiring: cross-business-unit collaborations and performance in multi-business organizations. *Academy of Management Journal*, vol. 53, no. 2 April, 2010.

11 Stephan Haeckel. *Adaptive Enterprise*. Harvard Business School Press, Boston, 1999, p20.

12 Michael Hugos. *The Greatest Innovation Since the Assembly Line*. Meghan-Kiffer Press, Tampa, 2007, pp18–19.

13 Michael Hugos. *The Greatest Innovation Since the Assembly Line*. Meghan-Kiffer Press, Tampa, 2007, p13.

14 Michael Hugos. *The Greatest Innovation Since the Assembly Line*. Meghan-Kiffer Press, Tampa, 2007, pp47–48.

15 Michael Hugos. *The Greatest Innovation Since the Assembly Line*. Meghan-Kiffer Press, Tampa, 2007, pp55–56.

16 Michael Hugos. *The Greatest Innovation Since the Assembly Line.* Meghan-Kiffer Press, Tampa, 2007, p59.
17 Joseph H. Bragdon. Profit for life. *Society for Organizational Learning*, Cambridge, MA, 2006, p175.
18 Joseph H. Bragdon. Profit for life. *Society for Organizational Learning*, Cambridge, MA, 2006, p175.
19 Based on an article by Rajan R Kamath and Jeffrey K Liker. A second look at Japanese product development. *Harvard Business Review*, November-December 1994, pp154–170.
20 Jeffrey Liker and Yen-Chun Wu. Japanese automakers, US suppliers and supply-chain superiority. *Sloan Management Review*, Fall 2000, pp81–93.
21 James P. Womack and Daniel T. Jones. Lean consumption. *Harvard Business Review*, March 2005, pp58–68.

11   Principle #11 – Resources

1 Taiichi Ohno. *Toyota Production System.* Productivity Press, New York, 1988, pix.
2 Todd Datz. Portfolio management – how to do it right. *CIO Magazine*, May 1, 2003. www.cio.com/archive/050103/portfolio.html
3 Todd Datz. Portfolio management – how to do it right. *CIO Magazine*, May 1, 2003. www.cio.com/archive/050103/portfolio.html
4 Matthew Leitch. Open and honest about risk and uncertainty. July 7, 2004. www.internalcontrolsdesign.co.uk/honest/index.html
5 Mary Ann McNulty. Cisco virtually eliminates internal travel. *The Transnational*, February 11, 2009. www.thetransnational.travel/news.php?cid=Cisco-virtual-meeting-telepresence.Feb-09.11
6 Author's interview with Lennart Francke, 24 January 2005.
7 Quoted in Thomas Davenport, Sirkka L. Jarvenpaa and Michael C. Beers. Improving knowledge work processes. *Sloan Management Review*, Summer 1996, p54.

12   Principle #12 – Controls

1 Foreword by Peter Senge to H. Thomas Johnson and Anders Bröms' *Profit Beyond Measure.* Nicholas Brealey Publishing, London 2000, pxv.
2 John Goff. Drowning in data. www.cfo.com/printable/article.cfm/3010723
3 The law was named after Charles Goodhart, a chief economic advisor to the Bank of England. The law was first stated in the 1980s in the context of the attempt by the UK government of Margaret Thatcher to conduct monetary policy on the basis of targets for broad and narrow money.
4 Robert Simons. *Levers of Control.* Harvard Business School Press, 1995, Chapter 3.
5 David A. J. Axson. *Best Practices in Planning and Management Reporting.* John Wiley, New Jersey, 2003, p59.
6 Author interview with Ken Lever, 11 February 2005.
7 Mark Graham Brown. *Beyond the Balanced Scorecard.* Productivity Press, New York, 2007.
8 www.bus.umich.edu/FacultyResearch/ResearchCenters/Centers/Acsi.htm
9 www.greatplacetowork.com
10 http://www.solonline.org/com/AR98/index.html

11 H. Thomas Johnson and Anders Bröms. *Profit Beyond Measure*. Nicholas Brealey Publishing, London, 2000, p69.
12 http://www.solonline.org/com/AR98/index.html

13 Implementation insights

1 John Kotter. *Leading Change*. Harvard Business School Press, Boston, 1996, pp156.
2 Gary Hamel. HCL's CEO on its "management makeover." *Wall Street Journal* online, blog, August 24, 2010. http://blogs.wsj.com/management/2010/08/24/hcls-ceo-on-its-management-makeover/tab/print/
3 Gary Hamel. *The Future of Management*. Harvard Business School Press, Boston, 2007, p15.
4 John Kotter. *Leading Change*. Harvard Business School Press, Boston, 1996, p57.
5 Rosabeth Moss Kanter. The enduring skills of change leaders. *Leader to Leader*, No. 13, Summer 1999. www.leadertoleader.org/leaderbooks/l2l/summer99/kanter.html
6 Gary Hamel. HCL's CEO on its "management makeover." *Wall Street Journal* online, blog August 24, 2010. http://blogs.wsj.com/management/2010/08/24/hcls-ceo-on-its-management-makeover/tab/print/
7 Gary Hamel. *The Future of Management*. Harvard Business School Press, Boston, 2007, pp181–182.
8 John Kotter. Winning at change. *Leader to Leader*, No 10, Fall 1998. www.leadertoleader.org/leaderbooks/l2l/fall98/kotter.html
9 Rosabeth Moss Kanter. The enduring skills of change leaders. *Leader to Leader*, No. 13, Summer 1999. www.leadertoleader.org/leaderbooks/l2l/summer99/kanter.html
10 John Kotter. *Leading Change*. Harvard Business School Press, Boston, 1996, p90.
11 Gary Hamel. HCL's CEO on its "management makeover." *Wall Street Journal* online, blog, August 24, 2010. http://blogs.wsj.com/management/2010/08/24/hcls-ceo-on-its-management-makeover/tab/print/
12 Gary Hamel. HCL's CEO on its "management makeover." *Wall Street Journal* online, blog, August 24, 2010. http://blogs.wsj.com/management/2010/08/24/hcls-ceo-on-its-management-makeover/tab/print/
13 Author interview with Gary Crittenden, February, 14, 2005.
14 Gary Hamel. HCL's CEO on its "management makeover." *Wall Street Journal* online, blog, August 24, 2010. http://blogs.wsj.com/management/2010/08/24/hcls-ceo-on-its-management-makeover/tab/print/
15 Bill Gates. *Business @ The Speed of Thought*. Penguin Books, London, 1999, p18.
16 Gary Hamel. HCL's CEO on its "management makeover." *Wall Street Journal* online, blog, August 24, 2010. http://blogs.wsj.com/management/2010/08/24/hcls-ceo-on-its-management-makeover/tab/print/
17 John Kotter. *Leading Change*. Harvard Business School Press Boston, 1996, pp132–133.
18 Gary Hamel. HCL's CEO on its "management makeover." *Wall Street Journal* online, blog, August 24, 2010. http://blogs.wsj.com/management/2010/08/24/hcls-ceo-on-its-management-makeover/tab/print/

14 Make management change your legacy

1 W. Edwards Deming. *Out of Crisis*. MIT, Boston, 1982 (26th Edition 1998), p146.

2   Quoted in David A.J. Axson. *Best Practices in Planning and Management Reporting.* John Wiley, New Jersey, 2003, p89.

3   Randall Rothenberg. Arie de Geus, the thought leader. *Strategy and Business*, Issue 23.

4   Randall Rothenberg. Arie de Geus, the thought leader. *Strategy and Business*, Issue 23.

5   Bill O'Brien. From the "Assessment for Learning" Initiative conference on www.sol. ne.org/com/ar98/index.html

6   Jeffrey K. Liker. *The Toyota Way.* McGraw-Hill, New York, 2004, p71.

Index

Abrahams, Jeffrey 42
accountability 24, 123–4, 155
  boss or customer 143–5
  confusion over 140–5
  design jobs/projects to align flow/
    accountability 152–3
  flows toward the customer 145–6
  implementation guidelines 145–54
  individual 191
  key points 156
  matrix management 154
  peer reviews 148–50
  people 142–3
  reverse 150–1
  teams 146–7
  transparency and disclosure 153–4
action plans 259–60
activity-based costing (ABC) 241–2
ad hoc agreements 235
adaptive management model xi, 15–16
  contrasting models 17
  early visionaries 19–21
  features 20–1
  principles 16, 21–9
agency theory 11, 12, 21
agile organization 233–4
Ahlsell 101, 170, 175
AIG 2, 6, 29, 69
Akzo Nobel 42
Alcoa 45, 50
Alliance & Leicester 6
American Customer Satisfaction Index
  (ACSI) 277
American Express 20, 116, 198, 217, 244–6,
  297
America's Best Hospitals 91
AMR Research 244
analysts 167–8
analytics

grouping KPIs into 273–5
nine steps to analytics-based scorecard
  275–6
turning dumb KPIs into intelligent
  analytics 272–6
Anderson, Alistair R. 78
Argyris, Chris 187, 188
AT&T 168
AvNet 191

back-office 116
balanced scorecard systems 272–6
Bazerman, Max 25
Bear Stearns 6, 29
Beer, Stafford 29
behavioral systems 13–14, 187
Beinhocker, Eric 12, 13, 14
best practice 92, 98, 102, 145, 158–9, 175,
  176, 231, 270, 276–7, 280, 286, 293,
  300
Beth Israel Medical Center 89–91
Beyond the Balanced Scorecard 275–6
Beyond Budgeting Round Table 304–5
Bhopal disaster (1984) 58
Birchard, Bill 153
bird flocks 27–8
The Black Book of Outsourcing 299
The Blackstone Group 69
Blank, Arthur 81
boards
  diverse and empowering 65–6
  engage in risk management 66–70
  guild urgent case for change and
    convince the board 287–9
  recommended practices 70–1
  shareholder value 166
Bogsnes, Bjarte 51, 258–9, 261, 262–3
bonuses 6, 162, 175, 181–2, 183, 190, 191
Borealis 247–8

bottom line thinking 44
boundary systems
    knowledge of 268–9
    managing costs 262–3
BP 69
    failure to embrace risk at highest level
        59–60
    Gulf of Mexico disaster 57–8
    profits ahead of safety 58–9
Bradford & Bingley 6, 29
Bragdon, Jay 23
British Airways 39–40
Bröms, Anders 227
Brown, Mark Graham 275–6
Browne, John 59
budgets
    elimination of 240–1, 258
    managing costs within boundaries 262–3
    switching from annual to rolling
        forecasts 206–7
    switching from make-and-sell to sense-
        and-respond 231–2
    understanding costs 254
Buffett, Warren 82, 167
building societies 5–9
bureaucracy 144
    design organizations around small teams
        131–2
    eliminate 129–32
    fewer layers = lower costs 130
business partners 116–18, 145
business schools 11–12

Cameron, Kit 76–8
capacity 254
Caplain, Bruce 69
Capra, Fitjof 14–15
Carnegie, Andrew 225
casino banking 162–3
Chandler, Alfred 10
check–plan–act cycle 214–15
Cisco Systems 247
Citicorp 42
Citigroup 2, 6, 8, 42–3, 67–8
CMB Packaging (Carnaud Metal Box) 180
Coca-Cola 164, 167
Coloplast 20
command and control management model
        xi, 109
    accountability 144
    alternative model 16–31
    centralized and inflexible 4, 8, 115
    decline and fall of 3–9

differentiation 4
    employee engagement and
        empowerment 9
    leadership 21
    military metaphors 24, 129
    opposite of empowerment 133–4
    pressure on 4
    regulation and risk management 7–8
    rethinking 9–16
    shareholder value 5–6, 7
    targets and incentives 7
    transparency and trust 4, 8
communication 37, 49–50, 84, 134–5,
        294–6
compensation
    cynicism concerning 82–3
    exaggerated incentives encourage greed
        83–4
    firm size 86
    multiple of average pay 84–5
    pay differentials 84
    pay–performance link 85–6
    payment-by-results 109
    transparency 95
competition 176–7
competitive advantage 4
complex systems 13–14
continuous improvement 73–4, 205–6
controls 28–9
    annual reporting cycle 263
    best practice 276–7
    cost management 262–3
    flexible systems 262
    goals, measures and action plans 259–60
    implementation guidelines 265–81
    intelligent analytics 272–6
    internal 62
    key points 281–2
    KPIs 260–1
    market movements 276–7
    measurement mania 264–5
    peer knowledge 276–7
    performance management 257–65
    preparation of reports 270–2
    quality 62–3
    relative measures 261–2
    skepticism about measurement 280–1
    strategy 278–80
    team autonomy 265–8
    values and boundaries 268–9
coordination 27–8
    ad-hoc agreements 235
    designing 230–1

from push to pull 228
front-line teams and IT 232–5
implementation guidelines 229–36
key points 237
make-and-sell to sense-and-respond
 225–9, 231–2
management-measurement systems
 collision 229
strategic supplier partnerships 235–6
Toyota example 227–8
Correnti, John 94–5
cost centers 250–4
cost drivers 241–2, 250–4
cost management
 decision-making within flexible system
 262
 local accountability 246–9
 managing costs within boundaries 262–3
 set directional cost goals 247–9
 unit benchmarks 249
 which costs add value 247
Countrywide Financial 6
Creating the High Trust Organization 53–4
credit crunch 2, 5, 183, 303
Crittenden, Gary 217, 297
Crockett, Carter 78
Crosby, Sir James 67
Csikszentmihalyi, Mihaly 152–3
Cuba thinking 12
cultural change
 build urgent case and convince the board
 287–9
 communicate vision 294–6
 consolidate gains and maintain
 momentum 302–3
 create compelling and coherent vision
 291–3
 difficulties 284
 enable and encourage people to change
 296–7
 establish guiding coalition 289–91
 implementation 284, 285–303
 key points 304
 look for quick wins 297–9
 think like a revolutionary 286–7
 transparency and trust 284–5
 work around resistors 299–302
customer accountability 144, 145–6
customer needs 118–19
customer relationship management 143,
 278–9
Customer Satisfaction Index 81–2
customer service 36, 39–40, 141–2

DAF 106, 107
Data Warehousing Institute 100
Davidson, William 19
Deci, Edward 125
decision-making
 devolved 80, 132
 devolving within flexible control system
 262
 local 37–9, 122
 standardized 246
 strategic 210–12
 team autonomy 127–9
 transparency 95
Dell 51–2
demand chain 4
Deming, Edwards 168–9, 175
Descarpentries, Jean-Marie 179–81
devolution 51, 106, 109, 115, 125–6, 130
Di Micco, Daniel 84, 190–1
Diller, Barry 167
disclosure 153–4
Disser, Dan 204, 205, 206–7
Drucker, Peter 99
Dunlap, Al "Chainsaw" 166
DuPont 85, 195

earnings guidance 167–8
Ebbers, Bernie 65, 301
economics 12–14
EFCS (Employees First, Customers Second)
 program 290–1, 298–9, 301–2, 303
Egon Zehnder International (EZI) 83,
 176–7, 197
elephants and fleas metaphor 126
employees
 engagement and empowerment 9
 framework for 10–11
 hiring and developing 36–7
 involvement 40, 44
 recognition of 199–200
 satisfaction levels 298
 self-organization 209–10
 share ownership and profit-sharing 194–7
 as small cogs 18
empowerment 9, 50, 81, 153, 279, 302
 effective 30
 enabled by transparency 78, 94–5
 freedom multiplied by capability 124–5
 trust and confidence 133–4
Enron 2
Environment, Health & Safety Audit Report
 (2002) 50
Epstein, Marc J. 153

equilibrium 12
ethics 45, 51–3, 66, 77

Facebook 45
Fannie Mae 6, 69
FAS 123R 198
Feedback Consulting 299
Fernández-Aráoz, Claudio 83–4
Financial Accounting Standards Board 198
Financial Services Authority (FSA) 67
five forces theory 12
Ford, Henry 225
Ford Motors 225–6
forecasts xii
    effective 222
    fast, light-touch process 216
    implementation insights 217–20
    rolling 206–7, 215–20, 241–2
    targets and rewards 216–17
Formula for Failure 127–8
Fortune 500 85, 90, 116
France Telecom 181
Francke, Lennart 250
Friedman, M. 11
Froud, Julie 86

game theory 12
gaming behavior 25, 26, 52–3, 193, 206
Gates, Bill 99, 300
General Electric (GE) 51, 81, 166, 212–13
General Motors (GM) 69, 190, 226
de Geus, Arie 305
Ghoshal, Sumantra 11
Gillette 167
goals xii, 25–6, 73–4
    competition-cooperation balance 176–7
    directional costs 247–8
    divulging earnings promises 167–8
    Handelsbanken example 157–64
    implementation guidelines 164–77
    key points 178
    league tables 174–6
    medium-term high-level 205, 208
    peer comparisons 173–4
    pursuing the wrong one 42–3
    relative improvement 168–70
    shareholder value 164–7
    team-setting 170–3
    translating strategy into 259–60
    transparency 95
"Goals Gone Wild: The Systematic Side
    Effects of Over-Prescribing Goal
    Setting" 25

Goizueta, Roberto 164
Goldman Sachs 6, 69
Goodhart's law 264–5
Goodwin, Sir Fred 6
Google 93–4, 128–9, 298
Goold, Michael 212
Gore, Bill 19, 127–8
Gore (W.L.) & Associates 82, 127, 131,
    148–50, 153, 210, 298
governance 22
    appoint inspirational leaders 79–81
    build diverse and empowering board
        65–6
    define success in terms of continuous
        relative improvement 73–4
    engage board in risk management 66–71
    focus on person not pay 82–6
    implementation guidelines 64–86
    key points 87–8
    limitations of risk management 57–64
    promote culture of truth, transparency
        and trust 75–9
    promote leaders from within 81–2
    understand key drivers of risk 71–3
The Great Place to Work Institute 277
Greenpeace 58
Groupe Bull
    abandoning negotiated budget 180–1
    rescue of 179–80
    rethinking performance evaluation and
        rewards 181–2
    separating targets from rewards 182
Groysberg, Boris 190
Guardian Industries 129–30
guiding coalition 289
    engage right people 289–90
    grow strategically 290
    influence but don't control 290–1
    work as a team 290
Gulf of Mexico disaster 57–60

Haeckel, Stephan 42, 47, 133, 142, 144, 154
Haglund, Gunnar 101
Hamel, Gary 286
Handelsbanken 200, 298
    abandoning budgets 161–2
    accountability 153
    being the best 158–9, 276–7
    bureaucracy 132
    continuous improvement 161
    core values 45–7
    crisis in 157–8
    customer relationships 279

decentralization 159, 160, 161–2
internal market 250
leadership 80, 82
new management model 159–64
principles and values 51
profit-sharing 196
target-setting 74
teams 111
transparency 96, 100, 101
value centers 113
Handy, Charles 126, 132
Hanover Insurance 304
hare organizations 1–3, 6, 29
Hayek, Friedrich 11
Hayward, Tony 57–8, 59, 61
HBOS 6, 29, 67
HCL Technologies 20, 94, 100, 113, 150–1,
    290, 298–9, 301, 305
goal setting 172–3
online portal 114–15
planning process 172–3
Heisenberg's uncertainty principle 265
Herzberg, Frederick 185, 200
Hilti 20
Hilton Hotels 171
Home Depot 81–2, 236
Houston, Oberon 59
HSBC 45
Hugos, Mike 233, 234

IBM 179, 305
ICI 42
Implementing Beyond Budgeting 263
In Search of Excellence 305
incentives
    for and against 184–5
    command and control setting 1, 2, 3
    debate concerning 182–5
    executive 183–5
    golden parachute 183
    retention bonus 183
    scrapping of 183–4
    switch off most people 186
    target setting 192–4
    understanding purpose of 196–7
information 22–3
    availability 97–8
    clean and accurate data 100–1
    hiding and manipulating 99–100
    integrate 134–5
    one version of the truth 101–2
    as open and transparent 93–6
    peer scrutiny and review 279–80

sharing 91
understanding 97–8
information management 73
innovation 4, 123, 209, 210
Institution of Mechanical Engineers
    (IMechE) 106
Intel 52
internal market 28, 96, 250
investment 243–6
ISO 9000 63
Iverson, Ken 19, 50, 94, 210

JD Power 277
Jensen, Michael C. 184, 193
Joachim, Aubrey 240, 241, 242
job design 152–3
John Lewis Partnership 47–9, 194, 197
Johnson, H. Thomas 227
Johnson, Tom 165, 166
just-in-time 28, 107, 110, 229, 252–3

Kahneman, Daniel 13
Kanter, Rosabeth Moss 290
Kay, John 43, 188
Kelleher, Herb 19, 20, 33, 34–5, 37, 38, 40,
    196
Kelly, Gary 35, 36, 37
Kelly, Terri 131, 148
key performance indicators (KPIs) 95, 97,
    116, 122, 135, 161, 258, 259
    deriving the best 267–8
    effective tests for 268
    pressure-testing results 260–1
    setting goals 260–1
    turning dumb KPIs into intelligent
        analytics 272–6
key points
    accountability 156
    adaptive system 32
    coordination 237
    goals 178
    governance 87–8
    planning 223–4
    resources 255
    rewards 201
    teams 119–20
    transparency 103
    trust 137
    values 56
King, Rollin 33
Kmart 82
Kohn, Alfie 187, 188
Koslowski, Dennis 301

Kotter, John 289–90, 292

leadership
  aligning metrics with value propositions
      278–9
  appointment 82–3
  attributes 20
  CEO and CFO harmony 284–5
  coach and support 22
  command and control vs. adaptive 21–9
  compensation 82–6
  definitions 79
  heroic 18
  ideas and strategies 209
  inspirational 79–81
  leader's dilemma 19
  management cockpit 18
  one version of the truth 101–2
  performance in complex jobs 83
  promote from within 81–2
  risk management 22
  shareholder value 164–5
  strategy development 115
  value centers 115
Leadership and the New Science 13
league tables
  encourage wanted behavior 175–6
  peer comparisons 174–5
lean management 107–8, 109–10
Lehman Brothers 2, 6, 29, 52, 69
Leitch, Matthew 70
Lever, Ken 205, 206–7, 272
Levy, Paul 89–91
Lewis, Les 127–8
Leyland Trucks 301
  Additional Vacation Days 189–90
  influence of 109–10
  management change 106–7
  management layers 108–9
  Team Enterprise 107–8
  top-down targets and incentives 109
  transformation of 105–6
The Living Company 305
Locke, Edwin 25
Lowe's 81–2

McCurry, Robert 304
McGregor, Douglas 11, 186
Mackey, John 19, 43–4, 49–50, 53, 78–9, 85,
      113–14, 133–4
McKinsey 66, 167, 184, 199
Maheras, Thomas G. 67–8
manage by exception 135–6

management change 305–7
  see also cultural change
management model xi
  coaches 118
  commitment vs. calculating style 43
  importance of 162–4
managing by wire 232–3
Marcus, Bernie 81
Marshall Industries 191
Mårtensson, Arne 51, 80, 115
Maslow, A. 11
matrix management 154
measurement mania 264–5
measurement skepticism 280–1
mechanistic model 13, 18, 124
Merrill Lynch 2, 6, 29
Meyerson, Mort 79
Microsoft 99, 300
Miller, Jeffrey G. 226
Minours, Teruyuki 128
Mintzberg, Henry 43, 82–3, 183–4
mission statement 35–6, 43, 50, 209
Montalivet, Camille de 180
Moore, Paul 67
Morlidge, Steve 194
motivation 25, 77, 109, 161, 184–6, 188,
      191, 200
Motorola 181
MRP systems 107, 226
Murphy, 184

Nadler, David 66
Nardelli, Bob 81
National Health Service (NHS) 175–6
Nayar, Vineet 94, 113, 114–15, 150–1,
      172–3, 285, 290, 296, 298–9, 301, 303,
      305
NEC 181
negotiation analysis 12
Nelson, Horatio 80
Nicol, Jim 204, 205, 207
Nokia 134, 235
Northern Rock 6, 29
Nucor Steel 50, 84, 94–5, 111, 190, 209–10
NUMMI (New United Motor
      Manufacturing) 190

obedient machine 16–18
O'Brien, Bill 304
Ohno, Taiichi 19, 227, 229, 254
Oliver, John 106, 107–8, 301
O'Neill, Paul 45, 50
OODA loop 232–3

Ordóñez, Lisa D. 25
organizational culture 169
organizational purpose 43–4
The Origin of Wealth 12
O'Rourke, William J. 50
Ouchi, William 121–4

partnerships 235–6
peer comparisons 173–5
peer knowledge 276–7
peer pressure 176
peer review 148–50, 279–80
performance 44, 50–1
    complexity of job 83
    criteria 147
    evaluation 181, 263
    pay–performance link 85–6, 184
    relative improvement goals 168–70
    reviews 214
    stretching 171
Perkins, Doug and Mary 44
Peters, Tom 305
Pfeffer, Jeffrey 85
Philips 73–4
planning xii, 26–7
    budgeting 203–7
    business strategy as continuous process
        212–15
    continuous change means continuous
        planning 207–8
    corporate strategy as responsive 210–12
    focus on continuous improvement 205–6
    implementation guidelines 208–23
    inclusive process 209–10
    integrated 221–2
    key points 223–4
    rethinking targets 204
    rolling forecasts as guide to actions
        215–20
    scenario 220–1
    speed is strategy 180–1
    see also strategy
Polman, Paul 166
Poskett, Charlie 106
Power, Michael 62, 63–4
predict and control management 2–3, 7
Prince, Charles O. III 67–8
problem solving 127–9
process owners 117–18
procurement 252–3
profit 165–6
Profit for Life 23
profit-sharing 194–7

public schools 121–6

quality assurance 62–3

Rappaport, Alfred 197–8
red tape 95–6
Reed, John 42
regulations 7–8, 75–6
reports
    design to fit on a page 270–1
    KPI trends and forecasts 271–2
    relevance of 270
resistors 299–302
Resnick, Michael 27
resources 28
    align investments with best current
        business opportunities 243–4
    avoid spend it or lose it problem 240–1
    cost drivers 241–2
    dynamic resource management 244–6
    implementation guidelines 243–54
    internal market 250
    key points 255
    local accountability 246–9
    manage cost drivers rather than cost
        centers 250–4
    opportunity for cost reduction 242–3
    rethinking cost management 239–43
    rolling forecasts 241–2
    standardized decision process 246
revolutionaries 286–7
rewards 26, 46–7
    changing mindsets 179–85
    employee recognition 199–200
    evidence for success of 187–8
    with hindsight 192–4
    implementation guidelines 185–200
    key points 201
    motivated by self-fulfillment 185–8
    rethinking 181–2
    separate from forecasts 216–17
    separating targets from rewards 182
    share options and restricted stock grants
        197–9
    share-ownership and profit-sharing
        194–7
    team not individual 189–92
    value of incentives 182–5, 186
Riordan, Richard 121–2
risk
    culture pressure point 72–3
    dealing with 288–9
    growth pressure point 72

information management pressure point
73
key drivers 71–3
risk appetite 22, 66, 67, 69, 70
risk management 7–8, 22
  BP example 57–60
  contradiction at core of 63–4
  engage board in 66–70
  internal control 62
  paying lip service to 69–70
  quality controls 62–3
  risk manifesto 70
  standardized process 61–2
  team engagement with 70
  treating symptoms rather than the
    disease 60
The Risk Management of Everything 62
Roche 95–6
Rodin, Rob 191
Royal Bank of Scotland (RBS) 2, 6
Rubin, Robert 68
rules and procedures 62–3, 64
runningahospital.blogspot.com 90

Sarbanes-Oxley (SOX) Act (2002) 2, 35,
  75–6, 207
satisficing 14
scenario planning 220–1
Schein, Edgar 192
Schmidt, Eric 93–4, 128–9
Schrage, Michael 69, 70
scientific model 12
Sears Roebuck 98–9
Securities and Exchange Commission
  (SEC) 51–2
Seddon, John 63, 191
service level agreements (SLAs) 116–17
share ownership 194–7
shared service centers 116–17
shareholder value 5–9, 41–2, 198, 277
  maximization 11
  obsession with 7
  poor short-term target 164–5
  profitability goals 165–6
  pursuing as "dumbest idea in the world"
    166–7
shareholders 21, 71, 184
Shaw, Neil 58
Shell 183
short-term wins 297–9
  agile and responsive business 298
  attracts best people 298
  cost savings 297–8

entrepreneurial energy, innovation and
  growth 298
Simon, Herbert 13, 14, 187
Simons, Robert 84, 269
Six Sigma systems 107
Skinner, B.F. 187
Smart Service Desk concept 150–1
Southwest Airlines 53, 66, 82, 100, 101,
  111, 113, 153, 298
  corporate culture 34–5
  employee recognition 199–200
  hiring and developing the right people
    36–7
  information availability and
    understanding 97–8
  lessons learnt from 39–41
  local decision-making 37–9
  mission and purpose 35–6
  origin and development 33–4
  profit-sharing 196
  structure for success 37
Specsavers 44, 66
Stadelmann, Anton 175
stakeholders 21, 45
Stanford Business School 45
Statoil 20, 51
  Ambition to Action 257–64
  devolving decisions within flexible
    control system 262
  managing costs within boundaries 262–3
  measurement mania 264
  moving beyond annual reporting cycles
    263
  moving toward relative measures 261–2
  performance action 257–64
  translating strategy into goals, measures,
    action plans 259–60
  using KPIs to set goals/pressure-test
    results 260–1
Stern, Erik 198
Stern Stewart 198
stock options 197–9
strategic suppliers 235–6
strategy 26–7
  continuous process 212–15
  know if it is working 278–80
  responsive 210–12
  translating into goals, measures, action
    plans 259–60
  see also planning
Strategy and Structure (1962) 10
Sullivan, Scott 65
supply chain 4

supply network 235
Surowiecki, James 71
swarming behavior 234
Sydney Water Corporation
  avoiding spend it or lose it problem
    240–1
  cost reductions with no redundancies
    242
  focus on rolling forecasts and cost
    drivers 241–2
  rethinking cost management 239–42
systems theory 14–15, 28–9

target/s xii, 2–3, 6, 25, 73–4
  aggressive 7
  cost-setting 247–8
  incentives 192–4
  rethinking 204
  separate from forecasts 216–17
  separating from rewards 182
  shareholder value 164–5
  through accountability 123–4
Taylor, Frederick Winslow 74
teams 23
  accountability 24, 105–10, 146–7
  agree team-based success factors 266–7
  autonomy over decision-making and
    problem solving 127–9
  coach and support front-line teams 134
  communication of vision to 295
  efficiency and responsiveness 232–5
  executive 111, 114–16
  flexibility in 230–1
  goal-setting 25–6, 170–3
  implementation guidelines 110–19
  key points 119–20
  local accountability 246–9
  multi-disciplinary 210
  performance evaluation 26
  planning 208
  project management 267
  regulation of performance 265–8
  rewards based on 189–94
  risk scenarios 70
  salespeople 191–2
  self-managed 19, 23, 106, 108, 109, 110,
    113, 124, 128–9
  small 131–2
  standards and guidelines 47
  star performers 190–1
  support services 111–12, 116–18, 145, 266
  trust 24
  value center 112–14, 118–19, 147, 266

Telekom Malaysia 20
Telenor 20
Tesco 236
Theory X and Theory Y 186, 188
Tomkins 203–4
  focus on continuous improvement 205–6
  rethinking targets 204
  switching from annual budgets to rolling
    forecasts 206–7
tortoise organizations 1–2, 6, 29
total shareholder return (TSR) 277
Towers Perrin 9
Toyota 69, 109–10, 111, 113, 128, 134, 153,
    165, 169, 190, 199, 200, 235–6, 278–9,
    298
Toyota Motor Sales 304
Toyota Production System (TPS) 227–9
transaction cost economics 12
transparency 22–3, 38, 40–1
  accountability 153–4
  clean and accurate data 100–1
  enables empowerment 94–5
  human networks thrive on 91–2
  implementation guidelines 93–102
  information 93–6, 99–100, 279–80
  key features 95, 103
  one version of the truth 100, 101–2
  peer scrutiny and review 279–80
  promote culture of 75–9
  publish costs of everything 96–7
  radical 89–93
  share bad news immediately 98–9
  understand meaning of measures and
    reports 97–8
Travelers 42
Trofholz, Don 129–30
trust 4, 8, 24, 36, 38, 39, 40–1, 65, 277
  coach and support front-line teams 134
  decision-making and problem solving
    127–9
  devolution 121–6
  eliminate bureaucracy 129–32
  empowerment 133–4
  implementation guidelines 126–36
  as inspiring 92
  integrate information 134–5
  key points 137
  manage by exception 135–6
  promote culture of 75–9
  starting at the top 125–6
  strategic and operating boundaries 132–3
  unlimited 132
truth, culture of 75–9

Tversky, Amos 13
Tyco 301

UBS 68–9
UBS Wealth Management 175
UK Manufacturing Excellence Awards 106
Unilever 166
Union Carbide 58
unit cost benchmarks 249
United Airlines 195
University of California 45
USA Networks 167

value centers 112–14, 119, 220, 249, 266
value propositions 278–9
    customer intimacy 278
    operational excellence 278
    product leadership 278
value zone 113
values 21–2
    agree noble purpose beyond shareholder
        value 41–2
    clear and inviolate 45, 61
    communication 49–50
    core 45–7
    culture of love and care 53–5
    ethics before profit 51–3
    Handelsbanken example 45–7
    John Lewis Partnership example 47–9
    key points 56
    knowing 268–9
    organizational purpose that "grabs"
        people 43–4
    performance 44
    performance evaluation 50–1
    pursuing the wrong goal 42–3
    Southwest Airlines example 33–41
    written constitution 47–9
Van der Veer, Jeroen 183

Viable Systems Model 29
virtuous organization 77–8
    as high performer 78–9
vision
    awareness 294–5
    communicate 294–6
    compelling and coherent 291–3
    engagement 295
    team-building 295
Vollmann, Thomas E. 226

Wal-Mart 133, 236, 305
Wallander, Jan 19, 74, 115, 132, 158–64
Washington Mutual 2, 6
The Washington Post Co. 167
Waterman, R.H. 305
Web 2.0 30
Weill, Sandy 42, 43
Welch, Jack 51, 166, 169
Wellington, Duke of 140
Werner, Götz 19
Wheatley, Margaret 13, 15, 21, 79, 93,
    124–5
white spaces 132
Whole Foods Market 43–4, 49–50, 66, 78–9,
    82, 85, 100, 111, 153, 194, 197
    self-managed teams 113–14
    trust and confidence 133–4
"Why Incentive Plans Cannot Work" 187
William Mercer 184
Williamson, O.E. 11
wisdom of crowds 71
Woolard, Edgar 85
WorldCom 2, 65, 301
Wright, Laura 35

Yunus, Muhammad 44

Zehnder, Egon 19